Contents

CONTENTS

The Roman Empire and its Neighbours

Second Edition

Fergus Millar

with contributions by Richard N. Frye,
D. Berciu, Tamara Talbot Rice,
Georg Kossack

Duckworth

This impression 2001
Second edition 1981
Gerald Duckworth & Co. Ltd.
61 Frith Street, London W1D 3JL
Tel: 020 7434 4242
Fax: 020 7434 4420
Email: inquiries@duckworth-publishers.co.uk
www.ducknet.co.uk

First published in English
by George Weidenfeld and Nicolson Ltd, London 1967

Originally published in German under the title
DAS RÖMISCHE REICH UND SEINE NACHBARN: DIE MITTELMEERWELT IM
ALTERTUM IV by Fischer Bücherei KG

© 1966 by Fischer Bücherei KG, Frankfurt am Main

English translation © 1967 by Dell Publishing Co., Inc.
New York and George Weidenfeld and Nicolson Ltd, London

A catalogue record for this book is available
from the British Library

ISBN 0 7156 1569 6

Printed in Great Britain by
Antony Rowe Ltd, Eastbourne

Maps

Maps by Design Practitioners

Preface to the second edition

This book, written originally for the excellent German series the *Fischer Weltgeschichte,* was first published in English in 1967. It went out of print after a few years, but at least it avoided the fate of most of the thirty-four volumes of the series, which were never published in English at all.

I believe that the book still retains its uses and am grateful for the offer to reissue it. For economic reasons the main text has undergone only essential corrections. The notes have been revised and amplified, and new notes added. The bibliography has been completely revised and expanded to take in at least a selection of work published up to 1980. For other reasons it has not proved possible to secure any revision of the chapter on the Dacians by Professor Berciu and on the Germans by Professor Kossack.

If I had rewritten the book completely now, it would of course be very different. But I am not sure that it would be any better. I hope that the arrangement by subjects and areas, and the selection of concrete examples, will still allow it to be a clear and useful introduction to the Roman Empire and its neighbouring peoples.

University College London, 1981   F.M.

Preface to the first edition

'No-one will compare my *Annals*', wrote the historian Tacitus in the early second century, 'with the writings of those who recorded the early history of the Roman people. They had the grand subjects – great wars, the besieging of cities, the overthrow and capture of kings; or, if they turned to internal affairs, the conflicts of tribunes and consuls, land and corn laws, the strife of plebs and nobles. My theme is narrow and inglorious: peace unbroken or barely disturbed, a gloomy tale of events in the city, an Emperor unconcerned about expanding the Empire.' The contrast Tacitus saw was real; the history of the early Empire has none of the drama, none of the crowded sequence of events which marked the great days of the Republic. But there are other themes, and it is a significant fact in itself that Tacitus – his historical outlook still conditioned by the senatorial tradition of the Republic to concentrate on political strife in Rome and wars abroad – could not take them as a subject. Looking back now, we see that the major theme of Imperial history lies in a long social development by which the Empire lost its dependence on precisely those Republican institutions which provided the setting for Tacitus' *Annals*, and developed a new structure dependent on the Emperor alone but open to men from all parts of the Roman world. That development made it possible for the effective capital of the Empire to shift from Rome. But other factors had to come into play to determine that it was to the East, to the Greek half of the Empire, that the centre of affairs moved – and that it was this region which was to survive as the Byzantine Empire when Roman rule in the West was swept away. The New Rome which Constantine founded was a Christian city; thus the third major theme of the period is the development of the Christian Church.

Had Tacitus been alive to record the third century he could not have complained of the lack of wars and sieges or the overthrowing of rulers. For it was then that the Roman Empire endured, and with difficulty survived, fierce and prolonged conflicts on both its northern and eastern borders. In the north the Empire had achieved its last great conquest in 106 with the absorption of Dacia, whose history up to that point is traced by Professor Berciu. The violent struggles of the third century were against German and Scytho-Sarmatian tribes whose movements and social development, described by Professor Kossack and Mrs Talbot Rice in the light of the immense volume of new archaeological discoveries, had long been profoundly influenced by the presence of Rome. In the east the formidable but largely quiescent power of Parthia was replaced in the 220s, by the Persian Sasanid dynasty who saw themselves as the heirs of the Achaemenid dynasty which centuries before had confronted Greece. At the same time, as Professor Frye describes, there were rapid social and religious developments in the immensely rich and complex culture of the Middle East directly comparable to the changes within the Roman Empire itself.

The increased pace of the changes was in fact the most important result of the third-century wars, whose actual course is often hopelessly obscure. They provide the main theme of this book – and the excuse for compressing too much, written too rapidly between the summer of 1964 and the spring of 1966, into so brief a space – which is to trace the process by which, with no break in historical continuity, a pagan Empire ruled from Rome developed into a Christian Empire ruled from Constantinople. This process came to fulfilment in the fourth and fifth centuries. It is the primary thesis of this book that the fundamental social and administrative changes which made it possible had taken place before the end of the third century.

F. M.

1

Introduction

Roman history begins at Rome and ends at Constantinople. It is this simple fact which provides the framework for the period covered by this book, from the death of the first Emperor, Augustus, in AD 14 to the accession of Diocletian in 284. The institutions of the city state of Rome provided the setting and the definition of the legal powers with which Augustus, victor in a civil war between members of the Roman governing class, characterized his position as monarch. In 14 the Emperor resided in Rome, ruling the Empire with the collaboration, largely formal but still partly real, of the Senate. Those who governed the provinces and armies of the Empire went out from and returned to Rome where, as members of the Senate, they passed the main part of their lives. The Roman citizenship, universal in Italy, was still rare in the provinces. In 284 the vast bulk of the population possessed the citizenship; the administration, greatly swollen, was largely staffed by men who had no connection with the city of Rome, and though some provinces, but not legions, were still governed by Roman senators, Rome itself was becoming what it became in the fourth century, a privileged backwater visited on rare ceremonial occasions by the Emperor who ruled from elsewhere. Diocletian himself made his capital in Nicomedia in Bithynia (North-West Turkey), a convenient central point on the route between the two main frontiers on the Danube and the Euphrates. It was only a short step to Constantine's foundation in 330 of his New Rome, Constantinople, a short distance away across the Straits.

The main theme of this period is unification – political, social, cultural and religious. In the beginning, the provinces, large areas

1

created by conquest and organized for administrative convenience, were ruled by governors, mainly senators, sent out from
Rome and aided by a minute staff and by the presence, not
everywhere, of Roman legions. Internally, the provinces were
mosaics of largely self-governing cities, tribes or communities
which paid their taxes to Rome and were periodically toured by
the governor for the hearing of the more important legal cases.
There was no administrative hierarchy: the governor came out
from Rome with his staff and returned there after a year or a few
years; the officials of the local communities were local alone,
and had as yet almost no opportunity to rise into Roman posts.
In some but not all provinces there were leagues embracing all
or most of the communities; some, as in Greece, had residual
political functions remaining from their past history, others
were there mainly for the communal cults of Rome and the
Emperor. Their acquisition of important political functions, however, was a gradual growth culminating in the fourth century.

A number of influences soon came to break up this division
between Roman and local elements in the State. In the Western
provinces especially – above all in Africa and Southern Gaul
and Spain – there were many communities of Roman, or at least
Italian, settlers or colonists; and even apart from these the
process of Romanization of the native peoples – that is the
assimilation to Italians in language, dress, local institutions and,
most important of all, urbanization – was already proceeding
rapidly. The Eastern provinces were already dominated by that
network of Greek cities which had been established, where it
did not already exist, by the conquests of Alexander the Great
three and a half centuries before. These cities tended to be ruled
by an, in varying degrees, rich and cultured bourgeoisie, whose
more prominent members sometimes had close contacts with
the governing class in Rome.[1] In both West and East the upper
stratum of local society came progressively to acquire the
Roman citizenship, and then to be given the posts held by
Roman 'equites' (literally 'cavalry-men', the conventional term
for the order of society which stood next to the Senate and was
defined by a property qualification). From these they, or more
often their sons and descendants, could rise into the Senate

itself. By the end of this period the Senate, though its core remained Italian, had become also a class of men deriving from all the more urbanized parts of the Empire, of whom many retained their local roots and some perhaps never came to Rome at all. The diffusion of the Senate is mirrored with remarkable accuracy in the origins of the dynasties which successively occupied the Imperial throne: first descendants of the Roman Republican aristocracy (the Julio-Claudians), then of the Italian bourgeoisie (the Flavians), then of Italian settlers in Spain and Southern Gaul (Trajan, Hadrian and the Antonines), then Africans and Syrians (the Severans) and finally, for much of the last half-century of the period, men from the Danubian and Balkan area which was now becoming Romanized and providing a substantial proportion of the recruits for the army, and which was also one of the main theatres of the continual wars which filled the middle part of the third century.

These wars themselves greatly accelerated a development which had been implicit in the Empire from the start, the detachment of the Emperor from the context of the Republican institutions (which means largely the Senate) of Rome itself. The constitutional position evolved by Augustus in the course of his reign had been created in terms of various powers held by senatorial magistrates and governors, but had neither given the Emperor any precise place within the Republican institutions nor set any effective limit to his activities and powers. Thus even Augustus had been able to leave Rome for long periods spent in Spain, Gaul and the East, and to rule the Empire from these places with little or no reference to the Senate. Tiberius (14–37), the first Emperor of our period, spent the last ten years of his reign on Capri. Other Emperors like Trajan (98–117) spent substantial periods on campaign, or like Hadrian (117–38) in journeying round the Empire. With him the Emperor took his personal staff, and selected friends and advisers, and would issue edicts, write letters and receive embassies wherever he happened to be.

The importance of this freedom of movement was accentuated by the readiness with which the communities of the Empire would send representatives to press their demands on the

3

Emperor himself. We find this pattern established as early as 29 BC when the geographer Strabo met a fisherman from Gyaros in the Aegean on his way to petition Augustus at Corinth for a remission of tribute: it is clearly there in 115 when embassies from many places suffered in the terrible earthquake which happened when Trajan was at Antioch.[2] Various Emperors made attempts to pass on to the Senate some of the business which came to them, never with much success. To the inhabitants of the Empire the source of all benefits was the Emperor, and to him they went.

For all that, Rome remained, up to the latter part of the third century, the normal residence of the Emperors. When they were there they followed a pattern of life not entirely dissimilar to that of Cicero, moving from their palaces in Rome to a series of villas scattered mainly along the fashionable coasts of Latium and Campania. Even at these villas they could, and often did, carry on their official business; Cornelius Fronto, the friend and teacher of Marcus Aurelius (161–80), reproaches the Emperor for overtaxing himself in hearing cases through the night while on 'holiday' at Alsium.[3] What finally broke this 'senatorial' way of life of the Emperors was simply the fact of incessant wars in the third century. In 217 Caracalla was murdered while on campaign in Syria and replaced by the first *eques* to reach the throne, Macrinus. The opportunity came because Macrinus, as Praetorian Prefect, was with Caracalla at the time; in his short reign (217–18) he never came to Rome. A few years later, in 235, the pattern repeated itself: Severus Alexander was murdered by the soldiers on the Rhine and replaced by a Thracian soldier risen from the ranks, Maximinus. Thereafter, in the next half-century, it was the predominant pattern for Emperors to be produced by the army after (or before) the death of their predecessor and to spend most of their reigns in the field, often moving repeatedly from one front to another, and only rarely appearing in Rome to celebrate triumphs or distribute largesse. From the obscure and unreliable evidence available on the lives of the third-century Emperors it seems that Gallienus (sole ruler 260–8) was the last who can have spent any substantial period of his reign in Rome.

What happened was thus that in the last fifty years of the period the office of Emperor was by the force of external circumstances placed more and more in the context of the army. Of the Emperors from Claudius Gothicus (268–70) to Carus (282–3) only Tacitus (275–6) was a senator in origin. Moreover, the whole nature of the Court, of the imperial régime and of the administrative measures adopted seems to have been profoundly affected by this process, as emerged most clearly with the reign of Diocletian (284–305). The change is aptly symbolized by the fact that when Diocletian came to build at Split in Dalmatia a palace for his retirement it was built on the model not of the palaces or villas of Rome, but of a camp of the Roman army.

The army itself was, in a number of different ways, one of the most important factors in social development within the Empire. At the beginning of the period the core of the army was still the twenty-five legions of Roman citizens, recruited mainly from Italy; beyond that there were non-regular formations of non-citizens, known as auxiliaries. With the spread of citizenship the legions came to be recruited more and more – by the end almost exclusively – from the provinces; on the other hand, by the middle of the first century the auxiliary units were losing their local roots (though not their local titles, which remained), and service in them had become regularized at twenty-five years, followed by an automatic grant of the citizenship. In the second century we find some auxiliary units composed entirely of existing Roman citizens. In short the distinction between legions and auxiliaries became largely a distinction in size and type of unit.

The recruitment of non-citizens into the auxiliaries and their discharge as citizens was one factor in the Romanization of the provinces; others were the growth of towns around or near legionary camps and the settlement of legionary veterans either singly or in regular colonies in the provinces. In these ways the presence of the army came to be the dominating factor in creating a new 'Romanized' social pattern in the outlying parts of the Empire. But beyond that one of the most important developments in the period – one which signifies a substantial change in the nature of the State – lies in the ever-increasing employment of soldiers, both the lower and upper ranks, in what might otherwise have been civilian functions. This is true, firstly, of police duties in the provinces. The second and third centuries saw a rapid spread of small posts (*stationes*) of soldiers for the preservation of order, mainly along the main roads; in the Christian martyr-acts, which begin in the latter half of the second century, Roman soldiers are increasingly common, acting in concert with the local officials. But it is also true of a wide range of other activities, from land-measurement and engineering works, to clerical and other duties on the staff of provincial officials, or of judicial functions. This process runs parallel to the steady increase in the number of administrative posts – concerned with such things as mines, the official post service, taxes or Imperial properties – held in Italy and the provinces by *equites*. From the end of the first century we have also the appearance of the post of city overseer (*curator rei publicae*), a person appointed by the Emperor to supervise the financial affairs of a city in Italy or the provinces. These were commonly of senatorial or equestrian rank but some – mainly from Italy in this period – were councillors of the city itself. Under Diocletian the office reverted entirely to local dignitaries who were, however, still appointed by the Emperor.

All these developments represent a steady diffusion of the 'Roman' State into the area formerly left to the local communities. Histories of the Empire often represent this as a sinister process by which Rome destroyed the freedom and vitality of the cities. It took place, however, in parallel with the process referred to earlier by which Roman posts became open to men from the provincial cities. A substantial number of the individuals we know of who served as centurions in the army, or in equestrian military or civilian posts also held local office as magistrates in their own cities. The fusion went both ways; local dignitaries could be given Imperial posts (especially that of *advocatus fisci* – advocate for the Imperial Treasury) in their own areas; the commander of an auxiliary unit might be made a town-councillor or official of the place where he was stationed.

The central place in the process of fusion was occupied by the army. For not only did the army provide (since no other substantial body of State employees existed) the lower-grade personnel to carry out the extended functions of the State with regard to private persons; the great majority of the holders of posts of equestrian rank had also been through the army, either entering already as *equites* or being raised to equestrian military and civilian posts from being a top-grade centurion (*primus pilus*).

From the reign of Vespasian (69–79) it became common for some holders of equestrian administrative posts to be elevated into the Senate by the Emperor. In the second century, especially in the Danubian wars of Marcus Aurelius, which imposed a considerable strain on the Roman army and its commanders, some came to be promoted specifically to hold senatorial military commands. With the troubles of the third century there could be careers like that of Oclatinius Adventus, who rose from being a soldier in the escort of a provincial governor, a centurion of the *speculatores* (a corps of soldiers on secret police duties), Praetorian Prefect and, when his colleague Macrinus seized the throne in 217, a senator, consul and Prefect of Rome.[4]

This last case was bitterly resented in the Senate, as we know from the attitude of one contemporary senator, the historian Cassius Dio. When the strains of the third-century wars produced an even greater need for professional commanders, the final effect was not so much the accelerated promotion of equestrian soldiers into the Senate as the rapid exclusion, between the 260s and 280s, of senators from all military commands. The traditions and social cohesion of the Senate had resisted the pressure of the new Roman State which grew up round the army, resisted it at the cost of power. For the portent of the new order had been Maximinus, the Thracian peasant who joined the army, rose to a high rank and seized the throne in 235, without ever being a senator.

The remaining aspect of the importance of the army was that it had to be paid for. Ancient states had previously relied on citizen militias called up in emergency, or on hired mercenaries. The early Empire saw the final establishment of a regular army of long-service troops, paid in cash and maintained (not always very strictly) on a full war footing. Moreover, although client kingdoms were absorbed and frontiers pushed forward at various times and places, there were only two major conquests after AD 14, Britain in 43 and Dacia in 105–6; and of these only Dacia produced the substantial quantities of booty which had been the traditional means of financing ancient wars. The army, which grew steadily, had thus to be maintained from taxation, from whatever irregular means of acquisition, such as confiscation, as existed, or from direct exaction of supplies in kind. It seems, though we have no figures and no hope of arriving at any, that a predominantly agricultural economy simply could not produce the required surplus without intense strain and human suffering. Rich senators (whose domains in Italy, however, were protected from direct taxation by the privileged status of Italian soil) were always liable to summary condemnation and confiscation of property; at the other end of the social scale, as we shall see, the documents provide endless complaints of the exactions of soldiers and tax-collectors. In between, the landholders who formed the ruling class of the cities found themselves liable not only for the expenditure and munificence which local office-holding entailed, but also for the collection of taxes and their payment to the provincial officials. One of the best-known features of the Empire is the process by which, from the second century onwards, local office-holding turns from being a privilege into a burden which men struggled to escape.

From the reign of Hadrian (117–38) onwards, however, we find the development of a system of legal privileges separating local town-councillors (and also army veterans and the higher classes) from the rest; the system may indeed – it is not yet clear – have been developed specifically as a compensation for the burdens imposed on them. In it the higher class, *honestiores*, acquired a right to a range of lighter penalties than persons of the lower class, *plebei*, convicted of the same offences. By the end of the second century it was also obligatory on a provincial governor to consult the Emperor before punishing an *honestior* with deportation.

The precise origin and purpose of these distinctions remains obscure. But it is certainly significant that they developed at a time when the Roman citizenship itself was ceasing to have its original importance. Its rapid extension through the provinces culminated in the edict by which Caracalla (211–17), so our sources claim, gave it to the entire population of the Empire (documents suggest, however, that some large underprivileged groups remained outside). The passage of two centuries had thus seen the effective replacement of a distinction between local groups (Roman citizens, predominantly Italians – and others) by one, applicable, as far as we know, equally over the whole Empire, between classes. It is symbolic of the change that the word 'plebs', which originally signified the lower order in the city of Rome, should have come to be a technical term for the lower classes throughout the Empire.

The nature of this new legal distinction can be regarded as the reflection in legal terms of that cultural assimilation and unification which is so characteristic of the Empire. By AD 200 a traveller could have gone from Britain to Syria and passed all the way through cities of a substantially uniform type, with very similar public buildings (baths, theatres, amphitheatres or stadiums, meeting-houses for the city-council, temples). In the cities, two languages, Greek and Latin, would have sufficed for the whole journey, and in some places either would have been understood. Though there remained a fundamental division between the Greek-speaking half of the Empire (as far West as the West coast of the Black Sea, the South-East Balkans and present-day Libya) and the Latin-speaking half, the two cultures, both fundamentally urban, were very similar. Latin education and literary culture had from the beginning been heavily dependent on Greek; and links remained close, with incomparably more influence coming from the Greek side. As examples of this cultural fusion – and the predominance of Greek culture – we have for instance the remark of the second-century Greek orator, Aelius Aristides, that when he was taking a cure at the sanctuary of Asclepius at Pergamum he met there an African who was not only a Roman senator but a student of Demosthenes.[5] Towards the middle of the third century a teacher of rhetoric from Greece could move to Rome, and then pass on from there and settle down to teaching in Autun.[6]

The cultural and social unification of the Empire was the

product of the spread of a broadly similar type of Graeco-Roman town life throughout the Empire. To say this is to point to an essential characteristic of Graeco-Roman civilization, its fundamentally colonial nature. That is to say that, outside Italy and Greece, the society and culture of all areas of the Empire was formed by the importation, by conquest, emigration or assimilation, of a dominant alien culture, and its imposition on, or fusion with, the pre-existing native culture.

To understand the Roman Empire we must begin with its governmental superstructure, inherited from the Republic and greatly altered in the first three centuries AD; for without that superstructure there would have been no Roman Empire at all. But once that is done, if we wish to understand what the Roman Empire was as a society and a civilization, as a part of human experience, we must turn to the different areas of the Empire, to see the varied forms which the dominant Graeco-Roman civilization took in each. We must ask how far Graeco-Roman culture remained an alien importation confined to the towns; how far the rural populations retained their native culture and language; or how far a real cultural and social fusion took place. The different areas had very different backgrounds, from Greece or Egypt with their long histories, to Britain with hardly any. In an area like Southern Spain all trace of native culture had already vanished by the beginning of our period, in the face of the immigration of Italians and the adoption of Latin culture by the natives. In Egypt, on the other hand, the native language – the language of the hieroglyphs – survived 600 years of Greek and Roman occupation, to emerge in the third and fourth centuries as Coptic, the language of the Egyptian Church.

Some aspects of the complex patterns produced by the meeting of Graeco-Roman and native cultures in the Roman provinces can be traced from the conventional Greek and Latin literary sources; others from documents, that is inscriptions or papyri. From the Greek provinces, but not from the others, we have substantial quantities of literary and documentary material in languages other than Greek and Latin. For the rest we are dependent on archaeological material, which alone can provide evidence about the clothing, houses, pottery, burial-customs or temples of the people in the provinces. The immense richness and variety of the material from the Roman provinces was first displayed in its full range in M. Rostovtzeff's *Social and Economic History of the Roman Empire,* published in 1926 and still the only significant major work on the period. But if no historian of the Empire has surpassed Rostovtzeff, archaeological work has made great progress, especially since the last war, in every major area of the Empire except Spain. Attention has come to concentrate on the relations between Graeco-Roman and native cultures; precisely this was the theme of the VIIIth International Congress of Classical Archaeology, held in Paris in 1963.[7]

The interpenetration of cultures was essential not only to the material civilization or to the social structure, but also to the religious life of the Empire. It is not only that it was native cults – in Gaul or Britain as in the East – which most successfully resisted the dominant culture, but that Graeco-Roman paganism itself was increasingly infused with the cults of gods – like Cybele or Isis or Mithras – native to the East. One of these cults was Christianity, which arose as a sect among the 'subcolonial' Jewish rural population of Palestine, but within a few years had spread along the network of Jewish communities in the Greek cities and in Rome. With that it became, paradoxically, an element in the dominant Greek urban culture, produced no literature in Latin until the late second century, and spread only slowly and with difficulty from the cities to the countryside.

Moreover, in the end the evolution of the Roman State itself in the years between Augustus and Diocletian can only be understood against the background of the social development of the various parts of the Empire. That development determined who was qualified, and able, to enter the service of the State, from the lower ranks of the army, to the equestrian order and the Senate, to the Imperial throne itself. Secondly, it lay in the nature of the State that there were only very limited aims, mainly related to the army, which it actively pursued of its own volition. For the rest, apart from the preservation of order and the raising of revenue, the State and its personnel tended to

11

keep to the role of deciding disputes and dispensing benefits petitioned for by its subjects. This applied equally to the Emperor himself, who, while exercising absolute and arbitrary power, tended to do so in the form of judgments between parties or responses to petitions for legal or material benefits presented by communities or individual subjects; the consequence was that the Emperor often decided the most trifling of local or personal affairs. The question of which areas at which times had men with the wealth, confidence and political contacts to present themselves to the Emperor, and get favourable responses from him, was thus fundamental to the working of Imperial politics. Here, as in so many things, the Greek East predominated; the substantial majority of all known Imperial letters are to Greek cities. The largely hostile or contemptuous attitude to the Greeks expressed in Roman literature, as with the 'avaricious Greeklings' scathingly described by Juvenal, distorts our view of the historical situation. It was the Greek East which had the wealth and population, which displayed vitality in literature and the new religions, which produced popular resistance to the barbarian invasions of the third century, and which was to have its own Romano-Greek Empire and civilization down to its end in 1453.

2

Rome, the Roman People and the Senate

Rome and the Senate provided the framework around which the institutions of the Empire grew. Under the Republic the Senate, elected by the Roman people but largely hereditary in membership, had been the real government of the State; the people, the nominal sovereign body, had the final say but little active part in the formation of policy. Under the Empire the people lost all effective constitutional rights – in legislation or elections – and gained ever-increasing economic privilege instead. There was Imperial supervision of aqueducts and public buildings, Imperial care for the corn supply and the price of food, the continuance of free monthly distributions of corn (and later other foodstuffs), ever-recurrent distributions of cash by the Emperors, and a lengthening series of games and shows grafted by the Emperors on to the existing calendar of the city. The traditional right of the Roman people to the fruits of Empire was supplemented by the need on the part of the Emperors to demonstrate the success of their régime by display and munificence in the aristocratic tradition of the Republic. Moreover, as we shall see, the presence of the Emperor gave the Roman people the chance to exercise some real political power, even when formal rights had vanished.

The importance of Rome and the Roman people thus lies in two things, the fact that it was still largely in Rome that the profits of Empire were expended, and the fact that Rome was still, until the very end of the period, the principal stage on which the role of Emperor was enacted. The importance of the Senate was much greater and more complex. Formed of the

13

holders and ex-holders of the magistracies of the city of Rome, many of them in the early Empire themselves descended from Republican senatorial families, it set the standard of legality, and of observance of propriety and tradition against which Emperors were judged (it was, for instance, a deliberate sign of deference to tradition in Tiberius that he stood up to greet the consuls). Augustus himself, after the victory in 31 BC which made him sole ruler of the Roman world, evolved his constitutional position with careful deference to senatorial sentiment. Thereafter the Emperors, all of whom, down to Macrinus (217–18), were themselves senators before their elevation, on the whole tried – with notable exceptions – to work with the Senate, and to decrease the underlying tension which inevitably resulted from the conflict between senatorial traditions and the very fact of the existence of an Emperor. The nature of the tension, and of the attempts to resolve it are shown by the fact that most of the Emperors from Nerva (96–8) to Septimius Severus (193–211) took an oath (which they did not always keep) not to execute any senators without a vote of the Senate itself.

Furthermore, a vote of powers and titles by the Senate was an essential, if often formal, element in the elevation of an Emperor; and it was the Senate which voted either the deification, or the 'condemnation of the memory' of an Emperor after his death. Beyond that the Senate retained the legislative role it had acquired in the Republic, did a variety, not easy to define, of administrative business, and acquired a new function as a court of law for certain offences by members of the senatorial and equestrian orders.

Such was, in outline, the position of the Senate as a body. In our historical sources, in Tacitus in the early second, Cassius Dio in the early third, or the *Historia Augusta* in the fourth century, it is effectively by how he behaved towards the Senate that an Emperor is judged. It is a striking fact that all those Emperors, Nero, Domitian, Commodus, who offended most violently the susceptibilities of the Senate died violent deaths.

Individual senators, moreover, retained, except in the special case of Egypt, the monopoly of the command of the legions and the major provinces. The pattern thus imposed on the government of the Empire survived largely unchallenged until the last third of the third century. The significant change before this was of a different type, the steady extension of the recruitment of the Senate to all the more urbanized parts of the Empire. But although the new men could not enter without the permission of the Emperor, they and their descendants absorbed none the less the traditions of the Senate, and the sense of its corporate dignity which the Emperor should not impugn.

Rome and the Roman People

Under the Republic the public services of Rome had been all but non-existent. Augustus, however, in the course of his long reign (31 BC–AD 14) had gradually established various services headed by men of senatorial or equestrian rank, with subordinate personnel. First, in importance, was the Prefect of the City, a senator of ex-consul status, who had wide police and judicial powers and commanded the three Urban Cohorts, of a thousand men each. This office, which later became the crown, only attained by a few, of the senatorial career, gradually took over the bulk of jurisdiction in Rome and became the head of all the services of Rome. Among the services were the *vigiles* (night-watchmen and fire-brigade) commanded by an equestrian Prefect, again a creation of Augustus. He too exercised some jurisdiction, in the interests mainly of preventing fires or punishing those who started them. But it is typical of the vague demarcation which characterized Roman jurisdiction that the only full record we have of a case before the Prefect of the *Vigiles* is of a long-drawn out dispute (226–44) in which a corporation of fullers defended their right to the free use of a public place.[1]

Augustus had also established the senatorial post of *curator* (overseer) of temples and public buildings, which lasted until the fourth century; in the second and third centuries we also find Imperial agents of equestrian rank, *procuratores*, for the public buildings of Rome. Not much is known of what these officials did. But the functions of another comparable post, the senatorial Overseer (*curator*) of the Aqueducts, established by the

15

Senate in 11 BC on the initiative of Augustus, are very well known; for Iulius Frontinus, who held the post in 96–8, wrote a book *De aquae ductu urbis Romae*, in which he described the development of the aqueducts and the manner, down to the minutest details, of their functioning and administration.[2] No other evidence shows so clearly how much Rome owed to the care of the Emperors, and how closely the senatorial administration and the new Imperial employees interacted. The origin of the service was the gang of slaves which Augustus' lieutenant, Marcus Agrippa, had formed for work on the aqueducts while holding the senatorial office of aedile in 33 BC. On his death in 13 BC he left the gang to Augustus who gave them to the State; two years later he had the Senate vote to establish the post of *curator*. The attendants of the *curatores* and the now public gang of slaves were to be paid from the Aerarium, the State treasury. Claudius (41–54) added a second gang of slaves, which remained Imperial property and was paid by the *Fiscus*, the Imperial treasury – which also paid for all materials used.

These offices were concerned with the maintenance of existing temples, public buildings and aqueducts. Beyond these the Emperors constructed, largely at their own expense, an immense series of buildings – temples, theatres, baths, arches, new aqueducts and so forth – which continued unabated until the last half-century of the period, when little building can be traced. In this later period the most important public work was one of a very different type, the construction by Aurelian (270–75) of a twelve-mile circuit of walls, mostly still standing, round the City – the first that had been necessary since the early Republic.[3] This great series of buildings – of which the most famous is perhaps the Colosseum, begun by Vespasian (69–79) and completed by his son Titus – symbolized the munificence and stability of the Imperial régime. It might serve another purpose too, for when a man offered Vespasian a labour-saving device for lifting marble columns up to the Capitol Hill, he refused saying 'Allow me to feed my people'.

It was indeed such immediate benefits which interested the people. The most important thing was the supply of corn and other foodstuffs at a tolerable price. Twice in Augustus' reign, in 22 BC and AD 6 there had been difficulties over the corn-supply. On the second occasion Augustus had put two senators in charge; but by AD 14 a new, equestrian, office was in being, the Prefect of the Corn-Supply (*Annona*). His duties and powers were limited. The corn-trade was in private hands, and there is no evidence that any corn-carrying ships were owned by the State; even the corn – perhaps about one-third of the total imported – which came as tribute in kind from the provinces, chiefly Africa and Egypt, was carried in private ships. The Prefect and his staff checked the quality of the corn, controlled weights and measures, prevented fraud and made contracts with shippers for the tribute corn; later the Prefect came to exercise jurisdiction in cases involving shippers. But the full responsibility fell on the Emperor, as Tiberius explained in a speech to the Senate in 22 – 'This responsibility, senators, is exercised by the Emperor. Its neglect would utterly destroy the State.' Three years earlier indeed he had been forced by the complaints of the people to lower the corn-price and pay a subsidy to the dealers. Claudius, who in 51 at a time of corn shortage nearly lost his life when attacked by an angry mob in the Forum,[4] established rewards for shipowners who brought corn to Rome, and supervised the construction of the first proper harbour at Ostia; a second, inner, harbour was built by Trajan. Septimius Severus (193–211) was credited with managing so skilfully that at his death seven years' supplies were left in the granaries of Rome. Then we have an anecdote from the reign of Severus Alexander (222–35) of how the crowd, in the circus or theatre, demanded a reduction of prices. The Emperor asked through his herald which foodstuffs they meant; 'Beef and pork', they shouted – and measures were taken to ensure better supplies.

Apart from the general supervision of supplies and prices, there was the more specific task of distributing a free monthly ration of corn to the Roman people. This was not a measure of poor relief, but a political privilege which the people had won in the late Republic, and which the Emperors maintained. It went to a specific list of persons, established at 200,000 by Augustus, who normally had to be males over the age of ten, Roman citizens and domiciled in Rome. These persons held tickets (*tesserae*) which entitled the bearer to go for his monthly ration on a certain day to a certain door of the main distribution-point, the Portico of Minucia. Philo, the Jewish philosopher, records that Augustus allowed the Jews of Rome to change the day if it fell on the Sabbath. Although in theory a list of qualified persons was kept, it is clear that the *tesserae* later became almost an object of exchange in themselves, which could be bought, sold or inherited. The actual distribution (as opposed to the provision of the corn, about which we know nothing) was supervised by two senatorial Prefects of the Corn Distribution, who are attested until the 230s. In the third century the distributions actually increased in range and variety; Septimius Severus is said to have added a daily distribution of oil, while Aurelian (270–75) added pork, wine at reduced cost, and substituted for the monthly distributions of corn daily distribution of bread.

Closely linked to the food distributions were distributions of cash (*congiaria*) which were given to the same list of people, but took place irregularly on special occasions such as Imperial accessions, birthdays or triumphs. They were personal largesse from the Emperor to the populace of the capital city – when Marcus Aurelius (161–80) returned from the wars, the people demanded eight gold pieces each, one for each year of his absence.[5] The Emperor himself presided at the occasion of the distribution; an anecdote about Hadrian shows him hearing a complaint shouted out by an old woman as he sat at a *congiarium*; and coins issued for the occasion show Emperors seated on a tribunal while a functionary hands the coins in turn to the people who mount the steps separately to receive them.

These distributions affected only a limited class of privileged persons. There were other benefits of greater importance. As Marcus Aurelius' teacher, Cornelius Fronto, put it, 'The Roman people is kept peaceful by two things, the *annona* and shows; the Empire is judged by its entertainments as well as its serious business. . . . *Congiaria* are demanded with less menace than shows; for *congiaria* benefit only the individuals on the corn-list, but shows the whole people.'[6]

Spectacula (shows) were, as is well known, one of the most important and characteristic features of Roman life, filling, according to a mid-fourth century calendar, no less than 176 days of the year. Many of the games and shows on the calendar went back to the Republic, and were still given by various senatorial magistrates, partly at their own and partly at public expense. Others were added progressively by the Emperors, and special ones accompanied occasions such as birthdays or triumphs.

The giving of games and shows involved no small or trivial efforts. Animals had to be collected and trained – Plutarch saw performing dogs at a show in Rome, and has a charming story of an elephant which failed to perform a trick and that night was seen practising by itself.[7] The Emperors in fact established a monopoly in the hunting and possession of elephants, and had an elephant park at Laurentum near Rome. They maintained schools of gladiators in Rome and later elsewhere (as prominent persons had done in the Republic, and some still did). They took care to collect the best performers; after the suppression of the Jewish revolt of 66–70, the 600 fittest prisoners were shipped to Rome to meet their death in the arena. In the third century the lawyer Modestinus writes that if a provincial governor has condemned men to the beasts who by their strength or skill are suitable for exhibition to the people of Rome, he should consult the Emperor. In the second and third centuries the Emperors also formed a troop of *pantomimi*, or dancers; those who failed to win applause in Rome were sent on tour in Italy and the provinces.[8] The tradition of Imperial shows culminated in 274 with the great triumph celebrated by Aurelian for the defeat of Palmyra; after the triumphal procession, which included, according to the *Historia Augusta*, not only captives and booty but hundreds of animals (tigers, elks, giraffes) and 800 pairs of gladiators, shows were put on, theatrical performances, races, wild-beast hunts, gladiatorial combats and a mock naval battle.

Imperial celebrations were sometimes accompanied by dinners for the whole population, sometimes served as they sat in the theatre or circus, sometimes set out at different points in the city; on such occasions the equestrian and senatorial orders would be entertained personally by the Emperor. On other occasions the Emperor might scatter at random among the crowd tokens, called *missilia*, which entitled the bearer to gifts of various sorts. Nero (54–68) thus gave away birds, foodstuffs, tickets for the corn dole, clothes, jewellery, pictures, slaves, cattle, trained animals, and finally ships, apartment blocks and plots of land. Elagabal (218–22) distributed gold and silver, food, clothes, camels, asses, cattle and deer.

While all these economic benefits grew, the Roman people lost all constitutional function. The first year of the period, 14, saw the beginning of a system whereby the Senate was to fill by mutual arrangement (later by a formal vote) all the places for the annual senatorial magistracies for which candidates had not already been put forward with the personal 'commendation' of the Emperor, which ensured election. The people continued until the third century to meet for the electoral assembly; the rituals of the Republican assembly were preserved, but they acclaimed a single list of candidates.[9]

The second major constitutional right of the people was the passing of legislation, in the form of laws (*leges*) or plebiscites. Our sources use the term *lex* of various items of legislation up to the reign of Nerva (96–8); but there is no actual description of a legislative assembly from this period, and it seems that none took place.

The loss of constitutional functions did not mean the loss of all power. Pressure could be brought both on the Senate (in 14, again, the mob attacked the Senate-house and forced the Senate to vote a pay-rise for the dancers in public shows) and, much more important, the Emperor. Apart from occasions when riots broke out, it was at the circus or the amphitheatre that the temper of the people – gathered there in their greatest strength – could be judged, and where they could shout their complaints or demands to the Emperor, and on occasion have a regular dialogue with him, in which he would respond verbally or by signs or through his herald. The people's demands might concern not only trivia like the execution of criminals, the appearance of gladiators, the freeing of a favourite performer, nor merely, as we have seen, the preservation of their own privileges. They might demand a remission of taxes (the activities of the tax-collectors were severely checked after demonstrations in 58) or an end to wars; Cassius Dio witnessed a demonstration in the Circus in 196 when the people chanted in unison demands for the ending of the civil war.[10] They could demand, successfully, the execution of Imperial favourites, like Cleander, the favourite of Commodus, who was disposed of after a riot against him in 190. But, more than that, popular support was at times a material factor in determining who occupied the Imperial throne. The popularity of his family and himself was important in ensuring the accession of Gaius in 37; popular support was carefully cultivated by Agrippina before she murdered her husband Claudius in 54 and put her young son Nero on the throne. In 193 the people gathered spontaneously in the Circus (now their natural meeting-place) and demonstrated openly in favour of a pretender, Pescennius Niger. In 238 the mob demonstrated in arms against the Emperors chosen by the Senate, Maximus and Balbinus, and forced the appointment of a third Emperor, the young Gordian III (238–44); later that year the people showed their strength by fighting a pitched battle against the Praetorian cohorts. Right at the end of our period it is recorded that Probus (276–82) was not only supported by the army and chosen by the Senate, but demanded as Emperor by the acclamations of the Roman people.

The Senate

The importance of the Senate lay firstly in its functions as a corporate body, secondly in the role of its members as individuals. Taking the corporate functions first, it should be recalled that their significance does not lie in any real power of decision or innovation which the Senate possessed, for it had none. If the Senate had not existed it would not have had to be invented; but since it not only did exist but was the embodiment of the traditions of the Roman State, the various things it did were of great importance.

First there was its role in the accession of Emperors. In 14, the first occasion on which power was transferred, this role proved difficult and embarrassing, for Tiberius, while taking some steps which indicated his assumption of power, showed

21

himself hesitant and suspicious in his dealings with the Senate, and had prepared no formula which would allow his accession to be accepted gracefully. The consuls put to the Senate a motion (whose precise terms Tacitus fails to indicate) on the accession of the new Emperor; Tiberius, who was present, resisted attempts by some bolder senators to make him declare his intentions, and finally after a long delay, made his readiness clear.[11] On most occasions thereafter, when a son succeeded his father, or a successful coup d'état had taken place, the Senate's vote of powers and titles to a new Emperor was merely a formal act of recognition, which did not have to be taken as marking the actual beginning of the new reign. Vespasian's titles, for instance, were voted by the Senate at the very end of 69; but he dated his reign from his first acclamation by the troops on the first of July. At some point, however (as we know only from an inscription on a bronze tablet found in Rome), it was legally enacted that Vespasian should have certain specific powers – of making war and peace, summoning the Senate and so forth; the document calls itself a *lex*, but has the form of a decision of the Senate, by which it was presumably passed.[12]

Usually, as stated, the Senate's part came to be merely the voting of the Emperor's titles. Even this right was jealously guarded; Cassius Dio, who was in the Senate when Macrinus' first letter arrived in 217, complains bitterly that he had used the full Imperial titulature without waiting for the Senate to vote it. But there were occasions on which the Senate's role was more active, if not always successfully so. In 41, after the murder of Gaius, the Senate was summoned by the consuls, and debated the restoration of the Republic. Some prominent senators, however, preferred the notion of their own ascent to the throne, the people shouted for an Emperor, and Claudius was meanwhile proclaimed in the Praetorian camp. In 68, admittedly when a rising had already taken place in Gaul and the Praetorian cohorts in Rome had declared for Galba, the Senate declared Nero, now in flight, a public enemy, and proclaimed Galba Emperor. But in the third century, paradoxically, the Senate had two moments of real power. In 238 it recognized Gordian I, proclaimed in Africa as a rival to the barbarous Maximinus, then, after Gordian's death, met and elected as Emperors two senators, Maximus and Balbinus, under whom (along with the young Gordian III, proclaimed to placate the mob) it fought a war against Maximinus which ended victoriously with his death at Aquileia.[13] Then in 275, after the murder of Aurelian, an extraordinary interregnum occurred, for the army sent an embassy to the Senate asking it to appoint an Emperor. The Senate first declined, then later elected Tacitus, a wealthy senator of Italian birth. Tacitus lasted only six months – but the significant thing is that even at that late date the Senate, for all its real weakness, remained the embodiment of legality and the constitution.

The other aspect of the Senate's role *vis à vis* Emperors as the embodiment of legality was the action taken after an Emperor's death. Where power passed peacefully it could normally be taken that the Senate would vote the deification of the Emperor and the inclusion of his measures (*acta*) in the oath of loyalty taken each year on the first of January – which thus mentioned the existing Emperor and all 'good' past Emperors. On one occasion, however, when power was transferred peacefully, on the death of Hadrian in 138, his successor Antoninus Pius had the utmost difficulty in persuading the Senate (which hated Hadrian because of the execution of certain prominent men) to deify him: 'In that case,' he said in a speech to the Senate, 'I will not be your Emperor either, if he was a wicked man and a public enemy. For if so you will annul his acts, of which my adoption was one.'[14] In fact it was possible, as in the case of Tiberius, for neither deification nor 'condemnation of the memory' (*damnatio*) – with consequent annulment of measures – to take place; after the murder of Caracalla in 217 the Senate did not condemn his memory for fear of the army, which favoured him, but managed to avoid voting his deification until forced to later by the turbulence of the soldiers. Normally, when a hated Emperor was killed, *damnatio* would follow, sometimes amid violent scenes; after the murder of Domitian in 96 the senators rushed to the Senate-house, shouted insults against his memory, tore down the images of him placed there and annulled his acts. Such a vote not only meant (as we know from countless inscriptions and papyri) the erasure of the Emperor's name wherever it was written, and its omission from future oaths. It also had practical consequences: Claudius went through the measures of Gaius, all annulled in principle, confirming separately those which deserved perpetuation; similarly, to avoid confusion, Nerva confirmed all the privileges granted by Domitian.

Under normal circumstances the Senate met, under the presidency of the consuls, twice monthly, or whenever summoned by the consuls, praetors, tribunes or the Emperor himself. Attendance, except for those absent on public business or granted leave by the Emperor, was in principle obligatory; in September and October, however a quorum chosen by lot sufficed. The obligation does not seem to have been enforced rigidly in practice, and the few figures available show a gradual decline in attendance – 405–9 in 23 BC, 383 in AD 45, between 250 and 299 in 138; Severus Alexander (222–35) is said by a dubious source to have laid down a quorum of only 70.

The formal business of the Senate was conducted by *relatio* – when the presiding magistrate put a matter forward for decision – and *interrogatio* – when he asked those present to give their opinions (*sententiae*) in order, beginning with the consuls designated for the following year, ex-consuls and then ex-praetors. Magistrates in office were omitted, except when the Emperor himself presided, but could intervene without being formally 'asked'. At the end of the process, which seems to have stopped with ex-praetors – the more junior senators not being asked to speak – the Senate voted by division (*discessio*). Inevitably the presence of the Emperor, who if actually holding the consulate himself presided, and otherwise sat with the consuls, and had with him his attendants, including the Praetorian Prefects and a military escort, caused some difficulties both in the formal ordering of the business and in the free expression of opinion. Tiberius was disturbed by a senator asking him at what point he would give his *sententia* (since the established order naturally made no provision for an Emperor); Claudius, in clumsy oration preserved on a papyrus, urged the senators to give their opinions responsibly, instead of the consul designate repeating the *relatio* of the consuls verbatim, and the others saying just 'I agree'.

This formal stage was preceded, however, by an informal procedure, which in the Empire assumed considerable importance, in which the presiding magistrate or other senators who wished, put forward reports or requests on matters of importance. This stage was much used by the Emperors for giving the Senate information or putting forward legislation, either by letter – read by the quaestor of Caesar whose job it was – or in a speech (*oratio*). The *oratio principis* (speech of the Emperor) naturally determined in practice the vote of the Senate; after reporting Claudius' speech in 48 on the introduction of some Gallic notables into the Senate, Tacitus says briefly, 'the speech of the Emperor was followed by the decision of the Senate'. Ultimately a speech by the Emperor to the Senate came to be regarded as a legislative act in itself; thus the lawyers quote as authority the speech made in 206 by Caracalla, when co-Emperor with his father Septimius Severus, on the legal confirmation of gifts between husband and wife. Concurrent with these developments was that by which the Senate greeted the speech of an Emperor (and sometimes the *relatio*, or the speech of a senator) with shouted acclamations (*acclamationes*) which in time came to have an ordered and rhythmical character and to be solemnly recorded as a part of the Senate's proceedings.

We do, however, have one example of a speech in which a senator, without actually opposing, commented on and emended the proposals of the Imperial speech. In 177 the *oratio* of Marcus Aurelius and Commodus proposing measures to reduce the price of gladiators for games given by provincial priests was followed by the speech of a senator (recorded on inscriptions from Italica in Spain and Sardis in Asia) in which – prefacing his remarks with 'Although many think that on all matters referred to us by the Emperor we should give a single brief *sententia* (of assent)' – he discussed the points independently and in detail.[15] That is one good indication of the more secure relations established between Emperor and Senate in the second century.

The legislation passed by the Senate covered a wide range of topics – for instance the status of women who had sexual

25

associations with slaves, the rights of wards, penalties for the destruction of buildings, the regulation of criminal procedure or the punishment of slaves present in the house when their master was murdered. The last *senatus consultum* (decision of the Senate) actually quoted as a source of private law, with no *oratio principis* mentioned, is the *senatus consultum Orfitianum* of 178, which gave a woman's children preference in inheriting her property over her brothers, sisters and others.

Legislation apart, the Senate passed measures on a very wide variety of matters. It voted triumphs and other honours to Emperors, and other honours to individuals – as when in 52 the Senate voted to give the *insignia* (decorations) of a praetor, and a huge cash reward, to Pallas the freedman of Claudius; it received embassies from Italian towns or the provinces; it voted funds from the public treasury for the erection of buildings or the holding of games in Rome; it gave permission for the establishment of markets or festivals in the provinces. Thus we have records on inscriptions of the Senate in 138 permitting a certain senator to hold regular market days on his estate in Africa, or, probably in the same year, allowing the formation of a club of *neoi* (young men) at Cyzicus in Asia. It is important to note, however, that there do not seem to have been any areas of business which belonged exclusively to the Senate. In all areas we find the Emperor deciding exactly similar matters. Whether a matter came before the Emperor or the Senate might depend on to whom the interested parties turned. Thus the Emperor might refer a matter to the Senate, as when Tiberius diverted to the Senate a series of embassies from the Greek cities in 26 to lay claim to rights of asylum, or the Senate to the Emperor. When an embassy arrived from Cyrene in 59 to accuse a senator sent years before by Claudius to recover some public property, the Senate said it knew nothing of the matter and referred them to Nero.

Whether the Senate debated public business of immediate importance depended on the Emperor. Tiberius (14–37), a determined constitutionalist, allowed the Senate to debate freely about public finance, public works, the recruitment and discipline of the troops, provincial commands and correspondence with client kings. Vespasian (69–79) communicated all public business to the Senate, while Marcus Aurelius (161–80) took the by then extraordinary step of asking the Senate to vote the funds for a war. But these were acts of grace, of respect for constitutional precedent: they could not be imposed on the Emperor by the Senate.

The one serious function which the Senate had not had in the Republic but gained under the Empire was that of criminal jurisdiction, primarily in cases of *repetundae* – money illegally acquired by governors and officials in the provinces – and *maiestas*, treason or *lèse-majesté*. The origin of the full *repetundae* trials appears to lie in a procedure established in 4 BC by which provincials wishing to claim simple restitution of the money, but not to bring further charges, could come before the Senate and have a board appointed to assess the amount. From there the Senate seems to have come to hear such cases in the full sense. The best known of such trials, which happened frequently, are those between 98 and about 106 described in the letters of Pliny the Younger, especially the trial completed in 100 in which he and the historian Tacitus prosecuted Marius Priscus, the governor of Africa. The Senate first discussed whether the procedure for simple restitution would suffice, or whether as, Pliny and Tacitus argued, the savagery of Priscus' acts required a full criminal trial. Then the full trial began, and Pliny's opening speech was delivered under the presidency of Trajan himself, as consul of the year. Four speeches were delivered in all, two senators acting as *advocati* on each side; the whole procedure went on for three successive days, which delighted Pliny as recalling the lost glories of the Senate. The trial was concluded with *sententiae* in order, in which consuls designate and ex-consuls proposed various penalties, and then a division to decide.[16]

The legal origins of the Senate's jurisdiction in cases of 'treason' are obscure, but the jurisdiction itself is well attested as early as the reign of Tiberius (14–37). 'Treason' might be anything from an armed rising to consulting horoscopes about the Emperor's death, or taking a coin with his image into a brothel. This vagueness of application – which none the less could be limited by an Emperor if he wished – was especially dangerous when added to the rivalries and enmities inevitably present between senators and to the real doubt and suspicion as to what would be permitted in behaviour towards the Emperor; in consequence a charge of treason could be tacked on to almost any other charge, and in reigns where relations between the Senate and Emperor broke down – as in the latter years of Tiberius, Nero or Domitian – a regular reign of terror could ensue. Even in other reigns such prosecutions could occur; Cassius Dio describes in detail how a governor of Asia was condemned by the Senate and executed about 206 because his nurse was said to have dreamed that he would be Emperor, and because he had used magical rites to bring this about.[17]

The remaining important function of the Senate, the filling of the senatorial magistracies in Rome, brings us to its other aspect, the careers and functions of individual senators. The Senate was in essence a land-owning aristocracy, legally debarred from commercial activities (which precluded neither the investment of money via middlemen nor the development of semi-industrial operations, like tileries or brickworks, on landed properties); entry to the Senate required a minimum property valuation of 1,000,000 or 1,200,000 sesterces. Given that, the sons of existing senators assumed the broad stripe (*latus clavus*) on the toga which signified senatorial status on formally entering manhood at about sixteen or seventeen. Others could gain the *latus clavus* only by petition to the Emperor. Thus the Senate was fundamentally a hereditary body, heavily supplemented by Imperial patronage. The lives of individual senators were built round the holding of a regular succession (*cursus*) of offices, most of them important under the Empire not so much for their functions as for the status they conferred. First there were two 'pre-senatorial' posts, the vigintivirate (from the fact that there were twenty each year), held at about age eighteen, and the tribunate of a legion; both of these disappear by about the middle of the third century. A man actually entered the Senate on gaining his first full magistracy, the quaestorship, at age twenty-five. The quaestors, twenty in all, mostly served as financial officers of the provincial proconsuls, though two each year were quaestors of the Emperor and read out his communications to the Senate. From 47 they had the obligation – limited by Severus Alexander (222–35) – of giving gladiatorial shows at their own expense on entering office. That introduces an important element in the senatorial career; the posts in Rome not only were not paid, they were sources of considerable expense (the satirist Martial, writing in the 90s, mentions that a woman, fearing ruin, divorced her husband on hearing that he was to be a praetor). The next stage, at twenty-seven or twenty-eight, was to be tribune of the people (ten each year) or aedile (six). The tribunes still formally retained the right of veto on public business which they had exercised in the Republic; by a paradox typical of the Empire the last recorded veto was in 69 when a tribune used it to prevent the Senate discussing a matter in the absence of the Emperor. The aediles retained limited powers in connection with roads, markets and public order; neither office appears after the first half of the third century.

The praetorship, held at about thirty, was the important step which qualified a man for the lesser provincial governorships, the command of a legion or various (ever-increasing) posts in Rome – such as the prefecture of the Aerarium, the public treasury – and the provinces. Their most important functions while in office were judicial, presiding at the courts and appointing *iudices* (arbitrators) in civil suits; their numbers rose steadily from ten early in Augustus' reign to eighteen in the middle of the second century. Once again an essential aspect of the office was the general function, given them in 22 BC, of giving the public games in Rome; though part of the cost was borne by the public treasury, the post was still a heavy burden which at times required subsidy by the Emperor.

After the praetorship there was normally a long interval, filled with the posts mentioned above, until a man reached the consulate in about his early forties; those of very distinguished birth, however, might be given the consulate within three or four years. The consuls were escorted by twelve attendants (*lictors*) bearing the *fasces*, presided in the Senate and at the formal elections, exercised some jurisdiction, and gave important games (a fact which ensured the survival of the office until 541).

In the Republic two consuls had held office throughout the year; now the two consuls who took office on 1 January were known as *ordinarii* and gave their names to the year, but after two or three months they were followed by a varying number of other pairs (*suffecti*). The number fluctuated, but in a typical year perhaps ten or twelve men held the consulate.

This was a means both of satisfying senatorial ambitions and of qualifying men to govern the major provinces, with two or three legions, and to reach the two major proconsulates, the rich and civilized provinces of Africa and Asia. Thereafter it was possible to hold a second consulate (nearly always as *ordinarius*) and even, in rare cases, a third. A second consulate very often accompanied appointment by the Emperor to the Prefecture of the City, the most senior senatorial post.

After AD 14 the procedure for appointment to the senatorial magistracies up to the praetorship was that the Emperor received the submissions of the candidates, rejected some altogether and gave a list of the rest to the Senate; a minority of these received his 'commendation', were known as 'candidates of Caesar' and were elected automatically. The remainder of the places on the lists for each office had to be decided by the Senate, and here the well-known process of patronage, influence and bribery operated within the closed circle of the Senate as they had done in the open elections of the Republic. Trajan (98–117) ordered that candidates should not give dinners, send gifts or lend money. The operations of patronage, and the influence of the Emperor are finely exemplified in a letter in which Trajan's contemporary Pliny the Younger urges on a friend the candidature for the tribunate of a young protégé: 'I obtained for Sextus the *latus clavus* from Caesar, and then the quaestorship (i.e. as a candidate of Caesar); by my support he has obtained permission to stand for the tribunate, and if he does not get it in the Senate I fear I may seem to have deceived Caesar.'[18] He goes on to describe how he is visiting the houses of all his friends beseeching their support.

The governors of the 'senatorial' provinces (see Ch. 4) were appointed for a year by lot, officials in the 'Imperial' provinces and, normally, in non-magisterial posts in Rome, at the will of the Emperor. By the early third century it seems, though it is not certain, that the senatorial magistracies themselves were in the Emperor's gift. What seems clear is that the consulate itself was never open to free competition after the reign of Augustus, but had always been appointed at will by the Emperor; it was noted for instance that in 54 Claudius had nominated no consuls after October, the month of his death.

In such a situation, with the extensive though not universal patronage of the Emperor and the very limited powers of the posts themselves, the whole process might not have seemed worth the effort, expense and possible humiliation. That was the view of at least one contemporary, the philosopher Epictetus (who had observed the scene as the slave of an Imperial freedman). Speaking about 108, he said, 'If you wish to be consul, you must give up your sleep, run around, kiss men's hands . . . send gifts to many and daily tokens to some. And what is the result? Twelve bundles of rods, sitting three or four times on the tribunal, giving games in the Circus and distributing meals in little baskets.'[19]

There were indeed cases of men who preferred to remain *equites* rather than embark on a senatorial career. But the striking fact is the opposite, that the Senate attracted recruits from ever wider areas of the Empire, first from southern Spain and Gaul, then beginning in the later first century, from the Greek East and Africa and finally, beginning towards the middle of the second century, from Dalmatia and the Danubian area. On a very rough calculation, provincials made up just over half the Senate in the third century, just over half of these being Greeks.

New entries to the Senate required Imperial permission, either by grant of the *latus clavus*, or, from the reign of Vespasian (69–79) onwards, by 'adlection' – the granting of the status of ex-quaestor, ex-praetor or other office. But the influx of provincials resulted not primarily from Imperial 'policy' but from the pressure of the wealthy classes in the urbanized parts of the Empire; Plutarch, writing about AD 100, describes how Greeks from the East clamoured for senatorial office, regarding each stage in the *cursus* as still below their deserts. What senatorial status meant is illustrated by the numerous Greek inscriptions

31

where local dignitaries mention that they are related to senators – we can even find old ladies who call themselves 'grandmother', or 'great-grandmother of senators'.

The effect was, to some degree, to turn the Senate from an element in government, a deliberative body, into the highest of the various classes of the population throughout the Empire. We find Trajan (98–117) attempting to halt the process by ordering that all candidates for senatorial office should have one-third of their property in Italian land. Marcus Aurelius (161–80) lowered the requirement to a quarter; but the scanty evidence available would not suggest that even this was actually observed. The formation of a senatorial 'class' is reflected in the development during the second century of a formal appellation, 'clarissimus vir' (most distinguished man) – which was, significantly, extended to their wives and children – 'clarissima femina', 'clarissimus puer'. The lawyer Paulus, in the early third century, writes that a senator has a double domicile, Rome and his native city: the lawyer Hermogenianus, at the end of the century, says that a senator is exempt from *munera* (non-honorific functions involving expenditure) but is liable to hold office in his own city.

A senator's position was, in origin, entirely personal and he was in no sense the representative of his native place. But it is significant of the process of change that in the mid-second century the inhabitants of Trieste could claim that a young man from there had entered the Senate mainly to protect their interests; the process is completed when in 255 a senator is for the first time attested as taking part in an embassy from his native city, Philadelphia in Asia, to the Emperors, then at Antioch in Syria.[20]

This development, though important, remained only an aspect of the Senate. The Senate itself as a body, with its core of Italians, was even to regain some independence in the fourth century, when the Emperors had finally gone elsewhere. As the embodiment of tradition it provided a centre of pagan resistance to Christianity; and when the last of the Western Emperors disappeared in 476, the Senate was still there.

3

The Emperors

The Office and its Setting

The monarchy of Augustus had been created by victory in a civil war; it was secured and perpetuated by careful management of both constitutional forms and personal behaviour to meet the Republican traditions and the personal sensitivities of the Senate. Therein lay the paradox of the Empire as a political institution. Power, and responsibility, devolved on the Emperor from the start. But because the appearance of monarchy and its trappings had to be avoided, the Empire was slow to evolve any easy and workable means of transferring power from one Emperor to his successor, any staff and machinery of government (beyond the slaves and freedmen of the household) centred round the Emperor, or much of the apparatus and ritual of a Court.

The succession was the most difficult thing. The constitutional position devised for the Emperor (known normally just as *Princeps* – 'leading citizen') was built up of powers derived from those exercised by senatorial magistrates: the *tribunicia potestas* (the powers of a tribune), *imperium proconsulare* (the right of command held by a proconsul as governor of a province, but exercisable everywhere by the Emperor) – and perhaps (the point is much disputed) *imperium consulare*, the power of a consul; he had at least the formal trappings of a consul, being preceded by twelve lictors (attendants bearing the *fasces*) and sitting on the tribunal with the consuls.[1] The Emperor was also *Pontifex Maximus*, chief priest for the public rites of Rome. The Emperor might also, when he wished, be *consul ordinarius*. Claudius, in 47–8, Vespasian with his son Titus, in 73–4 and Domitian (81–96), who held it continuously, all took also the office of *censor*. After Domitian the Emperors all exercised the functions of censor – of which the most important was that of revising the list of the Senate – but did not take the title.

Beyond these powers with their titles there were honorific appellations – *Pater Patriae* ('Father of his Country') or *Princeps Senatus* ('Leader of the Senate') – which might occasionally be accepted by Emperors; more important was the term *Imperator* (General) used sometimes, by the Emperors alone, as a part (*praenomen*, or forename) of their actual name; and 'Augustus', used as a *cognomen*, or last name. A good example of the Imperial titulature might be that of Titus in 80–1: *Imperator Titus Caesar divi filius* (son of the deified Vespasian) *Vespasianus Augustus, pontifex maximus, tribunicia potestate X* (for the tenth year), *imperator XVII* (hailed as general, or conqueror, by the troops seventeen times), *consul VIII, pater patriae.*[2]

These powers and titles, however, were personal. To indicate his successor an Emperor could have some comparable powers voted to him. In 14, for instance, Tiberius had held the *tribunicia potestas* since AD 4 and the *imperium proconsulare* since 13. The essential step, however, had been of a quite different nature, his adoption by Augustus (who was in fact his step-father), also in AD 4. For reasons which still need explanation, the dynastic principle was immediately accepted, even within the reign of Augustus, as an essential element in the Principate. References to the Imperial 'house' (*domus*) and its members appear in documents of Augustus' time; and when in 14 the inhabitants of Cyprus took the oath of loyalty to Tiberius, they did so to him 'with all his house', and swore to vote divine honours to *Roma*, to Tiberius and to 'the sons of his blood and to none others at all'.[3]

Thereafter the history of the Imperial throne is a history of dynasties, some long-lived, some abortive. No Emperor who had a son living was ever peacefully succeeded by anyone else. The importance of the dynastic principle is only emphasized by the fact that where an Emperor did not have a son, he designated his successor precisely by adopting him. The first occasion of an adoption from outside the Emperor's family was in 69, when Galba adopted Piso Licinianus, shortly before they were both killed. The second was more successful, when Nerva bolstered his tottering régime in 97 by adopting a respected senator, Ulpius Traianus, then governor of Upper Germany. Adoption was the rule in the second century, when no Emperor until Marcus Aurelius (161–80) had a son to succeed him. When Septimius Severus reached the throne by a coup in 193, he claimed – or at least inserted as an element in his titulature – a fictitious descent from all the Emperors back to Nerva.

Family descent, whether natural or adoptive, thus provided the basis for continuity. It still remained for the designated successor to receive the titles and powers of Emperor. In 14, as mentioned in the last chapter, the ineptitude, suspiciousness and perhaps genuine reluctance of Tiberius delayed the process, which consisted simply of a vote of the Senate, for perhaps as much as two months (the Cypriots meanwhile inscribed a record of their oath, carefully leaving a blank space for the word *Autokrator* – the Greek for *Imperator* – to be filled in when the formalities were completed). Normally, however, when there was a son or adopted son already marked out by special honours – for instance, Titus during the reign of his father Vespasian (69–79) had held the consulship seven times, the censorship and *tribunicia potestas* – the Senate's vote was a simple formality. In less straightforward cases another element entered the process, the Praetorian cohorts. In 41 Claudius (the uncle of the murdered Gaius) was found by them, taken to the camp, and proclaimed; in 54, after Claudius' murder, Nero, his step-son and adopted son, went first to the Praetorian camp, distributed largesse, and was hailed as *Imperator*. The vote of the Senate followed.

The second century saw the development of a more definite system of appointing a successor. The first stage, from 136 when Hadrian adopted a senator, who soon died, L. Ceionius Commodus, under the name L. Aelius Caesar, was to use the name 'Caesar' specifically as a title to designate the heir to the throne. The final stage was for the Emperor to make his son joint

Emperor with himself in the full sense; thus Marcus Aurelius and Commodus ruled jointly in 177–80, and on Marcus' death in 180 Commodus simply remained as sole Emperor. Similarly, Septimius Severus had Caracalla as his colleague from 198 to 211, and his younger son Geta as third Emperor from 209–11. This system reappears repeatedly in the third century (as with the joint rule of Valerian and Gallienus in 253–60) but the hopes of stability it offered were destroyed by the fact, mentioned in the first chapter, that the endless wars meant that the Emperors were constantly on campaign, and therefore constantly exposed to the turbulence of the army and the attacks of rivals.

The primary setting for the Emperor's life and business – as for that of a senator – was his palaces in Rome and villas in Latium and Campania. These were privately owned residences; Augustus had lived first in a house near the Forum, then in one on the Palatine hill which had previously belonged to the orator Hortensius. This house alone took on in part the character of a royal palace (the word derives from 'Palatium'). In 36 Augustus had given part of it for the construction of a new temple of Apollo. In the libraries and porticoes attached to the temple the Emperor might hear embassies, and even the Senate sometimes met. In 12 BC, when Augustus became Pontifex Maximus, part of the house was made public property as the Pontifex' residence, and a new temple of Vesta was built on the Palatine. In the course of the first century the Emperors seem to have acquired all of the Palatine hill (which had been a favourite dwelling-place for the Republican nobility) and through extensive rebuilding converted the whole into a complex of palaces. The most extravagant development was that of Nero, who after the fire of 64, spread his 'Golden House' across a large part of Rome to the Esquiline Hill (Plate 3).[4] Vespasian restored much of this area to public use and began the construction of the Colosseum on part of it. Throughout Rome, the Emperors progressively acquired, by inheritance or confiscation, other residences each with parkland (hence known as 'gardens' – *horti*) – like the *horti Sallustiani* where Vespasian held receptions, where Nerva died in 98 and where Aurelian (270–5) preferred to stay when in Rome.

Outside Rome there were country retreats like the island of Capri, which Augustus had bought from the city of Naples, and where Tiberius lived from 27 to his death in 37, or Tibur, where Claudius sat in judgment during the summer months and where Hadrian built his famous villa. Philo describes how his delegation from the Alexandrian Jewish community followed Gaius fruitlessly round the villas of Campania in the spring of 40. Each villa had its own staff of slaves; a poem by Phaedrus describes how when Tiberius arrived at his villa at Misenum, and took a stroll along the lawns and avenues, one of the slaves there ran about officiously watering the grass and brushing the dust – in the hope, which was not rewarded, of being awarded his freedom. The Antonines had a taste for more self-consciously rustic pursuits than strolling in the grounds; Marcus Aurelius writes from a villa to Fronto to describe how, after a morning reading Cato *On Agriculture*, he joined Antoninus Pius (138–161) in helping to gather the vintage, after which they both had supper with the workers in the oil-press room.[5]

Originally the State provided the Emperor with no staff beyond the lictors who escorted him, and some military units. The most important of these were the Praetorian cohorts, which derived from the units on service at the headquarters (*praetorium*) of a Republican commander; originally scattered in towns near Rome, they were brought together early in Tiberius' reign in a camp, whose walls partly survive, on the Viminal hill in Rome. One of the nine, later ten, cohorts, each commanded by a tribune, stood guard at the Emperor's residence each night.[6] Also attached to the Emperor was a separate corps of mounted *speculatores*, who acted as both escort and messengers. From the end of the first century the function of the escort seems to be taken over by soldiers called *equites singulares Augusti*, recruited mainly from Germany and Pannonia; a little later (it seems) soldiers on special duties, known as *frumentarii*, began to be quartered in a separate camp in Rome and to serve the Emperor (as other *frumentarii* did provincial governors) as messengers and, more importantly, as spies or police.[7]

All other staff were in the beginning the employees or (as slaves) property of the Emperor. The Emperors from Augustus

to Galba (68–9) even supplemented the soldiers at their disposal
with a private bodyguard of barbarians recruited from Germany;
Caracalla (211–17) restored the bodyguard, recruiting them
from Germans and Scythians.

The number of slaves and freedmen in the Imperial household
cannot be calculated, but must have run into many thousands.
At Rome slaves performed all the menial tasks of the palaces;
the inscriptions on their tombstones show for instance a head
cook, who established the tomb for himself and his descendants,
and, if there were none, for the guild (*collegium*) of cooks in the
Palatium; or a chief mirror-maker who similarly leaves his
tomb in the second instance for the apprentice mirror-makers in
the Palace. Separate households of slaves and freedmen were
established for the various *horti* in Rome, the villas outside
Rome, the estates in Italy and the provinces. Freedmen and
even slaves of the Emperor might live in considerable state and
enjoy considerable honour in local communities, making bene-
factions and (in the case of freedmen) being honoured with the
honorary rank of town-councillor; a famous inscription shows
a slave from the treasury of the province of Gallia Lugdunensis,
who had sixteen sub-slaves (*vicarii*) of his own – secretaries,
cooks, footmen, a valet, a doctor and others – with him when he
died on a visit to Rome in the reign of Tiberius.[8] When Flaccus,
the Prefect of Egypt, was arrested in 38 he was dining at the
house of an Imperial freedman in Alexandria.

It was naturally in the immediate service of the Emperor that
the greatest position and influence was to be gained. We have
cases like Theoprepes who began as the slave in charge of glassware in the Palace, then of the Emperor's ornamental brooches
(*fibulae*), then of a dining-room, and then rose to manage estates,
to hold minor secretarial posts with the Emperor and to manage
the Imperial dye-works in Greece, Epirus and Thessaly under
Severus Alexander (222–35); or Ulpius Phaedimus who started
with the charge of Trajan's drinking-cup, came to be principal
lictor and in charge of the files of *beneficia* (Imperial favours)
and was with Trajan when he died in Cilicia in 117. Philo
describes in the greatest detail how an Egyptian called Helicon
gained influence with Gaius by being his chief *cubicularius*

(chamberlain) and then being constantly with him – exercising, bathing and eating with him, and attending him as he retired to bed.[9]

The most important household positions held by freedmen were those concerned with the public business of the Emperor – his letters, petitions, the accounts of public funds. Their greatest influence was in the reign of Claudius, when Pallas (accounts) Narcissus (letters) and Polybius (petitions?) dominated the political life of the Court, and amassed huge fortunes. Their position and influence offended more than anything else about the fact of an Emperor's existence against the conventions of Roman society. The Imperial biographer Suetonius records of Polybius the single fact that he was seen in Rome walking between the consuls; no more needed to be said.

Towards the end of the first century, as we shall see in the next chapter, the chief 'secretarial' positions came to be given to *equites* promoted from administrative posts – an indication of the degree to which posts with the Emperor were acquiring an official or public status. But the lower clerical posts attached to these secretarial positions all remained in the hands of Imperial freedmen. Among the chief posts, that concerned with Greek correspondence was quite frequently given directly to Greek orators or writers – who thus formed part of the considerable group of Greek *litterateurs*, doctors (like the medical writer Galen under Marcus Aurelius), tutors and philosophers who at all times clustered round the Court, and could exercise considerable influence. Furthermore, even if the chief posts were now filled from outside the household, *cubicularii*, eunuchs and others could still exercise great power. The most notorious was Cleander, who was brought from Phrygia to Rome as a slave, was bought into the Imperial household, became a *cubicularius* of Commodus (180–92), was made the freedman colleague of the Praetorian Prefects and made a huge fortune – which he partly dispersed in largesse to cities and individuals – from patronage and the sale of office, before being executed in 190 in the face of a popular riot.[10]

In the middle 40–50 years of the third century (238–84) our evidence, both literary and documentary, is much less good.

But the influence of the household, the slaves and freedmen of the palaces, must have been greatly lessened in the period when the Emperors were mainly with the army. We do, however, hear of *cubicularii* accompanying Carus (282–3) on campaign, or of one Dorotheus, later presbyter of the Church at Antioch, who as an educated eunuch had gained the confidence of an Emperor and then been placed in charge of the Imperial dye-works at Tyre in the late third century. It is only with the more settled conditions, and fuller evidence, of the period of Diocletian and after that the Imperial household re-emerges into the light of history.

The same lack of evidence hampers our picture of the Emperors and their setting in this 'military' phase of their existence. But we do have, from the contemporary historian Dexippus, a valuable picture of Aurelian in the field receiving an embassy from the Iuthungi. 'When he heard that the embassy from the Iuthungi had arrived, he said that he would deal on the following day with the matters about which they had come. He marshalled the army in battle order so as to dismay the enemy. When the parade was in order he mounted a lofty tribunal wearing a purple cloak, and arranged the army around him in crescent formation. Beside him he placed the officers to whom commands had been entrusted, all on horseback. Opposite the Emperor were the standards of the picked troops – golden eagles, Imperial images and banners of the legions picked out in golden letters – all raised on poles plated with silver. When all this was arranged he ordered the Iuthungi to be brought into his presence.'[11]

Essential to the question of the position of the Emperor in relation to the Republican institutions is the problem of Imperial property and income. Some aspects of the problem are clear; some are disputed, and for the moment insoluble. The Emperor appears not to have received any regular grants of public money. Instead, he relied on his own income, made up of the revenues from properties, legacies and inheritances from friends and others (the giving of legacies and inheritances to public figures was a Republican custom which hardened – especially under some rulers – almost into an obligation in the case of the

Emperor), spoils from wars (*manubiae*) and the 'crown gold' presented by cities and provinces. Both of these benefits came to the Emperor as they had to the Republican generals.

Beyond that the position is obscured by disputes as to the legal nature of the separate Imperial treasury, the *Fiscus*, which is attested in connection with Imperial properties, *bona caduca* (goods falling vacant on death), the confiscated goods of condemned persons – in the course of the first century the *Fiscus* came to share both of these with the public treasury, the Aerarium – and with various fines, penalties and extraordinary taxes. The author of this book has argued that all 'fiscal' funds and properties were essentially the private property of the Emperor – and that therefore the acquisition of such incomes represents a usurpation by the Emperor of properly public revenues. Others believe that 'fiscus' refers to public funds handled by the Emperor in his capacity as an agent of the State.

However, wherever the borderline between 'Imperial' and 'public' funds was drawn – and by the third century the distinction is barely traceable – the essential thing is that even in the Julio-Claudian period the Emperors had acquired a wide range of properties – palaces and villas in Rome and Italy, estates in Italy and the provinces – which then, though in theory private property, passed automatically to their successors on the throne as such, even where there was no family connection. Thus Otho and Vitellius, in their brief reigns in 69, could enjoy the delights of the Julio-Claudian palaces, and the '*horti Sallustiani*', left by a friend to Tiberius (14–37) could be used as a standard example of Imperial property by an early third-century lawyer. This change indicates the rapidity with which the position of Emperor as such took on a life of its own, irrespective of who occupied it. This is shown clearly in the action of Pertinax (193) who refused to have his own name inscribed on buildings which were Imperial property, saying that they belonged to the State, not to himself.[12]

Outside the realm of these complex technicalities which defined the relation of the Emperor to the surviving structure of the city state, his position was a personal monarchy. The soldiers took the oath to serve the Emperor by name, not the

Senate and People of Rome; their discharge certificates were granted personally by the Emperor. The coinage of the Empire bore the image and the name of the Emperor – 'Whose image and superscription is that?' Deceased and deified Emperors – and to a lesser extent living ones – received divine honours in the provinces, which involved temples and cult-rituals, run either by the cities or by provincial leagues which formed the chief meeting-ground for the leading men of the cities. Statues of the Emperors and dedications to them were everywhere. Images of the Emperors were carried by the legions and placed on the judgment-tribunal of provincial governors. A man could seek asylum by clinging to the statue of an Emperor; the importance of such images is illustrated by an inscription from Lycia dating to the mid-third century in honour of a local official who gave a show to celebrate the installation of a 'sacred image' (*eikon*) of the Emperor.[13]

Similarly, not only communities but ordinary individuals could and did turn to the Emperor personally for the settlement of disputes or the granting of privileges. The satirist Martial, late in the first century, mentions a man who had come from his native town to petition the Emperor for the privileges of a father of three children. In the second century Artemidorus, the writer on dreams, mentions the case of a shipowner who dreamed that he had been imprisoned by the Heroes on the Isles of the Blessed and had then been rescued by Agamemnon: what the dream foretold was revealed when he was seized for transport service by the Imperial procurators, petitioned the Emperor, and was released. In the second century also, as we shall see in the next chapter, there developed a regular system by which both officials and private persons wrote directly to the Emperor to consult him on legal questions and were answered in rescripts. The Emperor might be hostile – and might dispense punishment as well as reward – preoccupied, indifferent or just lazy, or else absent in a distant province or hidden in his palace. Access to him was vulnerable to influence or bribery. But none the less we see something essential about what the Emperor as an individual signified to his subjects in anecdotes like one recorded of Hadrian. A woman made a request of him as he passed on a journey; when he said he had no time she shouted, 'Then stop being Emperor!' – so he turned and gave her a hearing.[14]

Men and Dynasties

The Empire arose from political struggles, culminating in the civil wars, between the members of the Roman aristocracy. The first dynasty to occupy the throne was securely rooted in the history of the Republic, descending via Augustus, the adopted grand-nephew of Julius Caesar, from the patrician Julii, and via Tiberius, the step-son and adopted son of Augustus, from the patrician Claudii, who went back to the Rome of the Kings. In their personalities and way of life, familiar from the pages of Tacitus and Suetonius, the Julio-Claudians exhibited in their various ways the self-glorification, brutality, luxuriousness and eccentricity of the Republican nobility, whose final product they were. Their reigns were marked by continuous conflict with the Senate; men could still dream of restoring the Republic – and if there was to be an Emperor there were other men, constantly under suspicion and in danger of prosecution and death, who by virtue of descent from Republican families or Augustus himself might have as good a claim to the position as those who ruled.[15]

Nothing showed the rapidity with which the world was changing better than the events of 68–70. When the governing class, disgusted by the brutality, sexual aberrations and lack of dignity of Nero, also became alarmed by a long series of executions, the lead in getting rid of him was taken by a second-generation Gallic senator from Aquitania, Julius Vindex, then (probably) governor of Gallia Lugdunensis. He and the Gallic army he raised were suppressed. But he and the Senate in Rome had turned, significantly, to a rich, elderly senator whose first known ancestor had fought against Hannibal, Sulpicius Galba, the governor of part of Spain. After a brief reign (68–9) he succumbed to a coup in Rome and was succeeded by Salvius Otho, whose great-grandfather had been only an *eques*, and whose grandfather had reached the Senate by the patronage of Livia the wife of Augustus. He was swept aside when the Rhine legions invaded Italy and placed on the throne A. Vitellius, whose grandfather had been an *eques* and agent of Augustus, but whose father had been three times consul, and the chief senatorial ally of Claudius. The throne was finally taken, and a new dynasty established, by Flavius Vespasianus, then in command in the Jewish war. He was a first-generation senator, whose father had been a tax-collector and money-lender, though his maternal grandfather had been an *eques* and maternal uncle a senator.

The arrival on the throne of a modest Italian bourgeois family brought, as Tacitus noted, a significant change in the social climate of Rome. His old-fashioned strictness and avoidance of luxury and display set the tone for society; while Vespasian also brought in more men of his own type, from the towns of Italy or the provinces, whose 'domestic parsimony' was not altered by success and fame.[16] Vespasian maintained on the whole easy and unceremonious relations with the Senate, struggled apparently successfully with the financial chaos brought by Imperial extravagance and civil war, but did not entirely avoid a reputation for undignified greed and parsimony. The actor who by ancient custom played the role of the dead man at his funeral asked those in charge how much it cost, and replied, 'Give me the money and throw the body into the Tiber'.

In the reign of Vespasian's second son, Domitian (81–96), on the other hand, relations with the Senate worsened steadily, ending with a rising by a senatorial general in 89, an expulsion of philosophers – thought to be subversive – about 92 and an orgy of prosecutions in 93–6. Works like Tacitus' biography of his father-in-law Agricola, or Pliny's *Panegyric* of Trajan, written in the following years, look back on Domitian's reign as a period of humiliation and terror.

When Domitian was murdered by members of his household in 96, the conspirators turned (as they usually did) to a rich elderly senator of respectable descent, M. Cocceius Nerva, of an Italian senatorial family which went back to the Republic, and included two well-known jurists. In his brief reign of two years his most successful act was to adopt his successor, M. Ulpius Traianus, then governor of Upper Germany (it was not an accident that this was the nearest major military command to Rome). He was the son of a senatorial general of the same name who had governed Syria and Asia and been made a patrician by Vespasian; the family, however, came from the municipality of Italica in Spain which had been settled by Roman veterans during the Second Punic War. He was thus the first Emperor of provincial origin (though he may not actually have been born in Spain). Few Emperors, if any, were more successful in relations with the Senate. Pliny the Younger, who was in the Senate during his reign, has left not only the *Panegyric* (an expanded version of the speech of thanks to the Emperor which he delivered on entry to the consulate in 100), but his letters, which illustrate the tact Trajan showed both to the Senate and to the senatorial friends he invited to advise him. Moreover, Trajan conquered a new and wealthy province, Dacia, in two wars, 101–2 and 105–6, and made an invasion of Parthia (ultimately unsuccessful, in that his conquest could not be retained) in 113–17, dying in Cilicia in 117.

His successor, Hadrian, his nephew by marriage and ward, also came of a senatorial family from Italica, though in fact born in Rome. At the moment of Trajan's death he was governor of Syria, and it was announced subsequently that he had been adopted as heir and successor. That naturally aroused some disbelief, and the historian Cassius Dio was told by his father, who governed Cilicia later in the century, that the true story was that the Empress Plotina and the Praetorian Prefect had concealed Trajan's death for several days while the coup was effected. The atmosphere was not improved by the summary execution of four senators of consular rank for 'conspiracy' as Hadrian was on his way back to Rome.

Hadrian, in many ways the most interesting of all the Emperors, might be said to personify in himself the variousness and the limitations of classical civilization. Much of his reign was spent in tours of the Empire – through the western provinces to Britain and back via Spain in 121–3, Syria, Asia Minor, Pannonia, Greece (where he spent the winter of 124–5, in Athens) and Sicily in 123–5, Africa in 128, Greece, Asia Minor, Syria, Judaea and Egypt in 128–32. Hadrian composed verses, had

45

ideas on architecture, surrounded himself with orators and artists; on visiting Alexandria he debated with the scholars of the Museum. He founded cities on his travels, Antinoopolis in Egypt, named after his favourite Antinous who was drowned in the Nile, Hadrianoutherai in Asia Minor, Aelia Capitolina on the site of Jerusalem – which led to the last of the great Jewish wars, the revolt of Bar Kochba in 132–5 (Hadrian's varied sympathies did not extend outside Graeco-Roman culture). He busied himself actively with the discipline of the army – inscriptions preserve part of the speech of mingled praise and criticism which he made after watching some auxiliary units on exercises in Africa – and initiated the construction of the great wall named after him in the north of England. His greatest devotion was to the Greek world, especially Athens which he visited three times, where he built temples and other buildings, and which he made, the meeting-place of a new Panhellenic League.

Yet his complex, many-sided character aroused suspicion and distrust. The end of his reign was marred by more executions, his first choice for adoption and the succession, L. Ceionius Commodus, died in 138 and he finally resorted to a respectable middle-aged senator, whose grandfather came from Nîmes, T. Aurelius Fulvus Boionius Arrius Antoninus, better known as Antoninus Pius (138–61); he was instructed to adopt, as his prospective successors, his nephew by marriage, M. Annius Verus – Marcus Aurelius (161–80) – and the son of L. Ceionius Commodus, later called L. Verus (joint Emperor, 161–9). Antoninus Pius lived modestly in Rome and on his estates, never stirred from Italy and preserved excellent relations with the Senate. Very little is really known of him as a man. Much more is revealed of Marcus Aurelius both in the letters he exchanged with Cornelius Fronto, and in his *Meditations*, written in Greek, the fruit of the Stoic philosophy to which he had devoted himself since childhood. Nothing shows the modest and 'domestic' spirit of the Antonine régime better than the passage in the *Meditations* where Aurelius lists the things he learnt from his adopted father: 'Mildness, and remaining unshaken in decisions taken on due consideration; indifference to seeming honours; industry and perseverance; readiness to listen to those with something of public benefit to contribute . . . permitting his friends not to dine with him always or to be obliged to travel out of Rome with him . . . the check in his reign put on acclamations and all forms of flattery; his careful watch on the needs of the Empire, the husbanding of resources, the patience to endure criticism on such matters.'[17]

Two at least of the twelve books of the *Meditations* were written on campaign against the barbarians from across the Danube. For wars dominated the philosopher's reign, in the East the Parthian war conducted in 162-6 by L. Verus, whose returning troops brought a terrible plague in their train, and then wars against invaders from the north from 167 to 175, terminated by a revolt in the east. Finally there were aggressive campaigns across the Danube in the joint rule (177-80) of Marcus and his son Commodus.

Commodus, assuming sole power at eighteen when his father died on campaign, at once asserted his authority by rejecting the counsel of all his advisers to carry on the war, made peace and returned to the pleasures of Rome. The pleasure was not to be shared by the Senate (in a famous metaphor, Cassius Dio, who entered the Senate during the reign, says the change from father to son was a descent from an age of gold to one of iron); the reign produced some of the features of Nero's – conspiracies, the strife of favourites, self-glorification and exhibitions of gladiatorial prowess by the Emperor.

When Commodus was strangled in his bath on the last night of 192, the conspirators turned, in a way now familiar, to an Italian senator of advanced years, P. Helvius Pertinax. In origin, however, he reflected the changed conditions of the second century; born in Liguria as the son of a freedman, he had served in equestrian posts, mainly military, and was then elevated to the Senate and exercised military command in the reigns of Marcus Aurelius and Commodus. At the time of his succession he held the highest senatorial post of Prefect of the City.[18] His reign, entirely senatorial in spirit, lasted only three months until he was killed by the Praetorian cohorts.

There ensued a grim period when two senators bargained with the Praetorian guard for the nomination as Emperor, and when the winner was swept aside by Septimius Severus, the governor of Upper Pannonia, who then fought a four-year civil war before finally securing his throne against his rivals, the governors of Syria and Britain. Severus was an African from the old Punic town of Lepcis Magna in Tripolitania, which had been given the status of a Roman colony in 109/10. At that time his grandfather had become an *eques*; his uncles, though not his father, had been Roman senators. The first part of his reign, with the civil wars culminating in the victory of Lugdunum in 197 and with the persecution of hostile senators, left an ugly impression. From 197 to 202 he was in the East, making a moderately successful invasion of Parthia and traversing Syria and Egypt before returning via Asia Minor and the Danube. Thenceforth he led a relatively peaceful life in Rome until in 208 he went with his two sons, Caracalla and Geta, on campaign in Britain. When he died at York in 211, the two sons left as joint Emperors, returned to Rome where Caracalla murdered Geta late in 211. The familiar pattern of summary executions followed, broken finally by his departure on an expedition to the East which occupied the rest of his reign. Caracalla, if our hostile sources can be trusted, exploited the position of Emperor to the full, dressing up as Alexander the Great and trying to play the role, carrying out a ferocious massacre of the Alexandrians who had insulted him for the murder of his brother, and humiliating the senators who accompanied him. Cassius Dio, who was with Caracalla at Nicomedia in 214, describes how he would announce that he would begin hearing cases in the morning, and then keep his senatorial advisers waiting at the door till evening, while he practised as a gladiator or drank with his escort of soldiers.[19]

When the Court was in Syria in 217, the Praetorian Prefect, Macrinus, fearing execution himself, had Caracalla murdered and after four days' hesitation became the first *eques* to proclaim himself Emperor. It happened, however, that Severus had married into a Syrian family which held the hereditary priesthood at Emesa in Syria; and the great-nephew of Severus' wife, Varius Avitus (better known as Elagabal – the name of the Emesene god), was now pushed forward by his ambitious mother and grandmother, proclaimed to the troops (falsely) as the bastard son of Caracalla, and ended Macrinus' rule after fourteen months.

The accounts of Elagabal's four-year reign (he was only fourteen when it began) are a mere catalogue of immoralities and follies. By 222 his family was able to replace him by his cousin Alexianus, now named Severus Alexander, also aged fourteen, who was dominated by his mother Mammaea and by Ulpian the jurist, now briefly Praetorian Prefect, and who had of necessity to pay scrupulous attention to the Senate. Though the father of Elagabal had been a senator, and that of Alexander an equestrian procurator, it was still an accident of fate that it was these two youths, rather than any senators from the prosperous bourgeoisie of Asia Minor, who were the first representatives of the Greek East to reach the throne.

When Severus Alexander was killed in 235 on the Rhine, and replaced by the Thracian soldier risen from the ranks, Maximinus, a new era was beginning. Contemporary historical sources dry up, Cassius Dio's *History* ending in 229, Herodian's history of the Emperors from Marcus Aurelius onwards in 238. We are left with brief fourth-century and Byzantine histories, and the fourth-century collection of Imperial biographies known as the *Historia Augusta*, which is filled with fantasies – and moreover missing for the period 244–60. Incomparably less is therefore known of the Emperors in this period. Some are mere names; many of pretenders who are briefly sketched in the *Historia Augusta* may never have existed at all. Not all the Emperors need be mentioned, and it will be enough to talk about those of whom something significant is known.

The salient features of the period have been mentioned already, the dominance of wars and civil wars, the removal of the Emperor from a primarily 'senatorial' to a 'military' context, and the growing tendency for the Emperors to come from the army not the Senate, and (for that reason) to originate from the Danubian lands. Other influences were still at work, however; the proclamation in 238 of the proconsul of Africa Gordian as Emperor with his son, Gordian II, led to the Senate's successful war against Maximinus, and the six-year rule of Gordian III (238–44). Gordian's rule, filled with constant wars, ended when, like Caracalla, he was murdered by the troops on the Eastern frontier and replaced by his Praetorian Prefect, Julius Philippus, born in Arabia. The social development of the Roman world is aptly indicated by the fact that it was to him that it fell in 248 to celebrate, with magnificent shows in Rome, the thousandth anniversary of the founding of the City. He was replaced by a Pannonian proclaimed by the army on the Danube, C. Messius Quintus Decius, who was, however, a senator and married into an old Italian family. It was in his reign that the first general edict of persecution of the Christians was proclaimed. His death in 251 at the great battle of the Abrittus in the Dobrudja was followed by the brief régime (251–3) of Gallus and Volusianus and then by the joint rule of an Italian senator, P. Licinius Valerianus, and his son Gallienus. Their rule was marked by an endless series of disasters, invasions in West and East, the creation of an independent, but Roman, Empire in Gaul – extending to Spain and Britain – the rise to independence of Palmyra, and the capture and humiliation of Valerian in 260 by the Persian king Sapor. Of Gallienus (sole ruler 260–8) we know a little more than of the other Emperors of the time. He ended the second Christian persecution, begun by his father in 257, and, when wars permitted, spent his time in Rome, showing civilized tastes little known to his predecessors since the Antonines. He patronized the great philosopher, Plotinus, promising to build him a philosophers' city, called Platonopolis, in Campania, and (according to the *Historia Augusta*) was like Hadrian, *archon* – chief magistrate – at Athens, was initiated into the Eleusinian mysteries, and wrote verses in Greek and Latin.

When Gallienus was killed in civil strife near Milan in 268, Claudius (268–70) gained power and inaugurated the series of Balkan and Danubian Emperors – Aurelian (270–5) and Probus (276–82) – who in the course of long years of fighting restored the unity of the Empire and drove back, though they could not prevent, a series of barbarian invasions. Claudius, born in Dalmatia, and Aurelian, probably from Pannonia, were cavalry commanders of equestrian rank; Probus was also from Pannonia, but our scanty sources do not even reveal what military position he occupied at the moment of his proclamation. The reigns of these men were of fundamental importance in restoring the Empire to the point where the reforms of Diocletian (284–305) were possible; but it cannot be pretended that we know much about then beyond the barest facts of the wars they fought.

Between the murder of Aurelian in 275 and the proclamation of Probus in 276 came the last great moment of the Senate, when the army invited them to name an Emperor. After some hesitation they ran true to form and acclaimed Tacitus, a distinguished senator, probably of Italian birth and seventy-five years old. Finally, in 282, the Praetorian Prefect Carus was proclaimed, made his two sons 'Caesars' and after a successful invasion of Persia, died or was killed. Soon the troops proclaimed a Dalmatian soldier named Diocles, who as the Emperor M. Aurelius Valerius Diocletianus inaugurated a new era in the history of the Empire.

4

Government and Administration

The Roman Empire had no Government. That is to say there was no body of persons formally elected or appointed who had the responsibility for effective decisions. Nor was there any representative body, duly elected, to which the 'Government' might have been responsible, nor any sovereign assembly or list of voters. As we have seen, the people of Rome, though they retained considerable actual political power and privilege, no longer either elected the magistrates of Rome, nor (so far as we know) even formally passed legislation. The Roman Senate, filled by hereditary entry supplemented by Imperial patronage, represented neither the people of Rome, nor, when its sources of entry spread through the provinces, the local communities; for although a senator often did in fact further the interests of his local community, he was neither elected by nor responsible to them. Nor could the Senate, in spite of its very important role *vis-à-vis* the Emperors, and in spite of the fact that it did deal with a variety of legislative and administrative business, be described as the governing assembly of the Empire.

The Empire was in fact ruled by the Emperor, assisted by his 'friends' (*amici*). By long-established custom, any Roman magistrate or governor, when taking decisions or sitting in judgment, had with him a group of advisers, chosen by himself, whom he would consult. The actual decisions and verdicts, however, were his alone; he was not bound by the view of the majority of the advisers. Precisely the same pattern operated with the Emperors. Augustus had in fact set up a body of a more formal type, composed of the consuls, one each of the holders of the other offices and fifteen other senators chosen by lot for a six-month period, to prepare business for the Senate. This body however, did not survive his own reign, and later Emperors reverted to the previous custom. The essence of the system of consultation with friends was its informality. Firstly, although there tended to be some stability in who was consulted even from one reign to the next, and although the holders of certain posts, like the Praetorian Prefecture, always tended to be consulted, the Emperor was always in fact free to consult whom he wished (and conversely to ban from his counsels anyone whose advice was displeasing). If, for instance, the Emperor left Rome to go on campaign or tour the provinces, he took with him those whom he wished as his 'companions' (*comites*), and consulted them. Secondly he was, as stated, not bound by their advice. When Marcus Aurelius died on campaign on the Danube in 180 he entrusted the eighteen-year-old Commodus to the guidance of the friends who were with them there. They advised the continuation of the war; Commodus made peace (with rather successful results) and went home.

Alone of the Emperor's friends, the Praetorian Prefects had something approaching an *ex officio* place in the Imperial counsels. This was partly because a Prefect who lost the Emperor's confidence rapidly lost the post also, but also because of the nature of the post, in origin – under Augustus – the command of the Imperial *praetorium* (headquarters). The potentialities of the office were displayed at once, when Aelius Sejanus, sole Prefect after his father had been sent in 14 to the Prefecture of Egypt, gathered the Praetorian cohorts in a permanent camp, and, until his downfall in 31, exercised supreme influence with Tiberius, attacking members of the Imperial house, exercising patronage over senators, being awarded public statues, the 'ornaments' of a praetor and finally (though an *eques*) the consulate itself. Thereafter, the role of the Prefects, normally two at a time, tended to be more modest; they accompanied the Emperor most of the time, and from the latter part of the first century sometimes took an active command in the field, normally on campaigns at which the Emperor was present. They also kept prisoners under guard and in the second and third centuries are found exercising jurisdiction in Italy outside Rome, having some prisoners sent to them for judgment from the provinces, or, when delegated by the Emperor, reforming judgments of provisional governors. A few Prefects like Perennis under Commodus (180–92), or Fulvius Plautianus under Severus (193–211), followed the footsteps of Sejanus; Plautianus held the consulate in 203 and married his daughter to Caracalla before being executed in 205. Later in the third century, as we have seen, some Praetorian Prefects reached the throne. But their standing importance resulted from the fact of propinquity to the Emperor: it was recorded of Marcius Turbo, Prefect under Hadrian, that he never left the Palace even to go home to sleep. Since jurisdiction occupied so much of the Emperor's time, the Prefects' judicial abilities became as important as their military one. The great era of the Prefecture was the early third century, when it was held by the lawyers Papinian, Ulpian and possibly Paulus. By this time too the Prefects had come to have a formal status comparable, in some respects superior, to that of senators: two protocols from the reign of Caracalla (211–17) show that when the Emperor took his seat in council he was formally greeted first by the Praetorian Prefects, then by his other 'friends' and the chiefs of the 'secretariats'.

Further details about what the Emperor and his advisers did, and how, must wait until they can be put in the context of the structure of the Roman state. The fundamental feature of this structure was that it was a compromise between the governmental practice of the Republic and the fact that all real power, and responsibility, lay with the Emperor. In the Republic, the governors of the provinces had been senators, normally appointed by lot for a single year each. From the establishment of the 'Triumvirate' in 43 BC, the Triumvirs had had the power to appoint governors, a power which Augustus seems to have continued to exercise down to 27 BC. When in 27 he 'restored the Republic', one essential thing was that, for some of the provinces, appointment by lot of governors (all called proconsuls) for a year was restored; these were known as 'public' or 'senatorial' provinces. For the others, mainly those in which important military forces were stationed, direct appointment by the Emperor continued. The governors of the 'Imperial' provinces were all also senators, who, like the proconsuls, were either of ex-praetor or ex-consul stntus depending on the importance of the province, were called *legati Augusti* (delegates of Augustus), and served until the Emperor recalled them. The commanders of the legions, nearly all stationed in Imperial provinces, were also senators, normally ex-praetors, entitled *legati* of the legion, and appointed by the Emperor.

The major exception to this pattern was Egypt which, from its conquest in 30 BC, had always been governed by a Prefect of equestrian rank, the significant anomaly here being that he had under him legions of Roman citizens. There were also minor provinces like Judaea governed by men of equestrian rank (who at first had the military title of 'prefect' but in the middle of the first century came to be called 'procurators'); they, however, had under them only auxiliary units of non-citizens.

With these exceptions, however, the Empire retained the monopoly of provincial governorships exercised by senators, leaving, however, those which were important military commands in the patronage of the Emperor. The division between 'Imperial' and 'senatorial' provinces has often been regarded as an administrative one, with the Emperor ruling the Imperial half and the Senate (allowing for occasional 'interventions' by the Emperor) the senatorial half. But in fact, the method of appointment apart, the only administrative difference was the varying length of tenure on the part of *legati*. From the beginning, as it now seems, proconsuls, like *legati,* received instructions (*mandata*) from the Emperor.[1] Otherwise, both Emperor and Senate (predominantly of course the former) made regulations applicable everywhere, and passed measures relating to places in either type of province.

In a senatorial province the chief financial official was the quaestor, a senatorial magistrate appointed to the particular province by lot and serving there for his year of office. In an imperial province the same functions – the supervision of tribute-collection and the payment of troops and officials – were performed by Imperial procurators, usually men of equestrian rank, but sometimes Imperial freedmen. This post, along with that of Prefect of Egypt and that of prefect (later 'procurator') of smaller provinces, marks the beginning of that steady build-up of posts, appointed by the Emperor and held by persons outside the Senate, which is one of the fundamental developments in the nature of the State in the Imperial period. Slaves and freedmen of the Emperor are found all over the Empire, performing functions especially in connection with Imperial estates and properties – including mines and quarries – but also later with taxes, the Imperial post (*cursus publicus*), or roads. Freedmen sometimes occupied the more important provincial procuratorships mentioned above (for instance Felix, the brother of Pallas, the notorious freedman of Claudius, was procurator of Judaea 52–60). But these posts were normally the preserve, later in effect the monopoly, of men of equestrian rank. It should be explained that an *eques* was in principle any Roman citizen of free descent for two generations back who had a capital valuation of over 400,000 sesterces (one-third of what was required for a senator). *Equites* wore a narrow purple stripe on the toga and could sit in the front fourteen rows at the circus or theatre in Rome. In other words the equestrian 'order' performed at a slightly lower level, and on a much wider basis, the same function as membership of the Senate, of providing a specifically Roman status to which the propertied classes in the provincial cities could aspire.[1a]

During the period there was thus a steady growth from very slight beginnings of a pattern of equestrian posts, which came fairly rapidly to form a hierarchy not entirely unlike the 'cursus' of senators. At all times the majority of the holders of equestrian posts had previously served in the army; some of them entered already as *equites* and, as a rule, served in three posts, prefect of an infantry cohort of auxiliaries, tribune of a legion, prefect of a mounted squadron (*ala*) of auxiliaries. Others were centurions who had reached the position of *primus pilus* (senior centurion) of a legion, then went to Rome as a tribune of a praetorian cohort, were *primus pilus* of a second legion and then went on to equestrian civilian posts; in the course of the first century we see the formation of a regular career by which these men after their first 'primipilate' went as tribune in turn to all three units in Rome – the *Vigiles*, urban cohorts and praetorian cohorts – and then after their second 'primipilate' could be expected to rise rapidly to the more important equestrian posts.

In the Julio-Claudian period (up to 68) the number of equestrian posts grew steadily from the mere twenty-five attested under Augustus, mainly by the acquisition of new minor provinces (the two Mauretanias or Thrace) ruled by procurators, and the monopolization of the post of Prefect of the various fleets, in the early period often held by Imperial freedmen. From the reign of Tiberius onwards it gradually became more usual, and finally invariable, to fill the major Prefectures – of the Annona, the *Vigiles*, Egypt and the Praetorian cohorts – by promotion from procuratorships; in the early period they were still often filled directly by Imperial favourites.

The most important of the posts not yet mentioned was that of procurator in a senatorial province, who was in charge of all the Imperial properties and estates there. The historical importance of these men was that by virtue of being the trusted emissaries of the Emperor and of controlling a considerable revenue and a staff of slaves and freedmen they inevitably tended to burst the bonds of the theoretically private position they occupied, usurp a semi-public position, and challenge the authority of the senatorial proconsul. As early as AD 23, when accusations were brought against a procurator of Asia, we find Tiberius protesting that he had only given him authority over the Imperial slaves and funds; if he had usurped the power of the governor and employed the services of soldiers (as he evidently had), then he had ignored the orders of the Emperor.[2] Later, however, we find such procurators not only carrying out political murders on the orders of the Emperor but performing public functions like the construction of roads or the measurement of lands under dispute. As early as 88, moreover, we have a measure prophetic of the future, when the procurator of Asia acted as governor of the province, when the senatorial governor had been executed by Domitian.

From the Flavian period on, and especially in the second century, there was a further growth of minor equestrian posts which generally came to occupy a lower place in the hierarchy than those already in existence; such posts were concerned with inheritances coming to the Emperor, taxes, gladiators, the transport service, the aqueducts and the Mint. Under Hadrian (117–38) we find the new junior post of *advocatus fisci* (advocate for the Imperial treasury) which acted as an alternative, non-military, point of entry to the equestrian cursus. Some local dignitaries, or Greek orators, however, held this post alone, without going on to others; an inscription shows, for instance, a man and his grandson from a prominent family in Phrygia (Asia), who both held this post but no other. In other words, this is an example of the fusion of local and Imperial office-holding mentioned earlier.

An equally important development, which also dates fundamentally to the Flavian period, was the entry of *equites* into the chief 'secretarial' positions with the Emperor previously held by Imperial freedmen. The first step was in fact taken by Vitellius when proclaimed Emperor on the Rhine in January 69; one of the beneficiaries of his distribution of these posts to *equites* was serving there as a legionary tribune, who found himself with the title 'procurator for the patrimony and inheritances and petitions'.[3] More typical is for instance the career of Vibius Lentulus, who after equestrian military posts held various procuratorships and finished up as a *rationibus* (in charge of accounts) under Trajan.

These posts now began to go regularly to men promoted from lower administrative positions. But especially those involving diplomacy or correspondence were often given directly to intellectuals or literary figures, nearly always Greeks. This had happened earlier on occasion, as when Claudius (41–54) gave his doctor, Stertinius Xenophon from the island of Cos, what appears to be an honorary military rank – plus military decorations after he had accompanied him to Britain – and also put him in charge of Imperial replies written in Greek. About the end of the first century an Alexandrian grammarian, Dionysius, who had been head of the Museum at Alexandria, was placed in charge of Imperial libraries and was then responsible for Imperial correspondence, embassies and replies.

In the second and early third centuries a long line of Greek orators came directly to the charge of Imperial letters in Greek.[4]

Two careers might exemplify the two opposing currents in the administrative development of the second century. First there is a professional, promoted from the army, M. Bassaeus Rufus; born in poverty and devoid of culture, he became a *primus pilus*, then went to the three units in Rome as tribune, was *primus pilus* again, was a procurator in Spain, then procurator (governor) of Noricum, procurator (financial) of Belgica and Germany, *a rationibus*, and Prefect successively of the *Vigiles* in Rome, of Egypt and of the Praetorian cohorts (169 to about 177); he won military decorations and the *insignia* of a consul in the Danubian wars of Marcus Aurelius, after which the Senate, on the motion of Marcus Aurelius and Commodus, voted to have three statues of him erected at three different points in Rome.[5]

Aelius Antipater from Hierapolis in Phrygia was the son of a man who was *advocatus fisci* first in the district of Phrygia, then for the whole province of Asia, and grandson of a High Priest for the imperial cult for the province. After studying rhetoric at Athens he became a well-known orator and was put in charge of Imperial Greek correspondence by Septimius Severus (193–211), and also made tutor of his sons, Caracalla and Geta; writing to Ephesus between 200 and 205, Caracalla calls him 'my friend and teacher who is entrusted with the composition of the Greek letters'. Philostratus, in his Lives of the Sophists, records that Antipater wrote a history of Severus' reign and that in particular he was a master of the style appropriate to Imperial letters. Later he was elevated to the Senate with the rank of ex-consul.[6]

In between these two extremes falls another development which must be briefly mentioned here, the employment of jurists in equestrian posts and as paid advisers (*consiliarii*) of the Emperor. The known jurists of the early Empire, up to the first half of the second century, were senators, who were given individually the 'right to give replies (to legal queries)' – the *ius respondendi* – and who might or might not be 'friends' of the Emperor and among his advisers. From the mid-second century there is a significant change, and the known jurists are predominantly *equites* in the Imperial service. The first example is L.

Volusius Maecianus, who was a military tribune, then in charge of petitions for Antoninus Pius in 138 between his adoption and accession, then, after prefectures of the *vehicula* (transport service) and the libraries, held more secretarial posts with Pius before going on to the Prefectures of the *Annona* and Egypt, and finally being made a senator. Apart from writing legal works, he was the law-teacher of Marcus Aurelius, and legal adviser of Pius and of Marcus Aurelius and Verus (161–9).[7] Later, as already mentioned, jurists rose to the Praetorian Prefecture itself.

Such was the broad structure of the major posts as they were up to the second half of the third century. Its essential features are that the structure of senatorial provincial commands remained intact, but that round it had grown up a very diversified pattern of equestrian posts answering to the greatly extended activities of the State and interests of the Emperor. In the last half of the third century, however, the senatorial structure finally crumbled. Even before that, especially from the end of the second century, there were recurrent cases of procurators governing provinces *vice praesidis* ('in place of the governor'). In some third-century cases, especially with the long list of such posts held by Timesitheus, later the father-in-law and Praetorian Prefect of Gordian III (238–44), these do not seem to have been merely replacements resulting from death or absence, but regular substitutions. Similarly, even ordinary procurators, as we shall see below, steadily acquired greater power and independence *vis-à-vis* the senatorial governors. We have a vivid picture of what an important procurator in the second half of the third century looked like to his subjects, in the letter sent to Rome by the synod of Antioch about 270 about the heretical bishop, Paul of Samosata; among other things he behaved like a *ducenarius* (a high-ranking procurator) rather than a bishop – 'parading across the public squares, reading letters and answering them publicly as he went, surrounded by a large body-guard, some marching before him, some following behind . . .'; he had a *tribunal* and an elevated throne, and an office (*secretum*) 'like the rulers of this world'.[8]

The final stage began in the middle of the third century, perhaps in the reign of Gallienus (260–8) as later sources state, when senatorial tribunes and *legati* of legions disappear from the army; it was continued between the 260s and 280s when most senatorial governors of praetorian, but not consular, rank seem to have been replaced permanently by *equites*. The process was to be completed by Diocletian, who left only two regular senatorial provinces, the proconsulates of Africa and Asia.

The link between these major officials and their subjects was provided by the staffs, drawn from various sources, who served them in the provinces. First, there were as usual elements surviving from the Republic, the attendants (*apparitores*) – scribes, lictors, heralds, messengers and others – attached both to Roman magistrates and provincial governors. They were drawn from panels (*decuriae*) divided by function and magistracy, and in theory at least were appointed to specific posts by lot. In spite of their fairly humble functions, they might be (especially the *scribae*) of relatively high social standing, some belonging to, or passing into, the equestrian order; many of them are known from inscriptions honouring them as the patrons or benefactors of local communities. They do not figure very largely in our sources; but one inscription from Africa lists among the advisers (*consilium*) of the proconsul in hearing a case three *scribae* and a *haruspex* (interpreter of omens). More prominent than these are the soldiers detached to serve on the staffs of senatorial governors and procurators. A senatorial governor (whether a proconsul or *legatus*) seems to have had a military staff consisting of a centurion as *princeps praetorii* (chief of headquarters), three *cornicularii* (adjutants), three *commentarienses*, and then *speculatores* (spies and executioners) and minor grades (clerks, torturers, etc.) known as *beneficiarii* – the *beneficium* (privilege) being release from normal duties.

Procurators also had a military staff, though we do not know how many. The 'daily report' (*pridianum*) of an auxiliary cohort on the Danube about 105 mentions not only soldiers detached as the *equites singulares* – mounted escort – of the *legatus*, but also others detached to serve on the *officium* (staff) of the procurator – that is, financial procurator – of the province. Soldiers served and escorted even minor procuratorial officials; when Pliny was governor of Bithynia in 109–11, the 'Prefect of the Pontic Shore'

61

had a centurion, two cavalrymen and ten *beneficiarii*, while the procurator of the province had also ten *beneficiarii*.

Soldiers on staff duties differed from *apparitores* in that they were relatively permanent, not coming and going with each governor. By the third century these 'officiales' were coming to be regarded as a class separate from the army proper – a step towards the civil service, still called 'militia', of the fourth century.

On a higher social level, a governor would take with him friends from Rome, who could act as his advisers in giving judgment, and might have with him also some literary men (for instance the antiquarian writer, Valerius Maximus, went to Asia with the proconsul Sextus Pompeius about AD 27). The appearance of a minor court which this gave was heightened by the fact that he might also employ, as did the Emperor, learned men to help with his correspondence and other matters. The best example of this is the letter in which Cornelius Fronto describes to Antoninus Pius his preparations for going as proconsul of Asia in the 150s (which ill-health in the end prevented): he had summoned friends and relations from home (Cirta in Africa), learned acquaintances from Alexandria who were to have charge of his Greek correspondence (with the cities of the province), prominent men from Cilicia, whose interests he had previously defended before the Emperor, and a man (an equestrian tribune?) from Mauretania who was experienced at hunting down brigands.[9] Such positions with the góvernor might go to prominent men from the province itself; a first-century inscription from Miletus shows a man who not only held important local offices there, but had been an official *comes* (companion) of one of the governors of the province, and had charge of his letters, legal replies and edicts. Philo describes with some bitterness how a prominent Alexandrian, one of the leaders of the anti-Jewish pogrom of 38, had been keeper of the judicial records of the Prefect of Egypt, and had amassed a fortune by taking bribes to alter them.[10] Once again we see the fusion between local and Roman elements in the régime.

Such was the structure of the administrative hierarchy. What we know of the details of its working comes mainly from provincial sources, like the Gospels or the Greek orators, or from inscriptions put up by cities to record privileges or favourable verdicts granted them by governors or Emperors. Both of these types of evidence are naturally confined to those areas of the Empire – chiefly the Greek provinces, Africa and Southern Spain – where an urbanized literate society existed. It should be made clear that we know virtually nothing of the workings of administration in, say, Britain, Lusitania, Noricum or Pannonia Superior.

Given that very large limitation, we know in fair detail how a governor – whether proconsul, *legatus* or procurator made very little difference – carried on his normal business (the conduct of military operations belongs in a different context). Firstly, then, if he were going to a province like Asia or Africa, whose more prominent inhabitants had friends in Rome, he would receive letters, even before his departure, recommending individuals there for his interest and favour; Marcus Aurelius himself, when 'Caesar' in the 150s, wrote to Fronto before his expected departure for Asia, recommending a man who had been introduced to him in Rome; Fronto himself writes to Aufidius Victorinus asking him to get a certain orator a public post as a teacher in the province he was governing. By the early third century, when Ulpian wrote his *On the Office of Proconsul*, a proconsul (we do not know explicitly about *legati*) had to send on to the province an edict announcing the date of his arrival, commending himself to the people and formally requesting a minimum of disturbance in greeting him; the place of arrival was fixed by custom and as a privilege for the city concerned – Ephesus in the case of Asia.

Such diplomatic elements in the position of a governor are often ignored. But a provincial governor often had very limited force at his immediate disposal, and the job involved of necessity successful relations with the important men and important cities of the province; indeed it was only by creating a unity of interest between Rome and its emissaries and the provincial upper classes that the Empire survived. We see this most vividly in the New Testament; once exposed both to personal pressure by the High Priests and Sanhedrin, and to popular pressure from the mob, Pilate has no option (if he wishes to avoid serious disturbances) but to have Christ executed. Then in Acts we have another illustration of provincial politics and diplomacy. When the new procurator, Festus, arrived in 60, he heard the accusations of the High Priestly party against Paul and 'wishing to do them a favour' asked Paul if he were willing to be tried in Jerusalem; it was then that Paul appealed to Caesar. A few days later Agrippa (a descendant of Herod, now ruling only some districts in Syria, but with hereditary rights as representative of the Jews) and his sister Berenice arrived to pay their respects to the new procurator, and was invited to examine Paul's case; Paul's self-explanation was heard in the procurator's audience-chamber by Festus, Agrippa, the officers (of the auxiliary cohorts) and 'the leading men of the city' (Caesarea).

The prime duty of a governor was the preservation of order, and the basic form of his activities was that of going round the province on a fixed circuit holding judicial sessions at each of a certain number of cities. The judicial session was known as a *conventus* (from the fact that people gathered for it from a wide area) and the status of a *conventus*-city (*metropolis* in the Greek provinces) was much prized. Addressing the people of Apameia in Asia about AD 100, and listing the sources of their good fortune, the orator Dio Chrysostom said, 'What is more the courts are held here every year, and a vast crowd of people collects, litigants, jurymen, orators, governors, attendants, slaves, pimps, muleteers, merchants, prostitutes, workmen. So those who have goods to sell can obtain the highest prices, and nothing lies idle in the city neither beasts of burden, nor houses, nor women.'[11] On the governor's arrival at any important city he would be greeted with speeches commending the city and praising himself; Ulpian says that proconsuls should put up with such speeches without impatience. By contrast, Dio Chrysostom urges the people of his native town, Prusa in Bithynia, to greet the governor with applause when he visits their assembly, and not assail him with mutual accusations.

If a city wished to bring matters before a governor without waiting for his arrival, they sent an embassy to him and received a letter in return (it is one of the essentials of the pattern of Roman administration that the cities acted and were treated *in form* like sovereign states). Thus Tullius Geminus, *legatus* of Moesia Inferior 47–50, writes to the 'Magistrates, Council and People' of Histria: 'Your ambassadors (whom he lists) found me in Tomoi, handed over your decree, expressed their loyalty to the Emperor and their pleasure at my good health and presence here, and carried out most conscientiously the talks with me on the matters about which you had instructed them . . .'[12]

The business of a provincial governor was conducted by reference firstly to the *lex provinciae* – law of the province (where there was such a thing) – an enactment laid down at the time the province was established, which determined the constitutions, legal status, privileges, laws and territories of the cities, and which might have been emended by subsequent senatorial or Imperial decisions; and secondly an edict issued by himself on arrival, which stated a list of principles which he would use in giving judgments; the edicts, whose detailed contents are very little known, probably remained very stable from governor to governor.

Thus both changes of any kind in the status or constitution of a city, or disputes about these things, and also differences between cities over privileges or (most common of all) boundaries would come before the governor. Inscriptions from several provinces show governors, often assisted by Imperial procurators, settling boundaries. A long inscription from Sardinia shows the proconsul there in 69 delivering judgment in a long-drawn-out boundary dispute between two communities; the offending parties had been sternly instructed by one previous governor to vacate the land, and had not done so; another one had given them a fixed time to get a ground-plan sent from the Imperial archives, which again they had not done. So now the proconsul again ordered their departure.[13] On other occasions a governor was asked to intervene in the internal affairs of a city either to establish a point of law, such as the legal powers of the magistrates, or to deal with a particular crisis. Thus in 93 the magistrates of the colony of Antioch in Pisidia wrote to the *legatus* of Cappadocia saying there was a corn-shortage, and asking him to take steps; so he ordered all inhabitants to make available for sale all corn over and above their household needs which they had in stock, threatened penalties against hoarding, and fixed a maximum price.[14]

From about the end of the first century we find provincial governors taking a more systematically active role in the affairs of cities, especially with regard to finance. The documents show governors approving new endowments, and permitting distribution of cash or the establishment of festivals. Ulpian says that a governor during his stay in a city must inspect the temples and public buildings to see if they need repair, and have the work done, as far as the finances of the city permit; he should appoint men to supervise the work and, if need be, detach soldiers to assist them. These increased responsibilities must have been limited, however, by the establishment, from the same period of *curatores* – of senatorial, equestrian or lower status – for the finances of individual cities, or groups of cities, who were appointed directly by the Emperor.

Furthermore it was always possible for the cities to contact the Emperor. Sometimes a city appealed against a decision of the governor; sometimes a governor wrote spontaneously to the Emperor to consult him. In the first century this seems to have been done only by Imperial *legati*. But from the reign of Hadrian on proconsuls did so too; so for instance we find the proconsul of Asia in 125/6 writing to Hadrian about a dispute over sacred lands, and the rent from them, in the city of Ephesus; Hadrian writes back giving his decision, and the proconsul writes to the city enclosing both Hadrian's letter and his own letter to the Imperial procurator (and the latter's rather arrogant reply) asking him to get the lands measured.[15]

But there were also a large number of cases where cities went direct to the Emperor, sometimes on purely diplomatic errands (Pliny discovered that Byzantium sent an embassy to the Emperor every year at considerable expense), but often on serious matters. So also did the provincial assemblies, at least in the second century; Hadrian sent a rescript to the assembly of Baetica about cattle-rustlers, and Antoninus Pius to that of Asia on the immunity of orators and other public teachers. Many examples of embassies to the Emperor are given in the chapters on the various regions. How the Emperor dealt with them will be discussed below.

It can thus be seen that the real power of the provincial governor in dealing with the communities under him was limited both by the existence of the Emperor and by the growth of other posts whose occupants, appointed by the Emperor, operated in the provinces. Much the same pattern can be seen in the governors' jurisdiction over individuals. Of the governors civil jurisdiction (which will have been confined to the more important cases) we do not have much direct evidence. Our fullest evidence is indirect – the Imperial rescripts on matters of private law which make up the whole of the *Codex Justinianus* and are quoted occasionally in the *Digest*; these are directed both to private persons and to the governors taking the cases, and thus again show the degree to which the Emperor overshadowed the officials.

From at least the end of the second century, and probably before, cases about sums due (from fines, confiscations, vacant inheritances or commercial transactions) to the Imperial *Fiscus* were dealt with independently by Imperial procurators; the new position is summed up in the words of Ulpian, 'There is nothing in the province which is not the proconsul's concern. But if there is a case about money due to the Fiscus, which concerns the Emperor's procurator, he does better to keep off.'[16] Furthermore, second and early third century inscriptions from Imperial estates (especially those in Africa) and mining areas show the procurators exercising effective police powers and settling disputes. Even outside the area of the Imperial interests and properties, some items of late-second- and third-century evidence show procurators deciding ordinary civil cases.

The evidence for criminal jurisdiction is much fuller, especially in Christian sources, from the Gospels and Acts to the Acts of the Martyrs. Once again, much criminal jurisdiction from the provinces came to the Emperor. Sometimes accusations were brought before him directly without (it seems) the provincial governor being involved at all; for instance Trajan when in Rome took the case of a prominent Ephesian accused by his enemies. On other occasions governors sent men, mainly those accused of political crimes, for trial to the Emperor. When Pliny found Christians accused before him in Bithynia he had the others executed, but set aside those who were Roman citizens for despatch to Rome. The *legatus* of Gaul in 177, however, merely wrote to Marcus Aurelius about the punishment of the Christians. Consultation of the Emperor rather than despatch of the prisoner himself had also become the rule by the end of the second century in respect of the class of *decuriones* (town-councillors) and above; with the growth from Hadrian (117–38) of the system, mentioned in the first chapter, by which they were exempt from the harsh penalties reserved for 'plebei', it became obligatory for provincial governors to consult the Emperors before sentencing them to deportation.

There remains the vexed question of the right of Roman citizens as such to appeal to the Emperor. The best-known case, that of Paul, turns out not to be very clear. It is when the centurion arrests and is about to beat him in the temple that Paul proclaims his citizenship; his appeal to Caesar comes later, when Festus suggests moving his trial from Caesarea back to Jerusalem. The other known first-century case is equally unhelpful; when a man appealed from the tribunal of the *legatus* of Germany in 68, the *legatus* went through the mime of moving to a higher tribunal (i.e. playing the role of Emperor), made him plead his case and then executed him. The normal view that a Republican right of appeal to the people remained as a right of citizens as such to appeal to the Emperor may be correct, but rests on slender evidence.

Much better known is the second-century system whereby, once a provincial governor had given his verdict, the prisoner would appeal, whereupon the governor would send to the Emperor a statement about the case, with a *libellus* (petition) from the appellant. In this case, as with those of the deportation of *decuriones*, the execution of the sentence was delayed until the Emperor's answer was received.

In criminal jurisdiction too, Imperial procurators came to play a role, though, with two temporary exceptions, this represented an improper usurpation, and was the subject of a number of Imperial rescripts – evidently ineffectual – designed to prevent it. As early as the 60s we find procurators in the Imperial province of Tarraconensis (Spain) condemning people and confiscating their goods, while the *legatus* stood by helpless; and the revolt in Africa in 238 which led to the proclamation of the proconsul, Gordian, as Emperor, was sparked off by exactions and condemnations by a procurator. Typical of the Imperial rescripts is one sent by Caracalla in 212 – 'My procurator – if not acting in place of the governor – could not (properly) have sentenced you to exile; so you need not fear a sentence which has no legal validity' (but which had none the less been passed). The two exceptions were cases of kidnapping and adultery, in which Caracalla conceded the jurisdiction which procurators had long usurped; but a rescript of Gordian III, written in 239, firmly denies the jurisdiction of procurators in cases of kidnapping.

Such was the administration of the provinces, omitting the peace-time activities of the army, and, equally important, finance. Finance, as regards the taxes paid by individuals and the manner of their exaction, will be described in the next chapter, on State and Citizen. As regards the level above that, that is the question of how State funds were handled by provincial officials, what methods of accounting were used, how coin was transported and distributed for the payment of troops and officials, and how far there were shipments of coin or bullion from the provinces to Rome or the other way, we are in complete darkness.

The very faint traces of evidence available can best be considered along with two branches of the 'central administration' (the term is an exaggeration), the treasury (Aerarium) in Rome, and the mints in Rome and the provinces. The study of the Aerarium suffers from the disadvantage already mentioned, the total lack of evidence about the transport of funds to and from it. The Aerarium itself, however, is fairly well known. It was the temple of Saturn on the side of the Capitol hill, which had served since the early Republic as the depository for the treasure, including coin, and documents of the State. Among the documents were financial ones, State contracts and the accounts deposited by provincial governors on leaving their province; provincial governors also 'reported' their *apparitores*, *comites* and others to

69

the Aerarium, thus putting them on the list for pay, and (it seems) continued to do so even in the third century. But the officials of the Aerarium – quaestors in the Republic and then, after various changes, Prefects of ex-praetorian rank, chosen by the Emperor – never used these documents to make up general accounts or a budget for the State. Their functions were limited to keeping the cash and documents, to making payments on the authority of the Senate or the Emperor, and to some judicial activities, which they acquired in the Empire, over the recovery of debts. They did not administer or plan the finance of the Empire. The Aerarium is a prime example of the survival in the Empire – to the mid-fourth century, in fact – of the primitive and now inadequate institutions of the city-state. To meet the deficiencies five separate commissions of senators were set up in the course of the first century, with the task of calling in revenue or limiting expenditure; none of them is recorded as having done anything. The management of State finance was left – in so far as it was managed at all – to the Emperor and his assistants.

In spite of the immense volume of evidence provided by the many thousands of coins surviving from the Empire, very little is known of the mints themselves and even less of the processes of decision which governed their output. Here too there was a surviving Republican element, the *tresviri monetales* (moneyers) – three of the posts in the most junior senatorial, or rather pre-senatorial, rank, the Vigintivirate. These posts are attested until the mid-third century. Among the bronze and copper coins produced in Rome and circulating mainly in Italy and the West (bronze and copper coins produced locally in the Western provinces disappear by the middle of the first century) the majority are marked S.C. (*senatus consulto* – 'by a decision of the Senate'). The types on the coins, however, are very similar to those of Imperial coins – which include all gold and (in the West) nearly all silver – produced at Lyon until Caligula (37–41) and thereafter at Rome. The letters S.C. *may* indicate that the separate issues were decided on by the Senate and produced by the *monetales*; but there is no evidence for the Senate doing this, and equally no evidence for the activity of the *monetales*, apart from the appearance of the title on inscriptions.

Nor is there any evidence from the first century for officials of the Imperial mint at Rome. Under Trajan (98–117), however, a Procurator of the Mint appears; and from 115 we have some dedications by the workers there – *officinatores* (?), *signatores* (die-cutters?), *suppostores* (setters?), *malleatores* (strikers?) – all of them Imperial freedmen, aided by Imperial slaves. Under Aurelian (270–5) the mint-workers in Rome were numerous enough to stage a serious revolt whose suppression required thousands of soldiers. In the Greek provinces, apart from the local city mints striking bronze and copper coinage, there were provincial and some city mints striking silver coins on standards different from those of the Rome coinage. These mints are none the less regarded as 'Imperial', though nothing whatsoever is known about them except the coins themselves.

The question of who decided the frequency of issues, the standard of the coins (the silver coins especially show a steady debasement from Nero on, ending in complete collapse in the second half of the third century), or the type and legends to be put on them is totally obscure. The last point is particularly tantalizing, since the Imperial coinage carried propaganda for the Emperors in a vast variety of forms – representations of Imperial constructions (like the harbour at Ostia), largesses or victories – or slogans like AETERNITAS or PROVIDENTIA. Much of the history of the Empire can be seen reflected in the coins. Yet we are ignorant not only of who decided what should be portrayed, but to whom the new coins were issued and under what circumstances (in donatives to the army and *congiaria* to the Roman people?). The point is important, for coins remained in circulation a very long time after their issue: 64 per cent of the coins buried in hoards during the Flavian period (66–96) had been minted before 27 BC. Hoards show similarly that coins in circulation in the Antonine period (138–80) averaged about fifty years from the date of issue. Our only clue to the sources of decisions is two lines of a consolatory poem by Statius on the death in the 90s of a former Imperial freedman *a rationibus* (in charge of accounts); among his duties was to decide how much metal 'should be struck in the fire of the Italian (Roman) Mint'.[17]

That apart, we have two references in the historian Cassius

Dio to Imperial coinage; in one he says (as the coin hoards abundantly confirm) that Trajan called in old coins and issued new ones; in the other he says that his own contemporary Caracalla (211-17) gave debased coins to his subjects, but good ones to the barbarians across the frontier – whom by this time Rome was buying off. In neither case does he say anything of the processes of decision. More details about the Imperial coinage and its collapse in the third century will come in the final chapter; for the moment the coinage must serve as an example of how little we know of many aspects of the Imperial system.

When we come to the actual activities of the Emperor, his advisers and his assistants, the same warning must apply. In a famous passage Cassius Dio explains that, while in the history of the Republic the truth could be arrived at because affairs were subject to public debate, different accounts in historians could be compared, and public records checked, in Imperial history it was not so: 'After this time most things began to be done secretly and by hidden means; and if anything is made public it is disbelieved, since it cannot be checked. For it is suspected that everything is said and done by the wish of the Emperors and those who have influence with them. As a result many rumours spread about things which never in fact happened, many things which happened are unknown, and nearly all public versions of the events are different from the reality.'[18] That is a fair introduction to the state of our knowledge about the central decision-making processes of the Empire. There are some areas about which we are relatively well-informed; Imperial jurisdiction was very often – partly as a matter of propaganda – carried on in public, and descriptions of cases therefore find their way into the literary sources. Favourable decisions, given in the form of letters, to delegations from cities tended to be recorded in inscriptions; the literary evidence also has descriptions of how delegations were received. Petitions from individuals were also received in public, and beyond that the literary evidence contains a lot of details about the fortunes of individuals – including in some cases the writers themselves – at the hands of the Emperor. Finally the law-codes (the *Digest* and the *Codex Justinianus*) quote a large number of rescripts on matters of private law addressed to governors, magistrates and private persons, dating mostly from the reign of Hadrian (117–38) onwards; while some of the lawyers whose works make up the *Digest* occasionally retail legal debates on the Imperial council, on which they themselves sat.

In other words the type of Imperial activity we know about is essentially that in response to the needs or conflicts of individuals or communities. It cannot be denied, indeed, that such activity took up a large part of the Emperor's working life; this type of work will be discussed in the last part of this chapter. But beyond this there are substantial areas where, for all the basic inertia of the system, positive decisions must have been made, and about which we have almost no evidence. Tiberius, as a demonstration of his Republican attitude, allowed the Senate to debate about revenues, public works, the recruitment and dismissal of soldiers, military commands and letters to client kings. The implication must be that these things were normally decided by the Emperor, presumably with his friends. What evidence have we about decision-making on such matters?

The best evidence of a debate about finance is the occasion in 58 when the people complained of the exactions of the *publicani*; Nero, it is stated, thought of abolishing the indirect taxes altogether, but was dissuaded by his advisers, who said that the Empire would collapse if they were abolished – and the people would go on to ask for the abolition of tribute also.[19] The Emperor's friends apart, however, there was the freedman 'in charge of accounts' (*a rationibus*) superseded at the end of the first century by an *eques* (his subordinates however remained freedmen). Some of these subordinates had purely domestic functions; a *rationalis* mentioned by Galen had the job of supplying from the Imperial stores the herbs which Galen mixed daily for the antidote taken by Marcus Aurelius (161–80). As for the functions of the *a rationibus* himself, Augustus left in 14 a general statement of the finances of the Empire, adding the names of slaves and freedmen from whom more details could be obtained. He, Tiberius (until he left Rome in 26) and Gaius also published public accounts, but later Emperors did not. The accounts themselves presumably continued to be kept;

but our only evidence is the passage of Statius mentioned earlier in which he describes in poetic terms the functions of the dead *a rationibus*, 'Now was entrusted to him alone the control of the Imperial wealth (a list of revenues follows) . . . quickly he calculates what the Roman arms beneath every sky demand, how much the tribes (the people of Rome) and the temples, how much the lofty aqueducts, the fortresses by the coasts or the far-flung lines of road require . . .'[20]

About decisions on public works or recruitment and dismissal we have no evidence at all. From a related area, declarations of war or the making of peace, we have two examples, Nero's consultation of 'the leading men of the State' about war with Parthia in 63 and the occasion, already referred to, when Commodus disregarded his advisers and made peace in 180. About appointments, however – that is the 'commendation' of senators for magistracies, the appointment of senators to Prefectures, curatorships or governorships, or of *equites* and freedmen in the Imperial service – we have much better evidence, all of which shows that the appointments were made personally by the Emperor (Tacitus notes that Tiberius actually appointed some procurators whom he did not know, on the basis of reputation), influenced inevitably by the favourites of the moment and by personal petitions or letters from patrons of candidates. Pliny writes to Trajan asking for the praetorship for a friend; Fronto writes to Antoninus Pius to ask for a procur-atorship for an Imperial freedman ('If you do not recognize the man personally, when you come to the name Aridelus, remember that I have commended him to you') and another procuratorship for an *eques*, the historian Appian. There also may have been, at least for the lower personnel, a regular system of reports. Pliny at least sent from Bithynia what are evidently brief formal reports on the Imperial employees; and in the only clear bit of evidence on an Imperial 'secretary' concerned with promotions – again a poem by Statius, addressed to the *ab epistulis* (in charge of letters) – he is said to send letters of appointment as a *primus pilus,* or for equestrian military posts.[21]

The actual appointments were made by the Emperor (Dom-itian was overheard asking his favourite freak, 'Why did I give

Mettius Rufus the last appointment as Prefect of Egypt?') and was transmitted by a 'codicil' dictated by him, if not actually written in his own hand: an inscription contains the actual text of one of these, from Marcus Aurelius to a procurator: 'Having long wished to promote you to the splendour of a ducenariate procuratorship I now use an opportunity which has presented itself. Succeed therefore to Marius Pudens, with the hope of my lasting favour while you continue to display your probity, diligence and skill.'[22]

Modern books tend to assume, on the model of present-day bureaucratic procedure, that correspondence directed to an Emperor was digested by the 'bureau' of the 'ab epistulis' and an answer drafted, which would then be signed by the Emperor. This is not so. Firstly, ancient letters were not signed; secondly the evidence makes clear that letters were brought directly to the Emperor, who would read them and dictate a reply. Augustus had removed a *legatus* because when reading a letter from him he saw that he had written 'ixi' instead of 'ipsi'; Philo describes how Gaius read a letter from the governor of Syria, getting angrier as he read, and then dictated a reply. When Caracalla (211–17) was on campaign in Syria he directed his mother Julia Domna (not, it should be noted, a 'secretary') to read and deal with the routine correspondence. This she did; a recently published inscription contains a letter from Julia to Ephesus, the only one from an Empress to a city.[23] Reading letters and dictating the replies was part of the Imperial routine. Vespasian began his day by reading letters and the reports of the secretariats, and then admitted his friends to salute him; when he grew old his son Titus would do the dictation for him.

An Emperor's dealings with cities or provinces were conducted mainly by means of delegations. If the city's delegation was coming on a purely diplomatic mission, or to ask for some favour not opposed by any other party, the form was that they were admitted to the Emperor's presence, one of them (sometimes an orator hired for the occasion) made a speech, and then the decree of the city was handed to the Emperor, who seems sometimes to have read it there and then. When a delegation arrived either to make accusations or to contest some matter with a rival delegation, both sides spoke, and the procedure took the form of a judicial hearing. Many embassies came on diplomatic errands, congratulating an Emperor on his accession, bringing gold crowns on the occasion of a triumph, or consoling him on the death of a relative. Even these embassies were actually heard by the Emperor. When an embassy from Ilium (Troy) was making, rather belatedly, a consolatory speech to Tiberius on the death of his son Drusus in 23, he replied sarcastically, 'And I in turn offer my sympathy for the death of your fellow-citizen Hector.' Hearings before the Emperor became an arena in which fame and fortune might be won; for instance, an orator from Arabia, Heliodorus, travelled all the way to the German frontier to represent his native town before Caracalla, and on being called into court before he was ready by the official 'in charge of hearings' (*a cognitionibus*) managed to turn the occasion to his advantage, was asked by the Emperor to deliver an extempore oration (on the theme 'Demosthenes, after breaking down before Philip, defends himself on the charge of cowardice'), and was awarded with the post of *advocatus fisci* and the privilege of riding in the annual procession of *equites* in Rome.[24]

On other occasions the decree of a city might be sent on to the Emperor by the governor of the province. In either case, the decree would be read by the Emperor and an answer dictated following the order of the points in the original decree – which tended to begin with some point of a diplomatic nature and go on to matters of substance. Thus Claudius, writing in response to an embassy from Thasos in 42, deals in turn with their proposal to build a temple to him, the confirmation of privileges granted them by Augustus, and with questions about their revenues and the export of corn.[25] The last known Imperial letter in response to an embassy from our period (they appear again in the period of Diocletian and Constantine), was written by Valerian and Gallienus from Antioch in 255 to Philadelphia in Asia. The Philadelphians had complained that the *koinon* (council) of Asia had laid on minor cities like their own expenses of the High Priest and presidents of festivals formerly born only by the *metropoleis*. The Emperors granted their request to be excused, expressing in rather moralizing terms the hope that they would not use the favour to the detriment of other cities.[26]

In all this it is not clear what the Imperial secretaries 'for Greek letters' or 'for Latin letters' actually did. From what Philostratus says about Aelius Antipater, mentioned above – that he wrote Imperial letters in a more pleasing and suitable style than anyone else – it seems that the Greek secretary actually composed the letters to Greek cities in Greek, presumably being given a draft in Latin. Beyond that we are in the dark.

Such was the main form of Imperial contact with the cities. Individuals who wished to approach the Emperor often did so by presenting written *libelli* containing their requests (or on occasion denunciations of others). It is evident that at least in the early period *libelli* were presented personally to the Emperor at his regular audience-sessions (*salutationes*); Augustus is recorded to have said to a man who handed over his *libellus* with excessive timidity, 'You are like a man giving a coin to an elephant.' These too were read by the Emperor – the plan for Domitian's murder was that he should be handed a *libellus* and struck down while reading it – as he did *libelli* which, like letters from cities, might be sent on by a provincial governor. When Pliny sent on to Trajan a *libellus* from an auxiliary centurion in Bithynia, Trajan replied, 'I have read the *libellus* . . . which you sent; moved by his entreaty, I have granted his daughter the Roman citizenship. I have sent you the *libellus* with the rescript to give to him.'[27] The phrase 'the *libellus* with the rescript' is evidently a reference to the fact that an Emperor, like magistrates and governors, normally answered *libelli* by writing a brief answer (*subscriptio*) underneath. Thus, in answer to a long *libellus* from the tenants of Imperial estates in Africa, complaining that undue days of free labour were being exacted from them by middlemen, Commodus (180–92) wrote, 'The procurators, observing orders and my instructions that no more than two or three days labour (should be demanded), will see to it that nothing is wrongfully demanded from you in contravention of the standing arrangement.'[28]

A *libellus* might thus be a request for anything (there was no exemption from legal liabilities, no status, no release from a penalty which an Emperor could not grant purely as a matter of grace) from cash, to citizenship, to the righting of wrongs. As such, the *libellus-subscriptio* system shades indistinguishably into the rescript system, by which Emperors gave written replies on points of law. But before we come to that it is necessary to look at the Emperor's role in civil and criminal jurisdiction. The Emperor's jurisdiction, whose formal legal origins – if any – are not easy to discern, was part, in one respect, of his public role in settling disputes and righting wrongs, and as such is continuous with the hearing of embassies (which might in any case be bringing civil or criminal actions against individuals) or of complaints from private persons. In another respect, the private trial and condemnation of prominent men suspected of subversion, it was a weapon, often greatly abused, against the upper classes and possible rivals, and a source of great bitterness and tension in relations between Emperor and Senate.

These last cases were likely to be held in secret within the walls of the Palace. In routine jurisdiction, Emperors would sometimes make a point of sitting in judgment in the Forum (assisted as always by their friends), but would also take cases at a regular *auditorium* in the Palace, at their villas in Italy, or on campaign. The only indisputably genuine verbatim record we have of a case before the Emperor, is one brought by some Syrian villagers against a man who had usurped the priesthood of their local temple, heard by Caracalla at Antioch in 216.[29]

This case had not been heard by the *legatus* of Syria, but was taken by the Emperor as a matter of grace in response to a petition. In this it was not exceptional. Firstly, the Emperor tried rivals and conspirators himself. Some civil and criminal cases came to him as a result of appeals; some prisoners were sent from the provinces to be tried by him, and even some civil cases seem to have been referred to him spontaneously by governors; Fronto made a long speech before Antoninus Pius protesting against the action of a proconsul of Asia in referring cases of disputed wills to the Emperor, and pointing out the delays and inconveniences which would result if that procedure were adopted generally. But these types of case apart, there appears to have been no machinery whatsoever for choosing which cases were heard by the Emperor; plaintiffs or accusers put a case before him and, if he wished, he heard it. Pliny the Younger, for instance, was invited to the *consilium* of Trajan when he was hearing a number of cases at his villa at Centumcellae about 106; the cases were those of a prominent Ephesian accused by his enemies, the wife of a military tribune accused of adultery with a centurion (here the *legatus* of the province had referred the case to Trajan – and Trajan added in his judgment that he did not wish to call all adultery cases to himself), and of an *eques* and an Imperial freedman who were accused of falsifying a will – the heirs had simply written to Trajan when he was in Dacia and asked him to take the case. The hearings lasted three days, during which the Emperor's advisers were entertained at the villa, and afterwards rewarded with gifts.[30]

Even though, as mentioned earlier, professional jurists began to be employed in 'secretarial' positions with the Emperor, to rise to the Praetorian Prefecture (which meant being with the Emperors in court), or to be employed as paid '*consiliarii*' – the earliest case is a jurisconsult who was later also 'a libellis' and 'a cognitionibus' (in charge of hearings') under Commodus (180–92) – the actual judgments were always given by the Emperor himself. The lawyer Marcellus describes how Marcus Aurelius, when deciding a difficult case, dismissed his advisers, meditated alone and then reassembled the court to hear the verdict; the great legal writer Paulus relates how he urged an opinion on Septimius Severus, who listened but took the opposite view.

For the last half century or so of the period we have, as with other things, little evidence about Imperial jurisdiction at work. What we do have is the rescripts quoted subject by subject in the *Codex Justinianus*. These decline very sharply in number in this period – the *Codex* quotes a total of 369 from the decade 220–30, 67 from 250–60, 26 from 260–70, and 9 from 270–80; but though the volume of legal decisions thus declined dramatically in the most troubled years of the Empire, it is significant that the flow of rescripts never disappeared altogether.[31]

Rescripts begin to be attested in significant numbers from

Hadrian (117–38) onwards, and were addressed not only to magistrates and governors but also to private persons, including common soldiers, freedmen and even slaves. Sometimes the rescript is merely a directive to the addressee to go to the proper authority; thus the lawyer Salvius Julianus says, 'I have often heard Caesar (Antoninus Pius) saying that the rescript, "You can approach the provincial governor" does not impose on a proconsul or his *legatus* or the governor of a province the obligation to hear the case'.[32] Other rescripts, which, like cases and embassies, continued to be dealt with during journeys and campaigns, were answers on actual points of law. Thus in 283 we find Carus and his sons sending a rescript from Emesa in Syria to advise a man that a transfer of property to him was illegal, as a contravening a decision of the Senate.

This item of Imperial business, insignificant in itself, might serve to point to the main developments of the period, the continued existence of the Senate but steady exclusion of it and its members from the active exercise of power, the development of an 'Imperial' administration growing round the senatorial framework and eventually invading it, and above all the increasingly independent role of the Emperor as the sole real source of political decisions and of law.

5

State and Subject: the Cities

The New Testament provides the best starting-point from which to look at the relations of State and subject under the Empire. In the Gospels we have the reflection of the census carried out in AD 6 when Judaea became a Roman province; we find Christ and the pharisees debating the payment of tribute, and we see the tax-collectors at work, the procurator exercising jurisdiction and the Roman army keeping order. One of Christ's sayings relates directly to one of the key points of friction between State and people: 'If a man will have you go with him one mile, go with him twain' (Matthew v. 41); the word Christ uses is *angareuein*, the conventional Greek term for the exaction of services by soldiers and official travellers. Precisely the same situation is reflected in the instructions of Domitian (81–96) to the procurator of Syria about the conduct of soldiers, recorded on an inscription: 'Let no one take a guide who does not have my authorisation; for if the peasants are dragged away, the fields remain untilled'.[1]

With the travels of Paul in Acts we see a different world, that of the Greek cities, or the Roman colonies of Philippi and Corinth. Here the Roman presence is less immediate and the principal role is played by the authorities of the cities themselves. Here too we see the status and protection conferred in this early stage by the Roman citizenship, a value which it was to lose in the course of the period.

The fact that the Judaean narratives and that of Paul's travels provide different views of the Roman State is not accidental. For the whole nature of a man's contacts with the State was

81

bound up with the nature of the community to which he belonged. 'Community' normally meant city, that is an urban centre electing, or at least producing, its own magistrates, having (normally) a city council and a 'territory' containing villages which were under its jurisdiction. The essentials of the pattern are given in an Imperial letter from the very end of our period granting the people of Tymandus in Pisidia (Asia Minor) the status of a city (*civitas*): 'Since it is innate in us to desire that throughout all our world the dignity and number of the cities should be increased, and since we see that the Tymandenes long to receive the name and status of "city", and promise fervently that there will be a sufficient supply of *decuriones* (town-councillors) among them, we think the request should be granted ... let them exercise with our permission the rights exercised by other cities, of convening a city council, passing decrees and doing other business which the law permits; they will have to appoint magistrates, aediles, quaestors and whatever other posts are necessary.'² Villages might have their own officials and even councils; the technical distinction between a village (called normally *vicus* in Latin or *komē* in Greek, but also a variety of other names) seems to have been that by definition a city could not be in the 'territory' of another city, whereas villages nearly always were. Thus Septimius Severus (193–211) punished Antioch in Syria for its support of his rival Pescennius Niger, by reducing it technically to the status of a *komē* in the territory of Laodicea.

What we know of the life and functions of the cities relates mostly to the more obvious public or communal aspects, the erection of buildings and temples, the provision of festivals and games, the passing of decrees and despatch of embassies, distributions of oil or corn or the provision of corn in shortages. More precise questions about the role of the city are often not easy to answer. The income of a city came from a variety of sources, rents from public land (which might lie outside the territory of the city) or public buildings, tolls, legacies, fines imposed by the magistrates, the sale of priesthoods and, much more common, *summae honorariae*, sums paid by magistrates or city councillors on entry to the position. As evidence for the revenues of a city we have the letter Antoninus Pius (138–61) wrote to a city in Macedonia in response to an embassy asking him to let them tap various sources of income (new forms of city income had normally to be approved by the Emperor). He mentions tolls, apparently approving their imposition on non-citizens of the place, permits them to levy a tax of one *denarius* per head on the free population (this is the only known example of a *direct* tax paid to a city) and allows them to have a council of eighty members who will each pay an entrance fee of 500 Attic drachmas.[3] The regular incomes of cities were thus very limited. But the limitations were compensated for by the tradition, backed by heavy popular pressure, of large-scale munificence – in the form of buildings, shows, distribution and free services – on the part of the leading men.

Antoninus Pius concluded his letter by laying down that non-citizens (like citizens?) should be subject, as plaintiffs and defendants, to the jurisdiction of the city magistrates in cases involving up to 250 *denarii*. That is one of the rare items of evidence we have about the border-line of local and provincial jurisdiction. As regards local jurisdiction we can only point to examples of police action, like that taken in various cities in the case of Paul, or the power to impose fines. A document from Mylasa in Caria dating to 209–11 shows the magistrates and council of the city acting as a court to hear charges against persons acting illegally as money-changers, imposing fines, and having slaves flogged and imprisoned.[4]

Even less is known of the all-important subject of the relation of a city to the villages in its territory. We know in general terms that the cities collected from their territories the tribute due to Rome, their own indirect revenues, and later recruits for the army (or a tax in lieu). But we have direct evidence of the relations only for instance in a decree from Hierapolis in Asia forbidding the city police-officials (*paraphylakes*) of the territory to exact more from the villages than food, bedding and housing, or to make the village mayors (*komarchs*) offer them honorific crowns against their will.[5] Similarly, some villagers in Phrygia in 244–7 complain of the exactions not only of passing imperial officials but of 'the powerful men in the city'.

Some oppression is equally clear in the passage (quoted in Ch. 11) where Galen describes how the peasants starved after all the best crops had been removed to the cities. We do not know, however, whether this was in the form of rents, of official exactions or (perhaps) of supplies destined for Roman officials. A late third-century lawyer, however, does say that some cities had the privilege of collecting (apparently without compensation) a certain quantity of corn each year from the landholders in their territory.

The gradual extension of Roman rule, in various ways from conquest to alliance, to areas of very different levels of civilization, produced a variety of forms and statuses of cities, which fundamentally affected the degree of self-government, the payment of taxes and the citizen status of their inhabitants. Within this framework Italy itself enjoyed a privileged status. Its inhabitants paid no tribute and were all Roman citizens. The cities in Italy were all (depending on historical circumstances) either *municipia* or *coloniae*. A *municipium* was in origin a city with its own constitution and magistrates, whose inhabitants shared certain rights, but also duties (such as military service), with Roman citizens; *coloniae* were in origin colonies of Roman citizens established with a standard form of constitution. Now that all the inhabitants of Italy enjoyed the citizenship, the distinction was largely a matter of form (though the people of Praeneste asked Tiberius to change their status from that of *colonia* to *municipium*).

Outside Italy there were also *coloniae* (the first had been Narbonne in 118 BC) and, since the late Republic, *municipia*. *Coloniae* were settlements of Roman citizens, usually discharged legionaries, but occasionally from the civilian population, made as a formal act of State, which involved the assignation of a plot of land to each settler. This was done on the basis of a centuration, the marking-off of the entire territory into rectangular plots aligned normally on the two main roads which crossed at right-angles at the centre of the city. Inscriptions from Orange, founded probably in 35 BC for legionary veterans, preserve the map of the rectangular lots made on the orders of Vespasian in 77.[6] The soil of a colony gained the so-called *ius Italicum*

(Italian Right) by which no tribute was paid; all citizens of a colony were by definition Roman citizens. New veteran colonies continued to be founded until the reign of Hadrian, and very occasionally later. After this there remained only the custom which had grown up in the early Empire of granting the title of *colonia* to existing cities. This might sometimes, as when Hadrian made his home town, Italica in Spain, a colony, be accompanied by extension and rebuilding, but was normally only a gift of the title and rights. Even the rights did not always follow in full: Vespasian made Caesarea in Judaea a colony but remitted only the poll-tax (*tributum capitis*). The *ius Italicum*, carrying remission from the tribute on the soil (*tributum soli*), was added by his son Titus. Some titular colonies enjoyed neither right.[7]

Provincial *municipia* present a number of problems, some insoluble. They represent the extension to the Latin provinces (they are virtually unknown in the Greek areas) of a Romanized form of city constitution, which in the Empire seems to have been established in each case by a separate *lex* giving the duties of magistrates, qualification for *decuriones*, rules for conduct of elections and so forth, and which seems by this time to have followed a fairly uniform pattern. Municipal status conferred no form of immunity from tribute, but it was instrumental in conferring the citizenship – and this is where the difficulties begin. The standard form of *municipium* was one which enjoyed the 'Lesser Latin Right'(*Latium minus*), by which those who were elected to magistracies in it, and their descendants, automatically acquired the Roman citizenship; in the second century, but attested in documents only from Africa, we also find the 'Greater Latin Right' (*Latium maius*), by which all *decuriones* of the *municipium* received the citizenship. The other inhabitants of all such *municipia* were perhaps known as 'Latins' (*Latini*); there seems to be no clear evidence on how their status differed from that of ordinary non-citizens.

Beyond that there seem to have been provincial municipalities whose inhabitants (like those of Italian municipalities) were all Roman citizens; but it has sometimes been argued that no such communities existed, and the evidence for them is certainly very slight. Pliny the Elder (alone) also mentions 'towns of Roman citizens' (*oppida civium Romanorum*) in the Western provinces; but if these really existed as a legal category distinct from *municipia*, we know in effect nothing about them.[8]

The normal type of *municipium* is best known from two documents from the early 80s, the 'charters' (*leges*) received by two Spanish towns, Malaca and Salpensa, when they became *municipia* as a result of the gift by Vespasian (69–79) of *Latium minus* to all of Spain.[9] The surviving parts of the charter of Salpensa contain regulations about the acquisition of citizenship by magistrates, about the oath taken by the magistrates and about their rights of freeing slaves and appointing guardians; the charter of Malaca, of which much more survives, deals with the conduct of the elections, the choice of patrons for the municipality, the leasing of the collection of local revenues and Roman tribute to contractors, the imposition of fines by the magistrates, and the checking of municipal accounts.

Outside these types of city with specifically Roman institutions all other cities would be known just as *civitates*; in the latter part of the period the term *res publica*, applied in the Republic to the City-State of Rome itself, comes to be the most general term for a city (of any type) as an institution. A *civitas* might then be anything from a great city like Ephesus, to a 'cantonal capital' in Britain, like Silchester, Calleva Atrebatum – Calleva (the capital) of the Atrebates. Very little is known of the internal structure of *civitates* in the West. But it is evident that, if sufficiently developed, they tended to have institutions modelled in those of the colonies or municipalities; we know for instance of a 'praetor' at Bordeaux under Claudius; and Vespasian in 74 addressed a letter, in response to a delegation, to the 'magistrates and senators of the Vanacini' in Corsica.[10]

The situation is quite different with long-established Punic cities, like Lepcis Magna, in Africa, and even more so with the cities of the Greek East. Here Rome merely took over an existing pattern of cities. In a less Hellenized area like Pontus (central North Asia Minor) it had been necessary to establish a pattern of cities with large territories. Elsewhere a number of veteran colonies were founded and new Greek cities established, usually developed out of existing villages. But in general the social and

urban pattern was already set. The most noticeable change –
which for once followed a conscious policy operated since the
early second century BC – was to convert the councils (*boulai*)
of the cities into preserves of the upper classes, for which men
qualified by wealth and of which they remained members for life.
Similarly, the power of making effective decisions and of select-
ing the magistrates fell more and more into the hands of these
perpetual *boulai* composed of the richer citizens; the process was
of course uneven and we have scattered evidence of popular
assemblies continuing to meet.

The city-life of the Greek East is abundantly illustrated not
only by contemporary authors like Plutarch or Philostratus but
by thousands of inscriptions recording decrees of the council or
assembly, the erection of buildings, the offices held and services
rendered by prominent citizens, the despatch of embassies to
Emperors or governors and the text of letters from them. A
second-century inscription from Thyatira in Asia might be used
to illustrate the range of functions performed by local magistrates: 'The council and people honoured P. Aelius Menogenes
Pyrichus Marcianus (a typical name of a prominent Greek,
Roman names being added to the Greek from his having the
citizenship), the poet, *strategos* ("general" – chief magistrate),
agoranomos (market overseer), secretary of the council and
people, *ephebarchos* (in charge of the corps of young men –
epheboi), distributor of corn, *dekaprotos* (one of the ten men
charged with guaranteeing the tribute – see below), who supervised the erection of important buildings, for the nobility of his
character and the honour he has done to his native city.'[11]

Among *civitates* there were a few privileged categories,
created mainly in the wars of the Republic. *Civitates foederatae*
were those whose rights had been established by a *foedus*
(treaty) with Rome. *Civitates liberae* ('free cities') were cities
within the area of a province but in principle exempt from the
visits or jurisdiction of the provincial governor; *civitates liberae
et immunes* were both free and immune from the payment of
tribute. In the Empire all the conventional rights might be
retained as a matter of grace by the Emperor, but could be, and
often were, removed at his pleasure. New grants of such privileges

were rare: Nero proclaimed the freedom and immunity of all the cities of Greece; Vespasian removed both.

Citizens of *civitates*, unlike those of *municipia* or *coloniae* could only gain the Roman citizenship (if they were not citizens by birth) either by service in the auxiliaries or by a personal grant. In rare cases in the first century provincial governors seem to have exercised the traditional right of Roman generals to grant the citizenship to provincials. But mainly even in that period, and entirely later, these grants were a monopoly of the Emperor, extended like so many other privileges entirely as a personal favour. New citizens and their descendants took the name of their benefactor. The names of the first- and second-century Imperial dynasties, 'Julius', 'Claudius', 'Flavius', 'Aelius', 'Aurelius', recur in the names of thousands of individuals from the provincial cities, especially in the Greek East. By the end of the second century it is an exception to find a prominent local office-holder who did not have the citizenship. As mentioned earlier, it was from this class of Romanized local notables that the equestrian order and the Senate were increasingly filled.

The citizenship was the essential preliminary to equestrian or senatorial rank. But for a man who did not seek entry to these higher orders, the concrete benefits provided by the citizenship were remarkably few. Augustus had ruled in 7 BC that a grant of citizenship did not confer immunity from local obligations unless a specific grant of immunity from tribute had accompanied it; we see the distinction clearly in the case of the historian Josephus who got the citizenship from Vespasian (hence his name, Flavius Josephus) but immunity from tribute in respect of his land in Judaea from Vespasian's son Titus. In principle, therefore, a Roman citizen gained immunity only if his property was in Italy or in a colony with the 'Italian Right'. Furthermore, citizens paid, and non-citizens did not, the tax on inheritances other than those from close relatives (because inheritances by non-citizens were not recognized in Roman law). One side-effect of this was that persons newly granted the citizenship paid the tax on inheritances from their still non-citizen parents (whose status again was not recognized in Roman law); in his *Panegyric*

Pliny discusses in detail the measures taken by Nerva and Trajan to ameliorate the situation.[12] According to a hostile contemporary, Cassius Dio, Caracalla's 'universal' grant of citizenship was made solely in order to bring the entire population within the scope of this tax.

In the early part of the period the citizenship was still a rarity in the provinces, belonging mainly to emigrants from Italy or a few of the more prominent locals. The status and protection it conferred is best seen in the experiences of Paul (who was born a Roman citizen – though how his family had acquired the citizenship is a mystery). At Philippi, by revealing, only after he and Silas had been beaten by the lictors who attended the *duoviri* (*strategoi*) of the colony, that he was a Roman citizen, he was able to make the magistrates escort them humbly out of the city themselves. Later, in Jerusalem, he said to the centurion, 'Is it permitted you to beat a Roman citizen uncondemned?' The officer of the cohort was then told, the threat of beating removed, and later the tribune wrote to the procurator, and sent Paul to him. It is clear enough that Roman citizens were protected against summary beating by minor or city officials (it was also known for *civitates liberae* to lose their freedom for beating or killing Roman citizens). At a higher level, as mentioned in the last chapter, there is considerable doubt over the question of whether there was any effective right of appeal to the Emperor for citizens as such. But as late as 177 Marcus Aurelius wrote to the *legatus* of Gaul to say that Roman citizens among the Christian martyrs of Lyons should be beheaded, but non-citizens thrown to the beasts.

That is the latest concrete evidence we have for special treatment of a citizen in legal proceedings. Nearly half a century later than that, in 212 or perhaps a year or two later, Caracalla, as our literary sources say, gave the citizenship to all the inhabitants of the Empire. Further evidence is provided by an Egyptian papyrus with the actual text of Caracalla's edict; but unfortunately it is so fragmentary that nothing concrete emerges except that there is a mention of *dediticii* (a term which seems to have meant either a newly conquered and surrendered population, or persons belonging to no definite *civitas*, or freed slaves who had previously been branded by their master). The sentence, however, can be reconstructed either to mean that all statuses or orders of society received the citizenship except the *dediticii*, or that the status of *dediticii* (alone) was abolished.[13] This status, however, at least as regards freed slaves, survived until abolished in 530. If the first reconstruction is preferred, we are left with the question of whether *dediticii* were a numerically insignificant category of underprivileged persons, or whether the term in the third century would have applied to all the rural population of say the villages (*komai*) of Egypt or of the Balkan lands. All we can say is that papyri do show Egyptian peasants without Roman names in the third century, that inscriptions from the Rhine and Danube do mention Roman citizens as opposed to others, and that the *diplomata* issued to veterans of the Praetorian cohorts envisage their marrying women who were non-citizens, while those for veterans of the *equites singulares* and the fleet say also that citizenship is granted 'to those who do not have it' (but all the four third-century veterans from those units whose *diplomata* we have were in fact themselves citizens).[14] So the evidence suggests, but does not prove, that significant numbers of the population did not receive the citizenship.

If we turn to the demands which the State made on its subjects we see that these were to a large extent mediated through the cities. The principal demands were for tribute and indirect taxes, supplies and accommodation for troops and officials, the maintenance of the Imperial Post (*vehiculatio*), labour, mainly on road-building, and recruits for the army.

Of the indirect taxes two, the 1% sales tax and the 4% tax on the sale of slaves had been established by Augustus; the former was halved by Tiberius and abolished in Italy by Gaius; the latter is not attested after the first century. The 5% tax paid by slaves on the sums they paid their masters for freedom had existed since the early Republic and is attested until the early third century, when it was raised to 10% by Caracalla and reduced to 5% again by Macrinus (217–18). In view of the large number of slaves reaching freedom, this tax must have been important; but we know almost nothing of how it was collected except that collection was originally done by contractors (*publicani*) and that from the reign of Claudius to about 200 we have sporadic evidence of Imperial procurators concerned with the tax. Much more is known of the 5% tax on inheritances, already mentioned, instituted in AD 6 to provide revenue for the Military Treasury which paid the discharge donations for veterans, raised and lowered by Caracalla and Macrinus like the freedom tax, and finally attested about 240. Here too collection was in the hands of *publicani*, and then, in the second century, of Imperial procurators and their subordinate Imperial slaves and freedmen. The law required the formal opening and reading of a will in the presence of witnesses. One papyrus we have is the will of a veteran dating to 194, with the note 'Opened and read in the metropolis of Arsinoe in the Forum of Augustus at the office (*statio*) for the 5% taxes on Inheritances and Manumissions'; another papyrus, the latest specific evidence for the tax, is a declaration made in Oxyrhynchus in 237 that an inheritance is exempt from the tax (because between close relatives) and ends with an official confirmation by an Imperial freedman, a *tabularius* (clerk), evidently of the *statio* at Oxyrhynchus.[15] Both of these taxes, paid in cash, seem to have disappeared in the vast inflation of the later third century, and do not reappear later.

Most is known of the *portorium*, or toll on goods in transit, paid at slightly different levels (normally 2 or $2\frac{1}{2}$% on the value of the goods) in the different areas of the Empire; the *portorium* in Gaul, for instance, was known as the *quadragesima Galliarum* – 'the fortieth ($2\frac{1}{2}$%) of the Gauls'. These areas were in no sense customs units and the tax had no purpose beyond that of raising revenue; only at some points on the Eastern frontier – through which passed the luxury trade from India – do we find a rate of 25%; since the drain of gold to India was causing alarm as early as the reign of Tiberius, this high rate may perhaps have been intended to check the volume of trade. Here too we see a transfer from the Republican system of collection by contractors to direct collection by Imperial employees; broadly speaking, the companies of *publicani* were replaced by individual contractors (*conductores*) in the early second century and they in their turn by Imperial procurators in the late second century. The basis of the system was again posts (*stationes*) placed on the main routes, and manned, in the latest stage, by Imperial slaves and freedmen. Travellers had to declare all their goods but were exempted payment on goods (including slaves) needed on the journey. An inscription from Zarai in Numidia dating to 202 is the *album* of a *statio* there giving what is evidently a list of conventional charges for different classes of goods – slaves, horses, mules, various garments, an amphora of wine and so forth. The workings of the system are illustrated by a story in Philostratus' novel about the pagan saint, Apollonius of Tyana; when Apollonius came to a crossing of the Euphrates the toll-collector 'took him to the board (evidently like the one from Zarai) and asked him what he had with him'. "*Sophrosyne* (temperance), *Dikaiosyne* (justice) . . . and so forth",' replied the sage – which the ignorant tax-collector took to be the names of female slaves.[16]

Once again, our evidence about the *portorium* stops about 240; but the tax reappears in the fourth century and we cannot tell whether its actual operation ceased in the troubled third century. It is significant, and not entirely easy to explain, that these indirect taxes alone of all the forms of contact between State and citizen never seem to have been handled as intermediaries by the cities.

The most important taxes, however, were the two forms of tribute, *tributum soli*, on the products of the soil, and *tributum capitis*, the poll-tax. These were based in a comprehensive census whose original imposition might arouse resistance and popular disturbances among the provincial population, as it did in Gaul under Augustus. Luke's Gospel refers to the census taken under Quirinius, the governor of Syria, when Judaea became a Roman province in AD 6; this census brought on the earliest activities of the *sicarii,* who urged the people to resist payment to the foreign power.

Except for Egypt (see Ch. 10) we do not have much evidence of the actual process of making census returns. But Ulpian, in the third century, writes: 'It is laid down in the census regulations that land should be reported for the census in the following manner: Name of each farm. *Civitas* and village. Names of two nearest neighbours. Acreage of ploughland to be sown over next ten years. Vineyards – number of vines. Olive-groves – the acreage and number of trees. Meadowland – acreage to be mown over the next ten years. Estimated acreage of pasture land. Similarly woods for felling.'[17] The census also included animal stock, houses (a wax tablet from Dacia dating to 159 is a contract for the purchase of half a house on condition that the original owner should pay the tribute on it until the next census), slaves and possibly ships, as well as numbering the free population. The inscriptions show senators (sometimes the existing governors of provinces), equestrian officials and later Imperial freedmen concerned with 'accepting the censuses' of provinces or smaller regions. But the groundwork of the censuses (which except for the fourteen-year cycle in Egypt cannot be shown to have happened at regular intervals) seems progressively to have fallen on the city officials. From Mesembria in Thrace, for instance, we have an edict of the officials summoning all those who worked the land to come to the city and be registered. Certainly by the end of the period taking the census was one of the regular 'burdens' which fell on local officials. They will presumably then have handed the records over to the Imperial officials of the census. The Emperor Gaius, when in Gaul in 39, was able to demand the Gallic census-lists, and select the richest men for execution and confiscation of their property for himself.

The fact that the cities now did the basic work of the census merely reflected the fact that they now, broadly speaking, had the responsibility of collecting the fixed tribute in cash and paying it to the Roman officials. The old system of contractors (*publicani*) collecting a tithe of the produce as tribute in kind was already disappearing in the late Republic, and is barely traceable in the Empire; a handful of inscriptions seem to reveal *publicani* collecting such a tithe in the corn-producing lands of Africa and Sicily. Elsewhere the *publicani* had gone, and the cities paid their tribute to the provincial officials.

The *tributum soli*, as its name implies, was in essence a tax on produce. The task of the city officials was thus in effect that of going out into the territory of the city and collecting the tribute from the villages. We find the Jewish leaders doing this in 66 when faced with a demand for arrears of tribute. The exaction of tribute became a regular burden on local officials (one of the privileges of a veteran was to be exempt from this). Since city officials lacked both adequate force at their disposal and adequate legal powers, the task must often have been difficult if not impossible; the sort of procedure to which they might be reduced is illustrated by a rescript of Severus Alexander in 231 giving a man the right to proceed against an *exactor* of tribute who had seized and sold up a slave-girl of his as a way of getting payment.

In the Greek cities, and in Egypt, the task of exacting tribute produced a new class of officials, the *dekaprotoi* (literally 'first ten'). In some places these seem to have been regular magistrates with wider functions, but in principle their job was the collection and more important, guaranteeing, of the tribute. Inscriptions show that persons under twenty-five, and even women, could hold the post; the reason, as the lawyer Hermogenianus at the end of the third century confirms, was that the post counted as a burden falling on the estate of the person. By this period also they had to make up the tax deficits of persons who had died.

This apart, a number of inscriptions show rich men who paid the tribute for their cities or even whole provinces. This is particularly noticeable with the *tributum capitis* paid by all free persons; in Syria it was paid by females from age twelve and males from age fourteen, to age sixty-five, at a rate of 1 % of their capital valuation (the details for other areas are unknown). So we find one P. Popillius Python paying the entire *tributum capitis* of Macedonia while High Priest of the province; another man left a sum whose interest was to pay the annual poll-tax of Tenos.

The collection and guaranteeing of the tribute in cash thus became a significant burden on the leading men of the cities – a burden increased even further when Aurelian (270–5) ordered the city councils either to find landlords for deserted land or be responsible for the tribute from it themselves. In the inflation of the third century, however, the fixed cash tribute must have lost greatly in value. The fortunes of the tribute in this period cannot in fact be traced from our evidence. But it is clear that as a source of bullion for the State it was replaced by the so-called *aurum coronarium* (crown gold), which developed into a regular tax; and as a way of taxing the resources of the land the tribute disappears in the reforms of Diocletian to be replaced by a new system which (it seems) owed its origins to the irregular exactions in kind of our period.

The *aurum coronarium* was a customary gift of gold crowns, made by subject communities to rulers and conquerors. Republican generals had received such gifts, but in the Empire they came to be a privilege of the Emperor alone, first offered and later exacted on accessions, victories and other occasions.[18] After Claudius' conquest of Britain in 43 crowns of 7,000 pounds in weight were offered by Tarraconensis and of 9,000 by the Gallic provinces; a papyrus preserves the letter which Claudius wrote on the same occasion to a Greek association of athletes in reply to their delegation bringing a gold crown. Some Emperors remitted – often just to Italy – the *aurum coronarium* as an act of grace. Another papyrus contains the somewhat rambling edict in which Severus Alexander (222–35) announced that he remitted all sums due in respect of gold crowns from the cities of the Empire.

Egyptian papyri reveal in fact that by the end of the second century there was a regular crown-tax *supplemented* by special votes of gold crowns on extraordinary occasions. In the reign of Aurelian we find the council of the town of Oxyrhynchus discussing the manufacture by craftsmen of such a gold crown, destined for the Emperor. Our most vivid evidence about the *aurum coronarium*, however, is the story preserved in the Babylonian Talmud of how the tax was imposed on Tiberias about AD 200. The people demanded that the Rabbis pay a share. They refused, half the population fled and half the tax was remitted. Then they asked again and were refused. All now fled except one fuller. The money was demanded of him, he fled, and the demand for the crown money was dropped.[19]

The *aurum coronarium* survived as a tax into the fourth century. The major features of fourth-century taxation, however, had their roots in three different forms of exaction – closely linked with each other – practised by the State in the early Empire. The first, which went back to the Republic, was the practice of making forced requisitions of corn and of other supplies for the use of the army or officials at a price fixed by the officials. The system was clearly open to abuse: in Britain in the 70s the population might have a requisition of corn laid on them, and if they could not provide it have to go through the farce of buying corn already in the military granaries and selling it back at a loss; alternatively they might be instructed to deliver the corn not to the camps near them but to distant ones, and so be prepared to pay cash instead.[20] Pliny in his *Panegyric* to Trajan delivered in 100, says that now (as opposed to conditions under Domitian) the provinces were not oppressed by new requisitions (*indictiones*) before they had paid the tribute, and that whatever the State theoretically paid for, it did pay for. The system was not of course always abused: papyri, for instance, preserve the receipts given by a staff-soldier (*duplicarius*) of an auxiliary unit in Egypt in 185–6 for the corn delivered by local officials, and their receipts for the cash paid. But from the end of the second century it does seem clear that provisions (*annona*) for the army in Egypt were acquired in the form of a surtax in kind (including wine and vinegar as well as corn), collected by local officials, and not compensated. For the other parts of the Empire in the third century we have to rely on references in legal sources to *indictiones* or *intributiones*, that is, occasional requisitions (as opposed to the regular tribute) laid on landholders, with no indication that these were paid for.

Then there was the Imperial Post (*vehiculatio*) established by Augustus, a staging service of vehicles by which messengers (probably always soldiers) and official travellers could be transported rapidly and without payment across the Empire. In some places the staging points may have been provided by the State, as when Hadrian built a road equipped with *stationes* and forts across the desert from Antinoopolis on the Nile to Berenice on the Red Sea. But in principle this too was a burden which fell on the magistrates of the cities. Use of the service was confined in theory to those provided with *diplomata* (certificates) issued personally by the Emperor. Pliny wrote to Trajan from Bithynia in about 110 to ask if out-of-date *diplomata* could still be used; Trajan replied, 'Out-of-date *diplomata* should not be used. So I enjoin on myself as an essential duty to send out to the provinces new *diplomata* before they are needed.' Needless to say, there is evidence of persons without *diplomata* using the services, of persons forging *diplomata* and of *diplomata* being provided for unofficial travellers. As we shall see later, a mere *assessor* of the governor of Palestine in the 230s was able to have his wife and two brothers-in-law despatched to join him by the *cursus* all the way from Pontus in Northern Asia Minor. Pliny himself gave his wife *diplomata* to return to Rome on the death of her grandfather, and was excused by Trajan for so doing.

The difficulty with the *vehiculatio* is that we cannot tell whether the term refers only to a specific organization covering only certain major roads – as opposed, that is, to what follows, the general practice of the exaction of services by troops and officials on the move. If there was a specific network in the early Empire then we cannot draw a map of it. Our best evidence that there was in some places a regular service comes from an inscription from Phrygia published in 1956, which relates to a dispute, stretching over about the first forty years of the third century, between two villages over their obligations in providing vehicles and transport animals for the *cursus* (they had the misfortune to live near an important cross-roads).[21] The first stage recorded is a hearing, probably in 208, in which a procurator, probably an Imperial freedman, hears the statements (all the parties speak in Greek, but the protocol is in Latin) of the representatives of the two villages, examines them, and pronounces his verdict that each village shall be responsible for providing half the transport along the stretch of road involved. His decision will be enforced by an *optio* (non-commissioned officer). Then we have letters from the *optio* to the Elders of each of the villages ordering compliance. Then, from 213, we have another procurator ordering disorders over the question to cease, and allowing the request of one of the villages to have a *stationarius* – soldier on police duty – to be stationed there. Finally, in 237, a third procurator again orders compliance. No text illustrates more clearly the administrative patterns of the time, the role of Imperial procurators (these ones may be those of an Imperial estate), the employment of soldiers, the pressure of the State's needs on the population – and the ability of the people to offer resistance.

The *cursus* itself apart, there was endless strain, which reached its maximum when an army or the Emperor and his Court was on the move, over the making of provision for official travellers. Papyri from Egypt show requisitions for the visits of Germanicus in 19, Hadrian in 130, Severus in 199–201 and Caracalla in 215–16; inscriptions from the Greek cities honour men who had taken on themselves the provisioning of armies or the Court. In the early third century the lawyer Ulpian discusses the case of a tenant who had fled on the approach of an army, and returned to find that the soldiers quartered there had removed the windows and everything else. But similar difficulties arose with the movement of individual soldiers or messengers, reflected not only in the passage of Matthew's Gospel but, for instance, in the remark made by Epictetus about 108: 'If there is a transport requisition (*angareia*) and a soldier seizes your ass, don't resist or grumble; for then you will get a beating and still lose your ass.'[22] A number of documents from Thrace and Asia Minor in the first half of the third century contain complaints of exactions in passing by soldiers, *officiales* and Imperial slaves and freedmen.

This period seems to have seen some development of *stationes* along the main roads. The contemporary historian Cassius Dio complains that Caracalla (211–17) had stopping-places built for himself all along the roads, even those on which he never intended to travel. An inscription from Thrace in 202 (discussed in Ch. 12) shows a *statio* being developed into a so-called *emporion* with a garrison of soldiers and a population drawn from the surrounding district. Taken together with the appearance of the *annona* as a tax in Egypt, and with the legal evidence of *indictiones* or *intributiones* as a constant burden elsewhere in the third century, this evidence may indicate the origin of the tax-system under Diocletian. Diocletian instituted a census on a new basis, made *indictiones* (assessments) on a regular basis (five-yearly, later fifteen-yearly) and made the provision of supplies in kind (*annona*) the basic form of taxation; the supplies were delivered to *stationes* on the main roads, and were used by passing troops or officials, or carried to the armies by the heavy wagons of the *cursus publicus*.

The tendency to shift the burden of fulfilling the State's needs on to the cities is seen also in recruitment for the army. At all times there seems to have been a substantial volume of voluntary recruitment, but the obligation of military service never disappeared, and forced levies were held from time to time in Italy and the provinces. The three methods of recruitment appear clearly in Trajan's reply to a letter of Pliny from Bithynia about two recruits (*tirones*) who turned out to be slaves, and therefore legally debarred: 'It makes a difference whether they offered themselves as volunteers, or were levied, or were given as substitutes (*vicarii*).' We cannot trace the process by which the offering of *vicarii* grew into a system by which cities were responsible for producing a certain number of recruits when required. But even in the second century it is stated that a city might claim an estate as part of its territory in order to be able to produce recruits from it, while at the end of the third century the 'production of *tirones*' was a regular local obligation. In the third century we also find an Asian village using a sum of money 'for the recruit tax'.[23] These are evidently the early stages of the fourth-century system in which cities had the annual obligation of producing either a number of recruits or, in some areas, money – the 'recruit gold' (*aurum tironicum*) – instead.

The wide range of functions performed by the cities was in fact carried out, with inadequate aids and services, by the magistrates and councils of the cities or by other individuals on whom local *munera* (obligations) were laid. The fact that the functions were both essential to the State and extremely burdensome to those who performed them meant that there was increasing attention (reflected in the legal writers of the second and early third centuries who discuss in great detail the statuses or occupations which conferred immunity from such tasks) to the question of who was liable for offices and *munera*, and, broadly speaking, increasing unwillingness to undertake them. By the third century the method of appointment for local offices and functions had changed from popular election to appointment by the council, and even to nomination of individuals by others at their own peril. That is to say that one man, usually a member of the council or ex-holder of the post in question, would nominate another, but thereby be his guarantor and liable to make up the deficiency if the other proved unable to pay the costs of the post; throughout the third century (only) it was possible for the man nominated to escape by ceding two-thirds of his property to the nominator, who then had to perform the task himself. These processes were closely watched by the provincial governors, who could put forward names themselves for appointment by the councils, were appealed to in case of dispute, and often actually attended the meetings of city councils while posts were being filled. In other words, the pressure of circumstance had, to some extent, transformed the leading men of the cities into the reluctant servants of the State. The fear of public office finds its reflection even in the Talmud; as a Palestinian Rabbi announced at the end of our period, 'If they have nominated you for the *boulē*, let the Jordan be your frontier.'

There can thus be no doubt that the pressure of the State on the population increased in our period, especially towards the end. Such demands for economic or personal services apart, the State also required some personal expressions of loyalty from its subjects individually. The institutions of Emperor-worship, it is true, were communal, set up by cities or provinces and only in Gaul and Britain (the altars at Lugdunum and Ara Ubiorum – later Cologne – and the temple of Claudius at Camulodunum) was the initiative in establishing them from Rome. They involved rites and ceremonies performed by the leading men, but there is nothing to show that all individuals were required to participate. The known oaths of loyalty, however – from 3 BC, AD 14 and two from 37 – which involved swearing by the gods and (in 3 BC) by Augustus himself (afterwards by 'the deified Augustus') do seem to have been taken individually; but we do not know whether they continued to be taken after 37.

But municipal magistrates took an oath by Jupiter, by the deified Emperors and by the 'genius' of the ruling Emperor, and a large variety of legal proceedings involved oaths by the Emperor or by his 'genius' or 'fortune'.

The stage was thus set for a possible direct conflict between the State and Christians. In fact, however, though the conflict came, its causes were wider, the resentment by the population of the Christian rejection of the whole apparatus of gods, temples, cults and traditional rituals deeply ingrained in every aspect of the communal life of Antiquity.[24] Similar resentment had been felt against the Jews, even though the practice of their religion – as being a long-established communal faith – was officially accepted (only under Hadrian do we find an active prohibition of Jewish customs such as circumcision). But the resentment still existed, and the attitudes expressed in the first century by an Alexandrian grammarian, Apion – 'Why do the Jews claim to be citizens of Alexandria when they will not worship the same gods as we?' – bore fruit in action in Antioch in AD 70, when the population, led in fact by a Hellenized Jew, tried by violence to force the Jewish community to sacrifice 'in the manner of the Greeks'.

Christianity first came to the notice of Roman officials, in the persons of Christ himself and Paul, through provoking conflicts and possible disorders within the Jewish communities or their proselytes and sympathizers. But already Christianity was having its impact on the pagan world; the silversmiths at Ephesus who rioted against Paul had more reason for fear even than they knew.

As Tacitus' account makes clear, it was the background of popular hatred which allowed Nero to seize on the Christians in Rome as the scapegoats for the great fire of 64. This action, however, was neither imitated in the provinces at the time nor followed by any general law against the Christians. When Pliny the Younger found Christians accused before him in Pontus about 110 he wrote to Trajan to inquire whether it was the name of 'Christian' itself or the crimes supposed to accompany the belief, which deserved punishment. But it is significant that the procedure adopted by Pliny, and followed in later persecutions, was (as the Christian apologist Tertullian was to point out) not that of an ordinary criminal proceeding. Instead, those accused were invited to deny that they were Christians, to call on the gods, to sacrifice before an image of the Emperor and to curse Christ. Those who yielded were released (unless they were Roman citizens) without any serious inquiry as to their past practices. In other words, the procedure was an attempt to force them back within the framework of pagan society. Only in the martyrdom at Lyon in 177 (see Ch. 8), which began with popular violence and then denunciation to the authorities, was evidence, obtained by the torture of slaves, of obscene rites and unnatural intercourse, taken as a ground for punishing even those who under torture denied their Christianity. But in spite of the general hatred of Christianity – shared equally, for instance, by Tacitus, Fronto and Marcus Aurelius – the authorities kept to the relatively passive role of attempting, often by public torture before large crowds, to obtain recantations from those accused before them. Maximinus (235–8) is said to have instituted an active persecution, but only of the leaders of the Church. The first great general persecution came in the reign of Decius (249–50); in Alexandria at least it had been preceded by violent popular outbreaks against the Christians a year before. Prosecution of the leading men of the Church was followed by a universal order for all the inhabitants of the Empire to sacrifice to the gods, pour libations and taste sacrificial meat. Egyptian papyri (cf. Ch. 10) preserve the actual text of some certificates issued to those who declared that they had always sacrificed to the gods and had been through, watched by witnesses, the required rituals. Many Christians submitted, causing a fundamental crisis in the history of the Church; many of those who refused were executed.

The spread of Christianity, with the acute tensions it created in pagan society, must inevitably have brought positive action from the State. It was not an accident, however, that sporadic local persecutions initiated by the population were replaced in the third century by a universal order to return, at least by a symbolic act, to the worship of the ancient gods. The desperate military struggle of the mid-third century brought this attempt to restore the unity of society round the traditional rites, just as it accelerated the steady growth of the functions of the State and its pressure on the population.

6

The Army and the Frontiers

The reign of Augustus was the last great age of Roman conquests; when he died, he left Tiberius his advice not to extend further the frontiers of the Empire. Thereafter, there were only two major wars leading to permanent acquisitions, Britain in 43 and Dacia in 105–6. Trajan's conquests in Armenia, Mesopotamia and down to the Persian Gulf in the war of 113–17 were disintegrating before his death, and were formally abandoned immediately afterwards. The Parthian wars of Marcus Aurelius' co-Emperor, Lucius Verus, in 162–6 and of Septimius Severus in 194–8 did, however, bring a new province, Mesopotamia, and extended Roman power to the Tigris.

But even the relatively peaceful period up to the 220s was filled with constant change and development in the disposition and functions of the army, and the nature of the frontiers. At the beginning of the period indeed it could hardly be said that recognizable frontiers existed. In the West there were still three legions in the interior of Spain, finally conquered only in 26–19 BC. Legionary camps were grouped along the Rhine, but no permanent forts had yet been established beyond it. The land between the headwaters of the Rhine and Danube was not yet occupied, while the first legionary camp on the Danube itself – Carnuntum in Pannonia – was established only in about AD 15; on the lower Danube towards the Black Sea, Roman control was still episodic in the early years of Tiberius. The main development of the period in this area is the pushing forward from the upper Rhine and Danube first of forts and lines of communication, then of a fortified line with forts, look-out posts, a palisade or stone wall, and a ditch – the creation in other words of a fixed visible frontier. Here, as with the similar works in Britain – Hadrian's Wall and the Antonine Wall – military history depends essentially on archaeology. Especially since the last war, 'frontier-studies' have become a branch of history in their own right, embracing not only the physical structure of the frontiers, but the history and disposition of the military units which served there, the social development of the communities which grew up behind the frontiers and the arrangements for controlling the barbarians beyond them.

On the lower Danube and in Dacia very much less is known of the frontier works. But aerial photography in Africa has revealed a complex pattern of roads, forts and settlements related to the 'Fossatum', a ditch and fortified line stretching through the desert of southern Algeria.[1] As we shall see in Ch. 9, the social development of Roman Africa, that is in essence the extension of settled cultivation, depended essentially on the steady movement southwest of the legion *III Augusta*, its construction of roads and encirclement of mountain regions. The date (or dates) of the construction of the 'Fossatum', however, is still obscure and will depend on archaeological work on the ground.

Farther East, in Tripolitania, the three farthermost Roman forts were established in the first half of the third century. This area, however, offers a salutary warning. Associated with these well-preserved Roman forts in the desert are the wide-spread remains of farm-houses, apparently fortified. Earlier investigators believed that these were the settlements of people (who in fact are not securely attested until the late fourth century) called *limitanei* – that is 'soldier-farmers' settled on plots of land in the frontier area by the State, with the obligation of fighting in its defence. In fact, however, closer investigation has shown that the area, now desert, had been settled substantially before the Roman forts were built by a prosperous Punic-speaking agricultural population.[2] The chimera of the 'soldier-farmers' has bedevilled much of the study of the Roman frontiers; they have in fact no place in this period.

In the East Rome was faced until the 220s by the declining,

and on the whole quiescent, power of Parthia. The two powers contended for the dominance over Armenia and fought substantial wars roughly every half-century. But here the significant development was the steady absorption of the Hellenized client kingdoms, chiefly Cappadocia in 17, all of Judaea finally in 44, Commagene in 72, Nabataea in 106. The rich city-state of Palmyra was fully absorbed in the second century as was the kingdom of Osrhoene, with its capital at Edessa, which was made a Roman *colonia* under Caracalla (211–17). At the beginning of the period all the four Roman legions in the East were grouped in the interior of Syria. Something resembling a frontier began to be formed when Vespasian put two legions under a consular governor into Cappadocia and stationed another legion near Jerusalem. The absorption of Nabataea in 106 was followed by the stationing of a legion at Bostra and the construction of a road from Damascus through Transjordan to Eilat on the Red Sea. This frontier was extended farther down the Euphrates in the 160s and to the Tigris in the late 190s. Here, unlike elsewhere, the defence depended primarily on fortified cities, Nisibis, Singara and later Hatra.[3] But here, too, aerial photography has shown a dense pattern of Roman forts in the Syrian desert and in Mesopotamia; once again nothing certain can be said about the development of the system until there has been prolonged excavation on the ground.[4]

The broad lines of the development of the Roman frontiers are thus clear; the change in the first two centuries of the period is essentially from a reliance on legions grouped (at least in principle) for attack to one where legions and auxiliary units were spread out in permanent fortified positions along the actual frontiers. The weaknesses of the system have often been pointed out. Above all it was designed to prevent minor raiding and unauthorized movement across the frontiers, but not for dealing with a major break-through at one point. By the early third century none of the legions in Europe were stationed at strategic points behind the frontiers.

A quite new phase in Roman military history opens in the 220s with the overthrow of Parthia by the new Persian dynasty of the Sasanids who soon invaded Mesopotamia and Syria. In the 230s there began in earnest the series of barbarian attacks across the Rhine and Danube frontiers which was to continue throughout the rest of the period. Vital as the period is, the course of the campaigns – and even more the development of the structure of the army – can only be followed in the broadest outline, and sometimes not even that.

This chapter will now trace the development of the frontiers up to the early third century in each of the best-known areas – Britain, the Rhine, the Danube and the East – and then revert to discuss the internal structure of the legions and auxiliary units, their recruitment and conditions of service, the life of the soldiers, the organization of discharge and so forth. These details are of more than military importance. The well-documented social history of the army is of interest in itself; and, for reasons mentioned in the first chapter, the army was a significant factor in the wider social history of the Empire. Finally it will say something of the main military developments of the critical half-century from the 230s to 284; the details here, however, belong in the history of the separate regions, since the invasions fundamentally affected the social history of the provinces.

The invasion of Britain in 43 with three legions from the Rhine and one from the Danube was followed by the rapid subjugation of southern and central England (seriously interrupted only by the revolt of Boudicca in 60). Wales, Northern England and Scotland were a different proposition. In Northern England the client kingdom of the Brigantes, based finally perhaps on the immense earthwork fortress of Stanwick in Yorkshire, which eventually reached 600 acres in extent, lasted until 69, when internal dissensions forced the chief, Queen Cartimandua, to seek the aid of Roman auxiliary forces. The Brigantes were finally conquered in 71, and the possibility of using a buffer-state to avoid further fighting in the North was lost.[5] In the West, legionary fortresses had been established on the Severn, and attacks on the Welsh hill-tribes conducted in the late 40s and 50s, leaving traces of at least one Roman fort of the Claudian period, and culminating in the seizure of the Druid centre on the island of Anglesey in 60-1. The final conquest of Wales came in 74-8, when a legion was established in south Wales, at Caerleon, and

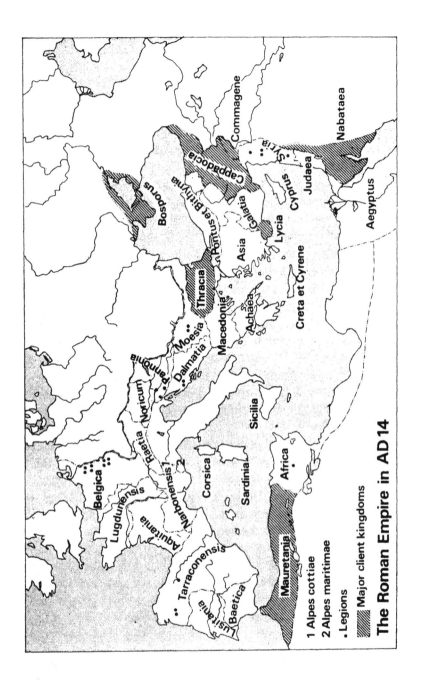

The Roman Empire in AD 14

1 Alpes cottiae
2 Alpes maritimae
. Legions
▨ Major client kingdoms

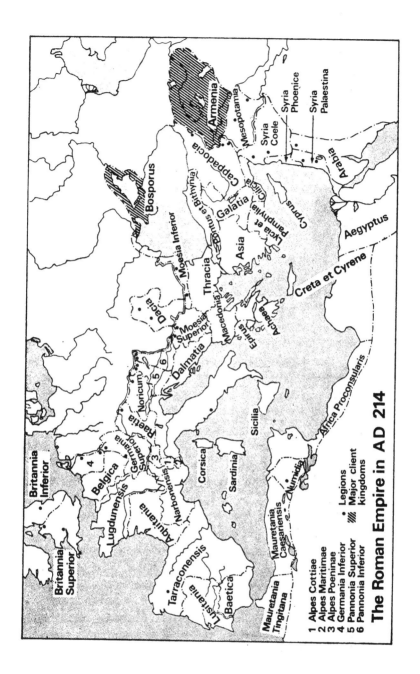

The Roman Empire in AD 214

- Legions
- Major client kingdoms

1 Alpes Cottiae
2 Alpes Maritimae
3 Alpes Poeninae
4 Germania Inferior
5 Pannonia Superior
6 Pannonia Inferior

Britannia Superior
Britannia Inferior
Belgica
Lugdunensis
Aquitania
Tarraconensis
Lusitania
Baetica
Mauretania Tingitana
Mauretania Caesariensis
Numidia
Africa Proconsularis
Sardinia
Corsica
Sicilia
Narbonensis
Germania Superior
Raetia
Noricum
Dalmatia
Moesia Superior
Epirus
Macedonia
Achaea
Creta et Cyrene
Dacia
Moesia Inferior
Thracia
Pontus et Bithynia
Asia
Lycia et Pamphylia
Galatia
Cappadocia
Cilicia
Cyprus
Bosporus
Armenia
Mesopotamia
Syria Coele
Syria Phoenice
Syria Palaestina
Arabia
Aegyptus

109

another at Chester in North-West England, near the Welsh border. In Wales itself, archaeology has revealed lines of auxiliary forts, connected by roads, at river mouths or strategic points in the mountain valleys. The later history of these forts is disputed; the standard view that many of them were evacuated (as being no longer necessary) in the second century is perhaps incorrect.[6] At all events there are traces of destruction at the end of the first century and again a century later; and, the military occupation apart, Romanization made no real progress in Wales.

In the North the campaigns of Tacitus' father-in-law Agricola in 78–84 spread a network of Roman forts up to the edge of the Highlands. Here recent excavations have disclosed the full plan of a legionary fortress built on the north bank of the River Tay, at the gateway to the Highlands, not earlier than 83, and systematically dismantled about 90. The camp, surrounded by a stone wall, was clearly intended to be permanent, but was never completed. The gateways were still of wood, not stone, the house of the *legatus* of the legion was never built, and the stoke-holes of the bath-house were never fired. When the camp was dismantled, its timbers apparently being shipped back to bases farther south, the soldiers carefully buried three-quarters of a million nails of all sizes, which remained undiscovered until a few years ago. This clearly reveals a change of plan, no doubt to be related to the removal of one of the four British legions in the 80s. The central point for the Northern defences now became the fort of Newstead in the Lowlands, manned by auxiliaries and legionary detachments. About AD 100 this and all the other lowland forts were burned, apparently by enemy action.

Thereafter the picture is obscure (though some further defeat is implied by the disappearance of the ninth legion at York by 122) until the construction of Hadrian's Wall.[7] Begun probably soon after Hadrian's visit to Britain in 122, it formed an eighty-mile link between the Tyne and the Solway, some fifteen feet in height, fronted by a ditch, with signal-turrets every 540 yards, and gates with turrets every mile. In the actual course of construction, the auxiliary forts, many for cavalry, which were placed behind the Wall, were moved up to the Wall itself. In the

West, forts continued the defence line along the coast; three other forts lay in advance of the Wall, and the largest unit in the area, a squadron (*ala*) of 1,000 cavalry, was stationed on the Wall itself. Behind the forts lay the so-called 'Vallum', a broad ditch with embankments and closely controlled crossing-places, which follows the whole length of the Wall; its purpose is still unclear.

Under Hadrian's successor, Antoninus Pius (138–61), the whole plan was changed. The frontier was moved north to the Forth-Clyde line, where a turf wall was built on a stone base, with a ditch in front and forts at intervals. On Hadrian's Wall the signal turrets were evacuated, the 'Vallum' frequently breached, the gateway doors removed, and civilian settlements began to develop round the forts. The Antonine Wall itself shows traces of destruction on probably two separate occasions and was finally assaulted and abandoned about 186–7.[8] Ten years later, a further invasion which swept a long way to the South brought great efforts actually to destroy Hadrian's Wall itself and its forts. Reconstruction and punitive campaigns followed, culminating in that led by Severus and his two sons in 208–11. At this point Hadrian's Wall was once again made the main frontier, with a reinforced garrison. The basis of the Severan system, however, was strongly garrisoned outpost forts beyond the Wall, manned by part-mounted cohorts and by irregular units of *exploratores*. The system brought peace. Along the Wall and round the outpost forts civilian settlements grew up; and if there is little trace of Romanization of the people of Southern Scotland, no further fighting is recorded for the rest of the period.

Roman activity on the Rhine and upper Danube was overshadowed by the great disaster of AD 9, when three legions were lost under Varus, and the hope of making Germany up to the Elbe a Roman province was abandoned. Inconclusive campaigns were conducted by Tiberius' nephew and adopted son, Germanicus, in 14–16, but thereafter the main reliance was placed on diplomacy, the support of Romanized leaders of the free Germans, and occasional shows of force. On the lower Rhine (the military districts of the Lower and Upper Rhine became the provinces of Germania Inferior and Superior under Domitian) the line of the river itself remained the frontier throughout the period. The garrison of four legions, supported by auxiliary units in forts along the river, was reduced to three under Domitian and two under Trajan, when the northernmost legionary camp, Noviomagus (Nijmegen), occupied since the Batavian revolt of 69–70, became an auxiliary fort. In the second century there were permanent legionary fortresses at Bonn and Vetera (Xanten). Along the Rhine, apart from auxiliary camps, there were the Roman veteran colonies of Cologne, established in 50, and Xanten (Colonia Ulpia Traiana) established under Trajan. In Holland, in the territory of the Batavi and Canninefates, two *municipia* were established, probably in the second century. These will have been swept away by the Frankish occupation in the 260s. The two colonies farther up the river, however, continued in full occupation into the fourth century.

On the Upper Rhine substantial developments took place in the late first and second centuries. Under Vespasian (69–79) there is evidence of fighting, of the advance of forts beyond the river, and the building of a road across from Strasbourg to the Upper Danube. The first great advance, however, came with the war of Domitian against the Chatti in 83, which contemporaries regarded as a farce; it led, however, to the establishment of a line of wooden watch-towers and stone forts in the area of the Taunus Mountains and the River Main. In the next half-century auxiliary forts were pushed forward from both the Upper Rhine and the Danube, and by 100 Tacitus could describe the area between the rivers as provincial land. Under Hadrian (117–38) there were three significant developments, the moving of all the auxiliary units up the frontier line itself, the building of a visible frontier in the form of a wooden palisade, and the appearance of irregular units called *numeri*. In the middle of the second century the Upper German frontier (*limes*) was moved 30 km. forward to form a straight line from the River Wörth to Lorch, where it met the Raetian *limes*. The Raetian frontier, a palisade (rebuilt as a stone wall in the early third century) backed by auxiliary forts, ran approximately westwards to meet the Danube south-west of Regensburg; here, after the Marcomannic Wars, a legion was established by about 175. By the second century the four legions which had guarded the Upper Rhine before 70 had been reduced to two, both still on the Rhine itself, at Mainz and Strasbourg.

In all this period there was little active fighting on the Rhine, though brief incursions are mentioned in about 162 and 174. Major fighting did not occur until 213 when Caracalla made a double attack from Raetia and Upper Germany on the Alamanni, now attested for the first time near the Roman frontier.

Along the middle and lower Danube, the provinces of Pannonia and Moesia, Roman control was still tenuous in AD 14. The three Pannonian legions were stationed in the south-west of the province, not far from the border of Italy. Auxiliary detachments manned the forts of Aquincum (Budapest) and Arrabona on the Danube, but the first legionary camp was established there, at Carnuntum, only in 14–15. Thereafter there was no strengthening of the Pannonian Danube frontier until the wars of Domitian (81–96). Here, as on the Rhine, reliance was placed on client-kingdoms. When the Marcomannic king, Maroboduus, sought refuge with Rome in 19, the control of the area north of the Upper Danube passed to the Suebi. A king given them by Rome lasted until 50, and his successors (one called Italicus) showed themselves still loyal in 69–70. In Moesia the legions seem also at the beginning to have been stationed well south of the Danube; but here the first legionary camp on the Danube, established in 15, was followed by three others in the middle of the century.

Major military developments did not come until Domitian's reign, and were a consequence of the growth of the Dacian kingdom (see Ch. 15) as a hostile military power. Fighting began in 85 with a Dacian invasion of Moesia in which the governor was killed. In the following year Moesia was divided into two provinces (Inferior and Superior) with two legions in each, Domitian came to Moesia in person, and the Praetorian Prefect Cornelius Fuscus was killed on campaign in Dacia. The first major success did not come until 88 with the great victory of

Tapae in Dacia. Peace was now made with Dacia, whose king received a diadem from Rome, money and technical aid; but further fighting was necessary against the Suebi, and also the Sarmatian Iazyges (now settled in the Great Plain between Dacia and the Danube on its central north-south stretch. See Ch. 16). They crossed the Danube in 92 and destroyed a legion, but were defeated by Domitian in the same year.

In this period a second legionary camp was established on the Pannonian Danube at Aquincum. But otherwise our knowledge of troop movements remains confused until after the two Dacian wars of Trajan, 101–2 and 105–6, and the establishment of Dacia as a province in 106. Of the course of the two wars little is known. The first ended with the occupation, perhaps by more than one legion, of all the southern part of Dacia including the capital, Sarmizegethusa. Then, when war was renewed after breaches of the peace-treaty by the Dacian king, Decebalus, the commander of the Roman occupation forces was captured. Fierce fighting was necessary before all resistance was crushed. Our most vivid evidence for the fighting (not, however, for the narrative of the campaigns) comes from the reliefs on Trajan's column at Rome – which show, for instance, the great bridge built across the Danube, the army pitching camp, battles in progress, the assault on Sarmizegethusa, Dacian prisoners in a camp, or a Roman legionary with the hair of a severed Dacian head clenched between his teeth.[9]

The results of this campaign established the permanent form of Roman defence on the middle and lower Danube. Pannonia was now (106–7) divided: Upper (Western) Pannonia had three legions on the Danube, at Vindobona (Vienna), Carnuntum and Brigetio, Lower Pannonia one at Aquincum. Ranged along the Danube between the legions were some twenty-three auxiliary units. Two legions remained on the Danube in Upper Moesia. In Lower Moesia one remained at Novae, another came from the Rhine to Durostorum near where the Danube turns north again, and one was moved from Oescus to Troesmis near the northernmost point of the river before it turns finally to the Black Sea. Dacia itself had one legion, at Apulum in the centre of the province, and some twelve auxiliary units. The Great

Plain to the west, and Wallachia to the east and south-east of the province, remained unoccupied, but closely supervised; Roman roads ran across to Dacia from Aquincum on the West and near Troesmis in the East. Half a century had thus seen a decisive shift of the military balance from Rhine to Danube, where now more than a third of the legions of the Empire lay. Except within Dacia, all of them, and the vast majority of the auxiliaries were stationed on the frontier itself.

Although there was spasmodic fighting in the interval, there was no major war in this area until the Marcomannic Wars of 166/7–75 and 177–80. Rome maintained close contact with the tribes across the frontier, for instance giving subventions to the Roxalani in Wallachia, or crowning the king of the Quadi in 140–2. But in the 160s considerable forces were drawn off for the Parthian War under Lucius Verus (see below). The 'Marcomannic War (a term of convenience – many different tribes took part) began with an invasion of Upper Pannonia by the Langobardi and Obii in 166–7, which was defeated, but followed by a much larger invasion by the Marcomanni, Quadi and Iazyges, which affected all of Pannonia and Noricum and reached northern Italy. The details of the fighting are again obscure. By 171 the Romans had regained the initiative and between 172 and 175 (the period portrayed on the Column of Marcus Aurelius in Rome)[10] Marcus Aurelius was able to defeat these tribes. Under the peace terms they gave back tens of thousands of prisoners and deserters, many of their own people were settled at points in the provinces and Italy, and they provided troops; 5,500 Sarmatian cavalry were sent to Britain, and cavalry from the Marcomanni, Quadi and Naristae were sent against the revolt of Avidius Cassius in Syria in 175. The frontier system was further secured by placing two newly-recruited legions on the Danube in Raetia and Noricum, and by moving one legion from Troesmis in Moesia Inferior to Potaissa in northern Dacia. The chief hostile tribes were forced to vacate the area bordering on the Danube; the Iazyges could meet only under supervision, and could not use their own ships, or land on the islands in the Danube. In 177–80 there was further fighting, during which a Roman force penetrated as far as Trenčin in

Czechoslovakia, and spent the winter of 179–80 there. Fighting ended substantially, though there was some further conflict in the 180s, when Commodus became sole Emperor and made peace in 180. The terms were similar, the return of captives and fugitives, the provision of soldiers, the holding of assemblies under Roman military supervision and the evacuation of forts in the demilitarized zone.

The next fifty years provide some evidence of clashes with the barbarians, more now towards the east, in Dacia and Moesia Inferior, and of rebuilding and strengthening of defences. But basically the defensive system remained as it was after the Marcomannic Wars until more serious invasions began in the late 230s.[11]

In the East there was, as mentioned before, no Roman frontier at the beginning of the period, though a stretch of the Euphrates opposite Syria was accepted as the boundary between Rome and Parthia. Elsewhere there was a penumbra of client-kingdoms, and in the north the kingdom of Armenia, the control of which was disputed between Parthia and Rome. A complex series of diplomatic exchanges over Armenia in the first century ended with a decisive demonstration of Roman control in Armenia in 63, and a compromise by which a member of the Parthian royal house was to be crowned as client king of Armenia, an event celebrated with great splendour in Rome in 66. More important were the measures of Vespasian (69–79) who perpetuated a temporary arrangement for the Armenian War by making Cappadocia (a client-kingdom which had lapsed to Rome in 17, and had subsequently been a procuratorial province guarded only by auxiliaries) and some neighbouring areas into a major military command under a senator of consular rank, with two legions on the Euphrates. At the same time the province of Syria was extended north along the Euphrates bank by the annexation in 72 of the client-kingdom of Commagene, which bordered on Cappadocia. Finally, as a result of the great revolt of 66–70, Judaea ceased to be a procuratorial province, and received a senatorial governor with a legion from Syria, stationed at Jerusalem.

In 106, under Trajan, came the annexation of another client-kingdom, Nabataea, with its capital at Petra. This too became a province with one legion, stationed at Bostra in Transjordan; under the first governor, Claudius Severus, a road was built from Eilat via Bostra to the border of Syria near Damascus. The work was done by the soldiers; in February 107 a legionary wrote home to his mother in Egypt, 'I give thanks . . . that, while all are labouring the whole day through cutting stones, I as a *principalis* (non-commissioned officer) go about all day doing nothing.'[12]

The formation of a continuous frontier along the Euphrates (supported by extensive road building in Asia Minor) and continuing through the Syrian desert past Palmyra – from near which we have a Roman milestone of 75 – to the Red Sea, along with the contemporary strengthening of the Danube frontier, meant that the Danube–Euphrates axis was henceforth the backbone of the military structure of the Empire. The first step had been taken towards the removal of the capital from Rome to the central point of that axis, Byzantium.

First, however, there was a major, if fruitless, Roman campaign, the Parthian War of Trajan in 113–17.[13] The excuse was the establishment by the Parthian king of his own nominee on the throne of Armenia. The details of the campaigns are much disputed; but it seems that Trajan conquered Armenia and made it a province in 114, Mesopotamia similarly by the winter of 115, and took the Parthian capital, Ctesiphon, and reached the Persian Gulf in 116, possibly forming a third province, Assyria, between the Lower Tigris and Euphrates.[14] In 116–17 came a major revolt in the northern conquered territories, which was suppressed at the cost of crowning kings for both Armenia and Parthia itself. Whether Trajan would have attempted a serious reconquest cannot be known, for illness forced him to retire to Roman territory, where he died in 117. His successor, Hadrian, immediately abandoned all claims to his conquests. The Roman nominee on the Parthian throne was deposed and given the minor kingdom of Osrhoene, losing even that a few years later.

Thereafter peace reigned, with minor diplomatic exchanges (Roman coins mention a king 'given to the Armenians' in the early 140s) until, on the accession of Marcus Aurelius and L. Verus in 161, the Parthian king declared war and gained considerable successes. But the campaign of L. Verus in 162–6 brought the re-establishment of Armenia as a client-kingdom, the sacking of Ctesiphon and (it seems) the occupation of all northern Mesopotamia to the Tigris. No regular province seems yet to have been formed, and the subsequent position is very obscure. But the Mesopotamian kingdom of Osrhoene began issuing coins with effigies of the members of the Imperial house, and from the new southernmost point of Roman control on the Euphrates, Dura-Europus (see Ch. 11) we have a vivid picture of the Roman occupation. The two auxiliary units, one of them from Palmyra, which occupied the city in the early years, were heavily reinforced in the early third century, when as much as one quarter of the town seems to have been walled off as a camp, a Headquarters and palatial residence for the commanding officer were built, and part of a temple used for military archives.

In the civil wars of 193–4 Mesopotamia was temporarily lost to Roman control. Septimius Severus regained the area in 195, making Nisibis a Roman 'colony', putting a garrison in it and making it the bulwark of the frontier. While he was engaged in further civil wars, ending with the victory of Lyon in 197, the Parthians besieged Nisibis. Severus returned in 197–8, and once again the Romans marched down the Euphrates and sacked Ctesiphon. Either at this time or in 195 Mesopotamia was made into a province, with two newly recruited legions, but under a Prefect of equestrian rank.

Finally in 216–17 Caracalla, in keeping with his impersonation of Alexander the Great, invaded Parthia, was murdered on campaign, and left it to his successor Macrinus (217–18) to resist a Parthian counter-attack and make peace. Two centuries of spasmodic fighting had thus seen a very considerable extension and consolidation of Roman control in the Near East – a far greater extension (if the absorption of client-kingdoms is included) than in any other area. It is significant that it was here and on the Danube that Emperors came to lead their armies in person. Two Emperors, Claudius in 43 and Septimius Severus in 208–11 had fought in Britain. But no member of the Imperial house since Domitian in 83 had fought on the Rhine frontier until Caracalla conducted a short campaign there in 213.

Such, in outline, was the pattern of wars and the development of the frontiers up to the early third century. When we come to the organization and life of the army itself, the principal developments of the period lay in the regularization of the auxiliary units and their predominant role in the manning of the new fixed frontiers. One aspect of this was the increasing importance of the new regular squadrons (*alae*) of auxiliary cavalry, 500 or 1,000 strong, for which Rome made use of the native skills of the Gauls and Spaniards, and later predominantly the Thracians, but also borrowed techniques from the barbarians, especially the Sarmatians, and the Parthian cavalry. A cardinal document for the process is the *Tactics* of Arrian, written in 136, which describes the cavalry exercises of the time, and ends by mentioning the instructions given by Emperors for the mastering of the fighting techniques of Parthians, Armenians, Sarmatians, Celts, Scythians and Raetians.[15]

The legions, however, remained the core of the army. By 215 the twenty-five legions of the Tiberian army had grown to thirty-two, established in permanent stone camps, or rather fortresses. A legion was formed in principle of some 5,000 infantrymen and 120 cavalry, divided into ten cohorts and sixty centuries, each commanded by a centurion. Among the centurions there was a complex pattern of promotion – based on the order of battle of the centuries – going up to the most senior, the *primus pilus*. Above these were six tribunes of the legion, all of equestrian rank, one of whom would be a young man of senatorial birth due to enter the Senate. The commander of the legion was a senatorial *legatus* of ex-praetor (in the early period sometimes ex-quaestor) status; where there was only one legion in a province the same man was *legatus* of legion and province.

Legionaries, who had in principle to be citizens, were recruited, as mentioned in Chapter 5, partly by forced levies and partly by voluntary enlistment. One of the most clearly defined features of the period is the way in which the legions (before about AD 70) began by being recruited largely from Italy or

Romanized Narbonensis and Baetica and ended by being filled up from the provinces in which they were stationed, and in particular from the sons of soldiers, born in the camps themselves. It is significant, however, that throughout the period, when entirely new legions were formed, they were recruited by levies in Italy.[16] In the beginning, service was for twenty years, followed by five years 'under the standards' (*sub vexillis*), i.e. attached to the camp but excused routine duties; by the second century the rule was twenty-five years of full service. The conditions of service are most fully illustrated by the complaints of the legionaries who mutinied in Pannonia on the death of Augustus: service might be stretched to thirty or forty years, and even formal discharge followed by the same duties *sub vexillis*; those who survived received as plots of land marshes or uncultivated hillsides; they were paid a mere ten *asses* a day, out of which they had to pay for their clothing, arms and tents, and bribe centurions for relief from duties. Ten *asses* a day was 225 *denarii* a year (a *denarius* equalled four *sesterces* or sixteen *asses*) paid in three instalments of seventy-five. The pay rose to 300 *denarii* under Domitian (81–96) and was raised again by Septimius Severus (193–211) and by his son Caracalla (211–17). A papyrus from the very end of the third century shows that legionaries then received about 600 *denarii* a year, still paid in three instalments. A papyrus of the 80s shows soldiers, apparently legionaries, receiving three *stipendia* per year, each of 248 Egyptian *drachmae*, with deductions for bedding, food, boots, banqueting fund and clothes. Cavalrymen seem even to have paid also for their horses; from Dura-Europus we have a file of letters dating to 208 from the governor of Syria to the tribune of an auxiliary cohort, assigning horses to individual cavalrymen, and giving the price. Deductions for food *may* have ended under Caracalla, though the evidence is not clear; but at the end of the third century it is certain that auxiliaries at least received a cash allowance in respect of rations amounting to some 200 *denarii* a year.

The regular pay thus did not allow for extensive savings. But it was supplemented by cash donatives given at the accession of Emperors (first by Claudius in 41) and on all major ceremonial occasions and anniversaries. The Praetorian cohorts received the largest donatives; in 202 Severus celebrated the tenth year of his reign by giving each of the Praetorian soldiers (and the people of Rome) 2,500 *denarii*, the equivalent of several years' pay. But for all soldiers donatives became a regular element in their pay.

The conditions of soldiers' life clearly improved in the course of the first two centuries, when legionaries tended to stay for long periods in the same camps, now regularly built of stone, round which civilian settlements (*canabae*) would grow up, sometimes at a short distance, sometimes immediately outside the walls. Bath-houses and amphitheatres are found regularly near the camps. Legions had their own 'territories', which legionaries seem to have been able to lease for grazing animals. There is ample evidence of soldiers buying and selling slaves; the law-codes even laid down that a soldier should be treated lightly if he overstayed his leave to pursue a runaway slave. A soldier could buy a house in the province in which he served, but not land – in case by attending to its cultivation he should neglect his military duties; but he could buy land in other provinces.

The most serious disability of a soldier was the fact that a marriage contracted by him was not legally valid. This rule was an archaic survival which had no moral overtones, but did seriously affect the legal rights of the *de facto* wives soldiers had, and their children. Hadrian, however, allowed the children of soldiers to petition for possession of their fathers' goods, to which they could have no legal right. The non-recognition of marriages persisted until the reign of Septimius Severus; an Egyptian papyrus, for instance, shows the Prefect of Egypt in 113–17 refusing the claim of a woman for the recovery of a sum given to her deceased husband under the marriage-contract: 'I cannot appoint an *iudex* on such a claim: for it is not legally possible for a soldier to marry.' The implication is, however, that the normal *forms* of a legal relationship between husband and wife were often observed. It was therefore a concession to established social practice when Septimius Severus (193–211) legalized soldiers' marriages.[16a]

121

On his final discharge a legionary received either a plot of land – either individually, or on occasions up to the reign of Hadrian, in a regular veteran colony – or a discharge donative fixed at 3,000 *denarii*. The question of how to settle soldiers on discharge, which had caused great difficulties under the Republic, had been solved first by personal grants of land or cash by Augustus, and then by the establishment in AD 6 of a special Military Treasury to provide the funds. It is recorded of Tiberius and of Nero that they put off the discharge of soldiers to avoid payment, but thereafter the system seems to have worked smoothly. Veterans were a privileged class. An edict of Domitian (81–96) exempted them from the payment of *portoria* and apparently from making provision for official travellers; the lawyers of the late second and early third centuries state that they enjoyed the same freedom as *decuriones* (town-councillors) from the harsher forms of punishment, and immunity from some local burdens. Documentary evidence, especially from Syria and the Pannonian towns, shows veterans as leaders of their local communities. The relatively good social position of veterans, and the cohesion between them, is well illustrated in a papyrus published a few years ago. A soldier, himself nearly due for discharge, writes to his brother at Karanis in Egypt, 'I ask you to receive with my recommendation the discharged soldier Terentianus who brings you this letter. . . . Since he is a man of means and desirous of residing there, I have urged upon him that he pay for my house for the current year (136) sixty drachmas, and that he have my field on lease for the coming year for sixty drachmas . . .'[17]

The most important development of the period was the formation of regular auxiliary units, which played an essential role both in manning the forts of the fixed frontiers as they developed and in providing mobile forces, especially of course the *alae* of cavalry, against barbarian incursions. At the beginning of the period the auxiliary forces seem to have been still predominantly temporary local levies commanded by their own chieftains. National levies from beyond the frontiers continued indeed to be used, the Moors under Lusius Quietus who fought in the wars of Trajan, the Sarmatians Marcus Aurelius sent to

Britain, and other barbarian units, known as *numeri*, which supplemented the *auxilia* in the frontier posts.[18] But even under Augustus there had been some national units from within the Empire commanded by Roman officers, and by about the 70s the *auxilia* had developed into regular units armed uniformly, with non-commissioned officers either promoted from their own ranks or transferred from the legions, commanded by prefects or tribunes of equestrian rank, and liable to serve anywhere in the Empire. The change is indicated by the appearance of *diplomata*, certificates, made of two inscribed bronze plates fastened together, which were issued to individuals and recorded that on honourable discharge normally after twenty-five years' service they had received the citizenship for themselves and their children and the right of a recognized Roman marriage with their wives (the wives themselves did not receive the citizenship). This was the formula up to 140; thereafter, for reasons which are not clear, only children born subsequently were given the citizenship. The disability with respect to marriage affected auxiliaries as it did legionaries; and even the grant of citizenship to existing children before 140 did not make the children legitimate. Auxiliaries also seem, however, to have benefited from Severus' legislation of marriages.

With the introduction of regular service, and the transference of units into distant provinces, the units retained their national names, but not (with some exceptions) their national recruitment. By the early second century auxiliary units on the frontiers were being supplemented predominantly by recruitment from the regions – a single province, or a group of provinces – nearest to them. Thracians, especially for the cavalry *alae*, continued to be recruited and sent to distant frontiers; and units originally from the East but stationed on the Rhine or Danube continued in some cases into the third century to be recruited from their home areas. For instance, the *cohors I milliaria Hemesenorum civium Romanorum* ('The First thousand-man Cohort of Emesenes, Roman Citizens'), stationed at Intercisa in Pannonia, continued to have soldiers with Oriental names who made dedications to their native gods from the mid-second to the mid-third century. This unit, like others of the period, formally entitled itself 'Roman citizens'. But throughout the auxiliaries, in principle recruited from non-citizens, citizen recruits become, as a consequence of the spread of citizenship in the provinces, more and more common. By about the end of the second century the great majority of known auxiliaries are citizens.[19]

We happen to have much more evidence for the life of auxiliary units under the Empire than we do for legions. We have for instance the letter of the Prefect of Egypt in 103 instructing the Prefect of a cohort to enrol six recruits – all Roman citizens – who are listed with their distinguishing marks (for recognition if they desert). Another papyrus, of 150, gives the full complement of a part-mounted cohort in Egypt, six centurions, three *decuriones* (non-commissioned officers), ninety-four cavalrymen, nineteen camel-riders, 363 infantrymen. From Moesia Inferior in 105–8 (that is during or near the time of the final conquest of Dacia) we have the daily report of another part-mounted cohort; it mentions men sent to the Moesian fleet, or to the army of Pannonia, one man drowned and another killed by bandits, others sent – apparently to Gaul – to requisition clothes, others to get horses, some guarding quarries, others escorting the governor or in the *officium* of the procurator, stationed in guard posts, on expeditions across the Danube, escorting the corn-supply or watching cattle.[20]

This document is however far exceeded in importance and vividness by the archives of the 20th cohort of Palmyrenes (a part-mounted cohort of 1,000 men) from Dura-Europus, dating to between 208 and 251.[21] These include the letters assigning horses already mentioned, daily reports – mentioning men sent to collect barley, taking letters to the provincial governor, getting wood for the bath-house, or absent without leave – and legal decisions by the tribune. The most important document, however, is the so-called *Feriale Duranum*, a calendar of the official Roman festivals and sacrifices as observed by the cohort in the 220s; the list, which is evidently the one observed throughout the army, is dominated by anniversaries relating to the Emperors themselves, accessions, deifications, victories or birthdays. Then, to complement the documents, the temple of the Palmyrene gods at Dura has a wonderful fresco of the tribune of the cohort sacrificing to the gods, with the standard-bearer holding the *vexillum* beside him, and ranged behind him the lower officers of the cohort.

For a picture of the settled life of an auxiliary cohort settled on the frontier at the other end of the Empire, one may go to the fort of the Saalburg in the Taunus Mountains, first occupied when Domitian pushed forward the Rhine frontier, and today partly reconstructed as it was when rebuilt in stone in the early third century. The stone wall, surmounted by battlements, enclosed barracks, store-rooms, a bath-house and a head-quarters-building with a colonnaded courtyard. Outside were large baths with central heating, a number of temples, and a village along the road leading to the main gate. The *limes* itself ran some 200 metres to the north.[22] Nothing shows more clearly the strength and settled conditions of the Roman frontiers immediately before the catastrophe of the third century.

The Roman army was thus deployed and organized fundamentally for frontier control and the checking and repression of barbarian movement in a zone beyond the frontier. Quite different problems were therefore presented, first when the aggressive dynasty of the Sasanids replaced Parthia in the 220s, and immediately attacked Mesopotamia, Armenia and Syria, and then when in the 230s the Alamanni began to move against the Rhine and Danube frontiers, and the Goths and others against the lower Danube. In the middle of the century other barbarian attacks, naturally of less importance, were made from the south on Africa and Egypt. The details of the fighting are traced – in so far as they can be – in the chapters on the regions. Here we may ask how the Roman army changed in half a century of wars fought largely within the frontiers of the Empire. But in this too we are almost in the dark. It does seem, however, that the fourth-century institution of the *comitatus* (from *comes* – 'companion') – a group of units accompanying the Emperor for field service – had its origins in the mid-third century, perhaps under Gallienus (260–8). Later authors mention units of Dalmatian and Moorish cavalry on campaign under Claudius (268–70) and Aurelian (270–5); and a Christian interrogated by the proconsul of Africa in 320 said that his grandfather, a Moor, had served as a soldier in the *comitatus*. Dura-Europus, again, reveals the earliest example of another characteristic fourth-century institution in the *dux ripae* (commander of the bank – of the Euphrates) in office before 240. Finally, as we saw in Chapter 4, the period 260–80 saw the exclusion of senators from all but consular military commands.

If the third century did see the formation of a regular field force, the reign of Diocletian did not carry the process much further; for the most marked military development of his reign was the construction of even stronger fortified defences along vast stretches of the frontier.

If we have in effect to admit ignorance about the third-century army, we can none the less discern significant patterns in the defence of the Empire. It was the East and the Danube region which claimed the attention of the Emperors. Severus Alexander in 231–4, Gordian in 242, Valerian in 256/7–60 (when he was captured by Shapur) then, after the domination of Palmyra in the East in 262–72, perhaps Aurelian in 272, and Carus in 282–3 all campaigned against Persia. By contrast, Severus Alexander came to the Rhine in 235 and was then murdered; his successor Maximinus led a campaign against the Alamanni and then took his army to Pannonia. Under Valerian, his son Gallienus commanded on the Rhine frontier in 254–8, but in 258 left to defend Italy, and in 259 his grandson Saloninus, left at Cologne, was killed, and Postumus inaugurated the line of Gallic Emperors which lasted until 274. Finally, Probus in 277 fought a successful campaign against the German invaders of Gaul. Gaul was not abandoned, though it suffered more severely than any other area. But the pattern of the Emperors' military activities shows clearly how the balance of the Empire had shifted to the Danubian and Eastern provinces. In the fifth century the 'fall of the Roman Empire' was in fact to be the fall of the Western provinces, and of Italy itself.

7

Italy

The history of Italy under the Empire is mainly the history of the gradual loss of the pre-eminent position she occupied at the beginning. In the early Empire, Italy retained the privilege, shared only by a few cities in the provinces, of exemption from direct taxation. But in the early third century the historian Cassius Dio could propose, what Diocletian nearly a century later was to put into effect, that Italy should be taxed like the provinces. Italy, again, was free from direct rule by Roman officials (except that until 44 three of the annual quaestors were appointed, with rather obscure functions, to districts of Italy); but in the second and third centuries there appear Roman officials appointed to individual cities, to districts, and finally to all of Italy. At the beginning of the period the citizenship, universal in Italy, was spreading only gradually in the provinces. In consequence, the great bulk of the citizen legionaries was recruited in Italy, especially in its most prosperous part, the Po valley. But even by the end of the first century the proportion of Italians in the legions was falling off so rapidly that it was once believed that Vespasian (69–79) had formally ended recruitment there. In fact Italians were still recruited, and when new legions were raised, as in the 160s, they were filled up entirely from levies in Italy. But the spread of citizenship had made possible the general practice of recruiting for the legions in the provinces or areas in which they served. The same process can be observed in office-holding by *equites*, where in the third century Italians seem (on very inadequate figures) to have occupied only about a fifth of the posts. Only in the Roman Senate do we find that, even in

127

the third century, nearly half the members of known origin were Italians. With the departure of the Emperor and the Court, completed by the foundation of Constantinople in 330, the Senate in Rome, with its core of Italian landowners, was to regain a position of considerable power and privilege.

Parallel to this process was a relative decline, by comparison with the other areas of the Empire, in economic position. The emigration of Italians to the provinces, as businessmen or settlers, which had been a marked feature of the late Republic and early Empire, seems to have dried up about the beginning of the second century. The red-glazed Italian pottery, known as 'Arretine Ware' from the main centre of production, Arezzo in Tuscany, was replaced as a luxury ware for export by Gallic pottery in the first century. And the fragments of some 40,000,000 amphorae containing wine and olive oil, mainly imported from Spain between the 150s and 220s, which form the Monte Testaccio in Rome, vividly attest the relative decline of Italian agriculture, and the ending of the predominance of Italian wines. Domitian (81–96) indeed attempted to restrict the cultivation of vines in the provinces (but not in Italy); his explicit aim was to encourage corn-growing, but behind that may perhaps have lain the desire to protect Italian agriculture.

Furthermore, it seemed to contemporaries that the manpower of Italy was failing. Nero (54–68) attempted to repopulate some South Italian cities with veteran soldiers. Nerva (96–8) set out (with what success we cannot tell) to buy plots of land for the poor of Rome. Trajan (98–117) instituted the only extensive social programme attributable to the Emperors, in a scheme – the *alimenta* – designed to provide for the upkeep of orphans in the Italian towns. Contemporary anxieties are reflected in what Pliny says in his *Panegyric* to Trajan about a cash distribution in Rome in which children were specially included – 'By your provision they will grow up to your military service . . . these are nurtured to be our strength in war . . . our adornment in peace . . . from these the camps, from these the tribes (of Roman citizens) will be replenished'.[1]

That said, it remains impossible to prove an absolute, as opposed to a relative, decline in the prosperity of Italy. In parts of the South, however, it is clear that some, though not all, cities declined, and large areas remained subject to recurrent disorders and banditry, mainly by escaped slaves. External dangers hardly touched Italy; only in the civil war of 69, briefly in about 168 and again in the civil war of 238 was there serious fighting before the raids and civil wars of the mid-third century; even these seem only to have touched the North. So far as we know, no Italian cities were destroyed in this period and none exhibit the contraction to a small area of the original city which occurred in a number of Gallic towns in the third century. Archaeology seems to show that Italy followed a pattern fairly characteristic of many other parts of the Empire, with urban prosperity and magnificence increasing up to the third century and then halting in the third. If the process is less marked, it is partly because no new cities were founded in Italy after the reign of Augustus, and because some of the existing ones had already reached their fullest urban development. One might take as an example Verona, where the magnificent surviving amphitheatre, the theatre and the street plan which still gives its shape to the centre of the city were in place by the time of Augustus. But if there were only minor adornments later, there was no contraction or decline. When Gallienus ordered the rebuilding of the city defences in 265, the new walls ran just outside where the old ones had stood, and were even extended to include the amphitheatre.[2]

Italy, even more than the provinces, has thus no 'history'. It can show neither the social changes which accompanied Romanization and the development of city life, nor, except to a very slight extent, the crowded military history of the third century which marks almost all other parts of the Empire. Instead, we have, especially for the early period, rather more information about agriculture and landholding than is available from other areas; and above all, two of the most fully known cities of the ancient world, Pompeii and Ostia, the former revealed as it was at the moment when Vesuvius erupted in 79, the latter, as it appears today, very largely the product of rebuilding and development in the first half of the second century.

From the beginning of our period we have a full description of Italy in the fifth and sixth books of Strabo's Geography, beginning with the prosperous Po valley, which produced corn, acorns (for feeding pigs), pitch, wine and wool, and its rich cities, among them Patavium (Padua) with more than 500 men who reached the property-qualification of a Roman *eques*; the mountainous Liguria with its population scattered in villages; the Sabine country up the Tiber from Rome, with its produce of olives, vines, acorns, cattle and the famous mules of Reate; then Rome itself, and to the south of it Latium and Campania, largely dominated by the estates and villas of the Roman aristocracy. The Greek cities of the South had by now largely lost their Greek institutions and culture, and had been absorbed by the Italians (a process Strabo refers to as 'barbarization'). But Naples especially retained its *gymnasia* and festivals, and was much frequented by Romans with a taste for Greek life – among them Augustus, who shortly before his death in 14 had been there to attend some games established in his honour.

The first century seems on the whole to have been a period of peace and prosperity. From the North, the foothills of the Alps, we even have evidence of the spread of Romanization to some hill-tribes there which still lacked the citizenship. For, in an edict issued in 46 from his villa at Baiae in Campania, Claudius settles the citizen status of some Alpine tribes, some formerly 'attributed' (attached for the purpose of jurisdiction) to the *municipium* of Tridentum (Trento), some not even that; their people had not only become inextricably mixed with the Tridentines, but had also been recruited, as if citizens, into the Praetorian cohorts, had risen to the rank of centurion, and even in some cases served as equestrian jurymen in Rome. Claudius announces that though their citizenship has no legal basis, the least harmful procedure is to recognize it as a fact.[3]

From central Italy we have some conception of the state of agriculture from Junius Columella, an immigrant from Gades who owned property at three places in Latium and probably another in Etruria, and who wrote a textbook on agriculture probably in the 60s. In it he gives advice on the running of every aspect of a fairly substantial mixed estate, with poultry, cattle, corn, olives and vines. He argues that the best system is direct exploitation by slaves supervised by their owner, but otherwise by a slave overseer (*vilicus*) – and describes, for instance, how to fit out a cellar for locking up slaves as a punishment. The alternative system, of leasing the land to tenants (*coloni*), is not recommended, except for outlying properties. At one point he mentions the exceptional productivity of the vineyard at Nomentum owned by Seneca, the philosopher and adviser of Nero. The story of this vineyard is told more fully in the *Natural History* of Columella's younger contemporary, the Elder Pliny. The land had been bought for 600,000 *sesterces* by a grammarian of Claudius' time, Remmius Palaemon; with the advice of an expert he had had the ground re-trenched, and within eight years had sold a single vintage, still on the branch, for 400,000 *sesterces*. This aroused the interest of the wealthy Seneca, who bought it for about 2,400,000 a couple of years later. Seneca himself emphasizes a different function of the property, describing how he went out to Nomentum to recuperate from the cares of the city.

The most vivid evidence for the economic life of Italy in the first century comes from a fictional source, the portrait of the rich freedman Trimalchio contained in the *Satyricon* of Petronius. The three heroes of the novel are invited to dinner at the house of Trimalchio in a town in Campania. At dinner Trimalchio relates how he came as a slave-boy from Asia, and, after many years as the favourite of his master, was freed, and later made his co-heir with Caesar. With the money he fitted out a fleet of five ships for trading with Rome, lost them all in a storm, built some more, and made (so he says) ten million on a single voyage, allowing him to buy up the rest of his master's former estate. At one point at dinner a clerk reads out a report on the estate (the figures may be exaggerated, but the picture is authentic): 'July 26th. Born on the estate at Cumae which belongs to Trimalchio 30 (slave) boys and 40 girls. Removed from the threshing-floor 500,000 pecks of wheat. 500 oxen broken in. On the same day the slave Mithridates was crucified for cursing the *genius* of our master Gaius . . .' Later, Trimalchio gives the specifications for the tomb he is having erected for himself: 'I beg you to put ships in full sail on the monument, and myself sitting on the tribunal in my *toga praetexta* (in his capacity as *sevir augustalis* – municipal priest for the Emperor-cult), with five gold rings, distributing coins to the populace from a sack . . .' The inscription was to run: 'Here lies C. Pompeius Trimalchio. The office of *sevir augustalis* was decreed to him in his absence. Although he could have been on any of the panels (of the magistrates' attendants) in Rome, he did not wish it. Pious, brave and truthful, he started from very little, left thirty million, and never went to hear a philosopher.'

If there were opportunities for the acquisition of wealth and status, there were still rumblings of social discontent, especially in the less prosperous south. In 24, for instance, a retired soldier of the Praetorian cohorts began holding secret meetings in the Brundisium area, and put up notices calling on the slaves who worked on the widespread pasture-lands to strike for freedom; but the revolt was soon crushed. Thirty years later, in 53, the charge was made against a woman of senatorial birth that she had allowed her slaves in Calabria to disturb the peace of Italy. The same disorders were to recur in the early third century.

Besides this, the occasional disorders in the towns did not threaten any serious unrest. Under Tiberius (14–37), for instance, the people of Pollentia prevented the funeral procession of a centurion from leaving the *forum* there until funeral games had been promised by the heirs – and were ruthlessly punished by forces sent by the Emperor. In 59, at a gladiatorial show given at Pompeii, a fight (depicted on a Pompeian fresco) broke out between the locals and people from Nuceria, and developed into a pitched battle with stones and weapons. The Senate exiled the ringleaders, dissolved illegal guilds (*collegia*) at Pompeii, and forbade shows there for ten years.

By reason of its nearness, of its historical privileges and of the needs of Rome, Italy tended to receive more direct attention from the Emperors than other parts of the Empire. The most striking example of this is provided by the harbours at Ostia, the first built by Claudius and completed by Nero, the second, inner one by Trajan. Before Claudius, ships bringing cargoes to Rome had to anchor off Ostia and either unload completely on to barges or else go up to Rome half-laden. The plan of Claudius' harbour, begun in 42 and completed by 62, has only recently been revealed by excavation. Over 1,000 metres across at the widest point, it was protected by two moles of some 760 and 600 metres in length made of marble blocks and concrete. At the end of the north mole a great ship, ninety-five metres in length, was sunk and filled with concrete to serve as the base of a lighthouse. The other mole carried harbour buildings. In 64, Nero issued a beautiful coin showing the harbour with its two moles, and ships riding at anchor in its shelter.[4]

Nero also began, but abandoned, a canal from Terracina to Ostia – to protect shipping on the last part of the journey up the coast to Rome – and also attempted to repopulate with legionary veterans Antium on the coast of Latium and the old Greek colony of Tarentum; but the majority failed to settle, and slipped away to the provinces in which they had served. Vespasian made a similar attempt, settling veterans of the Misenum fleet at Paestum. We know of this from the *diplomata* given to five of the men; since two of these were found in Bulgaria, one in Yugoslavia, one in Corsica and only one near Naples, it can be taken that here too the colonists preferred to go quietly home to their own provinces.

Before Vespasian could gain power, Italy had seen in 69, 'the year of the four Emperors', the first serious fighting it had experienced for more than a century. No major fighting had attended the march to Rome from Spain by Galba after the death of Nero in 68. But in January 69 the German legions proclaimed their commander Vitellius as Emperor, and invaded northern Italy, meeting forces from Rome supporting Otho who had murdered and replaced Galba. Even Otho's forces are said by Tacitus to have caused widespread devastation on their way north. But the main damage was caused by the troops of Vitellius, who besieged Placentia (Piacenza), destroying the amphitheatre outside its walls, and then, after the victory of Bedriacum near Cremona, ravaged the colonies and municipalities of Northern Italy; Tacitus describes how the locals took the opportunity to pay off old scores under the guise of soldiers, and how those soldiers who originated from there (as many still did) and knew the area, led the way to the richest estates and properties. Even worse slaughter and destruction took place in the second half of 69, when the Vitellian forces were in their turn confronted with the legions from Moesia and Pannonia which invaded Italy in support of Vespasian. A second battle, won by the invaders, took place at Bedriacum. Cremona, filled with people who had come from all over Italy for a fair there, was then besieged, taken and sacked. Thus, as Tacitus relates, a fine city was destroyed which had been founded 285 years before as a military colony for defence against Hannibal, and had prospered in the interval from its fertile lands and strategic position on the Po. Tacitus ends, however, 'Soon the surviving population returned to Cremona; the forums and temples were restored by the munificence of the citizens – and Vespasian gave his encouragement.'[5]

It was characteristic of the new Emperor, tight-fisted by nature and struggling with the financial losses of the civil wars, that he was less concerned with munificence than with increasing his revenues. One of his measures to raise cash was an attempt to reclaim for the State plots of land (*subseciva*) which formed part of colonies in Italy but had not been formally assigned in the allotments to the original colonists. They had all been occupied subsequently, and the reclamation will normally have taken the form of demanding money from the occupiers in return for full ownership. The result was widespread disturbance in Italy, and a procession of city delegations to Vespasian; he halted the scheme, Titus (79–81) carried it on on a small scale, but Domitian issued an edict formally abandoning the claims (the story is a good example of the limits of the power of the State in the ancient world). Domitian's edict seems to have been issued immediately on his accession in 81, for an inscription of 82 shows him judging a dispute over the occupation of such land between the people of Firmum (a veteran colony established by Augustus) and Falerii, in which no Imperial claim is mentioned.

The attempted recovery of *subseciva* was linked with a parallel programme of restoring to the cities their own public lands usurped by private persons. One reflection of this is one of the very latest documents from Pompeii, an inscription which records that on the authority of Vespasian a tribune of the

Praetorian cohorts, Suedius Clemens, after hearing cases and taking measurements of the land, had restored public property to the city. Within a few years, however, there came the eruption of Vesuvius in 79 which buried Pompeii in a thick layer of ash, under which it remained concealed until its location was revealed by the discovery of the inscription of Suedius Clemens in 1763. The excavations carried on since, especially those of this century, have revealed in the fullest detail the life of an old Oscan town, influenced by the Greek colonization of Southern Italy and dominated in its last two centuries by Rome.

Amid the infinite range of detail presented by Pompeii (as by its twin town Herculaneum, a few miles away), one may note that it presents a stage in urban development in which the single-storey 'atrium' house – that is one centred round a covered central court with an opening in the roof through which rain-water fell into a basin (*impluvium*) below – was still the basic unit, though colonnaded courts, further ranges of rooms, and gardens, had been increasingly added. Similarly, starting from the first century BC, second storeys had often been built on. But there is no trace of the many-storied apartment blocks characteristic of second-century Ostia, or of Rome itself. From the later period of the city's life there are traces of the conversion of town houses for commercial or small-scale manufacturing purposes (the rich evidently tended to move out into suburban villas). Both of these tendencies are apparent in a house of the first century AD in which the space normally used for a colonnaded court is taken up with a bakery, and the living accommodation is on the first floor, grouped around an internal gallery reached by a staircase from the atrium. Another variant is provided by the 'House of the Menander' (so called from a statue found in it), a rambling building dating originally from the third century BC and gradually extended, which has at the rear a stable-yard with a drinking trough and two light carts, a row of *amphorae* standing ready for filling, a room for the slave overseer or *vilicus*, and a line of rooms for slaves. In other words this is an example of something which was probably very common in the small towns of the Empire, a town house which also served as a farmhouse for working land in the area. More immediately attractive and interesting than these are houses like that of the Vettii, two merchant brothers, with its wonderful series of frescoes dating to the last decades of the city, or, on a suburban road, the Villa of the Mysteries – so called from its wall paintings of the first century BC, representing Dionysiac rituals. This elaborate and luxurious house was damaged in the earthquake which struck Pompeii in 62, and subsequently passed into the hands of a freedman, who at the moment of the eruption was fitting it out with wine presses and a wine cellar. In the area round Pompeii there are also a number of villas, one of which has slave accommodation and a prison for slaves with iron stocks in position, very much as recommended by Columella.

The communal life of the town is illustrated by the amphitheatre, built about 80 BC, the forum surrounded by a colonnade which masked the temples grouped around it, a basilica and a building for the guild of fullers, but above all by a feature unique to Pompeii, the hundreds of inscriptions painted on the walls recommending candidates for the local elections. A typical one runs: 'I pray you, neighbours, elect as *duovir* L. Statius Receptus, who is well worthy. Aemilius Celer, your neighbour, wrote this. If any opponent rubs this out, let him fall sick.'[6]

Immediately after the burial of the town some inhabitants returned, dug through the thinner layers of ash and removed valuables from the houses. Also, the Emperor Titus (79–81) provided funds for the restoration of the area. But nothing significant was achieved. Nor can we trace anything, beyond a single inscription and a reference in Pliny's letters, of the scheme by which Nerva (96–8) provided 60,000,000 *sesterces* to buy land-allotments for the poor of Rome. Very different, however, is the 'alimentary' programme of Trajan (98–117) by which funds were provided for the upkeep of children in the Italian towns. The procedure was that the Emperor provided a lump capital sum for each community, which was then distributed among local landowners in proportion (varying erratically around an average of about 8%) to the capital value of the land they registered with the authorities; on this sum they then paid an annual interest of 5% for the upkeep of the children. Some commentators have been led to believe that the scheme had a dual purpose, the other being the improvement of Italian agriculture by means of these capital grants. But in fact there is no hint of this in the evidence, and the system merely reflects the process of *obligatio praediorum* (the giving of landed property as a surety) by which the funds of municipalities were protected when handled by private persons. There is no clear indication that the 'loans' were welcome to the recipients, or even voluntary. The scheme seems to have continued, at least spasmodically, into the early third century, and inscriptions referring to it come from forty-six of the 400 or so Italian towns. But the main information about it is derived from two very long inscriptions from the reign of Trajan, one of 101 from the territory of the Ligures Baebiani near Beneventum, the other of 103–13 from Veleia in North Italy. The latter in fact shows an earlier stage in the process, in that it gives a very detailed list of the properties (as reported by their owners) on which the funds were to be secured, and a statement of the loan in each case. It is characteristic of the pattern of ownership that of the forty-nine landowners listed as reporting property (over 100 more are mentioned as neighbours in giving the details of location) nearly all list a number of separate items of property – cultivated land, uncultivated, woods – in different places; furthermore there are mentions of properties owned by the Emperor, by the Roman State and by neighbouring towns. The heading of the inscription gives the total amount (1,044,000 *sesterces*) lent at Veleia 'by the indulgence of the Emperor', the numbers of children to be supported – 245 boys of legitimate birth at sixteen *sesterces* per month, one illegitimate boy and thirty-four legitimate girls at twelve, and one illegitimate girl at ten – and the interest paid, 5%.

The inscription from the territory of the Ligures Baebiani has a different function, giving brief details of the properties, their value and the amounts secured on them, but adding opposite each entry the amount to be paid in interest every six months. In other words it is a record of the income produced by the scheme when established. The landowners mentioned on it provide a good cross-section of the propertied class, from private persons to members of the local aristocracies, to Roman senators.[7]

Another inscription records the decree of the town-council of Ferentinum praising Pomponius Bassus (one of two senators mentioned in the Veleia inscription as establishing the scheme) for performing the task in such a way as to earn eternal gratitude, and authorising the despatch of an embassy to ask him to be *patronus* of the town. As such, it typifies one aspect of politics and diplomacy under the Empire.

These documents deserve mention in some detail because they portray almost the only example of a major social programme carried out under the Empire. There can be no doubt of the scale and complexity of the operation; it is only unfortunate that we have no evidence as to how far it influenced the populousness of Italy.

The scheme involved, then and subsequently, the activity of regional officials, appointed by the Emperor, in the towns of Italy. Almost contemporaneously we have the first examples from Italy of a different type of Imperial official, the *curator* (overseer) of a town, a man, usually of senatorial or equestrian rank, appointed to check and control its public finances. Thus when in 114 the town-council of Caere wished to allot to an Imperial freedman a bit of public land on which to erect at his own expense a building for the *Augustales*, they wrote a formal letter to the *curator* asking his permission. *Curatores* are attested throughout Italy in the second, third and fourth centuries. In the course of the second century there appeared Imperial officials with a wider sphere of activity: first the four ex-consuls appointed by Hadrian (117–38) to exercise jurisdiction in Italy, then, under Marcus Aurelius (161–80), a number of *iuridici* (judges), usually senators of ex-praetorian rank. The first *iuridicus* of Transpadana (the area north of the Po) was Arrius Antoninus in the 160s, who is honoured by the town of Concordia for having helped its corn-supply (Roman officials rarely kept to any strictly defined sphere of duty). Cornelius Fronto, the orator and friend of Marcus Aurelius, also wrote to Arrius Antoninus, urging the claims of a man who was to come before him to defend his right to be a *decurio* of Concordia.

The first example of a post relating to the whole of Italy comes from about 215, when a senator who had previously been both a *curator* and *iuridicus* in Italy was appointed 'to correct the condition of Italy'. In the 260s or 270s another senator was appointed, with the title of *corrector* for Italy, and at this point the post of *iuridicus* disappears.

Such was the development of direct Imperial control in Italy. For a picture of its social and economic life we must revert again to the reign of Trajan, to the letters of Pliny the Younger, a senator from Como in North Italy.[8] At Como itself Pliny had property inherited from his mother, and owned a number of villas along the lake. He writes for instance to his friend Calvisius, a *decurio* of Como, about whether he should buy some property – fields, vineyards and woods – adjoining his own. The advantages would be the saving in house and garden slaves, carpenters and hunting equipment and in having to keep up only one villa in full order; the disadvantage was the decay of the land under the previous owner, who had responded to delays in payment by the tenants by selling up their equipment, thus further reducing their productivity. In consequence, the price had fallen from 5,000,000 to 3,000,000 *sesterces*. Or again he describes, not without self-congratulation, how he had remitted part of the price of his vintage to merchants who had purchased it and then found that they could not re-sell as well as they had hoped. As an important local figure, Pliny not only gave gifts to Como – for instance a third of the cost of a school, or land whose revenue was to provide *alimenta* for children – but also kept up a wide circle of acquaintance with people from Como and elsewhere in the north, among whom there was a recognizable fellow-feeling, and pride in the possession of old-fashioned virtues. Thus Pliny writes to a friend recommending a prospective son-in-law, 'His home-town is Brixia (Brescia) in that Italy of ours which still retains and preserves so much piety, frugality and even old-fashioned rusticity. . . . His maternal grandmother is Serrana Procula from Patavium (Padua). You know the manners of that area; Serrana is a model of severity even to the Patavines.'

Pliny had property also at Tifernum Tiberinum in Tuscany,

perhaps inherited from his maternal uncle, the encyclopedist, Pliny the Elder. In 98 we find him writing to Trajan asking permission to leave his post to visit these estates (which brought him 400,000 *sesterces* per year), where the beginning of a new five-year period required him to go and settle with new tenants. He also wished to build at his own expense a temple for the statues of the Emperors. This would be in the town of Tifernum, of which he had been made *patronus* as a boy; the inhabitants, he says, celebrated his arrival, mourned his departure, and rejoiced at the progress of his career. He also describes going to the estates, making a tour of inspection on horseback, and hearing the interminable complaints and disputes of the tenants. In another letter, in which he does not indicate the locality, he announces that he is changing his previous system of charging a fixed rent in cash – which had caused the tenants, despairing of making up arrears of payment, to seize and consume whatever was produced; in future he will demand a share of the produce in kind, which should be more equitable, though it will mean appointing some of his slaves to watch the crops and exact his share.

Finally, like other members of Roman society, Pliny had a villa outside Rome, at Laurentum on the coast. He describes its delights in a long letter, its porticoes, dining-rooms, bath with hot-water system, tower-rooms with views over the sea and the coast lined with villas, its formal garden and pavilions. Here Pliny would retire from the cares of official life, to rest and write.

Among the many scenes of official business Pliny portrays is his visit to the villa of Trajan at Centumcellae (Civitavecchia), where the Emperor was supervising the construction of a harbour. That site has not been explored. What is well known is the great hexagonal harbour (each side nearly 400 yards in length) excavated under Trajan inland from Claudius' harbour north of the Tiber and connected to it and to the river. The harbour was surrounded by warehouses and was evidently intended to provide for the main import of foodstuffs for Rome. Round the two harbours a town (yet to be properly excavated) grew up, which was sufficiently important to have its own bishop in the early fourth century.

140

The growth of this town – known simply as Portus, the harbour – meant the eventual eclipse of Ostia which lay between the south bank of the Tiber and the coast.[9] Ostia was originally founded in the fourth century BC as a Roman colony, whose rectangular plan continued to give its shape to the centre of the town. Extension and rebuilding especially in the second century BC and the Augustan period was followed, beginning perhaps in the reign of Domitian (81–96), by a large-scale reconstruction of the town which continued into the middle of the second century. The building-level was raised by about a metre, and 'atrium' houses, probably not unlike those of Pompeii, were largely replaced by apartment blocks built in brick, three, four, or even five storeys high, with shops lining their street fronts on the ground floor. In the same period a new temple to Jupiter, Juno and Minerva was built beside the forum, and the forum itself enlarged and given a *basilica* (market-hall) and meeting-house (*curia*) for the council; at least eight new public baths appeared. The inscriptions show a parallel change in the composition of the Ostian governing class. The local offices, which in the first century had been largely the preserve of a few established families, became open to new immigrants, to men who had risen through the guilds (*collegia*) and even the sons and descendants of freedmen. The new social order is typified in an inscription of the late second century of Marcus Licinus Privatus, a freed slave who held office in the guilds of bakers and builders, was a clerk of the city magistrates, was honoured with the *insignia* of a town-councillor and a seat of honour at public functions (having contributed 50,000 *sesterces* to public funds) – and had sons who were town-councillors and even Roman *equites*. By his time rebuilding at Ostia had virtually halted, while in the third century there are even traces of the abandonment of some sites, or, in one case, the destruction of a bakery by fire and the making of a path through the ruins. The third-century evidence does not reveal any sudden collapse; but it indicates something more than a shift of population to Portus, and shows that Ostia, untouched by any invasion, shared the decline in urban activity noticeable in all parts of the Empire.

Ostia reveals in abundance the popularity of Eastern cults in the Roman West under the Empire. There is a temple of Cybele, the Great Mother, built in the first half of the second century, and linked to it temples of the associated deities Attis and Bellona; inscriptions record the sacrifice of bulls and rams and the annual ceremony of a procession escorting a pine tree, symbolizing the dead Attis, to the temple of Cybele. This cult and those of Isis and Serapis seem to have lost ground by the mid-third century before the worship of Mithras; no less than fifteen shrines for this cult have been discovered in Ostia. Excavations in 1961 and subsequently have also brought to light a synagogue, situated near the coast outside the town. The surviving structure is mainly of the fourth century; but underneath part of it there are traces of an earlier synagogue, dating to the first century AD, and thus (with that discovered at Masada) the earliest one known.[10] The evidence for Christianity is less clear; some items from Christian cemeteries in Ostia and Portus may date to the third century, there are traditions of martyrs at both, and both places had bishops in the early fourth century.

For the rest, Italy in the second, and even more in the third, century presents little coherent evidence – partly a reflection of the fact that Latin literature had no major Italian representative after Pliny. A few items of evidence cast some light on the scene. For instance, an inscription from Trieste honours a young man from there who, it is said, had entered the Roman Senate primarily to defend the interests of the city, had represented it frequently before Antoninus Pius (138–61), and had finally gained Imperial permission for members of two tribes 'attributed' to the city to become town-councillors and local magistrates; they would then, when elected, gain the citizenship for themselves and, more important, share the burdens of local office with the original inhabitants. But though local office was a burden to its holders, they in their turn could oppress those below them. A case of this kind came to light in about 170, when the city officials of Saepinum and Bovianum began to harass the shepherds bringing flocks across the Abruzzi Mountains, claiming that the flocks were stolen and the shepherds fugitive slaves; the abuse was only ended because some of the flocks were Imperial property, and Imperial officials complained to the

Praetorian Prefects, who issued a stern warning to the city magistrates.

The years before that, however, had seen more ominous events, the levying of two new legions in Italy in the 160s, the spread of a plague brought back by the troops of the Emperor Lucius Verus in 166, and then (perhaps in 168 or 169) an invasion of tribes from beyond the Danube, who besieged Aquileia and burned Opitergium before retreating – the first foreign invasion of Italy for more than two and a half centuries. That danger over, Italy was disturbed again in the 180s (if we can believe the Greek historian, Herodian) by rebels from Gaul and Spain under Maternus (see Ch. 8) who made their way to Rome and were discovered before attempting to murder Commodus. In 193 came the murder of Pertinax, the proclamation of Didius Julianus and the march on Rome by the *legatus* of Pannonia Superior, Septimius Severus (193–211). He broke with tradition by establishing a legion near the Imperial palace at Alba, south of Rome, and replaced the existing Praetorian cohorts, mainly composed of Italians, by men from the Danubian legions – thus, as the contemporary Cassius Dio states, forcing the youth of Italy to live as gladiators or bandits. The following years did indeed produce a famous bandit, Felix Bulla, who ravaged Southern Italy with a band of 600 men, rescued two of his men from prison by pretending to be a local magistrate who wanted to put them to the beasts in a show, captured a centurion and sent him back with a message to Severus that he should feed his slaves so that they did not turn to banditry, and was finally captured about 206 and sent to the beasts himself.[11]

Further disturbance occurred in 238, when the Emperor Maximinus, proclaimed on the Rhine in 235, marched into Northern Italy and besieged Aquileia, which held out for the Senate and its Emperors, Maximus, Balbinus and Gordian III. Herodian's account of these operations reveals the continuing prosperity of the area, based on the vineyards which stretched round the city and produced wine for export; Maximinus' troops found large wooden barrels standing in the fields ready to be filled, and used them for crossing the river. The population fled into Aquileia from the surrounding villages and hamlets, repaired the walls which had largely collapsed from disuse, and successfully stood siege. They were able to resist, with ample supplies within the walls, until Maximinus' soldiers, driven by hunger, killed him and brought the war to an end.

The bare and uninformative narratives of the middle years of the third century provide only meagre details of events in Italy. Such as they are, they indicate that the North, though not the rest, was recurrently subject to invasion and civil war. The Emperor Philip was defeated and killed by Decius near Verona in 249; the Alamannic invasion of 258 ended with Gallienus' victory at Milan; Claudius defeated the great Gothic invasion of 268 at Lake Garda; some two years later the Iuthungi won a victory over Aurelian at Placentia (Piacenza) but were then defeated at Fanum Fortunae and Pavia. It was at this point that Aurelian began building his great defensive wall for Rome itself. The record of fighting in Italy is completed in the reign of Carus (282–3) with the bloody defeat of a pretender in the area of Verona.

These events do not seem to have disrupted ordinary life in Italy as a whole (though Italy reveals the same decline in the volume of known inscriptions from this period as do other areas). In central Italy at least it was possible to preserve a peaceful existence, unaffected by the turmoils elsewhere. Such an existence is portrayed, for instance, in the *Life* of Plotinus, the great neo-Platonist philosopher, by his pupil Porphyry. Plotinus was born in Egypt about 203 and came to Rome in about 244. There he remained, teaching and writing, until his death in 269/70, retiring on occasion to the estates of his friends and admirers in Campania. We see him in Porphyry's account with a wide circle of devotees both from the Greek provinces – Syria, Arabia, Egypt – and from the nobility of Rome. One senatorial friend, turning to the philosophical life, gave away his possessions and, as praetor, sent away his lictors and refused to ascend the tribunal. The orphan children of noble families were often entrusted to Plotinus, who cared for them in his house and carefully checked the accounts of their estates and revenues when presented by their legal guardians. He was also in favour with Gallienus (253–68) and, according to Porphyry, only obstruction at Court prevented the Emperor founding for Plotinus philosophers' city in Campania, to be called Platonopolis.

Italy had by now become something of a backwater, and was near the point reached under Diocletian, when she received in effect provincial status. But the traditional dominance of Rome and the Senate and, under its shadow, the life of the Italian cities, continued as before. It is hard to remember the struggles of the third century when we read, on an inscription, the decree passed in 289 by the *decuriones* of the colony of Cumae in Campania appointing a man to a vacant priesthood, and the letter in which the senatorial board of priests in Rome approved the appointment, and permitted the new priest to wear his robes while within the territory of the colony.

The Western Provinces: Gaul, Spain and Britain

In AD 14 Gaul and Spain had finally emerged from the period of Roman conquest. Southern France, indeed, colonized in places by the Greeks six centuries before, and a Roman province (hence 'Provence') since 121 BC, was long settled and Romanized – 'Italy rather than a province' in the words of Pliny the Elder. The fine monuments of the Roman cities in Southern France – such as Nîmes, Arles, Orange – date broadly to the Augustan age; and a long line of orators and senators from there entered Roman life in the first century AD. The conquest of the rest of Gaul – the 'Three Gauls', Lugdunensis, Aquitania and Belgica – had been carried out by Julius Caesar in 58–51, and since then only disturbances on the introduction of the Roman census under Augustus had broken the peace of a land where Romanization was already under way, and was very largely to survive the barbarian settlements of the fifth century. It is, however, a mystery why the Three Gauls with their evident prosperity were to contribute so few men to the equestrian and senatorial orders of Rome.

In Spain too, the Mediterranean and Southern coasts had received Greek and also Carthaginian settlements, and there the Roman conquest had begun in the wars against Carthage in the late third century. It was not completed, however, until the subjugation of the Cantabrian and Asturian tribes of the mountainous North-West between 26 and 19 BC. Romanization was effectively complete in the highly prosperous southern province of Baetica (Andalusia), and extensive along the urbanized Mediterranean seaboard of Tarraconensis. Men from these

146

areas already had an established place in Roman life; Baetica had already produced the first provincial consul, Cornelius Balbus from Gades (Cadiz), in 40 BC, and was to produce the first provincial Emperor, Trajan (98–117), whose family came from Italica. Central and Northern Tarraconensis and Lusitania contained a number of veteran colonies established by Augustus, but must otherwise have been little Romanized. We can deduce that peace was maintained by the fact that the three legions still stationed in Tarraconensis in 14 had been reduced to one by the year 70. But our knowledge of the social background in all parts of Spain, and especially in the less Romanized areas, is hampered by the very slight progress of archaeology there compared to Gaul or Britain.

Britain, invaded briefly by Julius Caesar in 55 and 54, remained free, but in close contact with the Roman world. The geographer Strabo mentions her exports of corn, cattle, gold, silver, iron, hides, slaves and hunting dogs, and the reverse traffic is indicated by finds of Gallic and Roman pottery in pre-conquest Britain. British chieftains had political links with Rome. The *tumulus* of a chief near Colchester (Camulodunum) contained not only a number of small bronze figures imported from Italy, and perhaps Gaul, but a medallion of Augustus made by cutting out and mounting the head from a silver coin of 17 BC. Others minted coins, patterned on Roman types, some with the Latin title of *rex*. The conquest itself was delayed until 43; the history of Roman Britain belongs in the last part of this chapter.

In Gaul, the southern province of Narbonensis, very largely Romanized, still retained the imprint of Greek settlement. The charming site of Glanum (St Rémy de Provence), which had been a flourishing Greek town in the second century BC, had later been Romanized, and also endowed with Roman monuments, such as a triumphal arch, in the Augustan age. But Massilia especially retained its Greek character; Julius Agricola, born in AD 40 at the *colonia* of Forum Julii (Fréjus), the son of a Roman senator and grandson of two Imperial procurators, studied at Massilia, which was marked, in Tacitus' words, by a combination of 'Greek charm and provincial modesty'. There were other Roman colonies, Narbonne dating to as early as 118 BC, or Arles founded by Caesar in 46 BC; its theatre was completed probably in the reign of Augustus, the well-preserved amphitheatre by the end of the first century, while its *forum* incorporated the rare feature of a *cryptoporticus*, or arched underground gallery running underneath the surrounding colonnade. Situated on the Rhône, it replaced Massilia as the commercial centre of the area. Nîmes (the *Colonia Augusta Nemausus*) contained the beautiful Augustan temple now known as the Maison Carrée. Like Vienne farther up the Rhône, it seems to have had the status, rare in this period, of a 'Latin' colony; Strabo notes that Nîmes had twenty-four villages in its jurisdiction and had the 'Latin' right by which magistrates of the town gained the Roman citizenship (see Ch. 5). He notes also that Vienne was now the political centre of the Allobroges, and that the chief men of the tribe had taken up residence in it. The prosperity of these cities is mirrored in the rise of their leading citizens into the Roman Senate, the earliest being Domitius Afer, an orator from Nîmes who was praetor in 25, consul in 39 and owned valuable properties near Rome, and Valerius Asiaticus from Vienne, consul twice, in 35 and 46. There were also important *equites*, like Afranius Burrus from Vaison, who became Praetorian Prefect in 51. This process reached its culmination in 138, when Antoninus Pius became Emperor, the grandson of a senator from Nîmes.

In the Three Gauls, Lugdunum (Lyon) provided the centre for Romanized institutions. In 12 BC, Drusus, the brother of Tiberius, had set up there an altar and temple to Rome and Augustus, placed on a fine esplanade of 400 by 100 metres adorned with statues set up by the sixty communities of Gaul whose representatives met there. The first High Priest of the cult was an Aeduan, Julius Vercondaridubnus, whose Gallo-Roman name aptly symbolizes the new era. Under Tiberius another High Priest, Gaius Julius Rufus from the Santones (Saintes), constructed the amphitheatre near the temple, for annual shows on 1 August.[1] At Saintes itself he erected a triumphal arch in 19 (Plate 8), inscribing on it his descent, taking us back to the tribal aristocracy of pre-Roman Gaul – 'Gaius Julius Rufus, son of C. Julius Otuaneunus, grandson of C. Julius Gedemo, great-grandson of Epotsiorovidus'.

Both the progress of Romanization and the tensions it produced are illustrated by the rebellion which broke out in 21, provoked by debt (probably to Italian merchants) and the extension of tribute. It was led by two men who themselves possessed the Roman citizenship, Julius Sacrovir of the Aedui and Julius Indus of the Treveri. Significantly, Sacrovir's first act was to take Autun, and seize as hostages the sons of the Gallic nobility gathered there to be educated in Graeco-Roman culture. The revolt was rapidly suppressed, however, by the single Roman cohort from Lugdunum, reinforced by two legions from the Rhine.

In the middle of the first century we find the Arverni (from Auvergne) hiring a Greek sculptor – later employed by Nero – to make a colossal statue of Mercury, or, more significant, the leading men of the Aedui and other tribes approaching Claudius in 48 with a request to be allowed to stand for office in the Roman Senate. A large part of the speech to the Senate in which Claudius supported their claims is preserved on the famous bronze tablet from Lyon, discovered in 1528. Yet though the Senate, not without reluctance, accepted Claudius' proposal, there is almost no evidence of senators from the Three Gauls, then or later. One example is Julius Vindex, the descendant of a royal line in Aquitania, whose father, it is said, was already a senator, and who, as *legatus* of Gallia Lugdunensis, began the revolt against Nero in 68. Thereafter there is evidence of only a very few senators or even *equites* from Gaul until we come to the Gallic Emperors of 258–74 (and even these were Roman officials whose Gallic origins are precariously deduced from their names) The cultured landed aristocracy enjoying senatorial rank found in Gaul in the fourth and fifth centuries could trace no senatorial ancestors in our period.

None the less, archaeology shows abundantly how Romanization itself progressed in Gaul. Of the towns, for instance, the North provides a classic instance of urban development in Amiens.[2] The Gallic town of Samarobriva was replaced in the first century by a Roman town of the characteristic rectangular street-pattern, made up of *insulae* (blocks) of some 147 by 110 metres each, with an amphitheatre just outside the built-up area. In the second century the area of *insulae* was more than doubled, incorporating the amphitheatre and now including baths, built over a cemetery which previously had been outside the town. Then came the third-century invasions, and the town contracted to a tiny fortified area round the amphitheatre, which now served as a fortress.

Amiens may be compared with Trier (Augusta Treverorum) which began as a civilian settlement round an auxiliary post, and was then made a Roman colony and laid out with the usual rectangular street plan early in the reign of Claudius (41–54). In the early second century came an amphitheatre and the huge public baths (the 'Barbarathermen') of at least three stories. The city walls built in the early or middle third century seem to have enclosed an area more than three times that of the Claudian colony. With the Gallic Emperors, who had at Trier a mint and finally their capital, Trier began its most flourishing period, when it was the political, and Christian, centre of Gaul. From the fourth century date, for instance, the surviving Constantinian basilica, and an Imperial palace replaced in the middle of the century by the cathedral.[2a]

In rare cases we can trace accurately the development of a farm-dwelling from native huts to a Gallo-Roman villa, often of the type known as the 'winged corridor' house. A by now classic example was excavated at Mayen near Coblenz. Here a wooden Celtic hut was reconstructed, still with a wooden frame but with stone walls, in the early Roman period, then in the first century AD acquired the normal outside corridor, and projecting wings of one room; by the end of the century it had main walls of masonry, a bath and a granary. From the other extreme of Gaul there is the villa at Chiragan near Toulouse, which developed from a single farmhouse, with rows of outhouses for workers, in the first century, to an elaborate complex of courts with a galleried façade, porticoes and even a *cryptoporticus* (basement portico), covering some forty hectares in all, in the late second century.

The prosperity of Gaul is reflected also in the progress of

pottery production there (given that we can never estimate the importance, not likely to be large, of any industry in the predominantly agricultural economy of Antiquity). At the beginning of our period the potters of La Graufesenque near Toulouse had just begun to rival the red-glazed ware of Arezzo in Tuscany, which was widely imported in Gaul as elsewhere. By the 70s they had monopolized the market in Gaul, the Rhineland and Britain and were exporting their wares into Italy itself. A case of ninety decorated bowls and twenty lamps from La Graufesenque had arrived in Pompeii in 79, and had not yet been unpacked when Vesuvius erupted. A second, even larger, centre of pottery production, at Lezoux (Puy de Dôme), had been in operation since before the Roman conquest, but did not begin to export widely until the second half of the first century. In the second century the products of these potters, stamped with their names, are found in Gaul, the Rhineland and Britain; production seems to have ceased at the end of the century.[3] In this period the dominant centres of production were in North-East Gaul, including Trier, which continued in production until the middle of the third century. The Gallic potteries thus show, along with a steady decline in quality, a gradual shift towards what was now the most important market, the military area along the Rhine.

Much is revealed about the political structure of Gaul, and the extent of its integration into the Roman Empire, in the events of 68–9. The fall of Nero in 68 was precipitated by the Aquitanian Julius Vindex, who as governor of Gallia Lugdunensis summoned an assembly of the Gauls to proclaim not a revolt but action against Nero, as unworthy to be Emperor. But while he sent messages to other provincial governors – and issued coins with Roman Republican slogans – the army which he raised was crushed by the Rhine legions.

The following year showed the persistence of local loyalties and tribal differences among the Gauls. The Treveri and Lingones of the North-East, ignored in the favours which Galba (68–9) showed to other tribes, supported the Rhine legions in their march on Rome which put Vitellius briefly on the throne. The march revealed bitter enmity between Lyon, which sided with Vitellius, and nearby Vienne, which was loyal to Otho, and narrowly avoided the sack. Later in 69 the semi-Romanized Batavi revolted and were joined by the Treveri and Lingones, and by German tribes from across the Rhine – and called on the rest of the Gallic communities to form an 'Empire of the Gauls'. The leaders of the revolt, by which the remaining Roman forces on the Rhine were defeated and even forced to swear loyalty, were tribal leaders who had commanded tribal units in the Roman service, and had Roman names (Julius Classicus, Julius Sabinus) and the citizenship; at the height of their power they took the titles and insignia of Roman Emperors. But at a meeting called by the Remi at Durocortorum (Rheims) the delegates of the rest of Gaul determined to remain loyal, and aided the legions sent by Vespasian in the suppression of the revolt.

Amid these great events a small local disturbance has a significance of its own. One Mariccus, from the small tribe of the Boii, believed by the people to be their divine champion, raised a following of 8,000 and attacked the neighbouring Aeduan villages. The revolt was crushed by the Aedui with Roman aid, and Mariccus' claims to immortality dispelled by his execution. We know no more than that, from a brief paragraph in Tacitus; but it is rare in our sources for the Western part of the Empire to have even a hint of the hopes and beliefs of the common people.

These events raise the question of how deeply Romanization had penetrated, or (which is slightly different) how far there had been a fusion of two cultures in a distinct Gallo-Roman culture. Little trace remains of pre-Roman Celtic monuments of any definable architectural type – though excavations at for instance Bibracte and Gergovia show that Celtic towns uninfluenced by Roman types of construction persisted into the early first century. But what is striking is that it is the most flourishing period of Roman Gaul, from the late first to the mid-third century, that produces constructions of a distinctive Gallo-Roman type.[4] There is, for instance, the 'winged corridor' house, and also temples of a type found only in the Three Gauls and Britain, with a high central room, either square, circular or irregular (but not an oblong rectangle as in the Graeco-Roman temple) surrounded at ground level by a covered passage with a roof supported by pillars on a low wall – apparently used for ceremonies in which the worshippers circled in procession round the god in the central room. Also distinctive to Gaul is the combined theatre and amphitheatre, which had a stage for performances but also an arena for gladiatorial shows and wild-beast fights. Gallo-Roman private houses are distinguished from those of the Mediterranean area by having large masonry-lined cellars, and (as is known from a couple of sculptural representations) high, steeply-pitched roofs.

The North-East produced also a distinctive local art-form in the magnificent funerary monuments, rectangular pillars ornamented with sculptured panels illustrating the life of the deceased. The most famous example, which dates from the early third century, is that which still stands at Igel near Trier; erected for a family of rich cloth-merchants, its sculptures show for instance a scene in their shop, tenants on their land bringing gifts, and pack-animals carrying bales of cloth over a hill.

In the decorative arts and pottery, whose details cannot be followed here, there seems to have been a revival of Celtic forms from the second century onward.[5] The fortunes of the Celtic language are also difficult to trace; Celtic documents disappear in the first century, and even of these the only extended one is the calendar of Coligny, in Celtic written in Latin lettering of the first century. Latin was clearly widespread; even in the potters' marks, for instance, *fecit* ('made') replaced the Celtic *avot* in the first century. But there are indications that Celtic survived; the Celtic word *leuga* ('league') appears even on official milestones in the third century; Irenaeus, bishop of Lyon in the late second century, may imply he has to use Celtic in his work; and Septimius Severus (193–211) allowed wills to be made in Celtic.

With the language, there persisted the native religion. Druidism, whose powerful caste of priests had been described by Julius Caesar, was forbidden to Roman citizens by Augustus, and suppressed altogether, according to Roman sources, by Tiberius and Claudius. But Druids prophesied the fall of Rome, and world-wide domination for the Gauls, when the Capitol burned in the civil wars of 69; they appeared again in the third century. Then there were the native gods, Teutates, identified with Mercury, and once the object of human sacrifices; Esus or Cernunnos, portrayed on monuments as a cross-legged figure with beard and antlers; Taranis identified with Jupiter, often portrayed in the act of slaying a dragon on sculptured columns found all over Gaul, but especially in the North-East. The history of the Gallic religion, as of others, is subject to an infinity of theories and disputed interpretations; a recent study, however, concludes that the third century saw the re-emergence of the Celtic gods from behind the Graeco-Roman disguises earlier imposed.[6]

Alongside them there had been imported, as elsewhere, the gods of the Graeco-Roman pantheon, especially the official triad of Rome, Jupiter, Juno and Minerva. These were followed by cults from the East, Isis, Cybele, and, especially along the Rhine where the legions lay, Mithras. Among the Eastern cults was Christianity, which appears with dramatic suddenness in the martyrdoms at Lyon in 177; the long letter in Greek in which the Christians at Lyon and Vienne sent an account of these events to those of Asia and Phrygia is preserved in Eusebius' *Ecclesiastical History*. The account shows that there was already a bishop at Lyon and a deacon at Vienne. The Gallic church, as the letter itself implies, had its roots in Asia Minor; one of the martyrs was a Roman citizen from Pergamum, another a doctor from Phrygia long since settled in Gaul. The martyrdoms began with mounting hostility from the population (whom the letter refers to as 'fierce and barbarous tribes') leading to exclusion from public places, imprisonment by the city authorities and accusation before the *legatus*, and ending with public tortures and executions, some as part of the shows put on in the amphitheatre of the Three Gauls for the annual assembly on 1 August.[6a]

The bishopric of Lyon then went to another immigrant from Asia, Irenaeus, whose theological works in Greek do not tell us much of the Gallic Christians as such; though in his *Exposition and Refutation of the false Gnosis* he mentions that the gnostic heresy had found adherents even among Christians, especially women, in the Rhône valley. Beyond a brief reference in

Irenaeus to Christian communities in the German provinces, and a Greek Christian inscription in verse from Autun, dating to the late second or early third century, we have no further evidence until 254, when Faustinus, bishop of Lyon, wrote to the bishops of Rome and Carthage (Cyprian, from whose correspondence our evidence comes) about the rigorous attitude taken by the bishop of Arles on the re-admission of those who had lapsed in the persecution of Decius (249–51). At about the same period came the martyrdom of Saturninus, the first bishop of Toulouse, related in a text, probably reliable, of the fifth century. On his way to the church each day Saturninus passed the Capitol (temple of Jupiter, Juno and Minerva) and his presence 'rendered the statues mute' (that is, omens could not be obtained from the sacrifices). Finally a crowd waiting for the ritual sacrifice of a bull seized Saturninus as he passed and killed him by tying him behind the bull and driving it down the hill. A number of other less reliable martyr-acts relate to the same period; but it is clear that by the middle of the third century there were bishops also at least at Paris, Rheims, Vienne and Tours.

The second half of the second century saw some forerunners of the wars and civil wars that were to follow in the third. In about 162 and 174 (the period of the great wars on the Danube) there seem to have been German raids into Gaul, and archaeology reveals some traces of destruction at Strasbourg. Then there were internal troubles, the rising of Maternus in the 180s (see below), and the civil war between Septimius Severus and his rival Clodius Albinus, the governor of Britain, which culminated in a bloody victory by Severus at Lyon in 197, and was followed by widespread confiscations in Gaul and Spain.

Thereafter peace reigned until towards the middle of the next century. Much is revealed of the institutions of Gaul, of the role of its leading Romanized citizens and of their connections with the Roman governors by a long inscription of 238 set up by order of the congress of the Three Gauls in the *colonia* of the Viducasses near Caen.[7] This honours Titus Sennius Sollemnis who had held all the offices in the colony and erected baths for the citizens, leaving an endowment for their repair; he had also

155

been priest of Roma and Augustus at the altar at Lyon, where he had put on thirty-two gladiatorial shows. He had been a friend of Claudius Paulinus, the *legatus* of Gallia Lugdunensis and had been his adviser when he was transferred about 220 to be *legatus* of Britannia Inferior. The inscription quotes verbatim a letter written by Paulinus from Britain sending him gifts of clothing and promising him a tribunate, with a salary of 25,000 *sesterces*, to be paid in gold. He was also a client of the succeeding governor of Gaul, who afterwards wrote a letter from Rome to his successor recommending Sollemnis (who had come to see him there) and informing him that Sollemnis had prevented the Gallic congress from bringing an accusation against Paulinus. Such a document, which has many parallels from the Greek provinces, vividly attests the growing integration of the Gallic upper class into the Graeco-Roman world. But before relating the storms which were to break over Gaul and the West, it is necessary to revert to the development of Spain and Britain up to this point.

Strabo the geographer gives a valuable picture of Spain at the very beginning of the period. In the South lay Baetica (roughly Andalusia) from whose rich plains foodstuffs were imported into Italy. The inhabitants had abandoned their native speech and customs, adopted Latin, and Roman ways of life, and had largely gained 'Latin' rights (see Ch. 5). Some parts were even more advanced; the rich trading city of Gades could show 500 men with the status of Roman *equites*, a number only equalled by Padua. In the two other provinces, Lusitania and Tarraconensis, both governed by Imperial *legati*, the veteran colonies, sometimes incorporating natives, settled by Augustus were the only islands of city-life except for the Mediterranean coast. Throughout central, northern and western Spain native customs and native tribal units persisted. We have an illustration of this in an inscription of AD 27 recording a compact between two *gentilitates* (clans) of the tribe of Zoelae in Asturia; all the persons named have native names – such as Turraion son of Cloutos – and there is no trace of Romanization beyond the fact that the inscription, as a public document, is in Latin. The people seem still to have *spoken* Iberian, as a native of Tarraconensis did when interrogated after murdering the governor of the province in 26.

Baetica provided some of the most important Latin writers of the first century, for instance, L. Annaeus Seneca, the orator, born at Cordoba about the middle of the first century BC;[7a] his son, Seneca the philosopher who was also born at Cordoba, came to Rome as a youth in the early years of Tiberius and was later the principal adviser of Nero; or the latter's nephew, the poet Lucan, also born at Cordoba and brought to Rome as a child. Junius Columella from Gades, the writer on agriculture, who immigrated to Italy (Ch. 7), mentions how his uncle Marcus Columella, who farmed in Baetica would prepare the ground for the cultivation of grain or vines, his methods of preserving wine, or his purchase for breeding of wild rams brought from Africa for use in shows put on by local magistrates. Then from Eastern Tarraconensis there was the orator Quintilian, born at Calagurris between 35 and 40, educated at Rome and given a public salary by Vespasian as a teacher of rhetoric, and the poet Martial, born at Bilbilis about 38–41. He too took the road to Rome, endured some years of poverty, but emerged at the end with a house in the city and a villa at fashionable Nomentum. Later, in spite of fame and Imperial favour, he retired in 98 to Bilbilis; from there he writes on one occasion of the lack of a cultivated audience, the loss of the libraries and theatres of Rome, the envy of his fellow townsmen – and on another of the profound peace and simple life of Bilbilis after the harassments of Rome.

In the reign of Vespasian the Romanization of Spain was recognized by the grant (recorded in a single sentence of Pliny's *Natural History*) of 'Latin' rights to all of Spain. A number of documents illustrate Spanish municipal life at this time, all, however, from Baetica. First there is a letter of Vespasian in reply to a delegation from Sabora in 77, permitting their town – now to be named after him (*Municipium Flavium Saborense*) – to be rebuilt in the plain, confirming revenues granted by Augustus and referring the question of new revenues to the proconsul. Then there is a letter of Titus (79–81) discovered in 1958, to the *municipium* of Munigua.[8] The municipality had appealed,

without justification in Titus' view, from a judgment of the proconsul in a dispute over payments to a man who had contracted
to collect the revenues there. Titus remits some of the money
due and orders the rest to be paid. From the reign of Domitian
(81–96) come the municipal charters of Salpensa and Malaca,
mentioned in Chapter 5. The vitality of Spanish community life
in this period is further illustrated by a monument from Lusitania, the great bridge (*Alcantara*) which still crosses the upper
Tagus River, built by the contributions of twelve local
municipalities and completed in 105/6. They employed a highly
literate architect, who inscribed there a poem in praise of his
own achievement in building a bridge built to last forever,
accompanied by a shrine for the Imperial cult.

As in other areas, it was the Imperial cult which provided the
only formal link between the communities of each province.
Tarraconensis acquired a provincial cult of the Emperor in 25,
when a delegation went to Rome to ask permission for a
temple to Tiberius and his mother Livia, Lusitania at some time
in the first century, Baetica not until Vespasian (69–79). The
provincial high priesthood, whose holder was elected annually
by the congress (*concilium*) of the province, was the crowning
position for the municipal aristocracies; most of the known
holders had filled offices in their native towns, and many gained
also Roman equestrian or senatorial rank. One fine example is
Voconius Romanus, who, as we know from the letters of Pliny
the Younger, was born at Saguntum of a rich equestrian family,
studied at Rome with Pliny (in the 70s or 80s) and was High
Priest (*flamen*) of Tarraconensis. 'You know how weighty the
judgment of that province is,' Pliny wrote, recommending
Romanus to a friend. Pliny gained for him from Trajan the legal
privileges of a father of three children, and petitioned Nerva
and Trajan to admit him to the Senate.

Another classic instance of the rise of Spaniards into the
Senate, and their role both at home and in the wider world is
provided by L. Minicius Natalis from Barcelona, consul in 106,
proconsul of Africa about 121, and his son L. Minicius Natalis
Quadronius Verus, consul in 139, and later also proconsul of
Africa. In the early 120s the two built for the citizens a bath and

porticoes on their own land at Barcelona and an aqueduct leading to it; in 129 the son (following the philhellenic tastes of Hadrian) won the chariot-race at the Olympic games in Greece; and some ten years later he was honoured as patron of the municipality by the people of Tibur near Rome, where he no doubt had a villa.

On a less exalted social level we have an inscription from Barcelona of a man who was a centurion in two legions and was honourably discharged under Marcus Aurelius and Verus (161–9). Once back in Barcelona he held magistracies and the municipal priesthood of Rome and the emperors. He left a legacy to the city to provide annually a display by boxers and a free distribution of oil at the public baths – on condition that his freedmen and their descendants should be freed from the burden of the sevirate (a lower grade of municipal priesthood). His inscription illustrates many important aspects of provincial city life, the connection between Imperial service and local office-holding, the role of munificence – and the early stages of the avoidance of office, as a growing burden.

So far as our evidence goes, the prosperity of Spain and the role of Spaniards in the Empire seems to have reached its climax in the first half of the second century. After that, as with Gaul, we are faced with the fact, which we cannot explain, that no more than a small handful of men originating from Spain is found in either the equestrian or the senatorial order. From the period of prosperity, however, we have the only example of a Spanish city which has been extensively excavated, Italica in Baetica.[9] An Italian settlement since 205 BC, it gained the rank of *municipium* only under Augustus, and that of *colonia* by petition to Hadrian, a native of the place. Hadrian did more – he enlarged the town and adorned it with magnificent public buildings – and it is the Hadrianic Italica which excavations have revealed. The new city was laid out in the classic rectangular pattern, with main streets sixteen metres wide (eight for traffic, four each side for pedestrians); all the streets in the excavated area were lined with porticoes to give shelter from sun and rain. The excavations have shown some fine *atrium*-type houses of purely Italian pattern; for instance there is that known, from its mosaic floors, as the 'House of the Birds', which centres round a patio of 22·40 by 18·30 metres containing two wells, and has a large dining-room, with an ornamental fish-pond beside it. Within the walls of Italica were two public bath-buildings, and outside it a theatre, not yet excavated, and an amphitheatre built to hold 25,000 spectators – one of the largest in the Empire, in size halfway between the amphi-theatres at Nîmes and Arles and the Colosseum at Rome.

Less is known of rural dwellings. But we have, for instance, a fine *atrium*-type villa of some thirty rooms, with baths equipped with hypocausts, and mosaic floors, excavated near Numantia in Tarraconensis; this was built in the mid-second century and evidently occupied continuously until the mid-fourth. On the other hand there are the primitive village houses excavated at Arguedas (Navarra), with their earth floors and brushwood roofs.

A wide range of productive activities lay behind the prosperity of Spain. Cattle-raising was well developed, and the *concilium* of Baetica wrote to Hadrian asking guidance on the punishment of cattle-rustlers; oil-jars from Italica are found not only in Rome, but in Northern France and the Rhine area; extensive areas of pottery-kilns have been found stretching along the banks of the Baetis (Guadalquivir). From the Atlantic and Mediterranean coasts of southern Spain, as from Morocco, was exported the highly-prized fish sauce known as *garum*; examination of the basins in which the fish was salted has shown that they were largely built in the Augustan age and ceased production in the third century.[10] The most important product of Spain was perhaps minerals – gold, copper, silver, lead and iron. Two inscriptions containing regulations for the mining are of Vipasca (Aljustrel) in southern Lusitania, dating to the early second century, give a vivid picture of conditions there. The mine-shafts were leased separately to individual contractors or groups of contractors, who operated them under strict conditions, being obliged for instance to see to the shoring of the shafts, and to carry away ore only between sunrise and sunset; the services for the mining area – the bath-house, shoe-making, barber's shop, fulling, auctioneering – were all leased as concessions to individual contractors. The contractor for the bath-house had, for instance, to keep it open from dawn until noon for women, and from one until eight p.m. for men, charging a fixed fee and being obliged to open every day and keep the heating apparatus in working order.

The religions of Spain show the normal pattern of a western province, the survival of some native gods – known only from their names on inscriptions, confined mainly to northern Tarraconensis, and not attested in Romanized Baetica – the importation of Roman gods (a notable example is the triple temple of Jupiter, Juno and Minerva which dominates the excavated remains of Belo on the coast of Baetica), and some traces of the Eastern cults, for instance, Serapis, Mithras and Cybele. From 287 we have a description, in the martyr-act of the saints Justa and Rufinus, of a procession celebrating the cults of Adonis and Salambo in Hispalis.

We cannot tell when Christianity arrived. St Paul expressed his intention of visiting Spain, but there is no evidence that he did. Legends apart, our first concrete evidence is as late as 254–7, when Cyprian, bishop of Carthage, wrote a letter to the Christian communities of Leon (Ad Legionem), Asturica and Emerita in reply to a complaint that the bishops of Leon and Emerita had lapsed in the Decian persecution. The church was evidently well established – the Spanish bishops were elected jointly by their own community and a congress of other bishops. A few years later we have the martyrdom of the bishop Fructuosus and his two deacons, burnt to death in the amphitheatre of Tarraco in 259. At the Council of Iliberris in the early years of the fourth century, twenty-three communities from Baetica and fourteen from the less civilized remainder of Spain were represented.

For the first century and a half there is no evidence (apart from a single reference to fighting under Nero against the Asturians of the North-West) that the peace of Spain was disturbed. By 70 there was only one legion in the whole country. But under Marcus Aurelius, probably in 168, Moors from North Africa crossed into Baetica. The province was put under the *legatus* of Tarraconensis, and the procurator of Mauretania Tingitana also operated there; an inscription from Italica

161

honours him for slaughtering the enemy and restoring the peace of the province, and another at Singilia Barba says that he freed the place from a long siege by the Moors. In the 180s came the rising of Maternus, a deserter from the army who gathered a force of bandits which grew into a regular army which overran Gaul and Spain, besieged cities and even attempted to attack the Emperor in Rome; unfortunately, our only source for these events, Herodian, is equally vague as to the local origin of Maternus, the social causes of the rising and the geographical extent of his operations. Then, as mentioned above, Spain suffered from the after-effects of the civil war of 196–7. A general of Severus fought (as an inscription records) against 'rebels' as governor of Tarraconensis; and the confiscations in Gaul and Spain seem to be reflected in the fact that it is from this moment that the mark of the Imperial patrimony appears on the Baetican pottery-fragments from Rome.

The civilization of Roman Spain remains, to a considerable extent, an untrodden field, which will produce rich results when proper attention can be devoted to it. But here even more than elsewhere, a brief account can be no more than the indication of some isolated features.

Roman Britain, on the other hand, has been intensely studied both in its military and its civil archaeology, though its surviving monuments are few and slight compared to those of Gaul or Spain. The military history of the province – which occupied four and then three legions, a number quite disproportionate to its size – has been sketched in Chapter 6. These pages will be concerned not with the traces of Romanization in the frontier area,[11] but with the civilization of the substantially Romanized part, that is the southern two-thirds of England.

The subjugation of England began with the invasion of 43, leading to the capture of Camulodunum (Colchester), the capital of the strongest tribe, the Trinovantes, and to an advance south-westwards by a legion under the future Emperor Vespasian. Recent excavations at Fishbourne near Colchester have revealed wooden buildings of this period, which seem to be military store-houses. These were followed by a civilian harbour settlement, incorporating a bath-house and possibly shops, and then in its turn replaced about AD 75 by an enormous palace built of masonry, marble being brought from as far away as Italy; built in three wings round a colonnaded courtyard, it occupied an area of at least five and a half acres.[12] Its owner is unknown; it could perhaps have been the client king Cogidubnus, whom the *collegium fabrum* (Guild of metalworkers) at Colchester honoured in a Latin inscription as *rex magnus* ('great king' of Britain).[12a] Another client king of the early period was Prasutagus of the Iceni in East Anglia; when he died about 60 his property was expropriated and his widow, Boudicca, led a revolt which only the utmost ferocity enabled the Romans to crush. Tacitus' account reveals an early stage in the development of Romanized town-life in Britain. The rebels sacked Camulodunum, established as a *colonia* of legionary veterans in 49. The town already contained a temple of Claudius, intended for the provincial cult, a senate-house for the councillors of the colony, and a theatre. However, the town-walls had not yet been built, and the place was sacked; beneath the stone and masonry buildings of the later Roman town there are indications of the burning of timber buildings, and, at two places, of stocks of pottery and glass. A similar fate befell Verulamium (St Albans) where again excavations have shown a line of timber-framed shops fronting the main street, which date to before 60 and are clearly Roman work, probably by military engineers. Here too there are extensive traces of fire, and the site was not rebuilt until 75–80. In these two places and London, where a large number of traders were gathered, 70,000 people are recorded to have been killed.

The last thirty years of the first century saw both an extension of Roman power into both Wales and the North (the absorption of the client-kingdom of the Brigantes and the establishment of a legion at York) and the development of Romanization. Tacitus describes how his father-in-law Agricola, governor in 78–84, encouraged the natives to build forums, temples and houses and to give the sons of the chiefs a literary education; we know of one Greek grammarian, Demetrius of Tarsus, a friend of Plutarch, who came to Britain in this period, and left two Greek inscriptions at York. Archaeology confirms the development of

British towns at this time. The forum of Verulamium was dedicated in 79, and the town now had a temple and market-hall of stone, though private houses were still half-timbered. By the early part of the second century the town had expanded over the earthwork which had formed its defences. Construction continued, with the first stone theatre and the first masonry-built houses appearing probably after a fire about 155. The town wall built at the beginning of the third century enclosed some 200 acres.[13]

Three more *coloniae* were founded, Lincoln and Gloucester in the 90s, York perhaps not until the early third century. Most Romano-British towns were what are termed 'cantonal capitals', the urban centres for tribes, Calleva Atrebatum – of the Atrebates – or Corinium Dobunnorum. Calleva (Silchester) is the best known, and its development can be traced, somewhat conjecturally, from its original existence as a native town of scattered huts enclosed by an earthwork. The first century saw the construction of a forum and *basilica* and even public baths, though the private houses were still irregularly spaced wooden huts. Then, perhaps in the reign of Hadrian (117–38), a regular grid of streets was laid out, and, perhaps at the same time, a much larger earthwork – too large as it turned out – enclosing 290 acres. Finally, at the end of the second century, a wall and ditch was built enclosing about 175 acres. A tiny reflection of the spread of literary culture is afforded by a tile which has scratched on it a two-word quotation from the Aeneid of Virgil.

Rural dwellings also show the process of Romanization (though even in the lowland areas native-type huts were still widespread in the Roman period). A classic case is the excavation at Lockleys near Welwyn, which showed a round native hut of the early first century, replaced successively by a large native hut in occupation from before the conquest to about 60–70 (with Roman pottery becoming more and more predominant), and then by a rectangular, five-roomed house with a verandah, walls of flint and mortar, probably timber-framed in the upper part, and faced with painted plaster. Finally, this was replaced in the late second century by a stone-built 'winged corridor' house of more than three times the size, which continued in use until a fire in the early fourth century.

The most common type of Romanized farm-house in Britain was a substantial building of some 50–100 feet long, often of the 'winged corridor' type, with a concrete and stone foundation and half-timbered walls. They were still far from luxurious, normally lacking hypocausts, mosaic pavements and baths. There is indeed a bath, dating to about 180, at the well-known villa of Lullingstone in Kent. But even here the impressive mosaics, hypocausts and other features belong to the early fourth century, the true period of the development of the luxurious Roman villa in Britain.

The religious life of Britain was the usual, infinitely complex, intermingling of the native cults, native gods, the Graeco-Roman pantheon and the Eastern religions, largely associated with units of auxiliaries. From Woodeaton in Oxfordshire, for instance, there is a square native temple surrounded by a covered ambulatory (so of the normal Celtic type) and set in a square enclosure. It was built in the first century, and the large number of coins found there show that it remained in use until the fourth, and suggests that a fair or market may have been held there.

By contrast there are the cults from the East, of which the most striking monument is the temple of Mithras in London. The temple, sixty-eight by twenty-six feet, was divided by two lines of pillars into a central nave, where the rituals took place, and two side-aisles with banked seating. At the western end, on a raised floor reached by steps, there will have stood the relief sculpture of Mithras, of which the head was found on the site, in the act of slaying the sacred bull. The institutions of Emperor-worship are illustrated by an inscription set up at Bordeaux after a voyage in 237 by a British shipper who describes himself as *sevir augustalis* of the colonies of York and Lincoln. Christianity also must have penetrated to Britain in the third century, though we have no reliable evidence of it; but the synod of Arles in 314 was attended by bishops from London, York and Lincoln, accompanied by a presbyter and a deacon.

Britain remained a frontier area. There was a serious revolt in the North in the 150s and barbarian attacks from Scotland in the 180s and about 200. It is possible that many of the cantonal capitals received earth walls in the middle of the second century, and clear that all of them had stone walls built at the end of the century. But the troubles of the third century, at least until the end, passed Britain by.

It was Gaul which suffered worst from the barbarian invasions. Coin hoards, and traces of destruction at Selts in Alsace, might indicate that incursions began about 240. But the first great invasion came in 253, when Valerian (253–60) had marched the troops of Rhine and Danube into Italy to secure the throne. The Alamanni crossed the Rhine in the area of Mannheim and advanced into the Rhineland and the Pfalz, while the Franks perhaps went via Metz, Rheims and Paris. It seems to be at this time that coin hoards and signs of destruction begin at Paris and continue to the great invasion of 276 – ending with the almost complete abandonment of habitation outside the Île de la Cité, which was rapidly fortified about 280 with materials taken from the buildings of the town on the left bank.[14]

Valerian sent his son Gallienus to Gaul, who was able to regain the Rhine crossings. but not the *limes* to its east (see Ch. 6) which was now almost entirely lost; coins minted at Cologne in 257–8 call Gallienus the 'Restorer of the Gauls'. But when he left about 259, leaving his son Saloninus on the Rhine, another Frankish and Alamannic invasion spread through Gaul; a map of the coin hoards of the period shows that only western France remained untouched. Some of the barbarians crossed into Spain, sacked Tarraco (which was still in ruins when the Christian historian Orosius wrote in the early fifth century), and even reached Africa. It was at this point that strong town-walls were built at various places in Tarraconensis; at Lucus Augusti (Lugo) the entire circuit survives.

About this time a Roman general, Postumus, probably of Gallic origin, besieged Saloninus in Cologne, killed him and inaugurated the Gallic Empire which lasted under him and three further rulers until the reconquest by Aurelian in 274. Postumus' power extended to Britain, Spain and even northern Italy. The details of the reigns of the Gallic Emperors, the limits of their rule and their conflicts, apparently successful, with the barbarians, and with the Roman Emperors, can not be followed here. But two significant facts are the campaign conducted by Postumus in 266–7 against the first barbarian sea-raids (signified by a heavy concentration of coin hoards on the north coast of Gaul), and the revolt of the city of Autun against the third Gallic Emperor, Victorinus, in 269. The revolt can reasonably be taken to signify the division, already clear in the crisis of exactly two centuries earlier, between the central Gallic communities and those of the north-east. Our information on the siege, which ended after seven months in the capture and destruction of the city, comes from an oration delivered in 298 to plead for the restoration of the great school there (whose beginnings we saw when the youth of the Gallic nobility were captured there in AD 21). The orator, the grandson of a teacher of rhetoric from Athens who migrated first to Rome and then to Autun in the first half of the third century, describes how the place was attacked and besieged by 'the bandits of the Batavian rebellion' – the Batavian units being, as they had been in 69, the spearhead of the Gallic force.

The Gallic Emperors, from their capital at Trier, succeeded in combating barbarian invasions until the last of them, Tetricus, was defeated and captured by Aurelian in 274. Soon after, there followed the most serious German invasion yet which left its traces right across Gaul, and may have reached Spain (the archaeological evidence is not clear).[15] It led to the contraction of a number of Gallic towns, such as Amiens or Paris, into small fortified areas; the best-preserved of the massive Gallic fortification walls of this period, most of them using material from earlier buildings, are those of Le Mans.[16] The invasion was ultimately mastered by Probus (276–82), who seems to have used the technique of driving the invaders forwards into central and western Gaul, and slaughtering or capturing them there; according to one source 400,000 were killed, 60,000 settled on Gallic soil. Finally, in about the very last year of our period, came the first great popular rising of the Western Empire, the peasant movement of the so-called

Bagaudae, which continued spasmodically into the fifth century.

It seems to have been in the last quarter of the third century also that construction began in Britain of the forts of the 'Saxon Shore' against raiders from the sea.[17] The West thus remained at the end of the period in a state of insecurity. Yet the barbarians were repelled, and it was not until the fifth century that great further losses of territory took place.

9

Africa

Africa shows more clearly than any other area the creative force of Roman civilization. Literary evidence alone, in the persons of Apuleius from Madaurus, the author of the *Metamorphoses* and the *Apologia*, which is one of the finest documents of Roman provincial life in the second century, Cornelius Fronto from Cirta, the friend and tutor of Marcus Aurelius, or the Christian writers Tertullian and St Cyprian, bishop of Carthage, would hint at the rich development of Romano-African culture. But beyond that, the long decline of the intervening centuries has left relatively untouched the splendid remains of the densely-packed cities on the coastal plains of Tunisia, along the coast eastwards to Tripolitania and, more scattered, westwards to the Atlantic coast of Mauretania. Inland, along the military road which penetrated the Aurès Mountains, there is the site of Thamugadi (Timgad) just as it was laid out as a colony in a geometrical pattern in AD 100. For the most part the mountainous areas of Numidia and Mauretania could not support cities like those of the Tunisian plains. But they still show the remains of hundreds of villages and of many thousands of olive-presses – which indicate the source of the prosperity they enjoyed, and continued to enjoy in the third century.

The Romans had not been the first to establish city-life in Africa. The Punic civilization established by the Phoenician settlements with their capital at Carthage still flourished in the first century of our era. The Punic sanctuary at Hadrumetum, for instance, remained in use from the sixth century BC to the early second century AD, while the sculptures of the first century AD from the sanctuary at Thysdrus show people in Carthaginian dress sacrificing, the women wearing the typical high conical hat. Significant numbers of inscriptions in Punic (a Semitic language) survive from the first century, and to a lesser extent from the second and third: from Tripolitania we have also later Punic inscriptions written in Latin characters. Moreover, the evidence of St Augustine shows that Punic was still commonly spoken in Numidia in the early fifth century. As well as Punic, there survived the native Libyan, known from more than a thousand inscriptions of varying dates, mainly from Tunisia and eastern Algeria. The alphabet is related to that still used by the Tuareg, and the language possibly to the Berber of present-day North Africa.[1]

On this already complex cultural pattern had been super-imposed, since the conquest of the original province of Africa (roughly Tunisia) in 146, a heavy Roman, or rather Italian, immigration, in the form both of regular colonies and of groups of private persons, like the Italian merchants Julius Caesar had found at Hadrumetum in 46 BC. Africa thus contained Roman *coloniae*, Latin *municipia*, Punic *civitates* – some of them freed from tribute for service to Julius Caesar – and native villages and unsettled tribes. 'Africa' included the later provinces of Africa and Numidia, and the proconsul, with his seat at Carthage, commanded, unlike most other *proconsules*, a legion, the *III Augusta*; in 37 a separate Imperial *legatus* was to be appointed to command the legion, and about 200 the western part of the province (where the legion was) became the separate Imperial province of Numidia under the *legatus*.

Mauretania in AD 14 was still a client-kingdom, ruled by Juba, a scholar who maintained a Hellenized court at his capital Iol, renamed Caesarea, which he began to transform into a city of Graeco-Roman type. Roman influence was further spread by the eleven or twelve Roman colonies which Augustus had established in Mauretania.

The prosperity of Roman Africa was largely the product of the work of the Roman army, not only in work of centuriation – the division and allotment of the land in rectangular plots aligned on the main roads – whose traces aerial photography reveals still imprinted over hundreds of miles in Tunisia, but the steady work of constructing the military roads, the most important running south-east from Carthage to cut off the Aurès Mountains, and that leading from Tacape, in a vast detour inland, eastwards to Lepcis Magna in Tripolitania. Associated with this was the progressive settlement of nomadic tribes, and finally the construction – perhaps from the reign of Hadrian (117–38) on – of a system of defences stretching from Tripolitania to southern Numidia.

In 14 an inscription reveals the legion *III Augusta* building a road from its camp, probably at Ammaedara, south-east to the coast at Tacape. The repercussions of Roman penetration appeared three years later with the beginning of the seven years' war waged by Tacfarinas, chief of the Musulamii. Tacfarinas, who had served in the Roman auxiliary forces, organized his people, nomads in central Numidia, into regular formations of Roman type. After several years of ravaging the villages and besieging the scattered forts of Roman Africa, he sent an embassy to Tiberius in 22, asking for land for his army to settle. The request was rejected, and Tacfarinas driven back by the construction of lines of forts. Two years later, however, he was able to attack the town of Thubursicu in central Numidia, but was then defeated and killed with the aid of forces sent by Juba's son and successor, Ptolemy. The victory was an essential stage in the development of the province. In the early second century we find inscriptions delimiting the land of the Musulamii from that of their neighbours, and the tribe itself governed by the 'Prefect of the tribe of Musulamii'. By that time too the legion had moved its permanent camp over 100 miles west-south-west to Lambaesis, leaving the Musulamii cut off to the north of the military road.[2]

In 40 Caligula executed Ptolemy, and the kingdom was annexed, though not without hard fighting against resistance led by a freedman of Ptolemy, Aedemon. When the revolt was crushed Mauretania was divided into two provinces, Caesariensis in the east and Tingitana, both under equestrian procurators. Not all Mauretanian communities joined the revolt; an inscription from the town of Volubilis honours Valerius

171

Severus son of Bostar who was *sufes* (a Punic term for official) and *duovir* and the first priest of the Imperial cult there, and had commanded auxiliaries in the war against Aedemon. He had then gone on an embassy to Claudius (41–54) and had obtained for the community the Roman citizenship (which perhaps meant the status of *municipium*) and immunity from tribute for ten years. The extensive remains of Volubilis, partially excavated, show the beginnings of construction in Graeco-Roman style under Juba, and the gradual development of the town up to its apogee in the early third century, when under Caracalla (211–17) a triumphal arch was built, a forum established and a fine basilica erected.

Some minor barbarian incursions and internal disorders – for instance the incident in the early 60s when Vespasian, as proconsul, was pelted with turnips in the market-place of Hadrumetum – troubled Africa in the rest of the Julio-Claudian period. Then, while a succession of Emperors disputed the throne elsewhere in 68–70, first in 68 Clodius Macer, the *legatus* of the legion, issued coins in his own right, raised a new legion, and stopped the corn for Rome, but was killed by a procurator. In 69 the procurator, Lucceius Albinus, then governing both Mauretanias, threatened to invade Spain in the name of Otho (significantly, it was also rumoured that he had assumed regal insignia and the name of Juba), but was killed while sailing – which shows the state of communications in mountainous Morocco – from Tingitana to Caesariensis. In 70 the proconsul of Africa was murdered, in the name of Vespasian, by troops sent by the *legatus*. While these struggles went on over their heads the communities of Oea and Lepcis Magna progressed from disputes over land to a full-scale war of their own, in which the Oeenses finally called in the nomadic Garamantes, who had to be driven off by Roman troops.

These troubles, and further fighting in Mauretania in the Flavian period, did not impede the steady development of urbanization and Romanization. We see these processes in the Punic-Libyan town of Mactar on a remote site in central proconsular Africa.[3] First-century Mactar had three magistrates called *sufetes*, and priests called *kohanim*; the people used distinctive chambered funeral monuments developed from the dolmens of the locality; they put up inscriptions in Libyan (though these are all possibly earlier) and Punic, in the latter of which Latin names begin to appear. At the end of the first century they could still erect a temple to the Punic goddess, Hathor Miskar. But more significant than that is the long Latin inscription of 88, the dedication by the *iuvenes* (corps of young men) of their basilica (training-hall) and store-houses. The sixty-five members are listed, none of them yet Roman citizens, all given by name and father's name, for instance Victor son of Balsamon. Latin names now come to half the total (the rest being Punic or Libyan) and are significantly more common among the sons. Thereafter Romanization was rapid. A forum with a monumental gate was dedicated in 115–6. The town was soon a *municipium*, and under Marcus Aurelius (161–80) reached the status of *colonia*. Early third-century Mactar produces one of the finest documents of Roman Africa, the funerary epitaph in Latin verse of a man who began as a poor peasant, worked twelve years as an itinerant seasonal harvester the length of Numidia, became the master of a gang of harvesters, and finally bought a house and land in Mactar, and was made a town-councillor and magistrate.

A quite different picture is presented by Thamugadi (Timgad), founded as a veteran *colonia* by Trajan, which, as an inscription shows, was being built by the soldiers of the *III Augusta* in 100. Aerial photographs show the rectangular plan, some 400 yards square, of the original colony, with its forum and theatre and chequerboard pattern of streets, and outside it the less orderly suburbs which grew up in the second century.

Different again is the Punic city of Lepcis Magna in Tripolitania, a port and the starting-point for the caravan-route to the Fezzan. The earliest known monuments, of the period of Augustus and Tiberius, already show prosperous development under Roman influence, a theatre, market-place and monumental arch of Augusta Salutaris. An inscription of AD 16 shows the proconsul of Africa building a road from Lepcis into the interior. Until the latter part of the first century, Lepcis was a non-citizen *civitas*, ruled by two *sufetes* with other magistrates and a council; public inscriptions were in both Latin and Punic. Punic names die out among the leading citizens towards the end of the first century (the latest example is Iddibal son of Balsillec who built a temple of Magna Mater in 72); magistrates from then on have Latin names and are Roman citizens. In the later first century the town became a *municipium*, and in 109–10 Trajan gave it the status of *colonia*, carrying with it the Roman citizenship for all; the *sufes* in office at the time was the grandfather of the Emperor Septimius Severus (193–211), who then became *duovir* and perpetual priest of the colony, and was also of equestrian rank and served as a *iudex* in Rome. Severus himself paid a visit to Lepcis probably in 202–3, gave it the *ius Italicum* (conferring immunity from tribute) and inaugurated a reconstruction and expansion of it on a magnificent, perhaps too magnificent, scale; the Severan monuments include a colonnaded main street, a new forum of 1,000 by 600 feet also lined with colonnades, a basilica which was converted into a Christian church in the sixth century, and a triumphal arch at the main cross-roads, whose carvings foreshadow the frontality of Byzantine art. But the splendid new harbour which Severus also constructed shows little sign of use, and seems to have quickly silted up.

Evidence of a different type for the town life of Roman Africa is provided by an inscription of 144 from Sala on the Atlantic coast of Mauretania Tingitana.[4] It is a long decree of the town council honouring Sulpicius Felix, the prefect of a cavalry unit stationed there, whom they had already made a town-councillor and honorary magistrate. Hearing that he is about to be replaced, they put on record his services in protecting their flocks from raids (evidently by neighbouring tribes), settling financial disputes, building a wall round the town and protecting its citizens while working in the woods and fields. They request the procurator of the province to allow them both to erect a statue to Felix and also to send an embassy to the Emperor (Antoninus Pius) to express their gratitude. The text illustrates many things, the relative insecurity of Mauretanian towns, the ever-expanding role of the army in the life of the Empire, the firm root taken by

Romanized town life, and the immediacy of contact between provincial communities and the Emperor in Rome.

Furthermore, it provides another item of evidence for the basic factor in African prosperity, the settlement, confinement or pushing back of nomadic tribes and the protection and expansion of agriculture. These processes occurred not only along the frontier zone but also in relation to tribes, like the Musulamii, within Roman territory; for instance, we find soldiers assigning fields, pastureland and springs in south-east Numidia in 198. Within this framework there seems also to have been another development of great importance, a relative shift from corn-growing (in the first century Africa provided two-thirds of the supply for Rome) to olive production. This seems to have resulted mainly through the making safe for agriculture of the High Plains; but olive-growing seems also to have invaded areas previously used only for corn, creating a mixed system. An important part in this development may have been played by the system of land-tenure inaugurated by the *lex Manciana*; this regulated the quota of crops, normally a third, payable by tenants to *conductores* (men who contracted to collect the rents) or the owners of estates, but also made provision for a five-year period free of payment when new fig-trees or vines were planted, and a ten-year period when an olive grove was planted on previously uncultivated land. It also gave provisional title to any tenant who cultivated land on an estate unallotted in the original centuriation, and provided for *conductores* to reclaim land left uncultivated. This *lex* is attested in our period only from regulations affecting Imperial estates (Imperial property in Africa, attested since Augustus, had been vastly increased by confiscations under Nero). We have a regulation made in accordance with the *lex* by Imperial procurators of estates in the Bagradas valley in 116–17; an extension by Hadrian of the right of possession and inheritance to centuriated land occupied and planted with olives or vines; and finally the petition of some tenants to Commodus in 180–3 complaining that the *conductores* had demanded more than their share under Hadrian's regulation, and also sent troops against them. The *lex Manciana* is also mentioned in documents of the Vandal period in the fifth century, and may therefore have been of general application throughout the province; its date and origin remain obscure. But it is certainly at least a reflection of a serious effort to bring under cultivation all usable land, an effort amply attested by the immense number of olive-presses whose remains survive in Africa.

The inscriptions illustrate also the complex organization of the scattered Imperial estates, administered from a central office at Carthage. Private persons also owned large estates (often containing whole villages), one of them a senator called Lucilius Africanus with an estate in the territory of the Musulamii. In 138 the Roman Senate voted that he should be allowed to hold a market on the estate twice a month, provided that no damage or disturbance was caused. The fear of popular gatherings is a theme which runs through all Imperial history.

Agriculture provided the basic wealth of Roman Africa, with its 500 cities, 200 of them in Proconsularis. Many of the cities seem from archaeological evidence to have contained only comparatively rich houses, and otherwise to have been mainly centres of assembly and entertainment for the country population. The characteristic features of Italian town life were reproduced in profusion, the aqueducts – like that of Carthage, stretching eighty kilometres – baths, theatres, amphitheatres – like the early third-century amphitheatre of Thysdrus, little smaller than the Colosseum – and the villas and town houses.

Our most vivid insight into this world is provided by Apuleius, born in the early second century as the son of a town-councillor at Madaurus in Numidia (a *colonia* of the Flavian period). His family was wealthy – his father left Apuleius and his brother each a million *sesterces*, the capital qualification of a Roman senator – and his education was begun at Carthage, where he learned to orate in Latin and Greek, and completed at Athens. About 156–8 he stopped at Oea in Tripolitania on his way to Alexandria, gave a public declamation in the basilica, and after a time married a rich local widow. Members of her family then accused him of securing her by magic; his *Apologia* is the speech he delivered in his defence before the proconsul, on judicial circuit at nearby Sabratha. In it we see the wealth of the African bourgeoisie and its sources. The widow was worth four million *sesterces* and had given her sons fertile fields, large houses, stores of corn, wine and olives, and 400 slaves. She and Apuleius had chosen to be married at a suburban villa of hers rather than at her town house – to avoid repeating the distribution of 50,000 *sesterces* to the populace which she had had to make on the marriage of her son. The son himself, now Apuleius' chief opponent, had been for his education to Rome and Athens, and on beginning to practise advocacy had been recommended by Apuleius himself to the proconsul. Now, says Apuleius significantly, he has so far declined as to spend all his time at the gladiatorial school at Oea, and to speak nothing but Punic. Apuleius, by contrast, pointedly displays his own classical learning, bestrewing his speech with the names of Greek and Latin authors, reciting a passage of Plato ('Which *you* will recognize', he says to the proconsul), and pointing out that his boorish opponents had taken as a magic formula what was in fact a list of the Greek names of various types of fish compiled in the manner of Aristotle.

Apuleius' wife and her relations were typical of the local aristocracies of the Empire in that their wealth lay in land, normally inherited, and was expended in luxurious living, or in munificence in the towns. Several hundred inscriptions from Africa attest expenditure by local citizens on public buildings or statues, distributions of cash, or shows or banquets for the people.[5] They were typical also in their close relations with Rome and their actual entry into the Roman equestrian and senatorial orders. A son of the widow by her first husband had died an *eques*; inscriptions show that a grandson of hers was a senator, and governor of Thrace under Septimius Severus. The first African *eques* had in fact appeared in the reign of Gaius, the first senator and consul, Q. Aurelius Pactumeius of Cirta, under the Flavians. In the middle of the second century Cornelius Fronto, also from Cirta, could write to the magistrates and council there about the choice of senatorial patrons, mentioning a couple of distinguished senators from Africa and concluding, 'There are also many other distinguished men from Cirta in the Senate.' At Acholla we have the villa built by Asinius Rufinus, who was brought into the Senate by Commodus and made consul about 184; the villa is built of brick, but richly decorated with stucco and mosaics, one of which portrays Hercules – with whom Commodus identified himself. In the third century perhaps one in eight of the Roman Senate was of African origin.

Towards the end of the second century, when the traces of native Punic cults begin to dry up, the dominion of the Graeco-Roman gods is interrupted by the first evidence of Christianity. This is the record (*Acta*) of the trial in 180 before the proconsul at Carthage of six Christians, some of whom from their names appear to be of native origin. The proconsul tries to persuade them to sacrifice to Caesar, discovering in the course of interrogation that they are carrying what they call 'Books and letters of Paul, a just man', and when they refuse has them beheaded. Some years later come the writings of the greatest figure of the early African church (and the earliest Christian writer in Latin), Tertullian, a convert from paganism. His long series of polemical writings covers the years from 196 to about 212, those after about 207 being coloured by his conversion to the rigorist prophetic sect of the Montanists, which had originated in Phrygia. Of his works one can mention the *Apologeticum* (defence of Christianity) of 197 or soon after, in which he attacks the condemnation of Christians for being such, and defends them against accusations of immorality or of disloyalty to the Emperor, while making clear that the State is to Christians something essentially foreign. His later works, to which no justice can be done here, show an increasingly violent rejection both of the State and of all aspects of pagan society.[5a]

Of the same period is the *Passion of Perpetua and Felicitas*, the record of a trial and martyrdom of some Christians at Carthage in 203. The text contains, embedded in a third-person narrative possibly by Tertullian, the account by Perpetua herself, a girl of twenty-two with a young baby, of their experiences in prison – where the deacons of the community managed to bribe the soldiers to give them a larger cell – including the dreams she had about the approaching martyrdom – and the interrogation by the procurator before a huge crowd in the forum of Carthage. The narrative then relates how they were brought to the amphitheatre of the military camp (the occasion being games to celebrate the birthday of Geta, the younger son of Septimius Severus) and thrown to the beasts before an eager crowd of onlookers.

The *Passion* indicates at one point that there was already a bishop at Carthage. Some years later, perhaps about 220, a bishop of Carthage called a council of seventy bishops from Proconsularis and Numidia. Our next information on the African church comes from the writings and letters (supplemented by the *Acts* of his martyrdom and a brief biography composed by a follower, the deacon Pontius, soon after his death) of St Cyprian, bishop of Carthage from 248-9 to his execution in 258, who lived through the persecution by Decius in 249-51. Cyprian's writings are dominated by the problems arising from the great crisis in the church in his time, the Decian persecutions (in which Cyprian himself went into hiding and vast numbers of Christians obeyed the order to sacrifice), the synod of 251 which established the conditions for the re-admission of the lapsed, and that of 255-6 (attended by eighty-five African bishops) which laid down that persons baptized by heretics must be re-baptized on entering the Catholic Church.[5b]

One of Cyprian's letters is addressed to eight bishops in southern Numidia, who appealed for help in ransoming members of their communities captured by the barbarians; Cyprian writes that he is sending 600,000 *sesterces* collected from his congregation. That must take us back to the long, but successful struggle of Africa, especially Mauretania, against the attacks of desert tribes in the second and third centuries. A Moorish revolt suppressed under Hadrian was followed by a considerable war in the 140s, in which military units were brought from Pannonia, Spain and Britain.[6] The insecurity of the times is reflected in the decree of Sala mentioned earlier, the building of walls at Tipasa, or an inscription in which a veteran of *III Augusta* describes how he was set on by brigands while on his way to direct the construction of a tunnel at Saldae in Caesariensis. In about 168 the Moors even crossed into Spain (Ch. 8), and about the same time there begins a long series of inscriptions stretching to 280 in which procurators of Mauretania record negotiations held with the chiefs of desert tribes, notably the Baquates. Diplomacy was not enough; the Moors were defeated again under Commodus (180–92), and towers and forts were constructed by him along the frontier of Mauretania. In Numidia, however, Roman domination reached its maximum extent with the occupation from 198 to about 240 of a desert fort, *castellum Dimmidi*, some 700 kilometres east-south-east of Carthage,[7] as it did in Tripolitania in the Severan period with the occupation of three forts on the routes into the interior, one of them several hundred kilometres inland.

In 238 the peace of Africa was broken by a civil war. The exactions of an Imperial procurator provoked the rich young landowners of the Thysdrus area (the centre of olive-production) to gather their slaves from the fields and attack and kill him. They' then seized the aged proconsul, Gordian, who was at Thysdrus on his judicial circuit, proclaimed him Emperor in opposition to the Thracian Maximinus (235–8), and escorted him with Imperial pomp to Carthage. The Senate in Rome accepted him gladly, but the *legatus* of Numidia, Capellianus, advanced on Carthage and massacred the untrained local forces with their swords, axes and hunting-spears. Gordian was killed, and Capellianus carried out executions of the leading men, and widespread confiscations in Carthage and other cities. Excavations at Thysdrus show what may be traces of destruction at this time; and an inscription from Theveste records a man 'seized by Capellianus'.

In revenge the legion *III Augusta* was dissolved by Gordian III (238–44), the grandson of the proconsul, and only reconstituted by Valerian in 253. This was necessary, for a series of inscriptions from Caesariensis and Numidia attest fierce but successful fighting in the years 254–60 against the incursions of the nomads; it was at this time that Cyprian was helping to ransom captive Christians. The last of these inscriptions honours Gargilius Martialis, the commander of a cohort and a force of Mauretanian cavalry at Auzia on the frontier of Caesariensis, by whose courage and vigilance the nomad chief Faraxen was captured and killed; but Martialis himself had been killed 'by the wiles of the Bavares'.

In the years between about 244 and 284 there are only slight traces of building and development in the cities of Roman Africa. The civil war of 238, the invasions of the 250s and the general, and still mysterious, economic decline of the whole Empire must have affected them. But the cities remained, only Lixus on the Atlantic coast showing evidence of large-scale destruction,[8] perhaps the work of the barbarian invasion through Spain about 259 (Ch. 8) rather than the Moors. There is nothing comparable to the contraction and fortification of many cities in Gaul. Moreover, the village economy of Numidia and Caesariensis seems to have flourished. It is not without significance that one of the last documents of the period, an inscription from Cirta, refers to a rescript in which Probus (276–82) permitted the holding of a twice-monthly market.

10

Egypt

Egypt fitted less easily than any other area into the Roman provincial system. Its capital, Alexandria, founded by Alexander the Great, had been the seat of the Ptolemaic dynasty, had been and still was the chief centre of learning in the Greek world, and contained a turbulent and abusive population which the Romans could only with difficulty keep in order. Behind Alexandria, along a narrow strip of cultivated land stretching up the Nile, lay Egypt itself, whose language, customs and art-forms, going back in a continuous tradition for some 3,000 years, had been overlaid but not destroyed by the extensive Greek settlement of the Hellenistic period. No other kingdom of comparable antiquity and coherence was incorporated in the Roman Empire; the fears and suspicions it provoked were accentuated by the importance of Egyptian corn, shipped down the Nile to Alexandria, and thence to Rome.

The contrast between Alexandria and the rest of Egypt is sharpened by the nature of our evidence. Alexandria produces major literary sources in Greek, especially by Jewish and Christian writers. The works of the great Jewish scholar, Philo, written in the first half of the first century, are the fullest expression of the intellectual outlook of the Hellenized Jewish community of Alexandria; he interpreted the Old Testament in Greek philosophical terms, sometimes writing explicitly for a pagan Greek audience. Then, from the late second century onwards, Alexandria became one of the main theological centres of the Greek church. The writings of Clement and Origen are followed by the letters of Dionysius, bishop of Alexandria

247–64, which are the main component of Eusebius' *Ecclesias-tical History* for the period 250–60.

The dry sand of middle and upper Egypt has preserved for us evidence of a quite different sort in papyri. Papyrus was the normal writing-material of Antiquity, but the thousands of papyri known from Egypt – often from rubbish-dumps or the stuffing of mummy-cases – are matched only by a few from Judaea or Dura-Europus (Ch. 11). By their very bulk they provide a unique view of society in a remote but culturally rich and complex part of the Empire. They include everything from fragments of Greek (and very few Latin) literary works – in which Homer predominates by far – to school exercises, private letters, accounts, official edicts, petitions to the authorities, census and tax returns, or certificates for completion of labour on the dykes. The vast majority of the papyri are in Greek; the Latin fragments are mainly literary, legal or military. But, beside the two classical languages, Egyptian survived, written and spoken. Egyptian temples in the traditional style and with hieroglyphic inscriptions continued to be built in the Ptolemaic period, and to be enlarged and adorned under the Romans; hieroglyphic texts were still being inscribed right through the first three centuries AD (the last known one dates to 296). Then there were two long-developed cursive variants of the hieroglyphic script, hieratic (used for sacred texts) and demotic, which in the Roman period appears mainly on tax-returns, written on papyrus or ostraka – fragments of pottery. But there are also demotic literary texts of the first century AD, for instance a papyrus with the ancient Egyptian legend of how Setme was taken by his son Si-Osiris to visit the Egyptian equivalent of Hades.

In the late first century AD a few papyri reveal the first attempts to write the Egyptian language in Greek letters; they are mainly magical texts where accurate pronunciation would be essential to the success of the incantation. In the third century we have some Greek Old Testament texts with marginal notes in Egyptian written in Greek letters. Egyptian written in Greek characters, with eight further characters added, now emerged as Coptic, the language of the Egyptian church. The main body of

Coptic texts (the word is also applied to the distinctive art of Christian Egypt, especially in textiles and sculptures) belongs to the fourth century and after. But in 1946 at Nag Hammadi near Luxor there came to light a collection of some forty-eight Christian texts, of some 1,000 pages in all, written in Coptic between about 250 and 350. Many, perhaps all, of the texts, which are heretical treatises or apocryphal New Testament works, are translations from Greek originals.[1]

When the rich but troublesome territory of Egypt came into Roman hands in 30 BC, Augustus' policy had been to preserve with minor modifications the administrative system of the Ptolemies, while extracting a maximum revenue in cash and kind, cutting down and controlling the privileges and revenues of the great temples with their corporations of priests, and introducing, along with a census on a fourteen-year cycle, gradations of privilege among the population, which determined whether they paid the new poll-tax (*laographia*). The administrative system bore little relation to that elsewhere in the Empire. The governor (*Praefectus*) was an *eques* – for any senator might see himself as the heir of Antonius. He ruled from Alexandria, making annual tours for jurisdiction and the inspection of accounts. The three main districts, the Delta, the 'Seven Nomes and Arsinoe' (Middle Egypt), and the Thebaid (Upper Egypt) were ruled by *epistrategoi*, and their subdivisions ('nomes') by *strategoi* ('generals' – though the office had lost all military function). The country contained only three Greek cities of the type known elsewhere, Alexandria, Naucratis and Ptolemais. Alexandria was deprived of, or kept without (the point is disputed) a city council and officials of the normal type. The chief towns of each 'nome', however, were known as *metropoleis*, and had some of the characteristics of Greek cities. Their inhabitants, or at least a privileged class known as *metropolitai*, occupied a middle position in the ladder of privilege. For the *laographia*, the flat-rate poll-tax imposed by Rome, was paid in full by the bulk of the population, in part (normally a half) by the *metropolitai*, and not at all by limited numbers of priests in each temple, by the citizens of the three Greek cities, and by Roman citizens. Within the class of *metropolitai* there was a further privileged class, called literally 'those from the gymnasium' from whom alone the officials of the *metropoleis* were drawn. The particular form in which this class was defined arose from the role of the gymnasiums as the centres of specifically Greek up-bringing. The qualification was in itself cultural (and financial) not racial; but, none the less, entry was gained by proving descent from ancestors who had been members. Thus from 127/8, for example, we have a papyrus containing the *epikrisis* (examination) return of a thirteen-year-old Graeco-Egyptian boy called Sarapion, showing that he was descended from *metropolitai* 'rated (for the poll-tax) at twelve *drachmae*', and also, separately, that his ancestors had been members of the gymnasium back to the census of AD 4–5 under Augustus.[2]

Sarapion's claims were lodged at thirteen because at fourteen payment of the poll-tax began, continuing to sixty or sixty-two. Hence also a census of the whole population was taken at fourteen-year intervals; returns were made by all property-owners, listing all their properties and the names, ages and statuses of the occupants. Thus in a papyrus roll with the census returns of two villages in the Prosopite nome in 174 a typical entry is: 'To Apion *basilicogrammateus* (a nome official) . . . from Tatithoes, daughter of Petephnouthis, of Thelbonthon Siphtha. I declare in accordance with the orders of the most excellent Prefect . . . for the census by houses my property in the village, that is a house and empty lot, formerly owned by Hartusis son of Petephnouthis and now by Tatithoes, daughter of Petephnouthis. Occupants: Tatithoes . . . widow, aged sixty, Thermouthis . . . her daughter, aged twenty . . . I, Didymas son of Psenamounis, have written this for her, as she is illiterate.'[3]

These census returns (which had to be addressed separately to four or five different officials) were only the start of the vast amount of documentation involved in raising the revenues and checking on the population of Roman Egypt. The papyri and ostraka attest a vast range of taxes in cash and kind, on land – based on reports of the annual extent of inundation – on differ-ent types of produce, and on trades, which defy all attempt at summary.[4] The documents show also an endless conflict between the State and its subjects, complicated by the general imposition in the course of the first century of the 'liturgical' system, by which the task of collecting and standing surety for the taxes, or of acting as tenant for various categories of state land, was imposed obligatorily on individuals, first by the officials of the different areas, and later collectively by the communities. The response of the taxpayers themselves was often flight; so for instance we find the collectors of the *laographia* for six villages in the Arsinoite nome complaining to the Prefect of 55-9 that many of the inhabitants have become impoverished, fled or died, so that they cannot collect the tax, and begging him to write to the *strategos* to tell him not to harass them until the matter can be investigated.

Our fullest description of Egypt as it was in the early Roman period comes from the geographer Strabo, who made a voyage up the Nile about 25 BC in the entourage of the Prefect. He describes Alexandria, with its double harbour and fine broad streets, the temple (*Caesareion*) of the Imperial cult, and the Museum, a centre for scholars founded under the Ptolemies and now under the patronage of the Emperor. Further inland, he saw the temple of Serapis at Canopus, where the god delivered his instructions in dreams to those who slept in the precincts, the legionary camp at Babylon (Cairo), with 150 prisoners employed on pumping water up to it from the Nile, and the Pyramids and tombs of the Pharaohs. At Arsinoe (formerly Crocodilopolis) he fed the sacred crocodile kept by the priests, and at Thebes heard – like many other travellers of this period whose names are inscribed there – the sounds emitted at dawn each day by the colossal statue of Memnon. Finally he reached the great temple of Isis on the island of Philae, which was built under the Ptolemies, and continued to receive additions, in the traditional style of Pharaonic Egypt, up to the reign of Hadrian (117–38).

Strabo also describes, but did not traverse, the routes which led from the Nile at Coptos to the Red Sea ports, from which, after the discovery of the monsoon, great fleets set off each year to trade in India. Goods were carried overland to the Nile, shipped down it, and exported from Alexandria to the rest of the Mediterranean.

Another traveller to Egypt, in AD 19, was Germanicus, the nephew and adopted son of Tiberius. At Alexandria he relieved a famine by opening the granaries where corn for Rome was stored; then he travelled up the Nile dressed in Greek clothes (as befitted an intellectual Roman tourist) and visited the temples, statues and pyramids. At Memphis the sacred bull Apis refused to eat from his hand, presaging his death. A papyrus published in 1959 gives a verbatim record of his speech to the crowd at Alexandria and his reception by them: 'The *exegetes* (chief official of the city), "I have given the Imperator himself both the decrees." The Imperator, "I who who was sent by my father, men of Alexandria . . ." The crowd shouted, "Hurrah, Good Luck, You will have blessings." The Imperator, "You men of Alexandria, who have set great store by my addressing you, wait until I have completed my answers to each of your questions before applauding." ' Another papyrus contains two edicts which Germanicus issued, one attempting to restrain the population from hailing him as a god, the other forbidding the forcible requisition of draught animals and boats from the people for use on his journey.

The turbulence of Alexandria was shown again in the reign of Gaius (37–41), when a wave of violence against the large Jewish community led to rival delegations to Gaius and Claudius (41–54), and to the latter's famous letter to the Alexandrines, written in the first year of his reign. The pogrom of 38 is described by Philo in his *Against Flaccus* (the Prefect at the time), with more details in his *Embassy to Gaius*, which mainly recounts the fortunes of the Alexandrian Jewish embassy which appeared before Gaius in 40. Trouble began with the arrival in Alexandria of the Jewish king Agrippa I (a descendant of Herod); offended by the sight of his royal entourage, the mob seized an idiot beggar from the streets, dressed him as a king and performed an insulting mime. Then they went on to a general movement against the Jews, demanding the placing of images in the synagogues and, after the Prefect had sought popularity by proclaiming the Jews to be foreigners in the city, driving them into one quarter, sacking their houses and workshops and beating or burning to death those they caught. Flaccus meanwhile arrested many of the Jewish council of elders and had them flogged to death in the theatre. This stage ended with the arrest of Flaccus for other reasons, but trouble continued, and in 41 two further embassies, of Greeks and Jews, from Alexandria came before Claudius. His letter to the Alexandrines, preserved in full on a papyrus, is in answer to the Greek delegation. He begins by recording the names of the twelve ambassadors (six of them Roman citizens) and then, clearly following the order of their requests to him, accepts some and rejects others of the religious honours they had offered him, and grants various privileges – though referring the question of a city council to the Prefect. Finally he comes to the Jewish question, on which there had been a confrontation before him between the two delegations. He orders both sides to keep the peace, and the Alexandrines not to disturb the ancestral customs of the Jews; the Jews were to keep to themselves, not to intrude on games given by Alexandrian officials, and not (as they evidently had) to bring in reinforcements from Syria and Egypt.

These issues, the conflict with the Alexandrian Jews and the claims of Alexandria to full city status, gave rise to some of the most curious local literature of the ancient world, the so-called *Acts of the Pagan Martyrs*.[5] These Acts come from a number of separate papyrus fragments, and have the form either of trials of prominent Alexandrines or of confrontations of Alexandrian and Jewish delegations, before a number of Emperors from Claudius to Commodus (180–92). How far they have any basis in fact is disputed; but, whether history or fiction, their tone is unmistakable, the heroization of the leading Alexandrians as against both their Jewish rivals and their Roman oppressors.

There was further violence in 66, when the Prefect, himself in fact an Alexandrian Jew, Tiberius Julius Alexander, the nephew of Philo, ended a conflict in which the Jews threatened to burn down the amphitheatre by sending in two legions and causing a massacre in which 50,000 people were killed. Two years later Alexander issued one of the most revealing documents of Roman Egypt, the edict detailing reforms consequent upon the proclamation of Galba on the death of Nero.[6] The edict was issued at Alexandria on 6 July 68; our main text of it comes from an inscription on the gateway of a temple in the Oasis of El-Khargeh, where it was promulgated on 28 September – which illustrates the slowness of communications. Alexander mentions that from the moment he entered Alexandria (in 66) he had been besieged by petitioners from both Alexandria and the country-side of Egypt asking for an end to abuses; he deals with, among much else, the forcing of people to contract for the collection of revenues or the renting of state lands, the process by which people who bought state land still found themselves compelled to pay rent for it, and the repeated resurrection by officials of cases against individuals of which Prefects had already dis-posed; similarly, the cultivators all over Egypt had complained of the imposition of extra taxes without authority.

Egypt also provides the only documentary evidence for the special poll-tax imposed on all Jews by Vespasian after the war of 66–70 (Ch. 11). Previously, adult male Jews had sent two *drachmae* a year to the Temple at Jerusalem. Ostraka – pottery fragments with tax receipts – from Edfu and a papyrus of 73 from Arsinoe, show that the tax, now paid to Jupiter Capitolinus in Rome, was laid on all, male and female, from the age of three – and back-dated from 72 to 70.

In about 73 also, refugees from the Jewish war arrived in both Egypt and the neighbouring Greek-speaking province of Cyrene (Libya), but their attempts to cause serious uprisings were opposed by the leaders of the Jewish communities in both provinces, and crushed by the authorities. But in 115–17 the Jews of Cyrene, followed by those of Cyprus and Egypt, rose against the Greek population, slaughtering enormous numbers, and causing, apparently in a deliberate crusade, widespread destruction. Inscriptions from Cyrene refer to roads and temples destroyed in the Jewish revolt; whole areas were de-populated, and had to be resettled with veteran colonists by Hadrian (117–38). In Egypt, the historian Appian, who came from a leading family in Alexandria, records how the Jews destroyed the temple of Nemesis there, and how he himself escaped by flight. We have also, for instance, a papyrus referring to a battle between the Romans and the Jews near Alexandria, and another with a petition to the Prefect from the *strategos* of Apollinopolis for leave to see about his property 'destroyed by the impious Jews'. Finally, in the words of Appian, Trajan 'destroyed the Jewish race in Egypt'. The papyri confirm this – only a single Jewish family seems to have survived in Edfu, and the Jewish community of Alexandria is heard of no more.[7]

In 130 Hadrian visited Egypt, disputing with the scholars in the Museum at Alexandria, sailing up the Nile and listening to the statue of Memnon at Thebes (where one of his entourage, Julia Balbilla, inscribed some verses which can still be read) and founding the only new city of Roman Egypt, Antinoopolis, in memory of his favourite Antinous, who was drowned in the Nile. The city, whose inhabitants were known as 'The Antinoites, New Hellenes', was an expression of Hadrian's philhellenism. It was laid out in the classic chequerboard pattern with two colonnaded main streets, twenty metres in width, intersecting at the centre, and the usual public buildings, baths, temples and theatre. The citizens, who received all the privileges of the inhabitants of a Greek city, were chosen partly by lot from Ptolemais and partly from the *metropolitai* of Arsinoe and elsewhere. Some at least received plots of land, and their children were supported from a fund established by Hadrian (the only example of an Imperial 'alimentary' system comparable to that of Italy).[8]

What it meant to be the citizen of a Greek city is highlighted by a papyrus of the mid-second century, the *Gnomon* (Handbook) of the *Idiologus*, the official in charge of the 'special account' into which certain fines and vacant inheritances were paid. A number of the more than 100 surviving clauses refer to distinctions of status, between Egyptians, *astoi* (the citizens of the Greek cities and also *metropoleis*?), Alexandrians and Romans. An Egyptian who claimed that his father had been a Roman citizen had a quarter of his property confiscated; if he enrolled his son as an ephebe (a youth who was a member of the gymnasium) he lost a sixth; Egyptian women married to Roman veterans were punished if they claimed to be Roman citizens themselves. In these circumstances an Egyptian might well wish to seem as 'Greek' as he could, even if his legal status was difficult to change; so from 194 we have a petition to the *Idiologus* from a man called Eudaimon son of Psois and Tiathres (Egyptian names) to have himself named officially Eudaimon son of Heron and Didyma (which were Greek names).

Social tensions occasionally emerged in serious disorders. Such a thing seems to have happened in 154, when the Prefect issued an edict promising an amnesty to those who returned to their homes, and describing his measures to restore order. Then in 172 the Boukoloi who inhabited the marshes near Alexandria rose under the leadership of a priest, defeated a Roman force and might have taken Alexandria but for the intervention of the governor of Syria.

The most noteworthy political event of the period, however, was the visit of Septimius Severus in 199–201. The visit, during which the Emperor made the usual antiquarian tour up the Nile, has left abundant traces in the papyri, a report of village officials to the *strategos* about the provision of supplies for the journey, and a large number of legal decisions, including a group of thirteen written out verbatim on a single papyrus, copies of ones posted in the stoa of the gymnasium at Alexandria in March 200. But the most important result of the visit was the establishment of city-councils both at Alexandria and in the *metropoleis*. Egypt retained its bureaucratic structure, and the most important function of the councils was that of finding people to accept the burdens both of local administration and tax-gathering; none the less a step had been taken towards the local autonomy characteristic of the rest of the Empire.

Though the Alexandrians had now gained what they had long sought, their conflicts with the Roman Emperors were not over. In 215 Caracalla arrived there in the course of his Eastern expedition, and, apparently in revenge for popular abuse of him for the murder of his brother Geta in 212, carried out a ferocious massacre. He also expelled all strangers from the city. The final sentences of his order, which is preserved in a papyrus, finely illustrate the contrast between Alexandria and the rest of Egypt: '. . . The persons who ought to be prohibited are those who flee from their own districts in order to escape rustic toil, not those who congregate here to view the beautiful city of Alexandria . . .

Genuine Egyptians can easily be recognised among the linen-weavers by their speech . . . moreover their habits and uncivilized way of life reveal them as Egyptian peasants.'

Among those who fled from Alexandria in 215 was the great Christian scholar and philosopher, Origen. The beginnings of Christianity in Alexandria and Egypt are very obscure. On the one hand we know the names of the bishops of Alexandria from the first century onwards, and the names, and something of the doctrines, of a number of Alexandrian heretics in the second century; on the other we have a tiny papyrus fragment of St John's Gospel, written perhaps in the 120s, which is thus the earliest known New Testament text, and a couple of other New Testament fragments from the later second century. But it is only towards the end of the century that Eusebius' *Ecclesiastical History* shows a well-established Christian community in Alexandria, with a bishop and a catechetical school whose head for some years up to 202/3 was Clement, a convert, possibly originally from Athens, whose brilliant and discursive writings used all the inheritance of ancient philosophy and literary technique to interpret Christianity. The greatest figure of the Alexandrian church, however, was Origen, born into a Christian family in Alexandria in about 185. After the death of his father in a persecution about 202/3, he devoted himself to an ascetic life and to giving instruction in Christianity, being recognized as their equal by contemporary pagan philosophers. In 215 he left Alexandria, as mentioned, and lived for a short time at Caesarea in Palestine, finally settling there in 230/1. His immense output of writings, some of which survive, included a work on the bases of Christian theology, commentaries on all the books of the Old and New Testaments, and the *Hexapla*, the Old Testament set out in six parallel columns, Hebrew, transliterated Hebrew and four Greek translations.

Origen suffered prolonged torture in the persecution under Decius (249–51) and died soon after, probably at Caesarea. At the same period there begin the letters of Dionysius, bishop of Alexandria, which are vivid testimony not only for the life of the Church but for events in Alexandria and Egypt. The persecution in Alexandria began with spontaneous popular violence a year before the edit of Decius. Christians were seized, beaten and tortured in the effort to make them apostatize, and their houses ravaged. When the edict arrived, a soldier was sent to arrest Dionysius, who escaped by flight. Later he was taken, but rescued from the soldiers by a group of Egyptian peasants on their way to an all-night wedding feast. The final form of the persecution was that all the inhabitants of the Empire were required to sacrifice before local commissions set up for the purpose; forty-three papyri survive from Egypt containing sacrifice-certificates obtained by individuals.[9] Many Christians sacrificed; many others, both in Alexandria and the towns and villages of Egypt, refused and were martyred. Others fled into the desert areas. This period saw the first Egyptian anchorite, Paul of Thebes, who was 'educated in Greek and Egyptian letters' and established himself in the desert during the persecution. His famous successor, St Anthony, who became a hermit about 270, seems to have known no Greek.

Dionysius records in detail the persecution under Valerian and its cessation by Gallienus in about 260 and also describes a civil war in Alexandria (followed by a plague in which he says the Christians cared for their sick while the pagans abandoned theirs) apparently during the revolt of Macrianus and Quietus (Ch. 11), who were recognized in Egypt in 260–1. Dionysius died in 264 and was succeeded by Anatolius who, typically of Alexandrian Christianity, was also head of the Aristotelian school there. Civil strife continued in his time. The new power of Palmyra (Ch. 11) invaded Egypt in 269–70, took it after fierce fighting and occupied it until perhaps 271.[10] Perhaps in the following year, there was a revolt in Alexandria, put down by Aurelian (270–5). In a siege of part of Alexandria by the Romans, which might belong to either of these episodes, Anatolius persuaded the council of Alexandria to expel all the non-combatants and arranged for them to be cared for by a Christian on the Roman side.

The Palmyrenes apart, Egypt seems to have suffered no external attack in the period except for a raid by the Blemmyes, briefly mentioned in the reign of Probus (276–82). Yet there is abundant evidence in the papyri that the third century was a period of great difficulty in Egypt. Prices rose sharply, brigandage seems to have been common, some land went out of cultivation (though Probus, as a papyrus of 278 records, ordered general forced labour for the restoration of the dykes) and, as elsewhere, the pressure of the needs of the State increased. The papyri illustrate the necessity of producing provisions for the soldiers (and, where necessary, bribing them) and above all the increasing difficulty of filling local offices. For instance, a papyrus from the Arsinoite nome, dating to about 250, records a hearing before the Prefect on the question of whether the *metropolitai* could impress people from the villages to hold certain offices. Severus (193–211) had ruled that the villages were exempt:

> 'The Prefect to Severus (advocate for the council of Arsinoe): What do you say to the law of Severus and to the judgements?
> Severus: To the law of Severus I will say: Severus ordained the law while the cities were still prosperous.
> The Prefect: The argument from prosperity – or rather the decline of prosperity – is the same both for the villages and the cities.'[11]

Yet the forms of local life continued; a papyrus from Oxyrhynchus, for instance, gives a list of poets and others who acquired some immunity as a result of victories in the annual festivals there between 261 and 289. And one aspect of the culture of Egypt, which contrasts with the spread of Christianity and the development of Coptic, is illustrated by a papyrus from the 260s, in which the town-clerk of Hermopolis welcomes a fellow-citizen on his return from an embassy to Rome by quoting a line from the *Ion* of Euripides.

11

The Greek Provinces

Compared to that of all the other areas of the Empire, the life of the chief Greek provinces – from Greece and Macedonia to Asia Minor, and Syria and its environs – is illuminated by an infinite wealth and variety of evidence. There is not only an immense quantity of contemporary Greek literature, pagan, Jewish and Christian, but, forming a complete contrast to it, the utterances of generations of Rabbis collected principally in the Mishnah, of about AD 200, and the Talmud. We have thousands of inscriptions in Greek, especially from Asia Minor, and also inscriptions and documents in Aramaic and its branches, Syriac and Palmyrene, and in Nabataean, a very early form of Arabic written in Aramaic script. Beyond that there survive extensive remains of cities, from Ephesus to the temples of Baalbek, to Caesarea, Jerash, Palmyra or Petra. Over the last few years our evidence has been enriched by entirely new sources, the excavations at the fortress of Masada, where the last survivors of the Jewish revolt committed suicide in 74, which have produced documents and biblical texts, and the earliest known synagogue;[1] the 'monastery' of Qumran and the Dead Sea Scrolls; and the documents and other finds – clothes, baskets, utensils, pottery – left in the caves of the Judaean desert west of the Dead Sea by the fighters in the Jewish war of 132–5.[2] Excavations between the two World Wars also revealed the wonderful site of Dura-Europus on the Euphrates, with its documents in seven languages, its temples, synagogue and Christian church.[3]

For this whole area Rome created a political framework, but little more. The regions were divided into provinces under

Roman governors, and the provincial system was steadily exten-ded to take in the client-kingdoms which ruled much of eastern Asia Minor and the Syrian area in the first century (see Ch. 6). Roman rule consciously favoured the creation in the cities of hereditary ruling classes, whose loyalty could be assured, and who could be held responsible for public order and the payment of taxes; the end of the first century also saw the beginning of a substantial influx of Greeks into the Roman Senate. Beyond that, however, Rome contributed only indirectly to the social and cultural history of the area. Greek civilization, where it was not native, had been spread by the conquests of Alexander the Great. Roman Emperors continued the tradition, already adop-ted by generals in the Republic, of founding more Greek cities. There were also a number of veteran colonies with Latin as their official language, mainly founded by Augustus; one of them, Berytus, even developed a school of Roman law. But in all the Greek-speaking areas there were only four Latin *municipia*. The use of Latin names spread very widely among the upper classes, mainly through the extension of the citizenship, which required the adoption of the Roman triple name; the result was usually a hybrid form, Tiberius Claudius Hermocrates, for example. Indi-vidual Latin names could be taken even without the citizenship; Simon the Cyrenaican, who carried the Cross, had given one of his sons a Greek name, Alexander, and the other a Latin one, Rufus (Mk 15, 21). A knowledge of Latin was much less wide-spread, though Claudius attempted to make it obligatory for Roman citizens. But individual Latin words gained a wide currency transliterated in Greek, as some did even in Hebrew.

Thus within the framework provided by the Roman Empire an almost purely Greek civilization persisted from the Hellen-istic to the Byzantine age, and enjoyed a new flowering in the second century. Its centres were Athens and the great cities of western Asia Minor, Ephesus, Pergamum and Smyrna. Its leaders were the rich landed families who, fostered by Rome, formed the ruling class of the cities and acted as local benefac-tors, paying for distributions of food, public buildings, musical and athletic contests (as well as the gladiatorial shows and wild-beast hunts which were one of the few imports from Roman culture). They sent off their sons to hear the fashionable rhetoricians (or 'sophists') and philosophers; the sons might become sophists themselves, or enter the Roman equestrian or senatorial orders, or both. The sophists of the late first century onwards were the most characteristic product of Greek civilization in this age; Philostratus' *Lives of the Sophists*, written about 230, is the most illuminating introduction to it. Originating themselves from as far apart as southern Gaul, Macedonia, Cappadocia and Arabia, the sophists tended to hold court in Athens or the great cities of Asia, gathering pupils from all over the Greek world.

Greek civilization, for all its attractions, remained throughout the Near East an alien importation. In Asia Minor, though it produced no non-Greek literature, scattered items of evidence reveal the survival, for instance, of Celtic in Galatia, and of Cappadocian and Cilician throughout our period; in Phrygia about a hundred inscriptions in the native language are known, written in Greek characters and dating mainly to the third century. In western Syria, near the Mediterranean coast, all the known documents are in Greek (plus a few in Latin), but a number of items of evidence indicate that certainly in the countryside, and in some towns, Aramaic was also spoken. Aramaic and its dialects was the *lingua franca* of the whole area from there southwards to northern Arabia and eastwards to the Tigris, and non-Greek documents come from Nabataea, Judaea, Palmyra, Dura on the Euphrates and Edessa – all of these being areas to which direct Roman rule was extended during our period. As is well known, Jewish religious writing in Hebrew and Aramaic flourished throughout this time. In Syriac, the dialect of Aramaic spoken at Edessa and written in a cursive script, the earliest known document dates to AD 6, and the earliest literature, which is Christian, to the latter half of the second century.

The best introduction to this world is the Gospels and the Acts of the Apostles. In the Gospels we see the life of the Jewish inhabitants of the villages and small towns of Galilee, in the tetrarchy of Herod Antipas, the son of Herod the Great. We also meet the soldiers of the client-kingdom with their borrowed Roman titles, centurion or *speculator*, or the Tetrarch entertaining his notables at dinner. Outside Galilee, Christ passes through the territory of the Greek cities of the coast, Tyre or Sidon, or of the Decapolis, but does not enter the cities themselves. For the great festivals they go up from Galilee to Jerusalem where the High Priests and the Sanhedrin hold sway, watched over by the procurator and his troops.

For a few years (41-4) the Judaean kingdom of Herod was restored in its entirety by Claudius to Herod's descendant Agrippa I, who managed briefly to balance the pressures from Rome, from his Graeco-Roman environment – for instance, he presented works of art to Berytus and built an amphitheatre there – and the Jews, observing the law in the Jewish areas of his kingdom. Towards the end, his ambitions brought Imperial disfavour, when he began to fortify Jerusalem, and called a conference of the client kings of the East. Both Josephus and Acts record his death at Caesarea; while giving a festival in honour of Claudius, he appeared dressed in a suit of silver, was hailed as a god, but soon fell ill and died.

After his death the whole Jewish area was ruled by Roman procurators, and the period up to the outbreak of the revolt in 66 was marked by increasing conflicts between the Jews and Greeks and Samaritans, and between the mass of the Jewish population and the upper-class group round the High Priests, who co-operated with Rome. Brigandage was rife (one earlier example was Barabbas, the bandit or terrorist – not 'robber' – released by Pilate), terrorists, known as *sicarii*, operated, and a number of popular prophets arose. One, followed by 400 people, marched to the Jordan, proclaiming that it would divide before them; another, an Egyptian, called a great crowd to the Mount of Olives and announced that the walls of Jerusalem would fall. Both were killed by Roman troops. In Acts, when Paul is arrested in Jerusalem, the tribune, hearing him speak Greek, asks 'Are you the Egyptian who recently led 4,000 of the *sicarii* into the desert?'

Before that, Paul had travelled in Syria, Asia Minor, Macedonia and Greece. In Damascus he fled (2 *Cor.* 11, 32) to avoid arrest by the 'ethnarch' (local governor) of Aretas – that is the king of Nabataea, the Hellenized Arab kingdom with its capital at Petra. On the first missionary journey of Paul and Barnabas to Pisidia and Lycaonia, the people of Lystra hailed them, in their native Lycaonian, as gods, and tried to sacrifice bulls to them. On the second journey they travelled through Asia Minor and crossed to Macedonia; at the Roman colony of Philippi a popular tumult caused them to be arrested by the officials, imprisoned, beaten and later released on the discovery that they were Roman citizens (Ch. 5). In Athens, the intellectual centre of the Greek world, Paul spoke daily in the Agora, disputed with Stoic and Epicurean philosophers, and made a speech on the Areopagus. In Corinth, also a Roman colony, he preached and was taken by the Jews there before the proconsul Junius Gallio (the brother of Seneca), who refused to intervene.

On his third journey Paul taught at Ephesus, where a riot was raised against him by the silversmiths who made models of the great temple of Artemis, and who feared the loss of their trade. A great crowd gathered in the theatre (the normal meeting-place of the people) and shouted the slogan, 'Great is Artemis of the Ephesians!' The riot was only quelled by the chief official of the city, the *grammateus* (Town Clerk), who addressed the crowd, saying that if there was any accusation to be made, the proconsul's court was available; if they wished to make any other demand, there were regular meetings of the city assembly.

No text illustrates better the city life of the Greek East, its passionate local loyalties, its potential violence precariously held in check by the city officials, and the overshadowing presence of the Roman governor. That presence is revealed equally in a long inscription from Ephesus of a few years earlier, containing the decree in which the proconsul, Paullus Fabius Persicus, acting in accordance with a decree of Claudius, regulated the finances of the temple of Artemis, abolishing the sale of priesthoods and cutting down the personnel that were maintained on temple funds.

The same local loyalties and the same supervision by the governor found expression in the *koina* – provincial leagues of cities, some pre-existing Roman rule, which represented the provinces *vis-à-vis* the governors and Rome, administering the Imperial cult, voting honours, and asking for the maintenance or extension of privileges. We have a record, for instance, of the meeting of the Greek cities in 37, when they took the oath to Gaius in the presence of the proconsul, and elected an embassy to congratulate him on his accession. The actual documents are inscriptions from Acraephia in Boeotia honouring a citizen, Epaminondas (the name of a famous Boeotian general of the fourth century BC), who represented Acraephia at the assembly at Argos, and, when many other rich and prominent men declined, volunteered to go on the embassy. The documents include the letter in which Gaius expressed his appreciation of the Greeks' loyalty.

Also from Acraephia we have an inscription with the text of the oration with which Nero, on his visit of 66–7 – during which he competed in the Olympic and other games as charioteer, singer and actor – addressed the Greeks gathered at the Isthmus of Corinth, and proclaimed their freedom and immunity from taxation. On that occasion Epaminondas, now High Priest for the Imperial cult, addressed the Acraephians and proposed that the city should erect an altar to Nero identified with Zeus 'the Liberator'. Vespasian (69–79) revoked the freedom of Greece.

In contrast to the deep peace of the other provinces of the Greek East, Judaea finally in 66 broke into open rebellion, symbolized by the ending of sacrifices in the Temple for the safety of the Emperor. When Jerusalem, besieged by Vespasian's son Titus with four legions, fell in 70, the temple was destroyed, more than a million casualties caused, hundreds of Jewish prisoners slaughtered in shows in the Greek cities of Syria and in Rome, and the seven-branched candlestick carried off as booty – it is portrayed as such on the Arch of Titus in Rome. Josephus, our main authority for these events, had been captured in 67, and from now on enjoyed the life of an Imperial favourite in Rome, writing his *Jewish War*, in Greek translated from Aramaic, in the late 70s and completing his *Jewish Antiquities* in 93. More important for the future was the action of a Rabbi, Johanan ben Zakkai, who escaped during the siege, obtained permission to found a school at Jabneh on the coast, and was thus able to carry on the Pharisaic tradition of continuous discussion, interpretation and development of the Law. The

Rabbis founded a new 'Sanhedrin' whose president, always from the house of Hillel, rose by the late second century to the position of a local dynast. Thus while the political identity of the Jewish people was destroyed, Judaism itself entered a new and important phase.

The revolt ended finally with the capture of Masada in 74; the Roman wall round the foot of the fortress, and the eight Roman camps, remain clearly visible in the rocky desert below.[4] As mentioned in Chapter 6, this period saw a legion under a *legatus* established at Jerusalem, two legions under a consular *legatus* in Cappadocia and finally the conquest of Nabataea, and the establishment of a legion at Bostra, in 106. Petra, however, the Nabataean capital, remained the metropolis of the new province of Arabia, and it is there that the impact of Roman rule can be most clearly traced. Building in Greek style had begun at Petra in the first century BC, and its famous rock-cut tombs (whose façades in fact imitate the frontal view of temples of local type) continue from then on into the Roman period. Under Roman rule the stream running through the wadi which leads to Petra was dammed, and directed through a tunnel; the main street was rebuilt on a higher level and lined with colonnades, and there also arose a triumphal arch of Trajan and the rock-cut tomb of a Roman governor.[5] To the evidence of archaeology we ought now be able to add that of a collection of documents found in 1961 among those of the Jewish revolt of 132–5 in a cave in the Judaean desert; this is an archive of family documents on papyrus dating from 93/4 to 132, and written in Nabataean, Aramaic and Greek. The documents concern, for instance, sales, deeds of gift, and a marriage contract, and refer to the census carried out in Arabia in 127 by the governor Sextius Florentinus. When fully published, they should illustrate vividly the coming of Roman rule.

While these documents illuminate the life of an obscure multilingual corner of the Empire, the same period, from the end of the first century, sees the beginning of the bulk of literary evidence for the main Greek areas. The solitary great writer produced by Greece itself under the Empire, Plutarch, lived and wrote in Chaeronea in Boeotia, his adult life stretching from the late 60s, when he was a student in Athens, to some time after 119, when in old age he was made *procurator* of Greece by Hadrian. His most famous work is the series of parallel biographies of Greek and Roman statesmen. But it is the huge collection of philosophical and scholarly essays known collectively as the *Moralia* which throw most light on his own time. Plutarch seems to have travelled to Sardis in Asia and to Alexandria, and visited Rome at least twice. His circle of acquaintances included Greeks from Macedonia and Tarsus as well as Greece itself. One of them was a highly typical figure of the age, C. Julius Antiochus Philopappus, the grandson of the last king of Commagene deposed in 72, who presided over festivals in Athens and, as his monument on the Hill of the Muses in Athens states, was made a Roman senator by Trajan. Plutarch's friends in Rome included a senator, L. Mestrius Florus – from whom he took his own Roman name as a citizen, L. Mestrius Plutarchus – and Sosius Senecio, one of the great generals of Trajan. But he chose as a matter of principle to live in his small native town, where his family had been prominent for several generations, carrying out minor local functions such as the care of buildings, and also acting as Priest of Apollo at Delphi some twenty miles away. Of his works the most important for his own time is the *Political Precepts* addressed to Menemachus of Sardis. He argues that political life even under Roman rule is still a serious pursuit, 'Now that the affairs of the cities do not involve leadership in war, the overthrow of tyrants, the making of alliances, what opportunities are there for a fine and brilliant public career? There remain public lawsuits and embassies to the Emperor, which demand vigour and courage and intelligence.' But the local politician must at all costs keep the people in check and prevent disputes which bring the intervention of the proconsuls. He should remember that he rules in a subject city, look from his office to the tribunal of the governor, and be conscious of the shoes of the Roman governor above his head.[5a]

This same period, however, saw the first major influx of men from the Greek provinces, mainly those of Asia Minor, into the Senate. When the influx began under Vespasian, some came

either from Roman colonies – such as C. Caristanius Fronto
from Antioch in Pisidia – or from Greek towns where there were
settlements of Italians. There were also the descendants of kings
and dynasts; C. Julius Severus from Ancyra, who entered the
Senate under Hadrian, describes himself on an inscription as
the descendant of Attalus of Pergamum and of three Galatian
dynasts, and as the relation of numerous ex-consuls. Most came
from the landed bourgeoisie of the cities, whose families combined office in the cities and provincial *koina* with posts in the
equestrian order and the Senate. A prominent example was the
Athenian orator and millionaire, Herodes Atticus, consul in
143, who among many other things built the stone seats which
still line the stadium at Delphi.[6] Perhaps the most significant of
the Greek senators is the historian, Cassius Dio, from Nicaea in
Bithynia, who was in the Senate from about 189 to his second
consulate, as *ordinarius* with Severus Alexander, in 229, and
governed Africa, Dalmatia and Pannonia Superior. His *Roman
History*, which goes from the arrival of Aeneas in Italy to 229,
reveals how it was possible to combine the Greek cultural
heritage with the political outlook of Rome, and thus fore-
shadows the Byzantine age.[7]

Cassius Dio was a descendant, probably great-grandson, of
the other great literary contemporary of Plutarch, the orator
Cocceianus Dio (Dio Chrysostom – the 'golden-mouthed') from
Prusa in Bithynia. He also came from a prominent family – his
maternal grandfather had been the friend of a Roman Emperor
and had been made a citizen – and hence a Roman citizen – of
the colony of Apamea nearby. Dio inherited vineyards and
pastureland in the territory of Prusa, and one of his early
speeches was made after a mob had threatened to burn his house
because he had hoarded corn in a shortage (Dio explains that
he does not grow corn for sale). Under Domitian (81–96) he
was exiled and took up the role of a mendicant philosopher,
visiting Rome, Greece and the Black Sea area. Restored by
Nerva (96–8), a personal friend, he quickly regained a prominent role in Prusa. A group of his speeches in Prusa early in the
reign of Trajan (98–117) illustrates many aspects of city life. An
embassy, including Dio, went from Prusa to congratulate

Trajan on his accession, taking the opportunity to ask for a larger city-council, for the right of local jurisdiction, for increased revenues, and (which they did not apparently achieve) freedom from taxation. When they returned rumours circulated that the embassy had been unfavourably received, that other cities had obtained greater benefits, and that Dio had used the occasion for personal advantage. Then there were great building-projects which Dio planned and began; the proconsul approved them, but some persons in Prusa called Dio a tyrant, resenting the pulling down of old workshops, tombs and shrines to make way for new colonnades, fountains and public buildings. Constant expansion and re-development of the cities is, as archaeology shows, evident almost everywhere in the Empire up to the early third century; only in Dio do we see the reflection of the resentment which this might cause. At any rate we find Dio threatening to withdraw from public life, and asking the people bluntly whether they wish him to proceed and ask the proconsul to collect the contributions of cash promised (by rich citizens) for the building works.[7a]

Dio himself reappears, and the same types of city disputes are dealt with, in the correspondence between Trajan and Pliny the younger, whom he sent as a special Imperial *legatus* to Bithynia, probably in 109. Pliny inspected the finances of the cities, apparently charged to do so more systematically than an ordinary governor, exacted money owed to the cities, and checked building projects. At Nicaea, for instance, he found a theatre under construction and already collapsing, with money promised by private persons still owing. At Claudiopolis, the people were constructing a bath-building, relying on the entrance-money of extra councillors granted by Trajan, and Pliny asked for an architect to check the work. Dio himself was accused before Pliny of not producing the accounts for public works at Prusa. There was also normal judicial business, such as in particular the hearing of accusations against Christians. Pliny put those who were denounced to him to the test of sacrifice and of cursing Christ; of those who persevered, the Roman citizens were sent to Rome, and the others immediately executed.

Pliny's letter to Trajan is invaluable evidence for the spread of Christianity, for the extent of popular hostility to it and for the indeterminate but repressive attitude of the Roman officials. Evidence from a Christian source (almost the first after the obscure 'sub-apostolic' period of the early Church) comes from the letters which Ignatius, the bishop of Antioch, wrote to the churches of Ephesus, Magnesia, Trailes, Philadelphia and Smyrna in Asia, and to the church of Rome, while he was being taken to Rome under guard to be thrown to the beasts under Trajan. He emphasizes repeatedly the importance of obedience to the bishops, and of avoiding heresies. Writing to the Roman church, he urges them not to try to save him from martyrdom – 'Let me be eaten by the beasts, through whom I reach God. I am the bread of God, and am ground by the teeth of the beasts, so that I may be found to be the pure bread of Christ.'

It is with the reign of Hadrian (117–38) that we reach the fullest flowering of Greek civilization under the Romans. Hadrian carried to its extreme the long tradition of Roman Philhellenism, outdoing Nero, whose devotion to Greek culture had been more egotistic and erratic, and expressed in behaviour offensive to Roman customs. Before his accession Hadrian had been *archon* (chief official) in Athens in 112, and during his reign made two journeys in the East, in 123–5 and 128–32. For all the attention and benefits he showered on other cities, it was Athens, where he spent the winters of 124/5, 128/9 and 131/2, that gained the most from him.[8] He initiated public works, an aqueduct and a bridge, built a Pantheon, the library of Hadrian and a *gymnasium*, and completed the temple of Olympian Zeus, which had been started six centuries before by the tyrant Peisistratos. He also founded a temple of 'Zeus Panhellenios', and established Panhellenic games and an annual Panhellenic assembly of deputies from all the cities of Greece and all those outside which could prove their foundation from Greece; an inscription preserves the decree of the 'Panhellenes' admitting the city of Magnesia on the Maeander in Asia. The importance attached to Hadrian's institution is best illustrated by an early third-century inscription from Thessalonica honouring a local magnate, T. Aelius Geminius Macedo, who had not only held magistracies and provided timber for a

205

basilica in his own city, and been Imperial *curator* of Apollonia, but had been *archon* of the Panhellenic congress in Athens, priest of the deified Hadrian and president of the eighteenth Panhellenic Games (199/200); the inscription mentions proudly that he was the first *archon* of the Panhellenic Congress from the city of Thessalonica.[8a]

That was one side of the picture, the development of Greek civilization and the conscious celebration of its unity and prosperity. In the native populations of the East it produced mixed feelings, nowhere better exemplified than in the conversation of three Rabbis of the second century, preserved in the Babylonian Talmud: 'Rabbi Judah said, "How fine are the works of these people! They have made streets, they have made bridges, they have erected baths." Rabbi Jose sat silent. Rabbi Simeon ben Yohai said, "All that they have made, they have made for themselves; they have built market-places to put harlots in, baths to rejuvenate themselves, bridges to levy tolls for them." '

For sixty years after the destruction of the temple Jerusalem lay mostly in ruins. The city was largely deserted, but some Jews still came, and tradition preserved the story of how the great scholar Akiba visited the deserted Temple and saw a fox running out of the Holy of Holies. When Hadrian came in 129–30, the site contained only a few houses. Hadrian determined to rebuild the place as a Roman colony, Aelia Capitolina, complete with a temple of Jupiter Capitolinus. That led to the last great revolt led by Shimon bar Kosiba (or bar Kochba), whom Akiba himself seems to have recognized as the Messiah. From classical sources and inscriptions we know that the war spread over some four years and involved 3–4 legions, with detachments of four others, some brought from Lower Moesia. One legion was destroyed, and the general Julius Severus, summoned from Britain, finally won a war of attrition, taking fifty major fortresses, 985 villages and causing over half a million casualties. The Jewish coins of the period have the slogans 'First Year' or 'Second Year' 'Of the Redemption of Israel', as well as 'Shimon' and 'Jerusalem'; some show the Temple, with a scroll of the Law inside.

The 1960s produced the now famous discoveries from the

wadis to the west of the Dead Sea, the Roman camps on the heights above, and the caves in the sides of the great ravines containing the skeletons of the defenders, their possessions, biblical texts, documents from before the war like the archive mentioned above, and especially the documents from the war itself, in Greek, Aramaic and Hebrew. Some contain orders from bar Kosiba – for the punishment of individuals, the confiscation of wheat, the sending of supplies. One Hebrew letter begins 'From Shimon bar Kosiba to the men of Engeddi (on the shore of the Dead Sea). To Masabala and Yehonatan Bar Ba'ayan, peace. You sit, eat and drink from the property of the house of Israel and care nothing for your brothers.' Possibly more important even than these are the leases in Aramaic and Hebrew, dated from the first to the third year of the Liberation, showing that there was a regular administrative system in the area under the rebels' control. Not all of these documents have yet been fully published.[8b]

The war ended with considerable devastation, the banning of Jews from a wide area round Jerusalem, shifting the centre of Jewish life to Galilee (though Jews still came to Jerusalem to lament over the ruins), and the establishment of the province of Syria Palaestina governed by an ex-consul with two legions. Political recovery was, however, remarkably rapid. The great patriarch of the early third century, Rabbi Juda ha-Nasi ('the Prince'), compiled the Mishnah in its definitive form, a code of rules in Hebrew built up from the sayings and discussions of earlier teachers, and relating to personal conduct, the Sabbath and even the rituals of the long-destroyed Temple. But he also played the role of a local dynast, with considerable landed wealth, a court – with a levée modelled on that of the Emperors – and wide personal jurisdiction. He acted as intermediary with the Roman governors, had students in his house study Greek as well as Hebrew, and had personal links with an Emperor whom Talmudic sources call 'Antoninus' – probably Caracalla (211–17).

If, beside the troubled history of the Jews, the rest of the Greek provinces enjoyed peace and a real degree of social stability, there were still signs of exploitation and social tension, with riots about the price of bread, as in Athens under Hadrian, occasional strikes, and scattered evidence of brigandage in Greece and Asia Minor. Before the third century, when there are important inscriptions, the evidence tells us little about the peasants. But we do have a remarkable passage of Galen, the doctor and medical writer from Pergamum, who became the personal physician of Marcus Aurelius. His book *On Good and Bad Diet* begins: 'The famine prevalent for many successive years in many provinces has clearly displayed for men of any understanding the effect of malnutrition in generating illness. The city-dwellers, as it was their custom to collect and store enough corn for the whole of the next year immediately after the harvest, carried off all the wheat, barley, beans and lentils, and left to the peasants various kinds of pulse – after taking quite a large proportion of these to the city. After consuming what was left in the course of the winter, the country people had to resort to unhealthy foods in the spring; they ate twigs and shoots of trees and bushes and bulbs and roots of inedible plants . . .'

Then we have an example of what must have been a very common form of disorder, in an incident related by the orator Aelius Aristides. While he was at Pergamum, some property he owned in Mysia (the nothern part of the province of Asia) was seized by his Mysian neighbours, who gathered a band of armed slaves and hired men and occupied the land by force. Aristides was able to appeal to the proconsul, then at Pergamum on his judicial circuit, and was restored to his property. But what could happen to Aristides could happen to lesser men with less chance of redress. For Aristides was one of the most famous orators of his time – and his orations one of the best sources for the Greek world of the second century.[9] There is for instance his oration in praise of Rome, which he delivered there in 143; his 'Sacred Discourses' which describe the long cure which Aristides, a life-long hypochondriac, took at the sanctuary of Asclepius at Pergamum – the god appeared in dreams to those who slept in the temple, and delivered his instructions; or the lament for Smyrna which he sent to Marcus Aurelius after the earthquake of 177/8, and which reduced the Emperor to tears, and led him to rebuild the city.

Other aspects of social and religious life are illustrated by the writings of Lucian the satirist, who came from an Aramaic-speaking background at Samosata on the Euphrates, and learned Greek as a second language.[10] One of his works, for instance, is a hostile account of a man Lucian regarded as a religious charlatan, Alexander from Abonuteichos in Pontus. Alexander set up as a prophet with the aid of a sacred snake, and, frequented by crowds from all over Asia Minor and Thrace, delivered answers to written inquiries about the tracing of runaway slaves, the discovery of thieves or brigands and even, to a Roman *legatus*, about the invasion of Armenia. Opposition was answered by the proclamation that Pontus was filled with atheists and Christians. He established his own mystery cult, and issued an oracle to all the nations on the plague brought back from the East by the armies of Lucius Verus in 166, and another on the Marcomannic War of Marcus Aurelius (Ch. 6). Finally he got permission from Marcus for his home town to be renamed Ionopolis (Ion being the name of his snake) – a fact which coin evidence confirms.

A rather different figure described by Lucian was the wandering philosopher, Peregrinus from Parium in Asia. On leaving home, he went to Syria where he learned the 'wisdom' of the Christians, and was arrested as one. What followed illustrates one essential reason for the success of Christianity, the cohesion and mutual assistance of the Christians. First they tried to get him released, then came to him in prison, brought food and sent money; delegates came from as far away as Asia to assist. Even after his release he was supported by them in his travels. Later, however, he left them, visited an ascetic philosopher in Egypt, travelled to Italy where he uttered public abuse of the Emperor and was expelled, and finally crowned his career by burning himself to death before a large crowd at Olympia in Greece, just before the games of 165.

These texts reflect the widespread hostility to Christianity, and the disturbance it caused in the social and religious life of the time. Even better evidence is the letter, preserved in Eusebius' *Ecclesiastical History*, which the church of Smyrna sent to the churches of Pontus to record the martyrdom of Polycarp the

209

bishop of Smyrna, who was burnt to death in the stadium there at some date in the middle of the second century. It is noticeable in the account, that the arrest of Polycarp was demanded by the crowd in the stadium, that a city official (the *eirenarch* – keeper of the peace) carried out the arrest, and that the examination by the proconsul was conducted in the stadium, before a large crowd, who were kept informed of the proceedings by a herald. They shouted repeatedly, 'This is the teacher of Asia, the father of the Christians, the destroyer of our gods, who teaches men not to sacrifice, or worship them.'

Evidence of a different sort for the spread of Christianity is provided by the site of Dura-Europus on the Euphrates, which came under Roman control as a result of the Parthian campaigns of Lucius Verus in 162–6 (Ch. 6). The excavations conducted in the inter-war period illuminated the life of this small Hellenistic foundation with its mixed Greek, Aramaic and Iranian culture, in close contact with Syria for a century before it was occupied by Roman forces in 165. Apart from the Latin documents of the army, the Roman period of Dura (165–256) produces papyri, parchments and inscriptions in Greek (the overwhelming majority), Pahlavi and Middle Persian, Safaitic, Palmyrene, Syriac and Aramaic. There is a small Jewish synagogue made just after the Roman occupation, and a much larger one of 244–5, adorned with magnificent frescoes illustrating biblical scenes, the crossing of the Red Sea, the Ark, Solomon's temple, or Elijah on Mount Carmel. There is also a Christian chapel constructed in one room of a private house; later, probably about 230, the whole house was converted for use as a church. Frescoes here show for instance the healing of the paralytic, or Christ walking on the water.

Lucius Verus' chief commander in the Parthian war was Avidius Cassius, the son of an orator from Cyrrhus in Syria who had been *ab epistulis* (in charge of letters) for Hadrian, and later Prefect of Egypt. Avidius remained as governor of Syria, and was also given charge of the whole East by Marcus. In 175 he rebelled and claimed the throne, lasting three months and being recognized as far away as Egypt before being killed by his soldiers.

210

This episode, of which we know little, was the beginning of even more frequent wars and civil wars in the Greek provinces. At Avdat in the Negev there are traces of Arab incursions in the second half of the century. More important was a raid by the Costobocci from the north-west coast of the Black Sea, which reached Greece in 170 and damaged the ancient sanctuary of Eleusis. Roman forces were brought against them, but the local population also resisted. At Elataea in Greece an Olympic victor called Mnesiboulos gathered a force, killed many of the barbarians, and was then killed himself; an inscription from the free city of Thespiae shows the despatch of a force of volunteers, almost certainly for this war. This raid seemed at the time a mere episode; the evidence about Mnesiboulos comes from a single sentence of the *Description of Greece* by Pausanias, a travellers' guide to the antiquities of the country composed between 160 and 180.

The years 193–4 saw the first major campaigns on the territory of the Greek provinces since the civil wars of the late Republic. Septimius Severus, who seized power in 193, had as rivals both Clodius Albinus, the governor of Britain, and Pescennius Niger, the governor of Syria. Severus' forces won major battles at Cyzicus, in Bithynia and at Issus in Cilicia, and began a siege of Byzantium lasting till 196. Further campaigns, probably in 194–5 and 197–8, were then launched into Parthia, resulting in the creation of the provinces of Mesopotamia and Osrhoene – the territory of Edessa, whose client dynasty appears to have survived a few years longer. The cities of Nisibis and (perhaps a little later) Singara in Mesopotamia now became Roman *coloniae*, and two legions were stationed there.

A number of significant items of evidence relate to the next Eastern expedition, that of Caracalla in 214–17. There are the complaints of Cassius Dio, who was with Caracalla at Nicomedia in Bithynia in 214, about the services exacted for the Emperor, and the necessity imposed of building stopping-places along all the roads for him. His words are reinforced by a number of inscriptions from Bithynia (the nodal point of the Imperial communications system) honouring local magnates who had borne the cost of supplying Severus, Caracalla and their armies on the way to the East. This evidence reflects merely one instance of the general pressure of State transport requirements on the population (Ch. 5). The same pressure is reflected equally in a growing number of inscriptions from Asia in this period complaining of the exactions of troops and officials. One of these is the petition sent by the villagers of Aragua in Phrygia to the Emperor Philip in 244–7: they complained that soldiers, prominent inhabitants of the cities, and Imperial slaves and freedmen had been harassing them, taking them away from their work, requisitioning their ploughing oxen and subjecting them to physical violence. A previous complaint to the Emperor, and his instruction to the proconsul, had brought no result.

For others, the presence of the Emperor was an opportunity. When Caracalla was at Nicomedia in 214/15, there arrived an ambassador from Ephesus who, as an inscription records, had already been as the city's ambassador to Severus in Rome and then in Britain (208–11), and to Caracalla himself in Germany (213), Pannonia (214), and later at Antioch and in Mesopotamia; the subject was apparently the status and rights of the city, about which he was later to go to Macrinus (217–18).[11] In Syria, probably at Antioch, in 216 Caracalla heard a case of which the verbatim record – the protocol in Latin and the proceedings in Greek – is inscribed on the base of a temple some forty kilometres east of Damascus. The case was taken directly to Caracalla by a petition, an irregularity which occasioned some debate among the parties. It was brought by the peasants of Goharia against a man who had usurped the priesthood of a local temple of Zeus, enjoying the immunity of a priest, wearing a gold crown and carrying a sceptre. The text breaks off at this point; had it continued it might have illustrated not only the triviality of the cases which might come to an Emperor, but much of the life of the Syrian countryside.

Before setting out for the East, Caracalla had summoned and imprisoned the king Abgar of Edessa, who may have been a Christian, and if so was the first Christian monarch. It is certain at any rate that Christianity was well established in Osrhoene in the late second century, and the first major Syriac writer was the Gnostic heretic Bardesanes (or Bar Daisan), a contemporary of Abgar. Other aspects of the culture of Edessa are illustrated by a beautiful mosaic floor from a building, possibly a palace, near the city. It portrays seven important persons in local dress – the men in long baggy trousers, the women in high head-dresses – who from their names, inset in Syriac, may be the wife of Abgar and her family.

The dynasty seems to have ended in about 213, and in 213/14 the city of Edessa became a Roman *colonia*. From 243 we have (from among the documents found at Dura) a contract for the sale of a female slave at Edessa, in Syriac with two signatures in Greek. The heading illustrates with unique vividness the impact of Roman rule: '. . . In the month Iyar of the year 554 of the former reckoning; and in the year 31 of the freedom of the renowned Antoniniana Edessa, Colonia Metropolis Aurelia Alexandria; in the residence of Marcus Aurelius Antiochus, Roman *eques*, son of Belsu, and in the second term as *strategos* of Marcus Aurelius Abgar, Roman *eques*, son of Ma'nu, grandson of Agga, and of Abgar son of Hafsai, grandson of Bar-KMR. . . .'

The accident of Caracalla's murder in Syria in 217, the fourteen-month rule of his Praetorian Prefect, Macrinus, and the successful rising against him in the name of the fourteen-year-old Varius Avitus (Elagabal), grand-nephew of Septimius Severus' Syrian wife, Julia Domna, and holder of the hereditary priesthood of the sun-god, Elagabal, at Emesa (see Ch. 3), temporarily projected a Syrian dynasty on to the Roman stage. Elagabal sent on to Rome a picture of himself performing his priestly duties in Syrian dress, and brought with him the black stone which was the cult-object of the religion of the Sun-god. These and other offences to Roman sentiment led to his murder in 222.

His successor, his cousin Severus Alexander, was more careful. In his reign, however, the situation of the Eastern provinces was totally altered by the fall of Parthia and the rise of Sasanid Persia in the 220s. The immediate threat to Mesopotamia and Syria was met by an inconclusive campaign by Severus Alexander in Mesopotamia in 231–4. But from this time on the security of the past two centuries disappeared. The effects were immediate; documents and coins seem to show that economic activity continued to some degree into the 230s, but declined sharply thereafter. From probably the early 240s also we have a priceless and neglected passage, in the address of Gregorius of Neocaesarea in Pontus (the later bishop Gregorius Thauma- turgus, 'the miracle-worker') to his teacher Origen, after five years of Christian instruction with him at Caesarea in Palestine. Gregorius describes how his mother had himself and his brother educated in Greek rhetoric, with a view to being orators; how one of his teachers, who taught him Latin 'not to a high degree but just so as not to be entirely ignorant of that language' sug- gested that he learn some Roman law; Gregory agreed reluct- antly, to oblige his teacher and because it might be useful if he practised in court. He might then have gone to Rome, but went in fact to study law at Berytus. The opportunity came because Gregorius' brother-in-law, who also knew some law, had been taken as *assessor* by the governor of Palestine; wishing to have his wife join him, he was able to send a soldier with *diplomata* for more than enough wagons of the *vehiculatio* (see Ch. 5) to accommodate both her and her brothers. It was thus that he came to Caesarea, met Origen, and abandoned Roman law for Christianity.

Few texts reveal so much of the Greek East, the education of a prominent family in a remote province, the unenthusiastic attitude to Latin, combined with a recognition of its usefulness, the intimate connection with Roman officialdom, the casually extravagant use of the *vehiculatio* by the officials and upper classes – which helps to explain how the burden which the peasants felt was created.

From the same period we have evidence of a persecution of Christians in Cappadocia and Pontus, from a letter written more than twenty years later by Firmilian, bishop of Caesarea in Cappadocia to Cyprian in Carthage (it is only with Christianity that we begin to get literary evidence from the remoter parts of Asia Minor). A series of earthquakes aroused a superstitious hatred of the Christians among the population; the governor joined in, churches were burnt and many fled. The crisis pro- duced a female prophet among the Christians, who announced that she could make the earth move, went barefoot in the snow as a sign of divine power, and challenged the authority of the church.

The Persian war was soon seriously renewed. In 240 the Sasanid king Ardashir was succeeded by Shapur I (240–72?), who advanced towards the Euphrates to be met by Gordian III (238–44) and his Praetorian Prefect, Timesitheus, in 242, who recovered Nisibis and Carrhae. Timesitheus died during the campaign, and his successor, M. Julius Philippus, murdered Gordian in 244. Greek sources claim that he made an agreement with Shapur before retiring to Rome. The great trilingual inscription of Shapur at Naqsh-i-Rustam has a different version: Shapur had defeated and killed Gordian, and Philip had brought peace by paying an immense sum in ransoms, and agreeing to pay tribute.

Philip, 'the Arabian', came from a village in Auranitis, east of the Sea of Galilee. Following the tradition of Kings and Emperors, he built a city, named Philippopolis, on the site, giving it the rank of a Roman *colonia*. The remains of the city have never been extensively excavated, but show an irregular rectangular pattern with porticoed main streets, baths, temples and a theatre, and with an aqueduct some twelve miles long. The city testifies to the continuance of the ancient tradition of urbanization, and, as the only example of a completely new city built in the mid-third century, has – or would have if excavated – a unique historical importance.

With the reign of Decius (249–51) we reach the most obscure and troubled period of the Empire, marked for the Greek provinces by invasions from Persia and from the coasts of the Black Sea, the rise of Palmyra in the Syrian desert to the status of an independent power, and by repeated struggles between pretenders to the Roman throne. Not all of these risings are mentioned here; but they are faithfully and vividly reflected in the words of a Rabbi of the mid-third century. 'A king entered the province. The people set up portraits of him, made images of him, struck coins in his honour. Later they upset his portraits, broke his images and defaced his coins.'

The reign of Decius saw the first great persecution of the

Christians. The bishops of Antioch and Jerusalem were martyred, and Gregorius, now bishop of Neocaesarea, fled. Our best evidence, however, comes from the *Acta* of the martyrdom of Pionius in Smyrna, which also casts a flood of light on the city-life of Asia at the time. Pionius and other Christians were arrested by a local official, the *neokoros*, and interrogated by him on the *agora* of Smyrna before a crowd of Greeks and Jews. In spite of the crowd's demands for their instant execution they were put in the city prison to await the proconsul. Various attempts to persuade them were made, a beating from the local police (*diogmitai*), and an address from an orator – who was silenced by Pionius with a reference to the death of Socrates. Finally, the proconsul arrived, interrogated Pionius and ordered him to be burnt, which he endured in the stadium of Smyrna along with a presbyter of the Marcionite heresy.

It was in the reigns of Valerian and Gallienus (253–68) that the most serious invasion reached the Greek provinces. About 253 the Goths raided the north coast of Asia Minor and penetrated as far south as Ephesus, while another force went through Thrace and attacked Thessalonica, whose inhabitants resisted strongly and defeated the siege. The attack spread terror throughout Greece, and led the Peloponnesians to fortify the Isthmus of Corinth, and the Athenians to repair their walls for the first time since 86 BC. Then the Borani sailed across the Black Sea and unsuccessfully attacked Pityous, but took it and Trapezus on a second raid. It was probably soon after this that Gregorius, now back as bishop of Neocaesarea, wrote his *Canonical Epistle*, the most vivid testimony to the social turmoil caused by the invasion. Writing probably to a neighbouring bishop, he lays down how to treat virgins raped by the barbarians, and how to deal with those who, despoiled by the enemy, had robbed others to compensate themselves, who had kept as slaves persons taken by the barbarians, who had joined the enemy and shown them their way, or who had kept booty left behind by them on their retreat.

A few years later a band of Goths marched down the west coast of the Black Sea, crossed the Straits and sacked and burned the prosperous cities of Bithynia. Turned back finally only by the accident of a swollen river, they departed with boats and wagons loaded with spoil. A few years after that, perhaps in 262/3, a further Gothic invasion reached the great cities of Asia, and burnt the temple of Artemis at Ephesus. It was perhaps on this occasion that the Goths besieged the city of Side in Pamphylia and were repulsed after heavy fighting.

About 267 the tribe of Heruli sailed from the Crimea in 500 ships, took Byzantium, sailed through the Straits, ravaged the islands of Lemnos and Scyros, and, reaching Greece, burned Athens, Corinth, Sparta and Argos and overran the Peloponnese. For these events we have some remaining fragments of the account by the Athenian historian and local office-holder, Herennius Dexippus, who himself led the resistance in Attica with a force of 2,000 men, and actually succeeded in inflicting a defeat on the barbarians; Dexippus' history of the Gothic and Scythian invasions in the third century included, as we know from one of the few surviving fragments, his own speech urging his men to defend their land.[12]

All this was, as Dexippus makes clear, after Athens itself had been sacked. Excavations have shown how the buildings round the Agora were burned and destroyed.[13] The kitchen of a house near the Agora was found to be filled with a mass of utensils, lamps, glassware, the skeleton of a donkey evidently driven in for protection, and a group of coins of which the latest date to near the end of Gallienus' reign (268). The destruction of buildings was carried further by the fact that the Athenians used masonry blocks from them to build a protective wall round a restricted area to the north of the Acropolis. The magnificent architectural complex of classical Athens was thus irrevocably destroyed. Yet on the protective wall itself we find verses with classical allusions inscribed by Athenians who helped to build it, and about the same time the Areopagus, council and people sanctioned the erection of a statue of Dexippus by his sons, whose dedication mentions his offices and priesthoods in Athens, his historical works, and only in passing his military prowess. Athens was to remain a centre for rhetoric and philosophy in the fourth century.

In the same years occurred the worst disasters on the eastern frontier. Shapur records in his inscription how, provoked by a Roman attempt on Armenia, he invaded Syria and captured a long list of cities. The date is obscure. But it seems that Dura-Europus fell in 256, and it was perhaps then that Shapur, as he records, took the great city of Antioch. Various sources have, with different details, the story of how Shapur was brought to Antioch by a renegade councillor from there, Mariades, who had been accused of corruption. It is perhaps at this moment that we should locate the famous incident narrated in the fourth century by Libanius and Ammianus Marcellinus: the people of Antioch were in the theatre when a comic actor on the stage shouted, 'If I'm not dreaming, there are the Persians!' They turned round and saw behind them the Persian archers.

Valerian now (perhaps 256/7) came to the East, re-took and rebuilt Antioch, and advanced against the Persians. What happened is best told in the words of Shapur: 'In the course of the third campaign, when we had attacked Carrhae and Edessa, Valerian Caesar came against us . . . (with) 70,000 men. And beyond Carrhae and Edessa we fought a great battle against Valerian Caesar, and we took Valerian Caesar with our own hands, and as for the others, the *Praefectus*, senators and officers who held command in the army, we took them and deported them to Persia. And the province of Syria and the province of Cilicia and the province of Cappadocia we burned with fire, and devastated, and made the people captive, and seized.'[13a]

Valerian was captured probably in 260, and the rock-cut sculpture at Naqsh-i-Rustam shows him kneeling before Shapur. While his son Gallienus was occupied in the West, much territory in the East was recovered by the generals Callistus and Macrianus. They, however, renounced allegiance to Gallienus, and proclaimed as Emperors the two sons of Macrianus, Macrianus and Quietus. The rising was quickly crushed, on the one hand at a battle in the Balkans won by a general of Gallienus, on the other by a new power in the politics of the East, Odenathus of Palmyra.

Since the early first century the great trading city of Palmyra in the Syrian desert had been closely linked with Rome, visited by Roman commanders since AD 17, garrisoned after the campaigns of Lucius Verus in 162–6.[14] The site, with its porticoed main street nearly 1,000 yards in length, its great temple of Bel, its sculptures showing sometimes heavily veiled women, sometimes men and women in costumes richly ornamented with jewels, is one of the most magnificent in the Roman world. Its inscriptions in Greek and Palmyrene (a dialect of Aramaic) testify to the dual nature of the local culture. Palmyrene auxiliary units served in the Roman army, and at some time in the first half of the third century the city had been granted the rank of a Roman *colonia*. Septimius Severus (193–211) had given the Roman citizenship to a leading Palmyrene, Odenath son of Hairan, son of Vahballath, son of Nasor. It was his grandson, Septimius Odenathus, now a Roman senator and ex-consul, who about 260 attacked the forces of Shapur and received from Gallienus, if he did not already have, the title of 'Corrector of all the Orient'; he also assumed a title which belonged in a different tradition, 'King of Kings'. In the following years he helped to suppress the revolt of Callistus and Macrianus, and seems to have fought two campaigns against Shapur, advancing as far as Ctesiphon, before dying in 267 or 268. His son Vahballath then succeeded to the titles of *Corrector* and 'King of Kings', but then in 270, backed by his mother Zenobia, went further and called himself *consul*, *dux Romanorum* and *imperator*. Palmyrene forces occupied Egypt, and Asia Minor as far as Ancyra in Galatia; in 271 Vahballath became 'Augustus' and Zenobia 'Augusta'. In 272 Aurelian finally marched East, and after fighting in Syria took Palmyra and its rulers; an uprising of the Palmyrenes in the following year was quickly suppressed.

Our best evidence for events in Syria in this period relates to the career of the heretical bishop of Antioch, Paul of Samosata. Elected bishop in 260, he scandalized the orthodox by preaching the unity of God and the manhood of Christ. A synod of bishops from Syria, Egypt and Asia Minor met at Antioch perhaps in 264 and made him promise to amend his teaching. When he did not do so, another synod of some eighty bishops met there about 269, were addressed by an Antiochene Christian with the Syrian name of Malchion, head of a school of rhetoric, and deposed Paul. Eusebius' *Ecclesiastical History* contains extracts from the letter written by the synod to the bishops of Rome and Alexandria. It describes how from poverty he made a fortune by bribery, how he conducted himself as a *procurator* rather than a bishop (see Ch. 4), gave shows to impress the congregation, demanded acclamations like those of the theatre, and had hymns in his honour sung at Easter. Finally they had to petition Aurelian to have him removed; Aurelian duly ruled that the church of Antioch should be the preserve of those in correspondence with the bishop of Rome and Italy. It has been supposed, without certain evidence, that Paul was a protégé of Palmyra. The incident is far more significant as the first occasion on which the Church asked the Emperor to intervene in its affairs.[15]

The campaigns of Aurelian (270–5) restored, except in Dacia and on the Rhine, the frontiers of the Empire. Further invasions were to follow. In 275 Goths from the north of the Black Sea ravaged all Asia Minor across to Cilicia, and were then defeated by Tacitus. The reign of Probus saw a brief military revolt in Syria, and a serious rising of Isaurian mountain tribes in southern Asia Minor, which involved the Roman forces in a full-scale siege of Cremna in Pisidia. But the military history of the East in this period ends with the triumphant invasion of Persia by Carus in 283, which reached Ctesiphon and compelled the new king, Varahran II, to make peace.

12

The Balkan and Danubian Provinces

Of all the areas of the Roman Empire, the provinces which stretched from the Black Sea to the Alps and Southern Germany offer by far the least information, by far the least possibility of understanding the nature of daily life or the course of social development. We do not have a single literary work written by someone living in this area between the 'Lamentations' and 'Letters from the Pontus' of the poet Ovid, exiled at Tomi (Constanza) from AD 9 to his death in 17 or 18, and the theological works of Victorinus, bishop of Poetovio (Pettau), who was martyred in 303/4. Furthermore, only the Greek cities of the Black Sea coast, and to a lesser extent Thrace, also Greek-speaking, produce extensive inscriptions which individually illuminate life in the area. For the rest we are left with a large number of minor inscriptions, useful mainly for nomenclature and references to institutions, and archaeological material. Especially since the last war, archaeological work has been carried on with considerable vigour in Eastern Europe; but no city has yet been fully excavated, and none could compare anyway with the great cities of Asia Minor, Syria or Africa.

A number of reasons, none the less, make this one of the most significant areas of the Empire. Roman rule was substantially established here only in the reign of Augustus (31 BC–AD 14), and did not reach its fullest extent until 106, with the conquest of Dacia, which was lost again about 271. It was imposed on a Celtic, Illyrian and Thracian population which, in spite of long contact and trade with the Mediterranean area, still seems to have largely retained its tribal structure and customs.

221

Our evidence for native society in this period is, however, almost negligible; we have no documents in languages other than Greek and Latin, and only the persistence of native personal names to indicate that other languages were in use; inscriptions indicate that non-urbanized tribes survived, but there is nothing beyond some native pottery, and, especially in Pannonia, portrayals of native dress on tombstones, to help us visualize their way of life. Greek culture was firmly established on the west coast of the Black Sea, where the earliest Greek settlements dated back to the seventh century BC, and in the client-kingdom of Thrace, finally annexed in 46. Elsewhere there was a steady development of Romanization during the period, largely the work of the Roman army, with its construction of roads and bridges, and its camps which attracted townships (*canabae*) of traders, and might either lead to the growth of *municipia* nearby or be transformed into *coloniae* when a legion moved on. The army also recruited men from these provinces, first into the auxiliaries then increasingly into the legions themselves, and discharged veterans, who settled either in groups as a *colonia* or singly, and in places formed a regular municipal aristocracy. It is also possible to trace on the one hand immigration by people from both Greek and Latin provinces, especially into Dacia after its conquest, and on the other the gradual abandonment of native names and local dress and the formation of urban communities on the Roman model.

The intimate connection between the Roman army and the life of these provinces resulted not only from the fact that they were newly conquered and still to be Romanized, but from the continual threat from the free barbarians beyond the Danube, manifest especially in inroads in 68–70, hostilities from the 80s to the conquest of Dacia, the Danubian wars of Marcus Aurelius between 166/7 and 180, and the prolonged invasions of 240–80. The consequence was the steady concentration of military force on the Danube, shifting the main weight of the legions to there from the Rhine (Ch. 6), and – with the growing tendency to recruit for the legions from the areas in which they were stationed – an increasing preponderance of men from these provinces in the most vital fighting forces of the Empire. These provinces, unlike Africa or Asia Minor, never enjoyed the prosperous city life which produced large numbers of men able to rise into the Roman equestrian or senatorial orders. But, via the army, they began suddenly in the third century to produce Emperors; Maximinus (235–8), a Thracian shepherd recruited into the auxiliary cavalry; Decius (249–51), Aurelian (270–5) and Probus (276–82), all allegedly from Sirmium in Pannonia Inferior; Claudius Gothicus (268–70) and Diocletian (284–305) from Dalmatia.

In AD 14 Roman rule of the area was just emerging from its formative stage – and had especially only just recovered from the great Pannonian and Dalmatian revolt of AD 6–9, which came near to endangering the continuance of the Empire itself. Raetia and the former kingdom of Noricum had been conquered in 16–15 BC and were now minor provinces ruled by *equites*. On the Magdalensberg in Noricum excavations have disclosed a busy trading centre of this period where traders came from many parts of the Mediterranean world to buy Norican iron ware; the shops there contain over three hundred inscriptions scratched on the walls giving details of names and purchases.[1]

Dalmatia, which under the name Illyricum had been under partial Roman control for nearly two centuries, was ruled by a senatorial *legatus* with two legions. Here the coastal strip, especially in the north, was substantially Romanized, with many immigrants from Italy, living in cities of colonial or municipal status; inland, Romanization had hardly begun. In Pannonia there were three legions, two still in the south-west, at Siscia and Poetovio, while the third moved to Carnuntum on the Danube about AD 15 (Ch. 6). In Moesia, which stretched along the lower Danube, Roman rule was only just established. The inhabitants are said to have paid tribute for the first time in the reign of Tiberius (14–37), and its defence still had to be assisted by forces from the client-kingdom of Thrace. Ovid, from his exile in Tomi, describes how Cotys of Thrace and a Roman force sent down the Danube had jointly defended the town of Aegisos against a Getic raid. His poems testify vividly to the insecurity of life on the Black Sea coast – the barbarians crossing the frozen Danube and carrying off beasts and captives from the fields, and the

223

inhabitants of Tomi, Ovid among them, rushing under arms to the walls at the sight of the enemy. Inside the old Greek colony little Greek was spoken, and that with a Getic accent. Getans and Sarmatians could be seen riding up and down the streets, and even the Greek inhabitants wore Getic trousers. Ovid claims that he learnt Getic and Sarmatian himself, and even wrote a poem in Getic on the apotheosis of Augustus. Even if Ovid is trying to arouse pity and gain his recall to Rome, his poems are still a unique testimony to the mingling of cultures and the harshness of life in a remote corner of the Empire.

The Thracian kingdom was in fact two kingdoms, the northern and southern, ruled by different members of a single royal house, who indulged in repeated strife until the annexation in 46. There were also other forms of strife – the tribes of the Geletae, Dii and Odrysae attacked Philippopolis (a Greek city founded three and a half centuries earlier by Philip of Macedon) in 21, and were driven off by Roman forces from Moesia, and Thracian royal troops. Five years later a revolt broke out among the barbarous Thracian mountain tribes, who feared that the national units they were accustomed to provide for local wars might be sent abroad as Roman *auxilia*; once again forces had to be sent from Moesia, and the war ended with a regular siege of a Thracian fortress.

When the kingdom was annexed by force in 46 it was placed under an equestrian procurator with 2,000 auxiliaries; under him were regional *strategoi*, or governors, an institution taken over from the kingdom. Such a hierarchy of regional governors was unknown in the Empire outside Egypt, and testifies to the primitiveness of the area and its lack of urban institutions. An inscription containing a dedication by thirty-three Thracian *strategoi* to an early procurator displays admirably the advancing Romanization of the Thracian upper classes; ten are still non-citizens, with mixed Greek and Thracian names, and of the rest, who are citizens, sixteen have taken a Roman name from Claudius (41–54), six from Gaius or a predecessor, one from someone unknown, and one from the procurator, M. Vettius Marcellus. Some of them are recognizably the sons of known *strategoi* of the regal period, and some have sons who were *strategoi* later in the century. Nothing shows more clearly how Rome could use and reward a local aristocracy.[2]

Romanization was pushed forward. Claudius established a veteran colony at Aprum, Vespasian another at Deultum; an inscription records the construction under Nero of hostelries and guard-posts along the military roads throughout the province. Trajan (98–117) transformed the administrative structure of Thrace into something resembling that of other provinces, founding seven new Greek cities, mostly named after himself or members of his family, on sites which may previously have been tribal capitals. The 'strategiai', originally fifty, seem to have been sharply reduced in consequence; only fourteen seem to have survived in the mid-second century.

Roman power in Moesia was meantime confirmed and extended. The *legatus* of Moesia in 57–67, Plautius Silvanus Aelianus, operated well beyond the Danube, bringing the Greek city of Tyra at the mouth of the Dniester under Roman control, defeating the Sarmatians (see Ch. 16), repelling the Scythians from the client-kingdom of the Bosporus (Crimea) and – a portent of the future – settling 100,000 'Transdanubians' on Moesian soil. He was also the first to send corn to Rome from the mouth of the Danube. Another side of the activities of Roman governors in Moesia is illustrated by a long Greek and Latin inscription from Histria on the Black Sea coast; it contains letters written to the cities by four governors between about 47 and 57, mainly concerned with a dispute between the city and the collectors of the import toll. The question turned on where the boundaries of the city territory lay, and the document begins with a statement establishing the boundaries made by the *legatus* of 100, Laberius Maximus. We find Plautius Silvanus Aelianus writing, '. . . You ask me also to preserve your rights at Peuce undiminished. For my part I am so far from diminishing any of those rights which have been long guarded for you that I should like to find new ways of honouring an ancient Greek city which is devoted to the Emperor and scrupulous in its dealings with ourselves.' We also have a detail, rare in official documents, about the economy of the city; Flavius Sabinus (50–7) writes that the revenue of the city is almost entirely derived from pickled fish.[3]

Roman city life began to appear now in the unurbanized central provinces. In Noricum five *municipia* were established under Claudius, and another under Vespasian. One of the Claudian foundations, Virunum near Klagenfurt, has been extensively excavated, and reveals a typical rectangular shape some 1,000 by 600 metres, with streets with lined underground drains separating the blocks of *insulae*, a forum with basilica, and a Capitol on artificially raised ground. In Pannonia the first colony, of veterans and Italian civilians, was established in about 15 at Emona, on the actual site of the camp which the legion *XV Apollinaris* vacated to move to Carnuntum. Another colony was founded by Claudius, and two more colonies and three *municipia* under the Flavians (69–86).

The second half of the first century was a disturbed period on the Danube, with incursions by the Sarmatians and Dacians during the civil wars of 68–70, and then serious fighting, stretching from the 80s to the conquest in 106, against the new power of Dacia (Ch. 15). The result, as detailed in Chapter 6, was the division of Moesia into two provinces in 86, and of Pannonia about 107, and the establishment of all the legions in the area in camps along the Danube, from Vindobona (Vienna) to Troesmis near the mouth. In Moesia there was also some scattered urban development: Scupi, far to the south near the Macedonian border, became a *colonia* in the Flavian period, as did Ratiaria and Oescus on the Danube under Trajan (98–117). Trajan also founded two new Greek cities in Moesia Inferior, Nicopolis and Marcianopolis, as he did in Thrace (which was now placed under a senatorial *legatus*). But in Moesia Romanization was always limited; four *municipia* at most are attested in Moesia Inferior, all of them in the military zone along the Danube.[4]

The final conquest of the kingdom of Dacia brought a vast booty of gold, silver, cattle, arms and prisoners. Paradoxically, Romanization, at least as regards formal institutions, was more intensive here than in the longer-established provinces on the other side of the Danube. The legion *XIII* was stationed at Apulum in the centre of the province, and as early as 108 we find a road being built from there up to Porolissum in the North. Sarmizegethusa became a *colonia*, established near but not on the site of the former capital. It displays the usual features of a Roman town, including a forum and amphitheatre; the military influence on its construction is, however, shown in the building for the *Augustales* (local priests of the Imperial cult), which seems to be modelled on the headquarters-building of a legionary camp.

One of the major attractions of Dacia was its gold mines, and among the immigrants from the Danubian provinces, Italy and Asia Minor attested in Dacia we find also the Dalmatian tribe of Pirustae, apparently transferred by Trajan to work the gold mines of Verespatak (Vicus Pirustarum – village of the Pirustae). These mines have provided some of the most interesting documents of the Roman period in central Europe, a series of wax tablets dating between 131 and 167, and concerned with such things as loans of money, the sale of half a house, the purchase of a female slave by a soldier of the legion stationed at Apulum, or a contract for hire between a labourer (who is illiterate and has the document written for him) and the lessee of a mine shaft. The tablets are in Latin, as are all the documents (except a few in Greek) from Dacia; only a few Dacian names appear.[4a] None the less, it is clear from other evidence, the unbroken occupation of farm steadings, the survival of native pottery or the continuance of burial customs, that – as one would expect – there was a substantial element of continuity in the forms of Dacian life through the period of the Roman conquest.

The same was clearly true in Pannonia, Noricum and Dalmatia. From Noricum and Pannonia we have carvings on grave-monuments showing people in native dress, especially women, who are shown wearing soft round caps, sometimes covered with a veil or wimple, large fur hats or a high round hat with a veil draped over it, thus very strongly resembling some forms of medieval dress.[5] In Pannonia and Dalmatia we have evidence on inscriptions of communities which continued into the second century to be known by their tribal names, such as in Pannonia the Azali, or the Eravisci who lived near the legionary camp of Aquincum, which became a *municipium* under Trajan; their areas are characterized by grave monuments showing people in native dress, sometimes adorned with a star, probably a symbol of Celtic origin. Similarly, most of Dalmatia beyond the coastal strip remained the territory of tribes such as the Iapodes or Mazaei; like the Pannonian tribes, they tended to be ruled by Roman military officials later replaced by civilians, often from the more Romanized aristocracy of the tribe itself.

Roman rule undoubtedly produced a cleavage between, on the one hand, those who were either integrated in Graeco-Roman society or who held official positions and on the other the lower classes, especially the peasants. We see this cleavage for instance in a couple of sentences with which the Greek orator Aelius Aristides describes a journey through southern Thrace in the mid-second century. After complaining of the vile weather, he says, 'There were no soldiers on messenger service to escort us . . . (so) I sought out guides myself, wherever necessary, and that was far from easy. For, barbarians that they were, they tried to get out of it, and had to be dragged out sometimes by persuasion and sometimes by force.' Much the same situation is reflected in a document from the territory of Histria at the mouth of the Danube; this dates probably to the mid-second century, and is a petition from the inhabitants of a village called Chora Dagei to the governor of Moesia Inferior complaining of the burdens and demands for services imposed on them because they live near a public road, and threatening to abandon their village if there is no remission.[6] But the fullest and most important document of this sort from the area, closely parallel to those from Asia Minor (Chs. 5, 11) is the petition from the villagers of Skaptopara in Thrace to the Emperor Gordian in 238 – which they were able to present through a fellow-villager who was a soldier in the Praetorian cohorts. They describe how they live in a village with hot springs two miles from a place where a market was held for fifteen days each year. People attending the market would come and force the villagers to provide for them without payment, as would soldiers travelling past on the road. Moreover, both the senatorial governors and the Imperial procurators of Thrace were in the habit of staying in the village to take the waters. This, they are careful to say, they do not mind, but repeated requests to have exactions by other persons stopped had had no lasting effect. So they ask the Emperor to intervene, saying that the number of householders in the village has already dropped, and threatening to decamp altogether if abuses did not end. Gordian tells them to put the matter before the provincial governor.

One type of measure which might be taken to relieve such conflicts is illustrated by a long Greek inscription of 202 about the establishment of a *statio* (staging-point) or *emporion* (market) on the road between Philippopolis and Hadrianopolis in Thrace. The procedure was to invite people from the neighbouring villages to settle there on the promise of exemption from the levying of corn, the supplying of guards and watchmen, and from transport service (exemptions which themselves indicate the normal lot of Thracian peasants). The function of the settlement, which was also to have a military garrison, was presumably to provide for passing soldiers. The inscription gives the names of 181 settlers. Thracian names predominate, with a strong mixture of Greek and a few Latin; less than ten of them seem to be Roman citizens.[7]

The uneven social development of the area may partially explain the persistence of brigandage, especially noticeable in the second century. References to brigands (*latrones*) may of course mean genuine social disaffection, or merely the persistence of unsettled mountain tribes. But gravestones from Salona on the Dalmatian coast, from Moesia Superior and from Dacia, especially the *municipium* of Drobeta, record people killed by bandits. Then it is recorded that Marcus Aurelius recruited brigands from Dalmatia and Dardania (the southern part of Moesia Superior) to fight in the Marcomannic war; and in about 175 or 176 an inscription records that regular Roman detachments were fighting brigands on the borders of Macedonia and Thrace.

The barbarian invasions and prolonged fighting under Marcus Aurelius (Ch. 6) had serious, though not permanent, effects on the Danubian provinces. Some evidence of insecurity even earlier is afforded by coin hoards from the 140s, 150s and especially 160s, mainly in Pannonia but also in Dacia and Noricum. From the period of the wars themselves there are substantial traces of destruction in Raetia, in Noricum, where for instance the town of Solva was burnt, and especially in Pannonia, where there was widespread damage in military camps, in towns such as Aquincum and Carnuntum, and in farmsteads. The tablets from Verespatak in Dacia, ending in 167, were apparently buried in view of an invasion. In Moesia Inferior the Greek city of Callatis was constructing or repairing walls in the early 170s, perhaps as a result of the Costoboccan raid which reached as far as Greece (Ch. 11). When the war ended temporarily in 175, the Quadi, Marcomanni and Iazyges returned 100,000 captives; the barbarians themselves demanded land, and unknown numbers of them were settled by Marcus in Moesia, Pannonia, Dacia, Thrace and even Italy. The war had also shown the inadequacy of the Roman defences on the upper Danube, and Raetia and Noricum now received a legion each, and were governed by senatorial *legati*. Some fighting continued in the 180s, and a series of inscriptions from the Danube bank in Pannonia Inferior under Commodus (180–92) attests the erection of watch-towers and guardposts to prevent secret crossing by 'brigands'. – which here means the barbarians.

The considerable damage and loss of life in these years did not halt the steady progress of Romanization and economic development. On the evidence available, it was in the late second and early third centuries that the local population in Pannonia began to erect villas of Italian type, and did so increasingly into the fourth century; the invasions of the 270s seem to have produced the first fortified villas.[8] A parallel development can be seen in a recently-excavated villa at Kolarovgrad in Moesia Inferior, constructed in luxurious style in the mid-second century, and fortified in the mid-third. From the towns, we have, for instance, a fragment of the constitution of the *municipium* of Lauriacum (Lorch) under Caracalla (211–17). From Solva, evidently recovered from the barbarian devastation, we have an Imperial rescript – the only one known from all the central European provinces – given by Severus and Caracalla in 205 on the privileges of the guild of *centonarii*, or firemen.

230

The rescript is followed by a list of ninety-seven members of the guild, of whom about half are Roman citizens; only sixteen Celtic names appear. The appearance of Imperial rescripts or letters among the inscriptions of a provincial town can be taken as a significant indication that the area is claiming an equal place among the regions of the Empire. It is noteworthy therefore that from Tyra at the mouth of the Dnieper we have a letter from Severus and Caracalla confirming the city's immunity from the *portorium*; they refer also to earlier letters sent by Antoninus Pius (138–61) and Marcus Aurelius and Verus (161–9). From Trajan's foundation Nicopolis in Moesia Inferior we have another letter from Severus replying to a congratulatory decree sent by the city on the occasion of a victory, and acknowledging their holding of a public festival to celebrate the news, and a contribution of cash sent by them.

Of all the cities in these provinces the best known are perhaps Carnuntum and Aquincum (Budapest) on the Danube. Both grew up in the neighbourhood of military camps, both were made *municipia* by Hadrian (117–38) and *coloniae* by Severus (193–211). At Carnuntum, while the remains of the camp two miles away have been fully exposed, the civil town has been only partially excavated.[9] But enough has been done to reveal that towards the end of the first century wooden houses gave place to stone, and that the town, once it had become a *municipium*, had an amphitheatre for 13,000 people, with seats reserved for the *Augustales*, baths and a huge building of several floors, with a colonnaded court, central heating and mosaic floors; its purpose is still unclear, but it may have been the residence of the governor of Pannonia Superior. A second, smaller, amphitheatre was built just outside the camp, probably in the late second century, by a town-councillor of Carnuntum, C. Domitius Zmaragdus, who originated from Antioch in Syria.

Something of the history of the town is revealed, for instance, by the excavation of a house there which was evidently burnt in the Marcomannic wars, then rebuilt slightly enlarged – the mosaic floors of the second period lie over a layer of burnt material – was altered again possibly in the third century, and remained in occupation until the late fourth. It is of some significance that even a town house such as this was not modelled on the Italian *atrium* house, but was of a type peculiar to Pannonia – probably derived from local farm houses -- with an open verandah on the front and a central corridor running back with rooms opening on either side.

Aquincum was similarly a double settlement, a legionary camp established in the late first century, a 'military town' immediately round it, with an amphitheatre larger than any other north of the Alps, and a civil settlement some two kilometres to the north where the first buildings appeared about AD 50 (when there was only an auxiliary unit at Aquincum); an amphitheatre was built here also about AD 150, and a town wall probably at the end of the century. Excavations in the civil settlement have revealed for instance a round Celtic temple of the type known in Gaul and Britain (Ch. 8), and near it a poor quarter with houses of one to four rooms; and on the other hand four or five shrines of Mithras. The most distinctive find from Aquincum is perhaps the portable organ with a bronze plate inscribed with the statement that it had been presented in 228 to the guild of firemen by a prefect of the guild, who was also a town-councillor of the *colonia*.[10]

Broadly speaking, it is only in places such as these, which had a long connection with the Roman army, in Noricum, which had had substantial trade connections with Italy since the first century BC, and on the coast of the Adriatic and the Black Sea, that we find anything that closely approaches the city life characteristic of most other parts of the Empire. From the Greek cities of the Black Sea coast, however barbarous the area might have seemed to Ovid, we find in the second century documents which would not have been out of place in the cities of Asia Minor. In Tomi itself, for instance, the council and people set up an inscription in honour of a man with a Roman-Greek name, T. Cominius Claudianus Hermophilus, who was a sophist, president of games, president of the league of six cities on the Pontic coast, and High Priest of the Imperial cult. In Histria a similar inscription, also from the second century, honours a woman called Aba, the descendant of distinguished local citizens who had held a variety of local offices, and who herself had acted as Priestess of the Phrygian cult of the Mother of the Gods, taking its expenses on herself; she had also, among other things, made a cash distribution to the town-councillors and others in the city. It is evident from this and other evidence that these cities possessed something like the rich landed bourgeoisie who dominated city life in the other Greek areas. The vigour of city life is shown by the determination with which, as we shall see, cities like Tomi or Marcianopolis or Philipopolis were to resist barbarian attacks in the third century. City life was to continue on the coast of the Black Sea long into the late Roman age; the urban civilization of the Greek part of Moesia provides a striking contrast with the very limited development of the Latin-speaking part further inland.

In Dacia the comparative strength of Romanization was shown by the fact that after the abandonment of the province in 271 (see below) urban life continued in the main centres, though in much reduced circumstances, until obliterated by the Huns in the fifth century. In Sarmizegethusa, for instance, the building of the *Augustales* was occupied as living quarters, and the amphitheatre converted as a defensive stronghold. Here and elsewhere, pottery and other archaeological evidence shows the survival of the forms and customs of the provincial period; and it is noticeable that the earliest evidence for Christianity (in the fourth century) is very largely limited to the surviving urban centres.[11]

Pannonia and Noricum also show some development of urban life and institutions. For instance, from the *colonia* of Mursa in Pannonia Inferior we have a second-century inscription recording that a town-councillor had commemorated his elevation to a local priesthood by building a row of fifty shops fronted by a colonnade, for the conduct of trade. From Carnuntum we have an inscription of 219 mentioning a man who was a councillor there and at the *colonia* of Savaria, High Priest of the Imperial cult of Pannonia Superior, and had also served as an equestrian officer in the Roman army. This area was also in increasingly close contact with the rest of the Roman world, especially with Gaul, regularly importing the Gallic pottery of the late first and second centuries. There was also immigration from other areas, and at Intercisa, for instance, apart from other settlers from the East, there was a Jewish community by the reign of Severus Alexander (222–35).

Immigration from the Greek East is especially noticeable also in the *colonia* of Salona on the coast of Dalmatia, which unlike the other cities of that coast, seems to have enjoyed an upsurge of prosperity in the third century; Christianity was established here certainly by the second half of the third century. This century saw also a certain development of Romanization in the hitherto largely tribal areas of inland Dalmatia.

Thus in the Latin provinces of central Europe there evolved a significantly Romanized provincial society with, at least until the end of the second century, substantial areas still inhabited by tribal communities. How such a provincial culture appeared to a Romanized Greek from Asia Minor is best seen in the description of the Pannonians given by the historian Cassius Dio, *legatus* of Pannonia in 226–8. 'The Pannonians dwell near Dalmatia along the bank of the Danube from Noricum to Moesia, and live of all men the most wretchedly. Both their soil and their climate is poor; they cultivate no olives and produce no wine except to a very slight extent and of a very poor quality, since the climate is mostly extremely harsh. They not only eat barley and millet but drink liquids made from them. None the less they are considered the bravest of all men. For having nothing to make a civilized life worthwhile, they are extremely fierce and bloodthirsty . . .'

Dio's remarks point to the most important role of the Danubian provinces in the Empire, the recruitment of their populations into the army, first as auxiliaries, then into the legions themselves. In the second and third centuries men recruited into the legions along the Danube and in Dacia came primarily from the province in which each legion was stationed and secondarily from the other Danubian provinces. Once in the army, they tended to retain their uncivilized manners. When Septimius Severus, after his march on Rome from Carnuntum in 193, replaced the largely Italian Praetorian soldiers with men from the Danube area, the result, according to Cassius Dio, was to fill Rome with a mixed crowd of soldiers savage in appearance, fearsome in speech and barbarous in manner. But, however distasteful such soldiers were to the civilized inhabitants of the Mediterranean, it was they and their native provinces that bore the brunt of the fighting which preserved the Empire in the third century. As an orator put it, addressing the Emperor Maximian (from Sirmium) in 289, 'Who can doubt that for many years, since its vigour was absorbed in the Roman name, while Italy has been mistress of the world from its ancient glory, Pannonia has been that by its valour? . . . And I shall recite how you were brought up and educated in that frontier region, that seat of the bravest legions, amid the manoeuvres of the soldiery and the clash of arms, whose sound mingled with your infant cries.'

By contrast, these provinces produced only a very few men of equestrian rank, outside the army, and hardly any senators. Raetia, Dacia and Moesia produced not a single holder of a civilian equestrian post that we know of until one from Moesia Inferior in the late third century. Noricum and Dalmatia each produced two equestrian officials known to us in the second century, and Pannonia three. One of these was Valerius Maximianus, the son of a local magnate and priest at Poetovio in Pannonia Superior, who after a long series of equestrian military and governatorial posts during the wars of Marcus Aurelius, was promoted into the Senate; he is thus one of the few examples from this area of what is so common elsewhere, the rise of local aristocracies into the Senate. For the rest, we have an inscription mentioning a couple of brothers from Pannonia who entered the Senate, and possible cases of senators from Moesia Inferior and Noricum.

Only Dalmatia – and then only the coastal cities – provides any fuller evidence. From the *colonia* of Aequum came Sex. Minicius Faustinus Cn. Julius Severus, suffect consul in 127, governor of Britain and commander in the Jewish war under Hadrian (Ch. 11), and also Cn. Julius Verus, consul in 153, presumably from the same family. The island of Arba on the northern Dalmatian coast provides one case where the rise of a family can be traced. We know of a centurion of the late first and early second century, Q. Raecius Rufus, who married the daughter of a municipal magistrate there; half a century later a senator called Raecius Rufus had property at Arba, and in 166 was *curator* of public buildings in Rome. Beyond that we have only the third-century Emperors already mentioned; the lack of documentation in this period does not allow us to decide whether they were striking exceptions, or whether significant numbers of men from these provinces entered the equestrian and senatorial orders in these years.

The barbarian invasions of the mid-third century began with an attack by the Alamanni about 233 against the upper Danube and Rhine, warded off by Severus Alexander (222–35) and, after his murder on the Rhine, by his successor, Maximinus, who then moved to Sirmium, where he remained in 236–8 and seems to have fought against the Sarmatians. In 238 there was an invasion by the Carpi and perhaps Goths on Moesia Inferior, which led to the destruction of Histria. In the 240s further attacks by the Carpi and other tribes were directed from the Wallachian plain, left unoccupied by Rome (Ch. 6), against south-east Dacia and Moesia Inferior. The Dacian cities of Romula and Sucidava were fortified at this period, while the nearby site of Cioroiul Nou shows extensive destruction followed by construction of fortifications on the ruins of previous houses.[12] At the same period widespread coin hoards in Moesia and Thrace reflect further barbarian attacks, possibly that of about 248 which left traces of destruction near Nicopolis and led to the siege of Marcianopolis in Moesia Inferior, whose inhabitants, as the contemporary Athenian historian Dexippus (Ch. 11) records, successfully resisted. In the reign of Decius (249–51) a Gothic invasion reached as far as Philippopolis in Thrace. Dexippus states that Decius, alarmed at the possibility of revolution if the inhabitants took too vigorously to arms, wrote a letter which the governor of Thrace, Priscus, read out in the stadium, urging them to show caution. They too, however, successfully beat off repeated attacks (archaeological evidence suggests that some suburbs of the city were now burnt), but were eventually taken. Decius himself came to Thrace and, after at least one defeat, ejected the barbarians from there and, it seems, Moesia and Dacia (an inscription of 250 from Apulum honours him as the 'restorer of Dacia'). But in a renewed Gothic attack he was killed in 251 at the battle of the Abrittus in Moesia Inferior. Further Gothic attacks, evidently through Moesia and Thrace, reached Thessalonica in perhaps 253 and Bithynia in about 256 (Ch. 11).

Thereafter little is known until 258–60, when a Sarmatian attack, reflected in numerous coin hoards, reached Pannonia, while the Alamanni attacked Noricum and Raetia. All the land between the upper Danube and Rhine was lost, and in Raetia there is evidence of a contraction of towns behind defensive walls comparable to that in Gaul.[13] Later literary sources state that Pannonia was ravaged, but add no reliable detail.

Then, about 267, the Heruli attacked Tomi and were driven off, as they were from Marcianopolis, and then took to the sea, eventually reaching Greece (Ch. 11). In 268 Claudius (268–70) won a great victory over the Goths at Naissos in Moesia, and forced the remnant of the invaders to submit, settling some on the land and recruiting others into the army. But raids and fighting continued, and about 271 Aurelian (270–5) abandoned the province of Dacia, and formed two new provinces carved out of central Moesia and northern Thrace, Dacia Ripensis along the Danube, and Dacia Mediterranea to the south, with its capital at Serdica (Sofia).[14] Somewhat surprisingly, the prosperous towns of central and northern Dacia seem to have suffered no attacks (none of them was fortified in this period), but to have been abandoned for strategic reasons, namely the insecurity of south-east Dacia.

In Pannonia there seems to have been comparative peace in the 260s; an inscription shows for instance that the baths of the legionary camp at Aquincum were restored after long disrepair in 268. About 270, however, came a major invasion of Iuthungi, Vandals, Suebi and Sarmatians, which penetrated as far as Italy. Aurelian (270–5) came to Pannonia and, after a drawn battle, forced the barbarians to sue for peace. Some surviving fragments of Dexippus (partly quoted in Ch. 3) show Aurelian parleying with the Iuthungi, and dealing with a peace embassy from the Vandals; they offered hostages, and a force of 2,000 cavalry for service with Rome, and retired across the Danube, being assigned – like the barbarian enemies of a century before – a fixed point for trade. Sporadic raiding continued, but was contained by the Roman forces.

From the reign of Probus (276–82) we have the information that he settled Bastarnae, and also Goths, in Thrace, and then had considerable difficulty in keeping them under control. His successor Carus (282–3) won a victory over the Sarmatians and Quadi on his way to the East – and fighting on the Danube was to continue unabated under Diocletian.

The Balkan and Danubian provinces thus remained relatively uncivilized and unurbanized compared with the other areas of the Empire. Their relative backwardness is shown, for example, by the fact that Christianity is attested only at Salona (which was to be one of the great Christian centres of the fourth century) before 284. The great persecution of 303/4 was to reveal, however, that Christianity had by then a strong foothold in the Danube area. None the less, the very backwardness of the area was essential to its military role. The Balkans and Asia Minor were to be the core of the Byzantine Empire, a fact already fore-shadowed when a Dalmatian Emperor, Diocletian, established his capital at Nicomedia.

13

The Empire and the Third-Century Crisis

In discussing the nature of the crisis which the Roman Empire suffered in the third century, we are not discussing why the Empire fell. For the Empire did not fall. On the contrary, the Greek half of the Empire survived, though with steadily decreasing territory, until the fall of Constantinople in 1453. In the west and north there were, it is true, considerable losses of territory in the third century, that is Dacia and the land to the east of the Rhine and between the upper Rhine and Danube. But it was not until the fifth century that Goths, Burgundians, Franks, Vandals and others occupied in effect all the Roman territories in Western Europe and Latin North Africa. Even here, Roman civilization, as opposed to Roman rule, survived in large measure, and profoundly influenced the language, customs and culture of the barbarians. All these barbarians were converted to Christianity, though none perhaps before their actual settlement in Roman territory;[1] of the fifth-century invaders, only the Huns, who never settled within the Empire, remained permanently pagan and effectively uninfluenced by Roman culture.

The greatest difficulty in the analysis of the third-century crisis is to determine exactly what we are trying to analyse. In other words, what happened? What changes took place? Much of the difficulty is caused by one feature of the crisis itself, namely the great scarcity of literary, documentary and archaeological evidence from the period. Our narrative sources are reasonably full up to 238, and we have a considerable body of evidence for the period of Diocletian and Constantine, that is from 284 onwards.

But for the political history of the half-century in between we have to rely on brief and bare Latin histories of the second half of the fourth century, and later Greek chronicles. It is particularly noticeable that the fourth-century – probably late fourth-century – series of biographies of the Emperors from Hadrian (117–38) to Carus and Carinus (282–3), the *Historia Augusta*, which has a missing section from 244 to 260, becomes more and more fantastic and unreliable in dealing with the later Emperors.

The first step is to describe in order some reasonably certain aspects of the period. Firstly, there was the acute instability of the throne itself. Every Emperor from Caracalla in 217 onwards died by violence, and the average length of reign in the half-century from 235 onwards was two or three years. As shown in Chapter 3, the Empire never evolved any secure political framework or any satisfactory means of appointing Emperors other than *de facto* family dynasties of varying stability. The fact that the Emperors of this period were constantly in the field against foreign invaders meant that they were constantly exposed to attack by other generals, either in their immediate entourage or in command of other armies. Thus civil wars were about as common as wars. Moreover, separate régimes were established in Gaul between 258 and 274, and in Palmyra and the East for a few years up to 272.

Then there were the invasions by the barbarians and by Sasanid Persia. The fact that these began at approximately the same period seems to have been a pure coincidence. The very existence of the Roman Empire, however, was undoubtedly one cause of the barbarian movements, in that they were drawn to it in the hope of land and booty. Similarly, the Sasanians, having destroyed the decaying rule of the Parthians, at once challenged Rome by laying claim to all the territories ruled by the ancient Persians. When these developments coincided, the Empire was exposed to heavy attacks broadly simultaneously on the Rhine, Danube and in the East.

The direct effects of the invasions were naturally very different in different areas. In Gaul, and to some degree in Spain and in Raetia on the upper Danube, there is widespread evidence of the contraction and fortification of cities. How profound a change this brought in the patterns of social life can as yet only be guessed. It is certainly the case that the life of the cultured Gallo-Roman aristocracy of the late Empire was spent on their estates rather than in the towns. But in Britain too, which suffered no invasions in our period, the fourth century seems to have seen stagnation, perhaps decline, in the towns, but a development of luxurious villas.

Repeated invasions also came to the Danubian area and central Europe, reaching down to Macedonia, Greece and Asia Minor. Sasanian invasions, and briefly, the power of Palmyra, reached to central Asia Minor and the coast of Syria. These must have caused great destruction and loss of life; we also know of prisoners carried off to Mesopotamia by the Persians. We can date the beginning of fortified villas in the Danubian lands to this period, and have scattered archaeological evidence of destruction; but only at Athens (Ch. 11) is such evidence detailed and systematic. Once again we have little clear evidence of the direct effects of the invasions. They may not have been lasting; Antioch was taken by the Persians in 256 and 260, and burned – and in the fourth century, as we know from a wealth of evidence, was one of the greatest and most flourishing cities in the Greek world.

In Egypt and Africa there were border struggles, prolonged in Africa, but no actual invasions. The civil war of 238 in Africa (Ch. 9) and the suppression of a pretender in Alexandria about 272 (Ch. 10) may have had, at least temporarily, more serious effects.

Though the direct effects of the invasions and civil wars can only rarely be assessed satisfactorily in the present state of our evidence, we can take it that they accelerated, though may not have caused, some other changes in the workings of the State and its relations with the population. The first and most clearly traceable of these was debasement of the coinage and inflation of prices. The two chief coins were the silver *denarius* and the gold *aureus*, worth twenty-five *denarii*. Debasement affected mainly the *denarius*, which was reduced to 75% silver under Marcus Aurelius (161–80), and 50% under Severus (193–211); after Caracalla (211–17) had issued a *denarius* of one and a half times the previous size, presumed to have been worth two earlier *denarii*, the silver content sank rapidly, reaching 5% in the middle of the third century. Aurelian (270–5) issued two series of silver-plated copper coins, whose values are still much disputed. Meanwhile, the bronze *sestertius* (four to a *denarius*) continued both to be issued and to be used as a common means of expressing prices and other sums until the 270s, and then disappeared in the face of the inflation of prices.[2] The inflation itself can be shown by the fact that the price of corn (expressed now in the debased *denarii*) was some 200 times higher in 301 than it had been in the first century.

It cannot, however, be pretended that we understand yet the details of the coinage system, especially in the period 270–300, or even essential elements of the background such as how the Imperial or city mints obtained their bullion. There are also indications that there was confusion and complexity at the time; a Carian inscription of 209–11 lays down penalties for the illegal changing of money; a papyrus of 260 orders money-changers in Egypt to stop refusing Imperial coins; another of about 300, is a letter from an official in Egypt to a subordinate ordering him to spend all the official 'Italian money' at once, as the Emperors are about to halve its value.[3]

We cannot yet state the causes of the progressive debasement and inflation. But it in its turn must have been a factor in converting the demands of the State on its subjects from cash to goods and services in kind (Ch. 5). The basic pay in cash of the troops in fact, though raised successively (Ch. 6), was not raised enough to keep pace with inflation, and in the late fourth century disappeared in favour of other forms of payment.

The evidence for the increased pressure of exactions by troops and officials in the second and third centuries is matched by similar evidence for the rapid spread, especially from around AD 200, of guard-posts for police purposes manned by soldiers in the Roman provinces. Similarly, we have a fair amount of evidence for brigandage in this period in many areas of the Empire.[4] But there is nothing to show that this should be regarded as a coherent social movement; the conditions and causes for popular movements (social oppression, economic

difficulties) undoubtedly existed, but only the peasant movement of the Bagaudae in Gaul, which did not begin until about
the very last year of our period, clearly had such a character.
The revolt of the Isaurians under Probus (276–82) was something different, the activity of an unsubdued mountain tribe
taking the opportunity of troubled times to extend their normal
brigandage. In short, what we have evidence for generally is
brigandage as a symptom or result of the third-century troubles,
not a class-struggle as a motive factor. The diffusion of substantial numbers of soldiers in scattered guard-posts may,
however, have been a factor weakening military resistance to
external invasions.

Similarly, it has been supposed that as a result of the plagues,
which are indeed widely attested in the second and even more
in the third centuries, there was a decline in population leading
both to the abandonment of fertile land and an inability to
maintain the army.[5] But we have no figures whatsoever for the
total population at this or any period of the Empire. It is true
that barbarians were settled in Gaul, Thrace and other areas in
the third century, which might suggest empty lands – but this
had happened in the first and second centuries also. We also
find, for instance, Aurelian making the city councils responsible
for paying the tribute on deserted lands; but this in itself proves
only a greater urgency in taxation on the part of the State. We
have in fact no basis for any statements about overall population
under the Empire.

The central and irrefutable element in the evidence for a social
crisis in the third century is the almost universal absence of
evidence, either inscriptional or archaeological, for construction
and development in the cities. As has been shown in the accounts
of the various areas, such development in the cities went on
continuously almost everywhere in the first and second centuries.
What did the cessation mean? Inscriptions relate almost
entirely to public buildings, and their absence shows merely that
new public buildings were not constructed. But there is similarly
little to show construction of private town houses in this period.
The cessation was not directly caused by war or invasion, for it
is visible, for instance, from the end of the second century at

Ostia, from about the 230s in the relatively peaceful province of Africa. Does this show a general economic collapse – or is it simply that, speaking very generally, the cities simply remained static, but did not actually decay, during the third century? This seems to have been the case, for instance, at Verulamium in Britain. Even so, we still cannot explain satisfactorily why development ceased. It should be noted, however, that, for instance, in Pannonia the construction of country villas seems to have continued in the third century (though on the other hand most of the villas known from Britain suffered a cessation comparable to that of the towns). It may be at least that in some areas what happened in the third century was the beginning of that shift of luxurious living to the villas of the countryside which is visible in the fourth century. As such, it is consonant with the depression of the status of *decuriones* or *curiales* (town-councillors) as opposed to the great landowners outside the town-councils, which is also characteristic of the fourth century. But such generalizations must be taken as posing questions rather than final answers.

The standstill in city activity is paralleled in many of the great pagan cult-centres, where inscriptions cease in the middle of the century; for instance at Olympia the last inscription of a victor in the games dates to 261 (though the games themselves are known to have continued), the last cult inscription to 265.[6] But if the practice of the pagan cults partially failed – to be revived under Diocletian – pagan religion itself developed. Aurelian in 274 established the worship of the Sun-God as the chief cult of the Empire, creating *Pontifices* for the cult, building a temple in Rome, and issuing coins with the Sun portrayed as 'Lord of the Roman Empire'. This official act mirrored aspects of the monotheistic mysticism of the time, and was to influence the earlier religious outlook of Constantine. The most significant religious development was precisely the growth of philosophical systems in which the pagan cults and legends were reinterpreted in mystical terms as symbols of, or stages towards, a single reality. These developments took place entirely in the Greek half of the Empire. From the West, we have only a few scraps of pagan Latin literature in this century before the Gallic panegyrics of Emperors delivered in 289 and after. But the Greek world had not only a considerable historian, the Athenian Herennius Dexippus (Ch. 11), or the philologist and rhetorician Longinus, who taught at Athens and later moved to the court of Zenobia of Palmyra, but the whole neo-Platonic school, whose greatest representative was Plotinus. The vitality of the culture of the Greek world in this period – and the ease of communications, which survived barbarian attacks and economic troubles – is seen best in the life of Plotinus' chief disciple, Porphyry. A native of Tyre, born with the Syrian name of Malchos in 232/3, he was re-named Porphyry by Longinus under whom he studied in Athens. In 262/3 he went to Rome, where he became a pupil of Plotinus. Other pupils came from Italy, Alexandria, the Decapolis and Arabia. In 267/8 Porphyry retired to Lilybaeum in Sicily, whence he also corresponded with Longinus in Syria. Later, after the death of Plotinus, he returned to Rome, where his pupils included Iamblichus from Chalcis in Syria, who later returned to Syria and taught neo-Platonism at Apamea, with pupils from Syria, Greece and Cappadocia. Before his death, perhaps soon after 300, Porphyry had completed a vast series of philosophical, moral, even historical, works including writing the *Life* of Plotinus, and editing his *Enneads*. His works included also *Against the Christians* in fifteen books, a serious and effective critique, perhaps written about 300, both of the books of the Old and New Testaments and of Christian doctrine, which was to be widely influential in the following century.[7]

The continued vitality of Greek culture was not the only aspect of the third century which must qualify the notion that the period was marked only by 'crisis' and decay. As emphasized before in this book, it was then that the decisive steps were taken towards the detachment of the Imperial system from the framework of the Roman Republican institutions, and, concurrent with that, then that the political balance of the Empire shifted to the Greek provinces and the Danubian and Balkan area. Within the society of the Empire there were equally significant changes. One is the emergence, in different forms and in varying degrees, of local cultures. In Gaul non-classical styles appear in pottery and decorations, and perhaps in the representations of the local gods; in Phrygia we find inscriptions in the local language; in Edessa there appears, before the beginning of the century, the first Christian literature in a non-classical language, Syriac; in Egypt there came the first works in Coptic, even if most, perhaps all, were translations of Greek Christian texts. Moreover in the official art of the Empire itself there appeared the first signs of that abandonment of the traditional classical art-forms which was to lead to the development of the very different art of Byzantium. The essentially naturalistic representational art in the classical style, inherited from and modelled on the art of classical Greece, was still practised – as it was in some forms into the Byzantine period – and indeed enjoyed a brief but real renaissance under Gallienus (260–8). But the essential change is the appearance of some characteristic features of Byzantine art, with non-naturalistic representation of individual figures, sometimes portrayed with rigid frontality – as Septimius Severus is on the arch he erected at Lepcis Magna in 203 – and a grouping of figures in formal patterns. The traditional explanation of this change – which was of course too complex and varied to receive any real justice here – is that it represents the victory of oriental influences, that is of art-forms produced in the Parthian and then Sasanian area. That is possible, though our knowledge of art in the Parthian period is very slight. It is equally possible that what took place was a rise to respectability of native styles in art, hitherto repressed by the predominance of the taste of the educated bourgeoisie for the classical tradition. Such a development could well have been accelerated by economic difficulties and (as we must presume) frequent interruptions of trade; very broadly speaking, it is indeed characteristic of third-century sites in the Roman Empire that they reveal fewer imported objects than those of the earlier period. They tend to contain instead locally made objects, of generally a lower technical and artistic standard. In these circumstances there was perhaps the opportunity for some local art-forms to gain currency and affect the main stream of artistic style.

The most important social change in the period, however,

was the development of Christianity. The significant aspect of this development is not further geographical extension, though that took place, but in organization, both within the individual churches and in the contacts between them. In the first half of the third century we have the earliest evidence of private houses being converted for use as churches; of these the most striking, and most clearly dated, example is that at Dura-Europus (Ch. 11). In the second half of the century, there appeared, probably, the first buildings designed specifically as churches. Christian catacombs and cemeteries appear in Rome in the second century, and by the end of it some seem actually to have been owned by the Church. By the middle of the third century the church of Rome itself was a substantial organization. In a letter to Fabius, bishop of Antioch, Cornelius, bishop of Rome (251–3), mentions that in Rome there were forty-six priests, seven deacons, seven sub-deacons, forty-two acolytes, fifty-two exorcists, readers and watchmen, and more than 1,500 widows and poor persons receiving support.[8]

More important still were the developing organizational links between the churches, grouped round the great centres, Rome, Carthage and Antioch. Sixty Italian bishops met in Rome in 251 to condemn the heresy of Novatian. Seventy African bishops met perhaps about 220, eighty-five in 256. The synods at Antioch in about 264 and about 269 which condemned Paul of Samosata (Ch. 11) were attended by bishops from Cappadocia, Pontus, Cilicia, Palestine, Arabia and (but for the illness of Dionysius in 264) Alexandria. Their decision on the second occasion was communicated to Rome, Alexandria and to 'all the provinces'. It is not an accident that while the earlier Christian literature is primarily doctrinal, scholarly or apologetic, that of the second half of the third century is made up largely of the letters of bishops, of Rome, Carthage, Alexandria and Antioch, and concerned with questions of discipline and the coherence of the Church as an organization. The correspondence of Cyprian, bishop of Carthage 248/9–58 (Ch. 9), reaches to Spain, Gaul, Rome and Cappadocia. It appears also to have been in the second half of the third century – when, as mentioned, the pagan cults suffered a significant decline – that Christianity both spread to all parts of the Empire, and reached broad sections of the country population. The church councils of the early fourth century demonstrated that Christianity, though still not the religion of the majority, was firmly rooted in all parts of the Roman world.

The third century thus saw a prolonged political and military crisis, from which the Empire still emerged as a political unity with its frontiers largely intact. It saw in all parts of the Empire a virtual cessation of the development and embellishment of the cities characteristic of the first two centuries, and in some areas, especially Gaul, the contraction of cities to walled strong-points. There was a collapse of the currency, and with it a tendency for the State to demand goods and services rather than cash from its subjects. Both of these developments may have assisted towards the growth of the large estate as an important social unit, in which the owner both had increased legal claims on his tenants and was responsible for producing services (or recruits) for the State from the tenant population.

The crisis was real. But an account of it does not exhaust the significance of the third century. It was a period of transformation, indeed of vitality, even within pagan culture, with new art-forms, the evolution of mystical, ultimately monotheist, interpretations of the traditional religion, and the last great representative of pagan philosophy in the neo-Platonist, Plotinus. Within Christianity there was the first major scholar and theologian of the church, Origen; while the later third century doctrinal disputes sowed the seeds of the great struggles of the fourth century. But above all it was the period when the church suffered its first great conflicts with the pagan State, survived them, and developed itself as a social organization ready to wield authority in the affairs of the world. Even from our inadequate evidence, it is possible to discern that the third century was one of the crucial periods in the history of Europe.

14

Parthia and Sasanid Persia

The first century of our era was one of great changes in the Parthian state. Although evidence is fragmentary, and overwhelmingly from Greek or Latin authors, nonetheless we can infer the changes from even the sparse data at hand. By the first century the Parthians had passed from an active, offensive policy, which made them the heirs of the Seleucids, to a defensive position against Rome. The aristocracy had won a strong position at the expense of the central authority, which a century previously had been dominant. The process of change, of course, was long in duration, but only in the first century can one see the results of a manifold development. For example, the title in Greek, 'King of Kings', was used sporadically first by Mithradates II (*c.* 123–88 BC) and again by Mithradates III (*c.* 57–54 BC), but during and after the first century it is no longer of exceptional occurrence but a fixed title of the Parthian rulers.[1] Likewise the use of Parthian letters on the coinage, together with Greek, begins in the reign of Vologeses I (*c.* AD 51–80), probably the same monarch to whom the fourth book of the *Denkart*, a later Pahlavi work, attributes the assembly of scattered fragments of the Avesta.[2] Vologeses I also built a new capital for the Parthians, Vologesokerta, north of Seleucia on the Tigris. Furthermore, it is to the first century that we may attribute the reappearance in literary sources of the native names of Iranian cities in place of Greek names, such as Merv for Antiochia Margiane. Finally, the new ideology of the Parthian rulers as descendants of the Achaemenid Artaxerxes II, may be tentatively assigned to the first century BC. This last development seems to have been widely promulgated in the first century AD as an attempt to strengthen the central government against rebels and against would-be usurpers of the Arsacid throne.[3] The Parthians, of course, had good reasons to consider themselves heirs of the Achaemenids after Carrhae (54 BC) and the raids of Pacorus in Palestine and Syria (40–39 BC). But the need for an ideology of legitimacy and continuity from the past was emphasized especially in the first century AD when troubles, and the breakdown of the central power, led to changes.

The reign of Artabanus III (c. AD 12–38) is a convenient period to examine and briefly assess the political changes in the Parthian state. Artabanus was probably a minor ruler of Hyrcania, east of the Caspian Sea, rather than of Atropatene, west of the sea, as is sometimes supposed. In any case, he led a revolt against the Parthian king Vonones who had been sent to Rome by his father Phraates IV and had lived there for more than fifteen years before becoming king c. AD 7. After several years of fighting, Artabanus was victorious and entered the capital Ctesiphon about AD 12. His attempts to reassert the central authority of the Parthian state against the nobility were not very successful, as we see from the many revolts against him. Josephus (Ant. 18, 339) tells of the independent rule of two Jewish brothers in Mesopotamia from about AD 20–35, when the Parthian government was powerless to suppress their robber kingdom and had to recognize it. The instability of the throne was such that Artabanus had to flee to eastern Iran about 36, and a Roman nominee Tiridates III was able to seize power for a few months. Artabanus soon reclaimed the throne and ruled several years until his death, but rebellions continued, including one in the city of Seleucia on the Tigris, which led to the independence of the city for seven years.[4]

One need not describe the political events following the reign of Artabanus, for they are not only confused, but also bear witness to the great disturbances and civil wars within the Parthian state, which for a time was split into an eastern part under Gotarzes II and a western under Vardanes. We should turn our attention to the internal changes in the Parthian realm, always keeping in mind the political and military events which attest the turmoil of the times.

Since our primary sources for Parthian history are written in Greek or Latin, it is easy to view that history as a series of wars between the Roman Empire and Parthia, with the advantage

Iran in the Parthian and Sasanid period

usually to the former. The concentration of sources on the Roman Empire, as the successor of the Achaemenid Empire and Alexander the Great, should not obscure the fact that the Parthian state had great problems on its northern and eastern frontiers which were frequently more important or more dangerous to the Parthians than relations with the Romans in the West. The end of the first century AD saw the rise of a powerful, new kingdom in Eastern Iran – the Kushans.

Evidence points to Kanishka as the real founder of Kushan power, the Darius of his empire. Unfortunately, the dates of

251

Kanishka's reign are unknown, primarily because of the lack of a fixed chronology for Kushan inscriptions. In fact there are several eras in Eastern Iran and North-West India which complicate the picture. The Indian Saka era began about AD 78, following an older Vikrama era which began in 57 BC, and now we have a local Khwarazmian era which began about the time of the Christian era and lasted more than seven hundred years.[5] From these we see that the Seleucid and Parthian eras had several parallels in the east. Whatever the dates of Kanishka, we find that during his reign Iranian legends in Greek characters appear on Kushan coins in place of Greek legends, an indication of a new direction in the cultural development of the Kushan Empire. He was also a great patron of Buddhism and we may suppose that in his time an important Buddhist missionary effort was fostered in Central Asia. It is significant that Chinese sources tell us that one of the chief Buddhist missionaries who came to China in AD 148 was a Parthian prince.[6]

Unfortunately, Parthian relations with the Kushans or with India remain a closed book, and we may only speculate about the numerous and varied coins from Eastern Iran which have survived, but which tell us little about the history of such a vast area. The coins seem to indicate that a number of small 'Indo-Parthian' principalities existed, several of them perhaps as buffer states between the Kushans and Parthians, subject to one or the other power and similar to those on Parthia's western border which are much better known.

It is important to remember that the Parthians never achieved the same degree of strong centralization as their predecessors the Achaemenids or their successors the Sasanids. Some of the semi-independent Parthian dependencies were only cities such as Seleucia and Hatra, while others were large states like Armenia in the north and Persis in the south. Between these two lay others such as Osrhoene around the city of Edessa, Gordyene, Adiabene, Mesene or Characene, and Elymais. It is no wonder that later Arabic and Persian histories characterize this period of history as one of many 'tribal kings', which also serves to explain why it is so difficult to recover the pre-Sasanid history of Iran. The political fragmentation of the Parthian state is thus the background against which cultural and religious developments should be examined.

As the Parthians moved westward from the Iranian plateau on to the plains of Mesopotamia, the Hellenistic and Near Eastern influences on their culture and art increased. Their earliest capital was in North-Eastern Iran, then came Hekatompylos, or Qumis near modern Damghan, followed by Ecbatana and finally Ctesiphon, although Ecbatana probably remained a summer capital. Ecbatana, modern Hamadan, probably became the Parthian capital under Phraates II (c. 138–128 BC), while the town of Nisa, in the Parthian homeland, became a cult-centre – the burial ground of former kings.[7] At Nisa, Soviet archaeologists have discovered many Parthian objects, including over two thousand ostraca (fragments of pottery), dating from 100–13 BC, written in Aramaic, but read as Parthian. The ostraca are primarily concerned with wine and vineyards and attest the importance of wine in ancient Iran, further evidence for which is supplied by the many Dionysian and Bacchanalian motifs on Parthian and Sasanian art objects. Many ivory rhytons were also found at Nisa, some carved with scenes in a purely Classical style, while others show a different, 'Oriental' influence.[8] These two influences are characteristic of early Parthian art.

It is tempting to assign the 'Classical' element in Parthian art to the royal court and the 'Oriental' influences to the nobility. This would coincide with the assumed royal patronage of the cities and the Hellenized population as a counterweight to the local aristocracy. In reality such a cultural division probably never existed, and we may suppose that both styles, if they may be so called, co-existed in both provincial centres and the capital. By the first century AD, however, the 'Classical' style gives way to that art which has come to be known among art historians as typically Parthian art. Two dominant features of this art are frontality, and the motif of the flying gallop. The latter is self-explanatory though not without problems, but the former needs elaboration since it represents such a marked change from both the previous Hellenistic and the contemporary Roman portrayal of the human form.[9]

Frontality in Parthian art means more than the presentation of humans *en face*. A strict symmetry and hieratic aspect of the representation are just as striking as the full face of the figure. In my opinion this art did not 'originate' in Syria, Greece or Parthia, but was a common development all over the Near East about the time of Christ. Only the Graeco-Roman world continued to copy the masterpieces of the Golden Age of Greece, and only when the Oriental religions, including Christianity, spread throughout the Roman Empire did the eastern style also spread. The popularity of frontality parallels the rise of Oriental sects which were for the most part mystery cults concerned with the personal salvation of the individual. Unfortunately, we know next to nothing of religions in the Parthian domains.

If we were to rely on archaeological remains in Iran from the Parthian period, we might infer that cults of Heracles, Dionysus and other Hellenistic deities flourished, most of them probably synthesized with local cults and deities.[10] It is difficult to believe, however, that such cults were more than modern lodges, fraternal orders, or drinking clubs. Both before and after the Parthians the worship of Ahura Mazda flourished in Iran, and we may believe that worship of this god was prominent also under the Parthians. Likewise, it is reasonable to suppose that the religious *malaise* of most of the Near East at this period also extended to Parthia, or at least to lands ruled by Parthians. Judaism, about which we know more than other religions, may be taken as a parallel for other faiths.

Thanks to the Dead Sea Scrolls we know that Judaism was far from monolithic and 'normative' at the beginning of our time reckoning. We know now of Essenes as well as Samaritans, followers of John the Baptist and of Jesus. We know of the conversion to Judaism of the royal family of Adiabene in the first century, and of large Jewish colonies in Mesopotamia and undoubtedly elsewhere in the Parthian domains.[11] Gnostic speculation, or the concern with special, intimate knowledge of the secrets of the universe, was widespread not only in Alexandria and Antioch, but surely also in Ctesiphon and farther east. It is most likely that the Mandaeans, who exist even to the present day in Southern Iraq, came into being as a sect in late

Parthian times. We have no information on the origins of the mysteries of Mithraism, Zurvanism and other Iranian movements, and evidence for their existence in Iran is lacking. Suffice it to say that the great popularity of time speculation, mystery religions, gnostic beliefs and saviour cults in the Roman Empire at least must have had echoes among the Parthians.[12]

The first century AD then was a period of change which continued into the second century – which century might be characterized as one of alienation from older forms of religion, society and culture. Furthermore, the Parthian state was at its lowest ebb politically and the Romans several times took advantage of this weakness to invade Mesopotamia. Ctesiphon was taken by Trajan in 115, in 165 by the general Avidius Cassius, and in 198 by Septimius Severus. The Parthians, however, remained throughout this period formidable enemies who inflicted several defeats on Roman armies. The centralization of authority in the Roman Empire contrasted with the opposite tendency under the Parthians, but the latter could frequently count on anti-Roman sentiment and even support at times from the vassal states in Mesopotamia, the Jews, Arabs or others in the Near East. We learn from Latin sources that both the mailed heavy cavalry (*cataphracti*) of the Parthians and the light armed cavalry, with bows and arrows, were feared by the Romans. The 'Parthian shot', whereby a fleeing horseman turned in his saddle and shot an arrow at his pursuers, aroused special attention among the Romans. It seems clear from Strabo, Tacitus and other writers, that the Romans considered the Parthian state as a worthy imperial rival to the Roman Empire.

The demand for luxury items from the East in the Roman Empire was a boon to merchants in Parthian lands as well as elsewhere, and the result of the trade in spices, perfumes and other luxuries was the growth of caravan cities such as Petra, Palmyra, Hatra and Charax on the Persian Gulf. Under the Parthians trade was maintained with China as well as the Roman Empire, and the direct Roman contact with India and the Kushan Empire was probably fostered by economic reasons, and the use of the monsoon winds by sailors, rather than because of political differences with Parthia. It is probable that during the long Parthian period of rule in Iran, many plants, fruits and products were exchanged between Europe and the Far East. For example, the pomegranate probably came to China from Iran in this period, while the peach and apricot came the other way.[13] The discovery of an ancient carpet in excavations in Siberia indicates the age-old pre-eminence of Iran in the art of rug making, further attested by embassies to China which brought lovely rugs and brocades as presents.[14] In short, we may assume that the artistic workshops of Iran continued to flourish under the Parthians, although their products may not be pleasing to many modern eyes.

The Parthian period was important in the history of Iranian literature. It is true that we have no contemporary productions save a few inscriptions, but traces of Parthian influence in later New Persian literature are not uncommon. It has been mentioned that the Parthian period is known in Arabic and New Persian literature as a dark age of many tribal kings. Yet the bulk of the *Shāhnāme* or 'Book of Kings', codified in verse by Firdosi, at the beginning of the eleventh century, reflects the tales, the chivalry and the mores of the Parthian era. I suspect that histories were not written under the Parthians but rather epic stories were sung by bards or minstrels called *gōsān* (Armenian *gusan*).[15] Although the Ashkanian (Arsacid) rulers, as the Parthians are known in New Persian, are given only a few lines in the national epic by Firdosi, the stories of previous rulers surely reflect the 'feudal' character of Parthian times, just as the hero Rustam reflects Heracles. The lack of reliable data, however, makes scholarly work in this area difficult and speculative.

The cumbersome system of writing Parthian was undoubtedly an important factor in the lack of records from the time of the Parthians. We have mentioned that the Aramaic language and script remained the vehicle of writing the Parthian language at least through the first century AD (parchment from Avroman and ostraca from Nisa). The Aramaic, it must be emphasized, was read as Parthian in Iran. By the third century, however, we find the Parthian language in semi-phonetic form written in characters derived from Aramaic, yet with many Aramaic 'ideograms' or 'masks', as attested by the inscriptions of the early

Sasanid rulers. Thus by the third century we have an established Parthian inscriptional alphabet; either a sudden new creation or the result of slow evolution. What happened in the second century to the system of writing? The most reasonable explanation is the decline in the number of scribes all over Parthian territory who could write traditional Aramaic. This decline was surely a continuous process from the time of the Nisa ostraca to the third century. We are only missing documentation from the second century to show the continuity which we must infer. The Orientalization of the Parthians, at the expense of Hellenism, may have contributed to the development of the Parthian system of writing as we know it from the third century, but this can be only speculation.[16]

The third century saw another series of changes in the Near East which completely reversed the roles of Iran and the Roman Empire, not to mention the new religious, artistic and other cultural developments. Fortunately our documentation increases enormously, for the Sasanids seem to have been conscious of their historical role to a much greater extent than the Parthians. Not only do we have classical sources on the rise of the Sasanids but also Iranian inscriptions, and later Pahlavi books, plus Arabic, Armenian, Syriac and New Persian books which preserve earlier traditions. One might say that the third century marks the beginning of a widespread literary activity in the Near East in many languages. If anything, the third century is even more important than the preceding centuries as the era of culmination of the changes previously in process.

The fall of the dynasty of the Arsacids to a rebel in Persis, the present Fars province, had many repercussions. The pressure of Roman arms on the Parthians must have contributed in some measure to a weakening of the Parthian state, but even more the internal divisions prepared the way for the Sasanids. The Parthian king Vologeses v had a rival in Artabanus v, but we do not know which areas were controlled by each ruler. An inscription from Susa dated 215, shows that Artabanus was recognized there as suzerain, while at least some of the time Vologeses ruled Ctesiphon and the north.[17]

The invasion of Parthian territory in 216 by Caracalla

coincided with the revolt of Ardashir the son of Papak, a vassal of the Parthians, in Persis. There are a number of accounts of the rise of Ardashir, an official version as found in Imperial inscriptions and in some later histories, a romantic folk version, reflected in the Pahlavi *Kār nāmak*, or 'book of deeds', of Ardashir, and in later Arabic works, and finally a Roman or enemy version. Needless to say, the first should be accepted as the most reliable, even with its exaggerations or pride in the dynasty, for it alone has contemporary documentation in edicts carved on stone.[18]

An inscription of Shapur, son of Ardashir, on a pillar from the excavations of the city of Bishapur, gives the date of the inscription in three forms: 'the year 58, of the fire of Ardashir, the year 40, of the fire of Shapur, the king of fires, the year 24'. Unfortunately, the dates of the early Sasanid kings are uncertain so we cannot determine the precise date of the inscription. One group of scholars supports 224 as the date Artabanus was finally defeated and killed by Ardashir, while another maintains 226, which date is now more popular. If the date of the fire of Ardashir is 226, then the Bishapur inscription was inscribed in 266. The term 'fire' probably means the beginning of a reign, or some important event, when a special fire was started and always kept burning to symbolize the reign or event.[19]

Papak ruled in Istakhr, near the ruins of Persepolis, while his son Ardashir held sway under him in Gor or modern Firuzabad south-east of Shiraz. Shapur, the eldest son of Papak, succeeded his father, but Shapur was killed in an accident and Ardashir became ruler of Persia possibly in 208, the first date of the Bishapur inscription. Ardashir consolidated his power and conquered the neighbouring districts of Kirman, Isfahan and Elymais before turning to his Parthian overlord. The struggle with Artabanus seems to have lasted about three years, but even after the death of Artabanus the Parthians continued the struggle and finally some of the Arsacid princes took refuge in Armenia where a collateral line of the Parthian royal family ruled until 428.

While it has been a commonplace among scholars to speak of the abrupt change from a feudal, fragmented state of the

Parthians to a centralized monarchy of the Sasanians, this process must have extended over a fairly long period. We know from inscriptions that Shapur considered himself a king over many kings, the names of some of whom are given. The old and important title of *satrap* had declined in significance until by Sasanian times it meant the equivalent of the mayor of a city and surrounding areas. The increase in titles at the court, evidence of a bureaucracy in formation, does remind us that the Sasanids were not just continuing Parthian institutions. Much remains to be done in the study of the varied Sasanian titulary and bureaucracy which should clarify many aspects of the question of the nature of the Sasanian state.

Perhaps the most important aspect of the new Sasanian state was its relation to religion. Thirty years ago, before the decipherment of the inscriptions of the high priest Kartir, little was known about the Zoroastrian religion at the beginning of Sasanian times. One tradition, found in later writings, claimed that a priest called Tansar had renovated the Zoroastrian religion at the command of Ardashir. Now, thanks to four inscriptions of the priest Kartir, we know more about the beginnings of the state church of Sasanid Iran. It has been suggested that Kartir should be identified with Tansar, but there is no evidence for this. Fortunately the four inscriptions, though not identical, correspond in parts, two being longer than the others, and thus they aid each other in reconstructing the message of Kartir to posterity. From his inscription at present-day Sar Mashhad, we learn that his full name was Kartir Hangirpe.[20]

His real career began under Shapur I, in whose inscription Kartir's name is found far down the list of notables at the Imperial court, with the title the *herbad*. Other evidence points to the meaning of *herbad*, at this time, simply as 'priest', one who was in charge of the cult and recitations. Kartir's position as court priest must have aided his rise, for he accompanied Shapur on his conquests in Western Asia, and probably was his spiritual, and general, adviser. In his inscription, carved on the same structure as the great inscription of Shapur – the Kab'ah of Zoroaster at Naqsh-i-Rustam – Kartir tells of his elevation to a high position of authority by Shapur, and how he,

Kartir, created new fire temples and helped to spread Zoroastrianism throughout the empire. Furthermore, he tells how he installed new fires and priests in territories outside of Iran, including Eastern Anatolia and the lands of the Caucasus. This new evidence for Zoroastrian missionary activity in Cilicia, Cappadocia, and elsewhere outside of Iran confirms the sparse literary evidence that Magi and 'Zoroastrian' cults existed inside the Roman Empire.

Kartir rewarded co-operative priests and punished those of heretical views. Kartir later initiated a pogrom against Jews, Buddhists, Hindus, indigenous Christians (called Nasoreans), Greek Christians (from Antioch?), called *Krstydan* in the inscription, Mandaeans (*Mktky*) and Manichaeans (*Zndyky*).[21] The remarkable inscriptions of Kartir reveal many new aspects of Zoroastrianism, with a multitude of details which need prolonged study to elucidate their significance.

The chronicle of the continued rise of Kartir is fascinating to follow in the inscriptions. Ohrmazd, son of Shapur (272–3) gave him a new title, Ahura Mazda *magupat,* 'leader of the Magi for the god Ahura Mazda', and increased his power and influence. As a sign of this he conferred a special cap and belt on him. Under Varahran I, brother of Ohrmazd (273–6), his privileges were confirmed and his authority increased. Varahran II (276–93), however, raised him even higher by giving Kartir a rank and station among the high nobility, thus elevating a priest to the highest social rank. He further made Kartir the chief priest and judge of all the empire. Although the title is not mentioned, this is surely the beginning of the office of *mobadanmobad,* literally 'chief priest of chief priests', parallel to 'king of kings'. Further, Kartir was placed in charge of the chief fire temple of the Empire at Istakhr, the homeland of the Sasanian dynasty, and sacred to the goddess Anahita, the patron saint of Ardashir, founder of the Sasanian Empire. To add to his appellations, Varahran gave him the personal epithet 'the soul-saviour of Varahran', indicating the close personal relationship between the priest and the king.

Kartir was not modest, for he continues to relate how he instituted many fires for his own house, presumably relatives and followers, and how he was always of great service to his religion as well as his king and himself. It should be mentioned that, under King Varahran I, the name Kartir does appear in Manichaean literature as a persecutor of Mani. In the Coptic Homilies this same person is called Kardel, in a Turfan Parthian fragment *qyrdyr,* and in a Turfan Middle Persian fragment *kyrdyr,* son of Ardavan (Artabanus).[22]

While one cannot continue in detail studying the history of at least two Kartirs, only one of which is the important figure who made the inscriptions, one more item deserves our attention, for it is different from the above notices. In his inscriptions at Naqsh-i-Rajab, Naqsh-i-Rustam (behind the horse of Shapur), and Sar Mashhad, Kartir gives a personal credo, remarkable for its simplicity and directness. He says that both heaven and hell exist and the good person goes to heaven after death, the bad one to hell. But the doer of good will also be rewarded in this life by peace of mind and happiness. Furthermore, the performance of rites and rituals is essential for salvation. In very poorly preserved passages of the Sar Mashhad inscription we obtain glimpses of some personal experiences of Kartir, a kind of *apologia pro vita sua,* with a certain quality like the story of Paul's conversion on the road to Damascus, or even Dante's descent into hell. Kartir wanted his name preserved for posterity, and the remarkable priest succeeded well in his aim.

We do not know what happened to Kartir, for his name is last mentioned in one of the inscriptions of Narseh at Paikuli, but in an unclear context which does not permit us to discern his fate. His name did not survive in later literary sources, so one suspects that there was some opposition to Kartir or to his work. His inscriptions, however, were not defaced or altered, which custom did obtain in Sasanid Iran.[23] There may be some reason other than merely opposition, maybe even trivial, which kept his name from literary sources, for his work of organization and building the Zoroastrian church as a partner of the government certainly did not cease.

The growth of the Sasanian church probably was spurred by competition from the religions mentioned above, which Kartir attacked. Perhaps the most threatening competitor was

Manichaeism, even though the others also engaged in missionary activities. Indications point to the rise of Manichaeism as the symbol of the new age which may be one reason why it was so hated by adherents of other religions. Manichaeism was a gnostic, synthetic religion, created by Mani, whose exact dates are uncertain but who flourished in the middle of the third century. He composed the books of recitation and reading for his followers and ordered them translated into all languages. Manichaeism has been compared with contemporary Bahaism and there are interesting points of similarity, but we cannot here discuss matters of doctrine and theology. Suffice it to say that the Manichaean insistence on the importance of writings, while it was hardly the origin of the concept of a religion with a holy book, seems to have had a strong influence at least on the Zoroastrians. The Avesta was collected and put in order, probably several times, under the Sasanians. A similar process began with the formation of the Talmud and other writings by the Jews in Mesopotamia, while the followers of other religions well may have engaged in similar activities in this time.

It is clear that the later medieval pattern of religions in the Near East was being set in the third century. This is the time of Origen and other church writers. It is also the time of the formation of religious communities, the exilarch (*resh galutha*) of the Jewish diaspora in Sasanian domains, and the grouping of the Christian church in Mesopotamia under bishops, with a systematic organization. The same was true of the Manichaean community, and others. Religions were organized on state or military lines to enable them to survive. The later minority, or *millet* system of the Islamic world, in which each religious minority lived under a supreme chief who was responsible to the central Islamic government for all of his community, seems to have come into existence in the third century in the Sasanian Empire. Although evidence is still circumstantial, many signs point to this development at this time. In other words, it appears that the Sasanians were blazing the trail for many institutions of the later Near East, whereas the Romans still clung to the glory that was Greece and the grandeur of the early empire. The pre-eminence of Iran in the middle of this century is nowhere better indicated than on the field of battle. For the first time a Roman emperor was taken prisoner by the Persians. Although Ardashir had clashed with the Romans in the consolidation of his empire, it was left to his son Shapur to inflict the greatest defeat suffered by the Romans at the hands of their eastern enemies.

We can now compare Roman sources with the trilingual inscription (Greek, Parthian and Middle Persian – the language of the Sasanians) of Shapur on the Ka'bah of Zoroaster, which provides a beautiful example of facts represented in different ways by the Romans and the Persians.[24] For the former the Sasanians opened the war and the Emperor Gordian III had to repulse the attack of the enemy. According to Shapur, Gordian attacked him. In this case Shapur seems to have started a campaign not against Rome but against several small independent states; in 240 the Sasanians captured Hatra which had withstood successfully previous Roman and Parthian attempts to capture it.[24a] He then turned to Osrhoene which submitted, and it is this event which probably incited the Romans. In a great battle, according to Shapur, the Emperor was killed and the new Emperor Philip the Arab sued for peace. The battle site of the Euphrates was renamed Peroz-Shapur 'victory of Shapur', later al-Anbar. Shapur says Philip paid half a million *denarii* as ransom but the Roman sources naturally are silent about this.

The second war began with the treachery of the Romans over Armenia, again according to Shapur. The Sasanians then annihilated a Roman army of 60,000, which is not recorded by Roman sources, after which they ravaged Syria and Cappadocia, capturing the eastern capital of Antioch and many other cities. The date of this expedition is much disputed, some scholars suggesting two campaigns in 253 and 256. Two events seem to point to 256 as more likely: one is the final capture of the Roman fortress on the Euphrates, Dura-Europus, by the Sasanians, and the other is the captivity of the bishop of Antioch, Demetrianus, which may be dated to 256 when his rule over Antioch ended.[25] There are still many unsolved problems but the events best seem to have followed the above chronology.

In the third war, when Shapur was besieging Edessa and Carrhae, the Emperor Valerian attacked. In the ensuing battle Valerian was captured personally by Shapur, according to the inscription, and the praetorian prefect and many other high Roman officers were also captured. This was probably in 260, after which the Persians again captured Antioch and many other cities of Cappadocia, Cilicia and Syria. Many captives were made and settled in the modern provinces of Fars and Khuzistan. The rest of the inscription of Shapur is concerned with the royal family and the court, which is of great importance for Sasanian history, but which cannot be discussed here.

The great influx of war prisoners had some interesting consequences, for the Christian communities in Southern Mesopotamia and Iran began from this settlement. Some prisoners were settled in a new city called 'Better than Antioch has Shapur (made this)', later the famous intellectual centre of Gundeshapur. Prisoners also built dams on the Karun River at present-day Tustar and Ahwaz, remains of which may still be seen. Finally, evidence of perhaps Antiochene influence may be discerned in the mosaics of Bishapur showing faces or more likely masks taken from the cult of Dionysus. Other effects of the influx of prisoners cannot be detected easily but undoubtedly existed.[26] Shapur commemorated his great victory by carving several large rock reliefs showing his victory over Valerian. It must have been a memorable event for the Sasanians, for it was not forgotten in later writings.

We have mentioned the church and the wars of Shapur, but now we can turn briefly to the state ideology of the Sasanians. In the inscriptions Papak is called a king, Ardashir king of kings of Iran, while Shapur and his successors are each king of kings of Iran and non-Iran (*Aneran*). This was a clear claim to universal rule, a return, perhaps not consciously, to the one-world of the Achaemenids. The process of centralization was hastened by the absorption of local dynasts and the replacement of them with members of the Sasanian ruling family. The concept of legitimacy was firmly established, so that allegiance to the house of Sasan was accepted everywhere in the empire, and only rebels who were members of the Sasanian family had any chance of success. The crown prince was usually made a king over an important area such as Gilan and Mazanderan on the Caspian Sea, or the East, to which we should turn.

The Kushans had been able to hold their own against the Parthians, but under Ardashir and Shapur the *Kushanshahr*, as the Kushan state is called in Shapur's great inscription, became subject to the Sasanians. The Kushan territory is described as extending from the plain of Peshawar, in modern Pakistan, to Tashkent in Soviet Central Asia, and to the borders of Kashgar in Chinese Turkistan, an enormous area which may have been more nominally than actually under the Kushans. For a long period the continuous nomadic threat to Iran from the north-east was ended and the powerful new Sasanian Empire re-established some borders of the old Achaemenid Empire in the east. This re-assertion of Persian power in the east, in place of the fragmented Parthian state, laid the foundations for the penetration of West Iranian cultural influences into Eastern Iran, which, after the fall of the Sasanian Empire, was to continue under the aegis of Islam until the New Persian language replaced the older Sogdian, Khwarazmian, Parthian and Bactrian languages as the predominant language of the entire Iranian world.[27] A short digression on the question of the division between Eastern Iran and Western Iran in the Sasanid period may be profitable.

Eastern Iran, east of the central deserts today called Lut and Kavir, was the homeland of the Parthians as well as other Iranian peoples mentioned above. Here separatist tendencies were strong, as well as local feudal cultures. This entire area was difficult for the Sasanians to control, and especially to integrate into their empire primarily based in Western Iran. So the military forces of the Sasanians were divided between the western frontier against the Romans, and their sometime allies the Alans, north of the Caucasus, as well as the Armenians, and the eastern frontier primarily against nomadic peoples from Central Asia, as well as against insurgent Kushans. In the third century the strong Sasanian kings were able to defend the eastern frontier and establish their rule on a firm basis.

In the wars with Rome the Persians may have had in mind

permanent conquests, but the resources of the Sasanians were not so great. Furthermore, the local inhabitants of the Fertile Crescent of Mesopotamia and Syria hardly preferred the Persians to the Romans as rulers. It was Odenathus, then his wife Zenobia, queen of Palmyra, who stepped into the vacuum caused by the temporary impotence of Rome in the Near East. For almost twelve years Palmyra dominated the Syrian and Mesopotamian frontiers of the Roman and Sasanian Empires until the Emperor Aurelian brought an end to Palmyra in 272. Iran during this period seems to have been exhausted, or at least concerned with internal affairs. Armenia, under an Arsacid dynasty, continued to remain a thorn in the side of the Sasanians and their hostilities never really ended.

The Romans soon recovered, and the Emperor Carus invaded Mesopotamia and captured Ctesiphon with little opposition, but his mysterious death at the end of 283 caused the Roman army to return home. It seems that the Sasanian king Varahran II was engaged in suppressing a rebellion of his brother in the East.

We have a complete set of Sasanian coins, which differ from the preceding Parthian coins in being flat and based on a different weight standard. On the coins we find characteristic crowns on the busts of the different kings, such that these distinctive crowns enable the student to identify the rulers portrayed on wall carvings, on silver vessels, or other works of art.[28] Sasanian art is also very distinctive, again differing from the previous period. The frontality, symmetric and rigid portrayal of humans gives way to profiles and the desire to tell a story. As always in Iranian art, decoration is an overwhelming principle. The later Islamic concern with geometrical designs and stylized flowers, and the like, had its prototypes in Sasanian art. Indeed the continuity between the Sasanians and early Islam is far more impressive than that between the Parthians and the Sasanians. Certainly there was a carry-over even between Parthian and Sasanian art, for example the flying gallop motif, but the new Sasanian culture was unmistakably distinctive.

The survival of many Sasanian silver bowls and cups from the third century, as well as superbly carved seals and other minor works of art, emphasizes not only the change from the past, but also the splendour and wealth of the new rulers. The monarch gave silver plates or bowls as presents to favourites after drinking parties, and the third-century specimens are masterpieces of art. The conscious attempt to impress and dazzle is ever present in these productions of imperial art.

So the third century AD in a sense marked the end of antiquity and the beginning of the 'Middle Ages' in Iran. Later the reforms of Diocletian were to have an influence in the neighbouring Sasanid state, but the early Persian rulers were confident of their own prowess to change the face of Iran and to create a culture and civilization which was a worthy competitor of the Roman Empire. The influence of the Sasanians was to extend far beyond the Iranian plateau, and was to continue for many decades after the fall of the Sasanids in the seventh century AD.

TENTATIVE GENEALOGICAL TABLE OF THE ARSACID KINGS

1. Arsaces I (*'ršk*) 247–?
2. Tiridates (*tyrdt*) *c.* ?–211 BC
3. Artabanus I (*'rtpn*) *c.* 211–191 BC
4. Priapatius (*prypt*) *c.* 191–176 BC
5. Phraates I (*prdh* or *prdty*) *c.* 176–171 BC
6. Mithradates I (*mtrdt*) *c.* 171–138 BC
7. Phraates II *c.* 138–128 BC
8. Artabanus II *c.* 128–123 BC
9. Mithradates II *c.* 123–87 BC
10. Gotarzes I (*gwtrz*) *c.* 91–87? BC
11. Orodes I (*wrwd*) *c.* 80–77 BC
12. Sinatrukes (*sntrwk*) *c.* 76–69 BC
13. Phraates III *c.* 69–57 BC
14. Mithradates III *c.* 57–55 BC
15. Orodes II *c.* 57–37 BC
16. Phraates IV *c.* 38–2 BC
17. Tiridates II *c.* 30–25 BC
18. Phraataces (*prdtk*) *c.* 2 BC–AD 4
19. Orodes III *c.* AD 4–7.

20. Vonones I (*whwnm?*) *c.* AD 7–12
21. Artabanus III *c.* AD 12–38
22. Tiridates III *c.* AD 36
23. Vardanes (*wrt'n*) *c.* AD 39–47
24. Gotarzes II (*qwtrz*) *c.* AD 38–51
25. Vonones II *c.* AD 51
26. Vologeses I (*wlgs*) *c.* AD 51–80
27. Artabanus IV *c.* AD 80–1
28. Pakores (*pkwr?*) *c.* AD 79–115
29. Oroses *c.* AD 109–28
30. Vologeses II *c.* AD 105–47
31. Mithradates IV *c.* AD 128–47?
32. Vologeses III *c.* AD 148–92
33. Vologeses IV *c.* AD 191–207
34. Vologeses V *c.* AD 207–27?
35. Artabanus V *c.* AD 213–26?
36. Artavasdes (*'rtwzd*) *c.* AD 226–7?

THE DYNASTY OF THE SASANIANS

1. Papak King (208–22?)
2. Shapur King (222?)
3. Ardashir King of Kings (226?–41?)
4. Shapur King of Kings (241–72?)
5. Hormazd Ardashir (272–3)
6. Varahran I (273–6)
7. Varahran II (276–93)
8. Varahran III (293)
9. Nerseh (293–302)
10. Hormazd II (302–9)
11. Shapur II (309–79)
12. Ardashir II (Brother?) (379–83)
13. Shapur III (383–8)
14. Varahran IV (388–99)
15. Yazdagird I (399–420)
16. Varahran V (420–39)
17. Yazdagird II (439–57)
18. Hormazd III (457–9)

19. Peroz (459–84)
20. Valash (484–8)
21. Kavad (488–531)
22. Zamasp (496–8)
23. Khusro I (531–79)
24. Hormazd IV (579–90)
25. Varahran Chobin (590–1)
26. Khusro II (590–628)
27. Kavad II (628)
28. Ardashir III (628–9)
29. Boran (629–30)
30. Hormazd V, Khusro III (630–2?)
31. Yazdagird III (632–51)

15

The Dacians in the First Century AD: the Roman Conquest

In the first century AD the Dacians embarked upon a new stage in the history of their material and spiritual culture and of their social and political organization. The natural resources of the region which lay between the Danube and the Carpathian foothills began to be exploited throughout on a technical level equal to that of the final era of La Tène. Agriculture was still one of the main occupations of the Geto-Dacians and they farmed not only on the plains and hillsides but even on the high ground in the mountains. Barns, store-pits and huge vases with carved motifs round the edges, used for the preservation of agricultural produce, and found inside various dwelling places or in specially planned outhouses nearby, provide us with ample and decorative proof of this activity. Cattle breeding can also be said to have played an important part in their economy. But the creative genius of this ancient people, part of the great family of Thracians, best found its expression in the widespread development of the different crafts: silver plating; ironmongery, which supplied them with a large variety of extremely individualistic weapons and tools; the construction of houses and citadels often so planned as to form a stronghold of defence, and built of freestone or fired brick. Geto-Dacian culture, as it was in the first century AD, while still assimilating certain Germanic and Sarmatian elements, the significance of which will be discussed elsewhere, was now subjected to the overpowering influence of the Roman factor, whose penetration was linked with the political changes that had been taking place in the regions of the middle and lower Danube from the reign of the first Roman Emperor onwards (see Ch. 12).

The Danube, sacred river of the Geto-Dacians, was destined to become Roman territory from source to delta. Dobrudja (Scythia Minor), which had been under Roman domination since the reign of Augustus, represented in the east a position indispensable to the Romans if they were to be sure of their supremacy in the lower Danube and in the coastal regions to the west and north of the Black Sea. Moreover, ever since the very beginning of the first century AD, this had been a region of intense Romanization, dependent on the federation of Pontic townships. Faced with the resistance of the indigenous Getic population, and with the forays of the Getic tribes of the right bank, of the Bastarniæ; and of the Sarmatians equipped with their chain mail breastplates, the first Roman Emperors had been forced to turn their attention to the lower Danube where the Roman province of Moesia had gradually grown to include Dobrudja and extend right down as far as the mouth of the Danube. Roman camps and strongholds multiplied all along the river bank, and during the reign of the Emperor Nero the Roman legate in Moesia, Tiberius Plautius Silvanus Aelianus, about AD 60 or soon after, transferred some hundred thousand transdanubians with their wives, children, kings and tribal chieftains to the land south of the Danube. He subsequently won over the Roxalani, Bastarnal and Dacians by restoring to them the kinsmen of their tribal chiefs, thereby not only proving himself a good diplomat, but also strengthening and spreading the cause of peace – (*pacem provinciae et confirmavit et protulit*) – beyond the river, without this actually involving the annexation of any foreign territory.

But the Dacians had yet to be subdued. During the civil war of AD 69–70, they began to gather together their forces, and Tacitus records that the victor of the ensuing battle, Mucianus, governor of Syria had at the time stood in fear of invasion from both sides: from the Dacians (*gens nunquam fida*) on the one, and from the Germanic tribes on the other.

Sure enough, even as the Empire was busy fortifying its positions in Moesia and in the lower Danube region, Dacian power continued to increase by leaps and bounds. The stronghold of this power was situated in the inner curve of the

Carpathian range among the foothills of Orăştie, stretching further along the southern line of mountains into the east and west, well past what could strictly speaking claim to be Dacian territory. An essentially immobile people, they were of the greatest danger to the Romans, first because of their own intrepidity as a nation, and second but no less important, because of the possibility that they might enlist the support not only of the Getae but also of other tribes both to east and west, such as the Marcomanni and the Quadi, who had been established in Bohemia since the beginning of the first century AD. One vast confederation of barbarians thus formed could have jeopardized the existence of the Roman Empire itself. In the light of these considerations, it is easy to grasp the full implications of the desperate struggle being carried on by the Romans during the respective reigns of the Emperors Domitian and Trajan, just when the fate of the Thracians depended on the strength of the northernmost reaches of their territory. The Dacians at this time were, to all intents and purposes, preparing to embark upon a period of independent civilization. Their culture in the first century AD, like that of the Getae, who spoke the same language as they, shows, within the limits of its own peculiarities, traces of a classical style, which could be termed the Decebalus style after the first-century Dacian chieftain who more than anyone personified the savage will of the Dacians to defend their land and their freedom. Throughout Transylvania and other regions of Dacia there are remains of fortified settlements described by Ptolemy as *poleis* (forty in number) economic, military, political and religious centres, certain of whose characteristics it has been possible to determine at closer range as a result of archaeological excavations.

Many centres of civilization, while continuing the life of the former *davae*, also show traces of a military and economic side to their existence. This supplies proof of their function within the framework of the vast tribal unions, or indeed within the State of Dacia itself; also of those links which existed between the different regions as a direct result of social and economic development. In fact, the aristocratic character of society in general was at this time becoming more and more clearly defined. The role of the nobles (*tarabostes, pileati*) became increasingly important as opposed to that of the commoners (*comati*). It may also be assumed that slave labour was employed, as much by the patriarchal and aristocratic families as by the State for the construction of fortresses, seats of government and refuge for the surrounding population.

As to the urban character of these centres, the word urban here must of course be taken in its ancient Greek or Roman sense, to denote a place of assembly for the various communities. Still, the progress of certain economic – *fora rerum venalium* – and political centres towards a so-called urban settlement has, thanks to archaeological discoveries, been proved beyond all doubt. This would have been during the reign of Decebalus, when Dacian oppidan culture was being swept towards a new stage in its evolution.

Similar fortifications may be found throughout Transylvania and beyond the Carpathian Mountains, although construction and dimensions vary slightly from one to the other.

An example of one such fortification may be seen in the fortress of Tilişca, near Sibiu. This is surrounded by two outer walls, one of which consists of a ramp made of earth and a moat, the other of a stone wall with two watch towers. The foundations of these towers are made of blocks of freestone, each divided into two and the gap between the halves filled in with rubble in the same way as the Greek *emplecton*. The walls were made of fired brick.

Another city is that of Piatra Craivei, situated to the north of the town of Alba Iulia, on a rock which towers over the Transylvanian plain at an altitude of 1,083 metres. Here fourteen terraces and a sanctuary with an *arx* surrounded by a *murus Dacicus* have been identified; here it was that excavators were able to determine the existence of an archaeological stratum 120 metres thick, which would point to an occupation dating back to the period between the second century BC and the first AD. It appears that this city could be identified as the city of Apoulon, which is mentioned by the Alexandrian geographer Ptolemy. Stone ramparts have also been discovered at Băniţa, Căpîlna, Covasna and other places in Transylvania, and to the east of the Carpathians on the site known as Bîtca Doamnei, near the town of Piatra Neamţ, as well as in various other places.

These settlements were often protected by a surrounding wall made of earthen hoardings, with moats for defence, after a tradition which dates right back to the Hallstatt period. But the originality of Dacian building is best illustrated by the *murus Dacicus*, a wall built of freestone, each one divided into two and joined together by beams, which in their turn were fastened to the stones by wedges made of swallow-tails. This contrasted strongly with the Celtic fortifications neighbouring on Dacia. It may be well to mention at this point that Trajan's Column, although it conveys the general characteristics of Dacian fortresses, particularly in its portrayal of the towers, betrays nevertheless in its bas-reliefs an imperfect knowledge of these important Dacian structures on the part of artists who, it would appear, executed this work for the express purpose of illus- trating Trajan's *Commentaries* on the Dacian War, a work which is unfortunately lost to us today.

Thus we may say that it is due to archaeological excavations, especially during the last fifteen years, that some light has been thrown on these settlements and in particular on those of the Orăştie hills which are of outstanding interest. It was here that the successive constructions during the first century AD of fortresses, castles, strongholds and watch-towers lent the settle- ment the appearance of a co-ordinated centre of defence planned around the royal residence of Sarmizegethusa. Both the idea behind this planning of defences within an architectural whole along the valley of one of the Mureş tributaries, at alti- tudes of up to 1,200 metres at Costeşti, Piatra Roşie, Blidaru and Grădiştea (the site of the capital), and the methods used to build the terraces – foundations made of freestone, divided, joined by two beams, and held in place by swallow-tail wedges in the manner of the *murus Dacicus* – and walls of fired bricks, each with its own bastion – are clear pointers to the high standard of technical skill reached by the Dacians, who had assimilated the basic elements of construction not only from the Celts but also from the Greeks and even from the Romans. Equally, both may be said to supply a clear indication of the Dacians' powers of organization as a people under a line of chieftains whose succession dated as far back as Burebista.

The religious character of this centre is demonstrated by its sanctuaries: two of circular and several of rectangular layout with stands or columns of stone. These bear witness to the important part played by religion in the Dacian State, a part often remarked upon by early writers in connection with the feats performed by the High Priests of Dacia. In the foothills around Orăştie, towers used as living places, and other more conventional houses, have been discovered, some planned rectangularly and others circular in form, made of bricks or of wooden beams and set on stone foundations. The roofs of this type of building would often have been tiled in the Greek manner. The rich variety of Dacian dwelling-places and tombs supply ample proof of the classic character of Dacian culture as it was in the reign of Decebalus. Quite apart from silverware, there existed also at this period a sort of painted pottery work of geometrically inspired design or decorated with motifs taken from animal and plant life, all of outstanding originality. Elsewhere the practice of writing – in Greek or Latin script – is yet another indication of the advanced stage of civilization which was gradually being attained by the Geto-Dacian peoples at a time when they were summoning up all their strength towards the final struggle as Rome's hold on the region grew inexorably tighter.

During the first century AD Dacian ironwork was developed into a fine art. In the settlements on the hills near Orăştie, for instance, a whole series of tools have been brought to light: scythes, sickles, hoes, ploughshares, coulters for the plough, various utensils used for welding iron, etc., etc. Whole depots of these tools have been found: obviously reserve stocks which were buried on the arrival of the Romans at Sarmizegethusa.

It was from iron that the Dacian artisans fashioned the arms that the Romans so dreaded, such as the curved dagger (*sica*), the swords and sabres, also curved (*falces*), and the arrowheads and lances. Equally, Dacian shields were lined with iron plates like the one found at Piatra Roşie, in the hills near Orăştie, which is richly decorated with motifs from plant life and has a figure of a wild boar depicted in its centre.

This economic development on the part of the Dacians was of some considerable danger to the Romans, since it left their opponents much better defended, able to shelter within their fortresses armed with their fearsome weapons. Moreover the military organization of the Dacians, in the face of Roman ascendancy, was becoming stronger and stronger.

This ascendancy was not confined only to the region of the lower Danube, but was also penetrating towards the Iron Gates of the river and around the middle Danube, where the Roman province of Pannonia was crucially positioned between the Dacians to the east, and the Germanic tribes to the west. Whatever the first Roman Emperor might claim in his *Res Gestae* about bringing the Dacians under Roman domination after crossing the Danube, the latter had continued their attacks throughout the first century AD, staging violent outbursts in Moesia across the frozen Danube, or even in Pannonia itself or on the territories of the Sarmatian Iazyges (who had been enlisted as allies by Tiberius probably in about the year AD 20 and were stationed between the Danube and the Tisa). These attacks led to a long-drawn-out war which took place under the Emperor Domitian, just when the Marcomanni and the Quadi were intensifying their pressure on the Romans from their respective positions on the borders of the Empire around the middle Danube. The reign of Domitian, despite the assertions of his enemies, represented a critical moment, if not for the future conquest of Dacia, at least for the strengthening of the Danube line, and for the application of the Roman policy *divide et impera* applied in order to ward off the combined danger of the Dacians and the Germanic tribes. This was the very moment at which the Dacians had for their leader Decebalus, son of Scorylo, whose moral character as set down by Cassius Dio, and whose physical likeness as carved upon the stone of Trajan's Column, bear witness to the harsh energy and praiseworthy qualities of the people he ruled, as they stood confronted by the greatest conquerors of the ancient world, preparing for the final struggle. After two battles in which

276

Cornelius Fuscus, the Praetorian Prefect, and Oppius Sabinus both met their death, the Dacians were beaten in their turn by the Roman general, Tettius Julianus, at Tapae, near the Iron Gates of Transylvania. Domitian, fighting the Marcomanni in Pannonia, and beaten by them, opened negotiations for peace in the year AD 89. By the terms of the peace treaty, which was concluded through a delegation of Dacian nobles (*pileati*) headed by Diegis, who had himself been crowned by the Roman Emperor, Decebalus became the ally of the Roman people, receiving in exchange financial aid and the labour force of a number of artisans to strengthen his defences. In addition, Dacian territory was opened to the Romans for their march on the Germanic tribes. However, this makeshift solution to the problem, arrived at against a background of very tentative goodwill, could only be temporary: the Dacians had by no means succumbed under the Roman yoke mentioned by Martial (VI, 76, 5). Well entrenched in the mountains, 'knowing quite well how to extricate himself from a position of defeat', Decebalus could shake the yoke off whenever he cared to, thereby placing the Empire in danger once more.

It was in order to fortify the frontiers of the Empire, at the same time seizing possession of the stronghold represented by the Carpathian crown, and also because of his greed to possess the great wealth of the country, especially its gold and silver reserves, that the Emperor Trajan undertook the Dacian Wars of AD 101–2 and 105–6. In the absence of direct sources, which have long since disappeared, we must rely on extracts from the writings of Cassius Dio for details of the events bearing on these two campaigns. These are corroborated by the carvings on Trajan's Column, the historical interpretation of which, however, is often open to question. Fortunately the archaeological aspect, of Adamclissi (Trophy, funeral altar, foundations of the Mausoleum and ruins of the town of Tropaeum Traiani) as well as various other archaeological discoveries are well placed to supply us with more exact details of this series of military feats. Indeed, in the first campaign, Trajan was forced to fight not only at Tapae and to the south of Sarmizegethusa, on Dacian territory, but also in Lower Moesia, where the fight against a coalition of Dacian, Germanic and Sarmatian warriors was particularly bloody. The severe peace terms forced upon Decebalus had been but an armed truce. Preparations were made on both sides for the final contest. The Dacian king sought to form a confederation with the neighbouring tribes who were also being threatened by Roman power. Trajan, who had annexed a part of Daco-Getan territory in Banaţ, Oltenia and Wallachia, commissioned the architect Apollodorus of Damascus to build the bridge at Drobeta, and gathered together a considerable force for a concentric attack on the heart of Dacian power in the hills around Orăştie where the gallant Dacian king was once more engaged in re-erecting the fortress walls which had been dismantled under the conditions of the peace treaty imposed on him by the Emperor. The campaign of AD 105–6 did not last long. Many Dacian tribes gave themselves up right from the beginning of the war, and the surrounding countries had already ceased to participate in what was for the Dacians their last struggle. The royal residence fell into the hands of the Romans, who destroyed the citadels, the population having already been evacuated elsewhere. Decebalus, pursued by his implacable enemies, committed suicide with a curved dagger and his head was sent by the victorious Emperor to Rome, where it was thrown down the Gemoniae steps. The Dacian State, progressing as it was towards consolidation, had ceased to exist.

Apart from the formation of a salient which ensured the safety of the Empire's boundaries, the Romans also acquired as a direct result of the Dacian wars all the gold and silver treasures amassed by former Dacian monarchs. This led to the considerable building up of the Empire's finances, and the execution of costly works of construction among which was Trajan's Forum, with the porches, basilica, library and famous column on which the episodes of this war were recorded. The number of prisoners was also considerable: for the autochthonous population who had stayed on this was the beginning of a new period, that of Romanization.

The continued existence of the native Dacians is shown not only by the names of persons, of places and of rivers, but also by more and more numerous recent archaeological discoveries.

Once exposed to the process of Romanization, they contributed to the creation of a popular culture which displays both elements of Roman civilization and certain features of the ancient native culture.

Moreover, these features were reinforced after the retirement of the Romans from Dacia under Aurelian in 271, when free Dacian Carpi invaded, and established themselves on the territory of the former province. The existing Daco-Roman population was thus reinforced by new native elements, who were themselves in their turn affected by the influence of Rome, since contacts with the Empire continued during the earlier migration period up to the end of the sixth century.

The free Dacians to the north and west of Roman Dacia, such as the Costobocci and Carpi of the eastern Carpathians, are attested by a number of ancient writers. Thus during the reign of Marcus Aurelius tribes of free Dacians and Costobocci along with Sarmatians invaded Dacia, whose governor, M. Claudius Fronto, was killed. When the territory of the Costobocci was occupied by the Asdings, they crossed the Danube and reached Greece (Ch. 11). But in the third century it was the Carpi who along with the Goths and other peoples presented a serious threat to Roman rule in Dacia and the Balkans. Their incursions into the Empire extended from 238, the most important being those of 242 and 245. A number of Roman Emperors, before and after Aurelian, bore the name *Carpicus* as a result of wars against this valiant people who continued the Dacian tradition of Burebista and Decebalus. After the withdrawal of Roman rule it was the Carpi who first established themselves in the former province, the Goths arriving only at the beginning of the fourth century.

From the point of view of archaeology the presence of the free Dacians is attested by the culture of Puchóv, in which there are Celtic elements, and of Lipica to the east of the Carpathians. From within the borders of Rumania the discoveries from Poienești in Moldavia are attributed to the Carpi in view of their funerary rites based on the insertion of the ashes in urns with lids, some of which reflect ancient Dacian styles. In spite of the powerful influence of Roman culture, especially as regards the style of ceramic vases, there evolved among the Carpi a culture of the La Tène type, which reveals also certain Sarmatian elements such as the typical Sarmatian mirrors, and handles in the form of animals.

The persistence of the native Dacians under Roman rule together with the reinforcement by the free Dacians provided the basic ethnic unity for the emergence of the Rumanian people. The free Dacians themselves were exposed to considerable Roman influence before being assimilated by the Daco-Romans inhabiting the area of intense Romanization. This explains the existence and 'renaissance' of certain styles of Dacian pottery which are found also in the Sîntana-Tcherniakhov culture of the fourth century. This is generally attributed to the Goths, but one must recognize in it some native Daco-Roman elements.

16

The Scytho-Sarmatian Tribes of South-Eastern Europe

The Sarmatians consisted of an association of tribes of central Asian origin. Like the Scythians and Cimmerians before them they were essentially nomadic, and most of them adhered to the last to a pastoral way of life. Even in the first century AD those who had penetrated into Dacia were, according to Strabo, still living as nomads in felt huts of the Asiatic type. Like the Scyths and Cimmerians, the Sarmatians were Indo-Europeans speaking an Iranian tongue which is believed to have closely resembled Scythian. Their recorded history starts in the sixth century BC when the majority of the tribes began slowly migrating westward across Asia. Some two hundred years later they had reached the foothills of the western Urals. The Roxalani tribesmen, together with the Iazyges, Aorsi and Alans, seem to have formed the spearhead of the advance, for the first of these tribes forged ahead towards the Volga, whilst the Alans who, with the Aorsi, had originally come from Sogdia, headed for the Kuban. Then the impetus of their advance slackened and the Aorsi dallied on the Volga till well-nigh the end of the pre-Christian period, when they moved to the north of the Sea of Azov. By the first century AD they had spread across Rostov's land, reaching Novocherkassk, where, in 1864, the rich Khokhlach burial, probably the tomb of one of their queens, was found by chance. It had been as sumptuously equipped as that of any nomadic king of similar rank since, throughout at any rate the earlier phases of their history, the Sarmatians were a matriarchal society. Included among its valuable contents were thirteen magnificent objects in gold. Most important of these were a diadem, a necklace, several bracelets and a tiny agate bottle of a type which is characteristic of the Sarmatians; it was set in gold and adorned with animal motifs. The silver vessels included two of Greek workmanship; a Greek terracotta figurine of Eros was also recovered from the burial. These imports serve to illustrate the closeness of the commercial links which, following the example set by the Scyths, the Sarmatians had by then established with the Greek colonial cities of the Black Sea's northern seaboard.

Like all the Scytho-Sarmatian nomads, the Aorsi were such splendid warriors that their bravery was commended alike by Strabo and by the Han Emperor Wu-ti. His decision to establish the western silk road strengthened China's contacts with the Eurasian nomads. The Aorsi constituted one of the larger Sarmatian tribes as well as one of the more adventurous. By 66 BC, according to Strabo, their army numbered some 200,000 men whereas that of the Alans consisted of only 20,000. Nevertheless, the Alans managed to conquer the Siracians who had come to the Kuban basin from Armenia. Eventually the two combined in occupying not only the banks of the Kuban but also the grazing lands stretching from the Sea of Azov to the Don.

The richest of the earlier Sarmatian burials have been found in the Kuban, whilst those of a somewhat later date are situated on the banks of the great rivers of southern Russia and the Ukraine. The Kuban burials cover a period which stretches from the fifth century BC to the third century AD. Many of them were excavated by Soviet scholars between 1929 and 1937, and again from 1946 to 1949. The finest burial of the flat type as yet known to us was found at Ust-Labinska. A great deal of jewellery, much of it in bronze, was recovered from it, together with numerous weapons, more especially spears, swords and arrow heads. Several small, oval-shaped barrows containing princely burials were found on the same site and on the neighbouring ones of Zubovsky and Vozdvizhenskaya. In all of these a shaft led either to a single burial chamber or to one in which a husband and wife had been buried. The objects which had been placed in the graves were similar to those found in the flat burials, but included as well numerous gold objects. A great many weapons were also found; especially notable are the long spears and long, very pointed swords mounted onto oval wooden hilts which differ radically from the spears and swords used by the Scyths. The helmets and corselets worn in battle both by riders and their mounts were also quite distinct from those which are associated with the Scyths. However, as in Scythian times, so in the Sarmatian period, gold plaques were being widely used as dress trimmings; yet these had become smaller in size, and designs of a geometric character had for the most part replaced the animal motifs favoured by the Scyths; even when an animal design did appear, the shape of the creature shown on the plaque, though still bearing Scythian characteristics, had undergone alterations to adapt it to the plaque's new dimensions.

The Alans were but a unit in the Sarmatian association. The culture of the bulk of the tribes in the early phase of their history, that is to say, from the third to the second century BC, is so well represented by the finds discovered by S. I. Rudenko in 1916 in a group of Ural burials called the Prokhorov, that the name is now ascribed to this period of Sarmatian culture. The largest grave in the group belonged to a chieftain who was buried in his iron chain mail, gold torque and bronze bracelets. As in Scythian burials, his gold-handled sword had been placed within easy reach of his hands and two magnificent vessels of Persian or central Asian workmanship – one inscribed in Aramaic with the words 'Cup of Atromitra' – were among the finds. Their presence in a tomb situated on the borderline dividing Asia from Europe is in no way surprising, for the Eurasian nomads had from early times kept in touch with their eastern neighbours and their commercial relations had strengthened with the years. The appearance of the Kushans in central Asia in the second century BC led eventually to the introduction into western Siberia of the Graeco-Indian elements which formed the basis of Kushan art. This took place more particularly among the Massagetic vassals of the Kushans, themselves the suzerains of the bulk of the neighbouring Sarmatians. Under their impact both the Sibero-Scythian and the Irano-Ionian elements which had for so long provided much of the inspiration for Sarmatian art started to give way to these new influences. Scholars have noted the presence of definite links between Kushan pottery and that of the Prokhorov and mid-Sarmatian periods, that is to say in the years stretching from the second century BC to the first century AD – the very ones, it is interesting to note, when contacts between the Sarmatians and the Greek colonial cities on the Black Sea's northern shores were strongest and enmity with the Scyths was at its height. In consequence, though Scythian metal work is of far finer quality than Sarmatian the reverse is true with regard to pottery. The fact that the Sarmatians were fire worshippers who sacrificed horses to their divinity, whereas the Scyths worshipped the elements, should perhaps also be ascribed to Iranian or central Asian influence.

The Sarmatians may well have owed their development into a State centering on the kingdom of the Royal Scyths in what is now southern Russia to the defeat inflicted in c. 175 BC on the Massagetae by the Huns, for it released the Sarmatians from the ties of vassalship which bound them to the Massagetae. In any case the speed of their conquests rapidly increased after that date, enabling them to found a kingdom which was known to their contemporaries as that of the Royal Sarmatians.

It is possible that the Sarmatians owed their victories to some extent to the invention, by the second century BC, of the metal stirrup and its use soon after in conjunction with the spur – advances with which they are often credited. Throughout the earlier phase of their history the Sarmatians were not nearly as skilled in archery as the Scyths had been. They therefore made use of these inventions to furnish their army with units of heavy cavalry. Several Roman writers describe this force, commenting upon the armour provided alike for rider and beast. It varied from the scale and ring to the plate varieties; the riders wore cone-shaped helmets and carried wooden or leather shields, using long spears and long, sharply pointed swords made of bronze or iron mounted on oval-shaped wooden handles terminating in a knob made of a semi-precious stone such as an onyx or agate, or of wood inlaid with gold; a large, oval-shaped semi-precious stone was fashioned into a guard. According to Tacitus only members of the aristocracy were permitted to serve in this force. The class qualification may well have served as a precedent for the Varangian princes of Kievan Russia who, at any rate to begin with, applied a similar rule in the case of their personal bodyguards. The bulk of the Sarmatian army was made up of mobile bowmen clothed in leather jerkins and caps. Their womenfolk doubtless fought in this force rather than in the heavy cavalry units, for in the early periods of their history the Sarmatians expected their maidens to take part in warfare, forbidding them to marry until they had killed an enemy in battle. It is their exploits which probably inspired the ancient Greek stories about Amazons. However, when Sarmatian society started breaking up into distinct social classes, a development which seems to have coincided with the formation of their heavy cavalry units, their matriarchal organization began evolving into a patriarchal one with chieftains gradually becoming more important than queens, and women doubtless ceasing to rank as the equals of men. The creation of Sarmatia's heavy cavalry led to the development of new fighting techniques; these proved so successful that gradually many major powers found it advisable to remodel their armies on similar lines. The Romans were eventually to go to the length of including in theirs Sarmatian detachments equipped and mounted in their native manner and encouraged to fight in their customary style. So far it has not proved possible to determine the breed of the horses which the Sarmatians used. Rudenko's excavations in the frozen Altaian burials at Pazyryk, dating from the fifth to the second century BC, showed that that group of nomads used both the thoroughbred Ferghana horses which the Chinese valued above all others and the rough Mongolian pony. Neither of these seems to correspond to the descriptions of the small, swift type of Sarmatian horse Hadrian was fond of riding when hunting over the hills and swamps of Tuscany; but, of the two, the latter is the more likely.

Though the heavy Sarmatian cavalry was undoubtedly superior to anything possessed by the Scyths, it nevertheless took the Sarmatians several centuries to eject the Royal Scyths from southern Russia and to confine them to the Crimea, whilst establishing their own state on the reaches of the lower Dnieper. At the time the Sarmatians still retained many customs and ideological as well as artistic conventions of Scythian origin. Some of these had belonged to them from time immemorial, others were introduced to them by the Scythian chieftains whom they had absorbed into their ruling class in the course of their advance westward. Nevertheless, in their art they subjected the Scythian preference for animal motifs to their own fondness for geometric designs and polychrome effects, achieving the latter as much by means of enamel and glass inlays as by the use of cabochon gems. With the exception of their Kuban burials, their mounds from the start bore a close external resemblance to those of the Scyths, though the graves which lay beneath them were completely different. Thus, in contrast to the elaborate tombs which the Scyths constructed for their chieftains, the Sarmatians did little more than dig a shaft which terminated in an oval or round hollow, only occasionally lined with rushes. The dead, wrapped merely in either a fur or leather sheet, were laid in these on the ground, but sometimes a rush mat was placed beneath the body; coffins and biers do not appear ever to have been used. The dead were sometimes laid out flat, sometimes placed in a crouched position and occasionally – as a result of the impact made on the Sarmatians by the native inhabitants – they had been cremated. Horses were almost invariably associated with the burials, but whereas in the case of the Scyths and kindred nomads the complete horse was buried beneath the same mound as its rider, the Sarmatians were generally content to place only the animal's trappings in the burial chamber; though sometimes, as for example at Starobelsk, they also included hooves and skulls. Sarmatian bits have fewer animal-shaped terminals and decorations than the Scythian, but they are instead provided with rings for holding the leathers. They were often of gold or silver, and what decorations they have generally take the form of bosses or geometric motifs. The saddles are hard and built with a high frontal of a type unknown in the Black Sea area prior to that date. These frontals were often faced with gold leaf stamped with bosses and adorned with jewels and coloured glass. The polychrome effect is characteristic of Scytho-Sarmatian art, but it becomes more marked when animal motifs of Scythian origin start giving way, first to geometric designs, then, under the influence of the Goths, to bird forms. Trappings such as these are found from the second century BC onwards in burials stretching right across southern Russia into Bulgaria and Transylvania. Equally characteristic of the period and area are the tiny gold bottles with rounded bases adorned with filigree and polychrome decorations. The presence in numerous graves of carnelian beads, glass pendants and vessels, together with some terra sigillata pottery and Egyptian scarabs and amulets, indicates that the Sarmatians were in close and regular contact not only with the Greek colonists of the northern shores of the Black Sea, but also with the Mediterranean world. The graves also often contained mirrors of oriental form made of a silver alloy and decorated with typically Sarmatian designs, as well as hemp inhaling outfits like those found at Pazyryk (Altai), bronze and iron cauldrons of the Scythian type, bronze objects of various sorts and gold plaques similar to those used by preceding generations of nomads as dress trimmings. The objects found in the graves clearly reflect the four main stages of development through which the Sarmatians passed. Thus burials dating from the opening phase of their history, that is to say from the sixth to the third century BC take the form of small mounds and contain very few objects. In the Prokhorov period, which extends over the next two centuries, the burials show that many Sarmatians had by then acquired considerable wealth. The mid-Sarmatian period, that is to say from the first century BC to the first century AD, is one of full development, and graves of that date reveal the existence of a class society in which feudal chieftains and barons played a prominent role. The last phase stretches from the second to the fourth century AD. Volgograd/Stalingrad area. Graves of that late date as, for example, those of Kotovaya, Novaya Norka and Shcherbakovka, to name but these, show that the old life persisted. Much polychrome jewellery, beads obtained from the north coast of the Black Sea, objects of central Asian origin and, at Shcherbakovka, a bronze Roman cauldron were present. However, in addition, the influence of the Goths is marked by the introduction of the cloak and the fibula which held it in place. In the late burials of the Crimea tomb paintings have been found showing Sarmatians dressed in this manner. Yet, simultaneously, the influence of the advancing Huns led to the introduction of cranial deformation at death.

Even when the Sarmatians were supreme in southern Russia they did not attempt to destroy the Crimean Scyths. Instead, following upon the death of Mithradates Eupator and the ensuing collapse of the Bosporan dynasty, they combined with the Thracians in establishing a Thraco-Sarmatian ruler on the Bosporan throne. Under Roman patronage the dynasty was to survive till AD 332 when the Goths conquered the area and put an end to its existence. Whilst these events were taking place in the Crimea, other Sarmatians, some of the Alans on the one hand, and the Iazyges and Roxalani tribes on the other, were on the move again. Although many Alans were to remain in the Kuban and the grazing lands to the north of the Sea of Azov till the period of the great migrations, when they pushed into the Caucasus where, by the ninth century, they had established themselves in Ossetia, surviving there to our day as the kindly and humorous Ossetians, others looked beyond these regions. As allies of Pharnaces, the son of Mithradates Eupator, together with the Siracians they contended against Rome. The nomads paid dearly for this act, for when Pharnaces died they found themselves obliged to recognize Roman suzerainty and to pay their masters a heavy tribute. However, the Alans quickly succeeded in regaining their independence. In AD 35 – as they were to do again in 72/3 and in 134/5 – they attempted to cross into Parthia and Roman Cappadocia; they failed to do either and when, in 64, under Nero, Rome annexed the Pontus they veered towards central Europe, but instead of heading towards Rome they turned in the direction of Poland and Bessarabia, whence they eventually penetrated deep into Europe. Yet during the first century AD the Romans paid little attention to the invading Alans or to the Crimean Aorsi, limiting themselves in AD 49 to obtaining Aorsi support for their candidate for the Bosporan throne, the founder of the Thraco-

Sarmatian dynasty. Nevertheless, as allies of the Crimean Scyths, both in the Caucasus and on the Don these tribes presented a real if undeclared threat to that kingdom and, as such, if only indirectly, they were a danger to Rome. In order both to guard against them in the Bosporan region and to protect Cherso- nesus from the Scyths, the Romans garrisoned Chersonesus and built a line of forts stretching from Tanais on the Don to the Taman peninsula. In addition they combined with the Bosporan rulers in maintaining a joint flotilla in the area. They also established a regular corps of interpreter-diplomats in Cherso- nesus, holding them responsible for all dealings with the Alans with a view to preventing the tribesmen gaining control of the Greek colonial cities. Yet, in reality, the nomads set far too much store on the Greek craftsmen and traders to wish to do anything of the sort; instead many of them settled in these cities, often intermarrying with the Greeks.

The Iazyges and Roxalani were largely responsible for Sarmatian penetration into central Europe. The Iazyges acted as the vanguard, abandoning their grazing lands to the north of the Sea of Azov and the lower Dnieper and Don to move westward. Some authorities believe them to be the group referred to by the Romans as Royal Sarmatians. Their decision to move westward may well have resulted from the pressure exerted on them by the Roxalani. Whatever the cause, the first century BC found them on the Dniester. They were not content to remain there and some contrived to cross the Danube, enter Lower Moesia (Bulgaria) and, as allies of Mithradates Eupator, proceed to attack Rome. However, it was not until *c.* AD 50 that the bulk of them had established themselves between the Theiss and the Danube.

Whilst the Iazyges were encroaching on Rome's borders, the Roxalani, as allies of the Scyths in their fight against the Crimean Greeks, had been defeated by the Pontic general Diophantus and had then joined forces with him in his fight against Rome. Their army is thought to have numbered some 50,000 men, but as they were ill-disciplined and but lightly armed the Roman legionaries had little difficulty in defeating them. Ovid, writing soon after AD 9, whilst living in exile at

Tomi, was able to leave us a description of their appearance and activities. By the year 20 they had crossed the Carpathians and had appeared in the Hungarian plain, and by 62 they had reached the lower Danube where they established friendly relations with the Germanic Bastarnae, and local Thracians and Dacians, and then proceeded to incite them to revolt against Rome. At the time Rome attached great importance to gaining control of the Black Sea and since the Scyths were in the process of besieging Chersonesus the Romans deemed it essential to reduce the tribes to submission in the Balkans and to restore order in the Black Sea's northern hinterland. Plautius Silvanus Aelianus was entrusted with the conduct of operations in Lower Moesia. By 63 he had succeeded in subduing the Sarmatians and was able to transport 100,000 of them across the Danube to resettle them on Roman territory and put an end to nomadic risings to the north of the Danube. He proceeded further to make his power felt in the Crimea where he managed to limit the independence of the Bosporan king Cotys I, possibly by deposing or having him killed, for Cotys, who had come to the throne in AD 46, cannot have been in power after Silvanus' victory, since a gold coin dated 62/3 makes no mention of him and a copper one of the same date displays the head of Nero. Yet, as J. G. C. Anderson pointed out, by 68/9 Bosporan coins were being stamped with the head of Cotys' son, Rhescuporis, together with those of Vespasian and Titus. In his passionate desire to prove himself a greater general than Alexander of Macedon, Nero had evolved a grandiose plan for expansion in the east. It hinged on the use of the Crimea as a base from which to capture the Dariel pass from the Alans and to use it as a pivot for Rome's conquests both in the Mediterranean and central Asian regions. However, Nero's successors did not share his ambitions, and aimed rather at containing than at conquering the Sarmatian assembly of tribes and so undertook no major campaigns in eastern Europe.

The truly astonishing success with which the nomads were able to stand up against so powerful a state as Rome should perhaps be ascribed, if only in part, to the fact that they were beginning to realize that the victories which the Huns were winning as they advanced westward were to some extent due to the superior quality of their bows. These were of the cross-bow type, but they were strengthened by a bone inlay which enabled their archers to use heavier, though still, as in Scythian times, trefoil-shaped arrow heads. This type of bow was so effective when used against heavy cavalry units that, in the second century AD, when engaged in a decisive struggle against Rome, the Sarmatians resorted to the use of mounted archers equipped with the Hunnic cross-bow with which, according to Parthian custom, they shot backwards. They are shown on Trajan's Column in Rome using the Hunnic bow in that way, wearing conical-shaped helms and armour of Sarmatian type but riding their horses without the aid of stirrups.

Though Plautius Silvanus had had his achievements commemorated by the grateful Senate in an inscription, his decision to transport so many Sarmatians on to the Roman bank of the Danube had created a void on the river's northern shore with the result that, at Nero's death, the few nomads who had been allowed to remain there became exceedingly turbulent. Thus, in about 67/8 Sarmatians from Moldavia and Bessarabia destroyed a Roman cohort and in the following year they managed to kill Fonteius Agrippa, Governor of Moesia. His successor, Rubrius Gallus, succeeded in restoring order and was able to build a number of forts at strategic points in Moesia, yet, regardless of Rome's need for troops, three cohorts had to be retained in the area. Soon even they proved insufficient. In 82 nomadic raids and incursions became so troublesome that Rome decided to purchase peace and security in Pannonia. She used the respite to build, probably in 85, an earth wall in the Dobrudja and to induce the Sarmatians to take part in the Dacian wars of 88 and 101, with the result that Dacia became a Roman province. Nevertheless, the Sarmatians were undermining Rome at times siding with her, at others crossing the Danube to raid her territory. In 93, Domitian found it necessary once again to take up arms against them. He subdued them, but only for a time and, in 117, Hadrian was obliged to defend Dacia from a two-pronged attack, the one directed from the west by the Iazyges, the other from the east by the Roxalani.

For the next sixty years the Iazyges were at war with Rome in Pannonia. Eventually, in 175, they were defeated by Marcus Aurelius in an epic battle fought on the frozen waters of the Danube. The statue which the grateful Senate erected on the Capitol still survives there. Aurelius' trophies included a number of standards similar to those depicted on Trajan's Column. C. V. Trever has shown that – like those used by all the Scytho-Sarmatian nomads as well as the Parthians – these standards were made of strips of coloured stuffs sewn only at the ends and shaped to represent dragons and reptiles. They were fixed to long poles; when motionless they could not be mistaken for live animals but at the slightest movement or breeze the strips of material fluttered, filled out and rustled, giving the impression of fierce, animated beasts. The captured standards must have appealed to the Romans for the procession formed in honour of the Emperor Constantius' entry to Rome included a double file of lancers carrying aloft dragons made of purple stuff studded with gold and precious gems.

In 172 Marcus Aurelius had won great renown by his victorious campaign in Germany. In celebration the year's issue of currency had been stamped with the words 'de Germanis'. His successes over the Sarmatians won him the title of Sarmaticus and the inscription on the year's coinage of 'de Sarmatis'. Furthermore, the peace terms which he imposed on the Sarmatians enabled him to despatch 5,500 tribesmen to Britain to serve in the Roman fort at Chester and on Hadrian's Wall in Northumberland. Yet these disasters did not break the fierce spirit of the nomads. Though, in the course of the third century, most of the Roxalani were absorbed by the Goths and the Alans, whilst others united with the Goths in raiding Western Europe, the Iazyges managed to remain distinct and autonomous and, as such, they continued to harass the Romans on the Danube. By the middle of the third century they had won certain concessions from the Romans. Nevertheless, in 236–8, war broke out anew between them, and this time the Iazyges were defeated. They recovered sufficiently to raid Dacia in 248 and again in 252, and Pannonia two years later, but were defeated by Carus in 282/3. Even at that late date they were still living there as nomads, burying their dead as their ancestors had done, in barrows of traditional form, as, for example, in the important burial at Szil, probably of a Sarmatian prince killed in battle, but with the signal difference that, in the manner of the Scythians, they now often included a chariot in their burials, though they had never done so when they lived in southern Russia.

In the fourth century the Huns conquered the Sarmatians. They killed most of them and assimilated a good many of the others; but some escaped westward and continued to harass the Goths and the Huns till, with the sixth century, they too disappear from the pages of History.

17

The Germans

History down to the Establishment of the *Limes*

There exists perhaps no better or more vivid introduction to the conditions in Roman-occupied Germany in the Augustan period than the account by Cassius Dio of the causes that led to the defeat and death of Varus in AD 9. 'The Romans held portions of the country, not entire regions but such districts as happened to have been subdued . . . the soldiers wintered there, and cities were being founded. Gradually the barbarians adapted themselves to Roman ways, getting accustomed to holding markets, and assembling peacefully. But they had not forgotten their ancestral ways, their inborn nature, their old proud way of life, their freedom based on arms. As long as they were unlearning their ancient customs gradually and as it were by degrees, they did not protest against these changes in their mode of life, for they were growing different without being aware of it. But when Quinctilius Varus was appointed governor of the area and in the course of his official duties attempted to take these people in hand, striving to change them, issuing orders as though they had already been subdued and exacting money as from a subject nation, their patience was exhausted.'

This passage aptly summarizes the changes which began with Drusus' conquest of certain sections of Germany, and it clearly regards the disaster of AD 9 as the result of a mistaken policy of occupation. The rising did not, as might perhaps have been supposed, originate in those sections of the country which were still free, but in the heart of the Roman-occupied territory. The

Romans themselves were well aware of the conflicts which then arose between the different tribes, even between members of one and the same tribe or indeed family, some siding firmly with the conqueror, some hoping to take advantage of their good relations with Rome to gain a paramount position among their own people, and some, including men who had seen service in the Roman army and even become Roman citizens, taking up arms. The complexity and potential tragedy of the situation is reflected in the accounts of the relations between the Cheruscan nobleman and leader of the revolt, Arminius, a constant companion of the Roman generals on their German campaigns, who had been made a member of the equestrian order for his services to the Empire, and Segestes, his father-in-law, a Cheruscan of note who remained unswervingly loyal to Rome but was unable to prevail against the feelings of his people.

In 12 BC when Drusus took his army to the right bank of the Rhine, he had made careful preparations to achieve his object – the conquest and exploration of the country and its conversion into a Roman province. From the second decade BC onwards Roman legions were posted to the north of the Alps and along the Rhine, and camps to provision and if need be rally the troops had been set up all along this line. The campaigns themselves were informed by an offensive spirit. The armies, according to the custom of the time, were marched down more or less passable roads into such centres of resistance as could be reached from the Rhine. Large-scale enveloping movements, as later on employed by Tiberius, were not yet used; for it would scarcely be correct to see as such the conquest of a coastal strip of Chaucan territory, an operation for which Frisian support had been secured. It had long been customary to explore unknown territory by water, and even Tiberius and Germanicus still made military reconnaissances by sea. From 11 BC decisive operations were concentrated on those vital strategic roads which until Germanicus' campaigns of AD 14–16 were regarded as the chief arteries of an eastern offensive: the Lippe Valley on the one side, the Wetterau with the trough of Lower Hesse on the other. In the west the adversaries to be met were thus first of all those old-established foes, the Usipetes and the Tencteri, and also the Sugambri. In the Main region a people still remembered on the upper Rhine from Ariovistus' exploits, the Marcomanni, had to be dealt with; on their defeat (which ended the campaign) their chieftain Maroboduus led them into Bohemia. Other tribes involved in this campaign included the Chatti of the Fulda, Lahn and Eder region, a people that lay across the route to the Cherusci, their northern enemies and neighbours, and who long remained a leading target for the Roman armies.

All these peoples inhabited an area which in language and culture had joined the nuclear regions of Germanic culture east of the Weser-Aller line only at a very late date, and even in the last century BC maintained extremely close links with the world of the continental Celts. Since Caesar's day this territory (at all events close to the Rhine) had time and again been entered by Roman soldiers: centurions trying to raise tribute, but repulsed in the process; punitive expeditions sent out to retaliate. Now the time had come to make good Rome's claim to Germany east of the Rhine. Yet in spite of an extensive field of operations (Florus refers to occupation troops and watch commandoes stretching from the Maas across the Weser up to the Elbe), by no means the entire country was affected. Whatever lay beyond the Elbe remained in the realm of fabulous rumour; it was here, in 9 BC, that a woman of superhuman size met Drusus and forced him to turn back by prophesying his imminent death – an apparition the Romans were to regard as the voice of Deity itself since Drusus died a bare month later. It was a momentous historical event when six years later Domitius Ahenobarbus crossed the Elbe, concluding treaties of friendship with tribes to the East of it. We hear on this occasion of the Hermunduri, a tribe which having left its homeland was settled by Ahenobarbus in the Main region, so recently abandoned by the Marcomanni. But this remains for many years the only information about these parts. Even Tiberius' German wars of AD 4 and 5 achieved little that was worth recording: a fleet sailed up the western coast of Jutland, a few Germanic tribal-names occur along the lower Rhine, north of the Lippe (Bructeri), and

on the lower Elbe, where Langobardi, Semnones and Hermunduri now entered the Roman range of vision.

Radically fresh developments took place only when there
arose, among the Marcomanni in Bohemia, a power-centre
which threatened to endanger all Rome's conquests east of the
Rhine. Maroboduus, according to Velleius Paterculus, had
assumed royal power and subjected or made dependent upon
himself by treaty all his neighbours: 'within a short while the
number of armed men guarding his kingdom, who by constant
drill had attained almost Roman disciplinary standards, rose to
vast and alarming proportions.' In AD 5 measures were put in
hand to destroy this Marcomannic threat. From the Rhine to
the Danube the legions launched a remarkable broadly planned
enveloping movement under the command of Tiberius. Five
days' march separated them from the enemy when to the rear of
the Danubian front news of serious revolts in the subject
provinces of Dalmatia and Pannonia forced Tiberius to break
off operations. It was, in effect, the end of a project which, had it
been successful, would have pushed out the frontiers of the
Empire from the Rhine and Danube to the March and Elbe; for
no politically significant results attended the attempts made after
Varus' death (notably under the confused command of Germanicus) to maintain the Imperial authority between the Rhine and
the lower Elbe. We read of widespread devastations, of a
butchery of the native population which in some areas seems to
have been carried out in barbarous fashion. But this did not
affect the situation as a whole, although the treaties of loyalty
to Rome concluded by most of the Germanic tribes within this
region remained valid and effective, at any rate until the middle
of the century. The winter quarters and military bases east of
the Rhine were given up and the legions withdrawn to the
Rhine-Danube frontier, a situation which remained unchanged
until the arrival of the Flavian dynasty in the 70s of the first
century AD.

A significant change did, however, occur inside Germany
within this period which seems in the first place to be due to
the achievements of Maroboduus who (notably, so it would
appear, after the failure of the Tiberian campaign) consolidated

his position inside his own kingdom, where the assumption of the royal title was to make him increasingly unpopular among his own people, and who managed to extend his influence over all the Germanic peoples in the Elbe region and some to the East of it. Among the other Germanic tribes his great confederacy, which included Langobardi and Semnones as well as Lugii, enjoyed enormous standing: the trophy of the victory of AD 9 was, as we saw, not kept among the victorious Cherusci but handed to Maroboduus. We shall see below something of the cultural impact of Maroboduus' kingdom, where ancient Germanic tradition mingled with Celtic achievement, and sutlers and merchants from the Provinces on the Rhine and the Danube spread Roman influences in material equipment as well as cultural forms. A new and distinctive culture now arose in Bohemia, a region where Germanic peoples had come to rule over an older native Celtic population, a culture that was to exercise a profound influence on the other Elbe-Suebic groups in Central Germany, Brandenburg and Mecklenburg, and Eastern Lower Saxony. But this influence did not long survive the departure of the legions, who by their very strangeness fostered among the various Germanic tribes a sense, if not of unity, at any rate of common interest. No sooner had the legions left the country than the ties linking the various tribes began to loosen. Arminius now became the champion of tribal independence against the oppressive domination of Maroboduus. Even his allies, the Langobardi and Semnones, turned against the king now that their freedom, seemingly threatened by the projected Roman Province, appeared once and for all secure. The decisive battle was fought in AD 17, in proper battle order on the Roman model. Maroboduus, induced to retreat, returned to his kingdom greatly weakened in prestige, and with little difficulty he was the following year expelled by Catualda, a Marcomannic exile returned from his sojourn among the Goths. Shortly afterwards Catualda suffered the same fate at the hands of the Hermunduri, and like his predecessor found refuge on Imperial territory. The retinues of both these leaders were settled on the northern banks of the Danube between the Waag and March and given as king Vannius, a man of the Quadi – the first we hear of this particular

Suebic tribe which, together with the Marcomanni, was long to form a constant threat to Rome's Danubian frontier.

Surrounded by a bodyguard of foot-soldiers and mounted Sarmatian Iazyges (a people who at about that time were moving westward from southern Russia into the plains of Hungary east of the Danube, Ch. 16), and in the habit, whenever danger threatened, of retiring to his various strongholds, Vannius was able to amass great riches through tolls and plundering raids. Having reigned for thirty years he was well on the way to becoming a despot when like all these rulers he fell victim to internal dissension and to the envy and hatred of his neighbours. The author of his fall, according to the reports, was Vibilius, king of the Hermunduri, who had formed an alliance with Vangio and Sido, Vannius' nephews and heirs. For Rome the significance of these events went very much deeper than the fate befalling one particular king. We read on this occasion of Lugii and other peoples from the East Germanic realm, as well as Hermunduri, peoples bearing down upon the Danube and with this upon the frontiers of the Roman province of Pannonia, drawn by the riches of Vannius' state. Vannius' defeat (his retinue was settled in Pannonia) did not destroy the kingdom of the Quadi. But the pressures from the north, which could not but endanger the Danubian frontier, became with time progressively more powerful, initially in the years 89 to 97, when Domitian, involved in costly wars with Dacia, engaged in heavy fighting with the Quadi and Marcomanni in order to secure a western frontier he saw threatened by both Suebi and Sarmatians. After the conquest of Dacia and its conversion into a Roman province in 106, and the establishment of military strongholds, some in extremely advanced positions, on the left bank of the Danube and on the March and Thaya, these outposts served as bulwarks against the pressures from the north.

We do not know what factors set in motion the Lugian peoples against the Suebi of the Danube. There is archaeological evidence to show that during the late years of the first century AD they considerably extended their area of settlement, towards Upper Silesia and the Upper Vistula, and also, in particular, towards the Bug and Dniester. Whether this spread was due to a migration of Lugian groups is something we cannot now be certain of, though it does appear probable on several counts. But the movement is presumably associated with those more clearly discernable re-groupings which are likely to be connected with the appearance of the Goths in the Vistula estuary region. The country between the Vistula and Oder had never been a theatre of war, and the written reports provide little information. They comprise, besides migration myths which are inconclusive for lack of parallel traditions by which to evaluate them, attempts made at tribal classification by ethnographically interested historians from Strabo to Tacitus and Pliny, who differ not only in the naming of the various tribes, but even in their accounts of the more important confederacies. Whereas for instance Tacitus, like Ptolemy, regards the Lugii as one of the larger confederacies and together with less significant tribes includes in it the Harii and Nahanarvali, Pliny bases his classification on the Vandals, a confederacy which appears to include among its members at least one Lugian people, the Charini, if this indeed resembles Tacitus' Harii in more than name. Among the Vandals Pliny numbers the Burgundians, located east of the Semnones by Ptolemys, and the Gutoni – the Goths, who in Tacitus and apparently also in Strabo form an independent group.

These discrepancies are likely to reflect historical developments. According to the Gothic migration myth recorded by Jordanes (551) the Goths on landing expelled first the Rugii 'inhabiting the ocean-shore' and then proceeded to subject their neighbours, the Vandals, 'whom even then they overcame and included among the conquered nations'. In view of the perennial strife of Goth and Vandal an air of hindsight may appear to permeate this statement. But it is likely to have a very early core and to reflect conditions in the newly settled Vistula country. The Silings provide a further instance of these shifting allegiances. By the time the name of Vandal had been extended to all the peoples living north of the Sudeten Mountains (unlikely to have happened before the Marcomannic Wars of the last third of the second century AD), the Silings were regarded as a sub-division of the Vandals. But Ptolemy, in a map which seems in part to draw upon far earlier sources, still places the Silings – without any further ascription – below the Semnones, a location where they could scarcely be included in the Lugian confederacy. It would therefore appear that we may postulate certain shifts and even changes in the alignment of the smaller groups, without being able to explain the details of the process.

It does seem fairly certain that with the arrival of the Goths in the Vistula estuary region, and the collapse of Maroboduus' empire which, according to Strabo, had numbered among its allies the Lugii, the older groupings began to disintegrate and the various individual tribes to form fresh groupings. The outcome of this did not become evident until the second century AD, the period of the Marcomannic Wars, when the great Gothic and Vandal confederacies moved directly within the range of the Imperial defences.

A further focus of unrest took shape as far back as the first century AD along the lower Rhine. Initially this was a matter of fairly insignificant raids and revolts. The Frisians, exasperated when a Roman governor laid down, as standard for the tribute they had to pay in ox-hides, the hide of an aurochs, gathered their forces and in AD 28 laid siege to a Roman fortress, inflicting appreciable losses. More troublesome were the Chauci, who under alien leadership had plundered the Gallic coast and broken into Roman territory on the lower Rhine. Soon after the middle of the century conditions in this part of the country deteriorated greatly. Changes in the nature of the landscape, and notably the flooding of the coastal marshlands, reduced the hitherto more or less intensively cultivated arable acreage and pastures. Since the numerous permanent military establishments of the Rhine frontier now prevented the coastal peoples from expanding westwards, the situation in central Germany began to have a very different impact on the lower Rhineland than earlier. The Chauci expanded at the cost of the Ampsivarii up to the country of the Frisians, while these expanded Rhinewards, occupying in AD 58 among other areas a coastal strip between the Rhine and Zuider Zee which was Imperial frontier territory. The Chatti somewhat earlier had plundered Roman territory on the upper Rhine, and been repulsed. All this goes to show that it was now no longer possible to speak of a pacification of Germany, as it had been – at any rate near the Rhine – until the reign of Claudius.

The troubles after the death of Nero set off a wave of uprisings which radically altered the relations between the Empire and the Germanic tribes. This time the impulse was provided by the Batavians, a sub-group of the Chatti, who had settled between the Old Rhine and the Waal, supplying several cohorts for the auxiliaries under the command of members of the tribal nobility. In 69–70 one of these leaders, Julius Civilis, took advantage of a favourable opportunity to call upon his people to secede. The response was immediate and immense. From Cologne to Mainz the Roman troops were faced with treachery, secession, protracted sieges, and sometimes even annihilation by the barbarians. Never had so many Germanic tribes fought in one camp: Canninefates, Frisians, Chauci and Chatti; the long-familiar Usipetes, Bructeri and Tencteri; even Tungri, provincial subjects from the Maas. But the object of the rising – presumably the formation of a state embracing both sides of the lower Rhine and also certain Belgic territories, a region that had long exhibited ethnic, linguistic and cultural traits in common – was not achieved by the rebels. The rising having spent itself in isolated actions, Vespasian was able to restore stability and the old situation along the frontier.

With these experiences behind him, Vespasian in the 70s decided to push the Roman frontier out across the Rhine and the Danube into the still unconquered section of Germany, and to shorten it by building across the Black Forest a highway to link the Danube with the upper Rhine (already in the late Tiberian-Claudian period this had been secured by forts). Domitian carried on this process, and his campaigns of 83 and 89 against the Chatti resulted in the earliest installations of the *limes* in the Taunus. South of the Main, corresponding bases were set up in the Odenwald and on the Alb. As *agri decumates* this newly conquered territory became part of the province of Upper Germany.

Further frontier extensions date from the reigns of Trajan and Hadrian until, by the time of Antoninus Pius in the mid-second century AD, a line had been reached which led from the Rhine north of Coblenz at a regressive angle across the Taunus ridge to the Lahn loop near Giessen, from there down to the Main at Seligenstadt and Miltenberg and straight ahead to the Rems near Lorch, where it took a turn eastwards to reach the Altmühl at Gunzenhausen and the Danube at Eining. Strategically somewhat odd, this frontier, falling between the Roman provinces of Raetia and Upper Germany, makes sense only when it is seen to be a consolidation of earlier lines of occupation, which had as it were become frozen at a period when the attention of Rome was directed elsewhere. In this its final form the *limes* secured the peace for only three generations: already in the first third of the third century it was breached along a wide front by Germanic peoples.

Distribution and Settlement

The period after the establishment of the *limes* and the conquest of Dacia, when the Imperial frontiers attained their farthest extension towards both east and north, may nevertheless be considered a period of consolidation and pacification. It is the period of Tacitus' *Germania*, a book published in the first year of Trajan's reign, which summarizes the situation after a period of rapid historical development. This work, though based in part upon earlier sources, also incorporated contemporary information and in its central sections it was by no means out of date. In conjunction with the archaeological material, which supplements and elaborates the text in many ways, the book provides us with something rare in history: the opportunity of taking a cross-section of a people at a point in time when the development of its various sub-groups was regarded as having been completed, and they had grown together into a historical body with sufficiently distinctive internal characteristics to set it apart from its neighbours both on the frontiers of the Empire along the Danube and the Rhine, and in the depths of eastern and northern Europe.

The *limes* region itself remained outside the precincts of this Germany, for all the peoples – including the Germanic ones –

who settled on Imperial territory were absorbed in the provincial Roman culture. The same holds good of the population of the *agri decumates* where, on the upper Rhine and also north of the Neckar, groups of settlers had been living even in the first half of the first century AD who bore the distinctive marks of contemporary Germanic culture; both archaeological evidence and the name 'Suebi Nicretes' (Neckar Suebi) on inscriptions of Trajan's reign attest their ethnic character and their origin in the region of the Elbe.

South of the Central Uplands the situation differed in that Germanic settlers appear at this time to have reached neither the *limes* nor the Danube (where this formed the frontier), confining their spread almost entirely to the Main Valley, and in the Bohemian basin to the Eger, Moldau and Elbe system. The Budweise trough provides the most southerly, and also the most isolated, signs of early Germanic settlements. Moravia, on the other hand, has up to the close of the first century AD yielded nothing worth mentioning, apart from a few traces around Olmütz. The archaeological evidence begins to pile up again in the wine-growing districts of lower Austria, and also east of the March in Slovakia where they nearly reach the Danube, and where, within close range of the Imperial province of Pannonia, we may locate the kingdom of Vannius. This region was doubly frontier territory, for from the mid-first century AD the Hungarian plains to the south-east began to receive those Sarmatian Iazyges who, moving westwards from the Black Sea steppes, left their earliest archaeological relics in the broad plains west of the Theiss around the turn of the first century AD. Indigenous peoples, best known among them the Osi and Cotini, closely linked by common culture with the Continental Celts, and later, in some unknown manner, to become members of the Lugian confederacy, still inhabited the neighbouring regions of the north-east: the Waag Valley (Puchóv Culture), and the upper reaches of the Vistula and Oder, where Germanic settlement did not set in until the close of the first century.

Even as late as the first century, *Germania libera* south of the Central Uplands shows with the exception of northern Bohemia no sign of widespread, unitary Germanic settlement. In the west the few Suebic groups were incorporated in the *limes* and soon lost their individuality; in the Bavarian Main Valley traces have been found of small, and archaeologically at present still isolated, groups of Hermunduri; while on the Danubian frontier, between the March and Waag, there lived the Quadi, allied with nomadic mounted Iazyges warriors and ruled by men of their own people, but under Roman supervision as it were, and under constant pressure from the north. While it retained its independence (up to 106) the Dacian kingdom made its influence felt as far as the March, as well as very powerfully in the Theiss region of Eastern Slovakia, and even more so northwards of the Carpathians along the Dniester in Podolia (Lipica Culture), where the possibility of Dacian settlements has to be taken into account.

No grounds exist for supposing Dacians to have been the only peoples settling hereabouts. But we can neither unequivocally locate, nor safely associate with any given set of finds, the names of other early peoples known to us from Eastern Europe, the Peucini, for example, or the Veneti and Bastarnae. Even in the first century AD the Sarubinzy Culture was still widespread in the regions between the Central Bug across the Pripiet to the Dnieper, a culture one would gladly ascribe to the Veneti if this term represented no more than a collective name for all the eastern neighbours of the Germanic peoples (which does not necessarily mean that the Venetan sphere of influence remained the same throughout this period). East of the Vistula estuary, providing a firm link in the chain of the Germanic frontier peoples, there lived the Aestii, ancestors of the Pruzzi, a Baltic people whose Germanic affinities, noted by Tacitus, have recently been confirmed by archaeologists.

At the northern frontier of the Germanic world, in Central Scandinavia, the situation again becomes unclear. Germanic finds worth mentioning of the early Imperial period have been discovered only on the Baltic islands, in Östergötland, and in the Oslo Fjord. Their shortage elsewhere may be due to the time-lag noticeable in the spread of culture northwards from the Continent, for everywhere in northern Europe cultural change set in belatedly and is most tellingly expressed in objects remodelling in later styles forms of pre-Roman origin. Large stretches of the interior – the extensive, densely wooded rock country of Småland, Uppland, Bohusläns and the parts of Norway distant from the coast – still remained without permanent settlement, and were not penetrated and occupied until the third and fourth centuries AD, later to attain in the period of the Great Migrations and the Vikings that stage in the outlying rural settlement-type that forms the economic and social background to the sagas. Nevertheless one may, at least around Lake Mälar, postulate very early beginnings of colonization, that is if the Suiones described at length by Tacitus are indeed connected with the Svear, later to be found here. Northwards of the line running from Oslo to Uppsala one may, however, be certain that nomadic ways persisted as much in the Imperial period as earlier; centuries were to pass before this zone became culturally a part of Europe.

The situation was very different in the interior of continental Germany. Disregarding for the moment sections of the Central Uplands which were difficult to approach and unsuited to the needs of contemporary settlers, and also disregarding southern Germany beyond the *limes* as well as certain sections of eastern Saxony, Further Pomerania and the Vistula region, the archaeological map shows (depending on the state of research) a more or less dense network of settlements, divided into groups and bounded by stretches empty of finds. These settlement-groups frequently show material cultural affinities which seem to be explicable in terms of inter-communication, and they have consequently been defined as social associations enjoying common trade. In this way a north Germanic group in Scandinavia faces a coastal group along the North Sea coast; this in its turn faces a western group extending from the Rhine up to the Saale and from the Weser bend down to the Main at Würzburg; and this faces an Elbe-Germanic group between western Lower Saxony and the Oder, and an East Germanic group between the Oder and the Vistula, the San and the Bug.

The question of course remains which of the Germanic peoples familiar from the ancient sources are likely to be represented by the various groups, a question upon which agreement is unlikely to be reached since the ancient writers (who anyway

cover only sections of Germany as a whole) quite clearly ba.
their ethnographic classifications upon a variety of principles.
Depending on the relative importance attached to factors such
as language, origin, tribal tradition, social and religious institutions, as well as, in particular, the shifting allegiance of the
various tribal members of the larger groupings, a number of
possible classifications did – and do – in fact present themselves.

Only where the classical accounts are particularly detailed and
dependable does it therefore seem possible to map precisely the
whereabouts of the peoples recorded by ancient writers, and to
co-ordinate them with modern archaeological attempts at
classification. But even allowing for numerous discrepancies and
uncertainties in detail, it does seem fairly certain that the North
Sea group included Frisians and Chauci and, north of the Elbe,
several of those smaller tribes listed by Tacitus and lumped
together as Saxons by Ptolemy. The West Germanic group
would have included besides the Bructeri-Tencteri group, the
Chatti, the Cherusci and a section of the Hermunduri. The
Elbe-Germanic group counted among its members the Langobardi, the Semnones, and besides Hermunduri, also Quadi and
Marcomanni. East Germanic, finally, were the Lugii (Silings,
Asdings, etc.), the Rugii, the Burgundians and the Goths.

Social Development

All these groups differed amongst each other in origin, size and
general external appearance, a fact which becomes particularly
evident if we look at them during the Augustan period, when
Roman impulses emanating from the Rhine and the Danube
came up against the different Germanic groups in a great variety
of forms, and many stages of development. The relative homo-
geneity in material culture, the outcome of this Roman impact,
was confined at first to the peoples that fell under the influence
of Maroboduus, the Marcomannic king whose political activities
prepared the ground for uniformity; the Elbe-Suebic peoples
between the Luneburg Ilmenau and the Oder, and the East
Germanic Lugii in Central Silesia and the Warta bend. The
Vistula estuary, the Elbe, Fünen, and certain parts of Jutland,

r hand, still remained fairly peripheral at this

details the response to this Roman-Marcomannic act naturally differed from place to place, depending on the ... ir of the local traditions, and the distance from the centres of these impulses. This is particularly noticeable where the nature of the country called for independent solutions to problems of settlement and economic and social life, though it is just as evident in certain aspects of the religious life, in the grave-gift customs associated with the funerary ritual for instance. But in the articles of clothing, the trappings for both horse and rider, the weapons and the table-ware – often costly Roman imports – and in the treatment of the bodies and the grave-gifts which mark the burials of members of the higher social groups, a remarkable uniformity, extending across the boundaries between the different groups and peoples, becomes at once apparent.

It would seem to follow that the bearers of this change were chiefly members of the nobility, and the far-reaching links revealed by many of the finds may up to a point be assumed to have been restricted to this particular class. Many parts of Germany remained outside this movement in its initial stages: Scandinavia, Further Pomerania, the Vistula bend and all of Western Germany between the Rhine and the Aller. But even here the Germanic culture distinctive of the Roman period was breaking through by the middle, and notably the second half, of the first century AD, to extend, homogeneous in style and repertoire of form, from the *Limes* to the Vistula and northwards up to the Oslo Fjord during the second century AD.

The factors behind this spread remain obscure, for we know as yet too little of such basic aspects even of contemporary life as settlement habits, and economic or social order. Around the time of Jesus' birth, for instance, movements become noticeable in certain sections of the North German plains which resulted on the one hand in the colonization of the marshlands east of the Weser, and on the other in the abandonment of quite large areas of the terminal moraine country (*Jungmoränenland*) which has today more fertile soils than the adjoining stretches of sandy soil. Yet we do not know whether there was any connection between these movements. Nor do we know why and in what manner these and other regions were then newly settled, while other, older areas of settlement were given up. Occasionally these shifts have been ascribed to the migration of particular tribes, a theory which leaves out of account the fact that settlement mobility (which had its parallel in the instability of the political associations of the time) appears to have been characteristic of prehistoric conditions, and no less potent a factor in the first few centuries AD than earlier in the pre-Roman Iron Age.

Population movements were normally still a matter of hamlets or group settlements changing their location from time to time inside a given area of settlement. But how precisely this proceeded, and whether such movements might involve changes in the inter-relationship of the various communities, are questions which cannot be determined until a good deal more is known archaeologically about these settlement-areas. Few of the finds of the first two centuries AD point to any social differentiation inside the settlements, and while it is self-evident that certain individuals and families would have enjoyed a higher social standing than the rest, it does appear that the small, short-lived type of settlement and loose social cohesion of the time were not, in general, conducive to the growth of rigid class distinctions. Even where, for one reason or another, settlements remained constant over generations, the emergence of classes based on property is scarcely noticeable: either the structure of the population by mode of production provided no opportunity for such developments, or peoples with a predominantly peasant way of life settled in large isolated farmsteads, which appear also to emphasize their independence by possessing separate burial-grounds. With any increase in the population, the dwellings in such settlements would be increased and added to. In the marshland *Wurten*, where stock-farming may have played a more important role than cultivation, a different solution was found; and here a large *Wurt* of more than thirty farmsteads would consist of prosperous and less prosperous farm enterprises, cottars with some domestic industry (e.g. comb-making), and, finally, a well-to-do local family performing the administrative functions of village *starosta*, or elder.

It is worthwhile taking a somewhat closer look at these *Wurten*, for the changes which took place in the course of the second century in the structure of their buildings and in the relationship between the individual farmsteads reflects in local and specific form developments then taking place throughout Germany. In the initial phases of the *Wurt* several farm enterprises were surrounded and marked out as a unit by a common fence or ditch, units which would differ in the number of their farmsteads, just as the farmsteads differed considerably in size and in material equipment. In time the individual farmsteads split off from their original units, and, as the individual *Wurten* amalgamated into a single large *Wurt*, attained their independence, or so one might deduce from the fence now often surrounding them. The disintegration of these older groupings must in some way have been connected with the rise of the *starosta* farm which, during the second century, gained a hall or mansion-house, designed exclusively for human habitation, as well as several more unit-farmsteads. This was soon enlarged and to the purely agricultural buildings were added workshops for craftsmen working in bronze and iron. In the third century these workshops were concentrated on an extension of the *Wurt*, i.e. transferred from the residential area of the hall to its periphery. By now the *Wurt* had grown into a complex social community containing a hall occupied (as is indicated by the constancy of its location) by an old-established local family still predominantly agricultural in its way of life although by now equipped with the means of manufacturing metal implements and entrusted with certain communal functions; as well as numerous farm enterprises, dependent or independent of the hall and differing in size; and also cottages, the inhabitants of which would have had some share in the communal stock of smaller animals and, for the rest, gained their living by fishing, minor handicrafts and, presumably, by working for neighbouring farmers and the great hall.

In this particular form the emergence from among the village communities of leading families may have been confined to the larger and longer-lived settlements of the coastal marshes. But it is also typical of developments throughout Germany, in that similar, mansion-like farms appeared elsewhere, first on the outskirts of the Imperial frontier on the lower Rhine, and somewhat later (the third and fourth centuries) in the interior itself. In one such instance we find a large farmstead, surrounded by a moat and palisade, facing three smaller unit-farmsteads, also fenced in, and, at some distance but still enclosed, a long structure without stables: a hall containing an elevated seat and other features marking out its special role inside the hamlet. At another site the living-quarters of a large unit-farmstead, forty-seven yards long, were converted into a spacious hall also equipped with a raised seat – beneath which was found a sizeable hoard of coins. This particular site also contained a number of smaller structures, and conveys as a whole the impression rather of an estate than a collection of independent farmsteads (as is indicated by the permanent settlements of the long buildings – see above).

This growing differentiation in social structure, perhaps already expressed in the internal village developments described above, and certainly apparent in the emergence of the hall/mansion-type of home as a distinctive form of settlement, was evidently due not only to economic change. Decisive, rather, were two entirely different factors: the arrival from elsewhere of dominant groups of a different ethnic origin (e.g. Maroboduus in Bohemia), and contacts with the Roman Empire. These contacts, which notably during the *limes* period became more marked with the extension of the Imperial frontier on the Rhine and the Danube, were strengthened by the custom adopted by Germanic noblemen since Maroboduus' time of serving with the Roman forces. In barbarian societies leading families have often been raised to positions of still greater eminence as a result of contact with highly developed civilizations; and in both settlement and funerary ritual (still to be described) the barbaric nobility of this period has left material proof of that desire for outward distinction, that borrowing of striking attitudes and deliberate attempt to set itself apart which produced in the cultural forms regarded as decisive features in common extending across tribal boundaries. This applies as much to Dacians and Celts as to the early Germans, for though

311

these various peoples responded very differently to the impact of Mediterranean civilization, and differed greatly in their degree of assimilation, in the fundamentals of the social life and the political activity of their leading families they basically agreed. Everywhere the leading men set up a following of dependents and a military retinue of free men for wars and plundering raids, and everywhere the people able to command the necessary means for such a costly increase in prestige kept up the external show proper to their distinguished position.

To judge from both the finds and early sources, far-reaching links were forged between these families through marriage, adoption and gifts, and from them sprang those military chieftains who on their return home from having made their fortune in the Roman service sought remunerative employment with their own or with some other people: Maroboduus and Arminius, Cruptorix, a leader in the Frisian uprising, Gannascus, a Canninefate serving with the Chauci, Julius Civilis among the Batavi. All these men secured for themselves the means of obtaining their ends, and they commanded retinues bound to them by special ties of loyalty and which, depending on size and importance, were allowed a privileged position by the Romans upon losing their leader (e.g. the followers of Maroboduus, Catualda and Vannius). We read in contemporary accounts of such chieftains becoming landowners: Cruptorix possessed a farm, Julius Civilis estates (*agri*) and country houses (*villae*). At once one thinks of the village with its great hall, and also of the villas inside the province. There can finally be little doubt that it was this social class which provided the leadership for the political association – the tribal confederacy, whether in the form of a constitutional principate or of a monarchy, as well as the military kings of later periods of Germanic history.

The social structure which (at any rate in its fundamentals) is reflected in the settlement-types of the time left its mark also on the funerary ritual. Whereas the ordinary population was buried in extensive urn-fields, the aristocracy was buried – often by inhumation – in small separate groups of graves, the men almost invariably without weapons and at best accompanied by horse-gear, knife and scissors. The characteristic grave-gifts consisted of articles of clothing (sections of belts and clasps), drinking vessels for wine and beer, drinking horns, and containers made of clay, glass and metal (the glass and metal vessels chiefly of Roman make and fashioned in the Roman manner), jewellery including neckrings, bracelets and charms, and parts of board-games, notably gamesmen.

But these lavish grave-gifts, though homogeneous over extensive distances, are geographically by no means uniform in any given period – no single site, not even any given single region, provides sufficient evidence to let us reconstruct without a gap the history of this usage throughout its lifetime. This indicates how lacking in tradition were the aristocratic funerary practices of the period. It also suggests a fundamental instability in the aristocratic position of leadership and establishes that the outward forms of distinction intermittently adopted by the nobility depended for their continuance on other factors too, on the nature of the cultural contacts and their power to penetrate, and on their readiness to accept borrowings from outside.

These graves supply, besides, some more specific information. To judge by the quality of the workmanship, the grave-gifts were the product of skilled craftsmen, and since with time they exhibit progressively more clearly marked regional features, they would appear to have been made by artisans who were in the direct employ of their patrons. It has been correctly noted that from the third century onwards we may speak of a 'court art', which could have moulded the style of the entire era.

From workshops such as one may imagine located at the great halls and the courts of the nobility, vigorous artistic impulses did in fact emanate. Borrowings from classical art now appreciably enlarged the artistic repertoire in both technique and subject-matter; the human figure joined the older animal and vegetable motifs. Artistic skill, if still devoted to decorating functional ware, began to vary in expression from place to place, as if adapted to the special requirements of given individual patrons. Like the great hall and the aristocratic grave, art too began to symbolize the individual and his class. Artisan's products were now inscribed with personal names and magic formulae (affording the owner supernatural protection) in runic lettering: mentally too the people of the time were changing.

Whereas the graves of the nobility show in both lay-out and material equipment a uniformity extending over wide areas, the larger popular burial-grounds (mostly urn-fields) exhibit appreciable regional discrepancies in ritual detail; which would seem to indicate that communities of tradition (as one might term the settlement-groups) were of local significance only. From the viewpoint of the changing social order the single most interesting aspect of these burial-grounds is their weapon-content. The evidence is certainly particularly patchy here, since it was only intermittently the custom to bury weapons with the dead, and that not everywhere. But since a study of the weapon-composition of the various graves reveals typical groups exhibiting a constant numerical inter-relationship, one may at least say that the fighting men were not uniformly armed, a conclusion permitting of certain deductions about troop-formation and fighting methods. Most numerous, accordingly, were the lance-bearers, followed by men carrying both shield and lance. The smallest group consisted of warriors fully armed with lance, shield and sword. Just as swords do not turn up in every male graveyard, so the equestrian spur, an object sometimes also found without accompanying weapons, is only now and again found in a sword-carrier's grave. The very rarity of the spur marks out its owner as member of a special class; the leading class, apparently, since horse-gear is also found with aristocratic burials unaccompanied by weapons, and one which in the funerary ritual was not necessarily marked by weapons.

Contemporary battle-accounts endorse the impression of a privileged position enjoyed, at all events initially, by the mounted men. At first encounter an élite of horsemen, each accompanied by a man on foot, would fight at the head of the attacking wedge. Besides the light spear opening the battle, the horseman also used a lance, and then fought, if this was lost and could not be replaced by the accompanying man on foot, with a short sword in hand-to-hand combat. Later the influence of neighbouring mounted Iranian peoples – Iazyges, Roxalani and Alans – led to the formation of mounted contingents (and sometimes even to the mounting of entire armies) operating independently, equipped with weapons and insignia including pike, bow, armour and dragon-banner modelled clearly on Iranian proto-types. How very powerfully the ethos of the mounted way of life was to seize hold of the nobility of early Germany became apparent during the period of the great migrations.

For both infantry and cavalry the chief weapon was the lance, and it is therefore the one most often found. The foot-soldier often though not invariably protected by a buckler (the point of which could become dangerous at close quarters) had to fight in closed ranks if on losing his lance he was not to be delivered helpless into enemy hands. Some, at best a quarter, of all the warriors also carried a sword, kept as short as possible for close combat, on the model of the Roman *gladius*. The long thrusting-sword, still generally employed for single combat in the pre-Roman period, ceased to be serviceable; concerted troop action, not individual valour, provided the only hope of standing up to the tactically-trained Roman legions. Even in Varus' day Germanic armies still thought it necessary to ambush Roman troops, rather than engage in open battle. Yet by the time the Langobardi and Semnones joined battle with Maroboduus, the rival armies faced each other in properly disciplined rank and file.

Further sub-divisions can on closer investigation be intro-duced into these military groupings, including divisions based on geographical differences arising even inside the boundaries of any given tribe or people. But no single settlement was clearly sufficiently populous to recruit the armies formed by the fighting men; the military sphere of organization therefore quite evidently failed to coincide with the local association as represented by the settlement. This is already apparent in the custom, inherited from earlier times, of having separate male cemeteries that are likely to have served several communities. Even plainer is the evidence of the extensive weapon hoards that have been found in bogs thought to have served as sacri-ficial sites for the larger confederacies, tribes, or tribal groups associated by religious ties. The custom of sacrificing weapons to the deity, although sporadically already known in the pre-Roman Iron Age among both Celtic and Germanic peoples, became more widespread in the second and third centuries, particularly in Jutland. For a number of reasons we may therefore assume the existence of extensive warrior confederacies, linked not only by military service but also by common religious practices.

Ancient sources clearly attest the supra-local significance of the early Germanic sacred places and the central position these occupied in the tribal life (which would explain why they tended to be especially subject to enemy ravages). The deities worshipped were predominantly female: Tanfana among the Marsi, Baduhenna among the Frisians, Veleda among the Bructeri, Ganna among the Semnones, Nerthus among the peoples north of the Elbe. The Lugian Nahanarvali worshipped a pair of brothers with rites conducted by a priest in female habit.

All these may have been vegetation cults designed to promote the life-force and fertility in man, animal and crop alike. Quite a number of sites, both large and small, have been found where foodstuffs including butter and other fats, hazelnuts, harvested crop and harvesting tools were deposited, as well as animals – pigs, sheep, cattle, dogs and even horses – and parts of animals. Wooden idols, mostly female, have been found in fenced-in enclosures which are interpreted as sacred places, as well as wooden oracle sticks employed in casting lots, and human skeletons and parts of skeletons.

Two types of sacrifice therefore existed. One, dedicated to growth, prosperity and fertility in general, bore chthonic features and with its carved idols, which in certain areas were predominantly female, it may have resembled the *terra-mater* vegetation cults so widespread in classical antiquity. The other sprang from the male sphere of life. The man sacrificed his weapons, marks of his dignity, to what was probably the god of war, and presumably also, judging by the weapon-sacrifices occasionally found in grave-fields, to the god of the dead. We do not know whether the gods were thought of in human form, although the classical accounts seem to suggest as much. What does however remain entirely uncertain is when precisely the barbarian Olympus in which the warlike element, with Thor and Wotan, took the place of honour, came into being; when the Germanic peoples began to see their gods as individuals, not just as anthropomorphic beings in some vague, general sense. Perhaps it is significant that the great sacrificial bogs of Jutland, where weapons by the hundred were dedicated to the deity, grew in importance and reached their zenith at a time when the human figure began to be portrayed in an art which evidently stood in the service of religious associations, a time, also, when writing, initially confined to personal names and magic formulae, began to make its first appearance.

These inner changes have an external parallel in the changing ethnic situation. The Germanic world of the late second and third centuries was no longer the world described by Tacitus. It was a world which witnessed the growth of those more extensive political confederacies composed of sections of earlier groupings, whose fortunes were to determine the history of the migration period. Some of these new groups, notably those which, while adopting novel forms of organization, managed best throughout the stormy years that followed to keep intact their ethnic composition, appeared under new names: the Alamanni, the Franks and Saxons. Others, among them notably the Goths and Vandals, preserved their old familiar name but, in spite of considerable adherence to ancestral tradition, often greatly altered their ethnic composition in the course of their great wanderings, by alliances and amalgamations of the most variegated kind.

Second- and Third-Century Developments

The new phase was inaugurated by the struggles between Rome and the Danubian Suebi in what is known as the Marcomannic War (166–80). By now the often-proved method of setting up provinces in enemy territory in order to secure the Roman frontier, a method still successful in the case of Dacia, miscarried entirely. This was due neither to a lack of striking power among the Roman forces, fighting deep in enemy country, nor the death, prematurely, with well-earned victory already in his hands, of Marcus Aurelius, nor to the determination of the Suebi in

Moravia and Slovakia to put up a defence. What proved decisive was rather the pressure exerted by the peoples of the interior upon the frontier population, a pressure culminating in large-scale population shifts. In the winter of 166-7, for instance, when thousands of Langobardi crossed the frozen Danube and broke into the province of Pannonia, they carried with them *en route* from their old home along the lower Elbe sections of some Lugian peoples – Lacringi and Victofali. As a few years later (in 171) did the Asdings, these people turned towards Dacia, to ask admittance to the Empire. This was denied to the Victofali as well as to the Asdings, who thereupon decided to settle in Northern Bohemia as neighbours of the Quadi, where they remained until the Asdings, in an attempt to spread their settlement into Banaţ, abandoned by the Romans (275), came up against Sarmatians and Western Goths. At the same time, in 278, Vandal Silings and Burgundians emigrated from Silesia into the Main valley, from where they broke into Raetia, to be defeated by Probus. Already at the time of the Marcomannic Wars the province had been threatened, and several fortresses on the Raetian *limes* had gone up in flames.

Far more disastrous, because more uncontrollable, was the development north of the Carpathians and to the rear of the Greek cities of the Black Sea littoral between the mouth of the Danube and the *regnum Bospori*. Its outcome is graphically summarized in the appearance of a people bearing the name of those same Goths who, according to their migration myth, had landed in the Vistula estuary around the time of Jesus' birth, coming from Scandinavia. Neither the written nor the archaeological sources allow us to trace the stages of their advance, a process that seems to have been completed by about the year 230; and shortly after the mid-century the split into a western and an eastern Gothic group seems to have taken place. About the year 271 Dacia was conquered and partially settled by the Western Goths; as would also seem to be indicated by the archaeological material of this and later periods (the Tcherniakhov Group), which extends in similar forms far across the Dnieper. Dacia itself became untenable for Rome once barbarian peoples in rapid succession had crossed the Danube, plundering and burning the frontier fortresses and coastal towns, rendering Moesia itself unsafe, and threatening and harassing even Thrace and Macedonia. Asia Minor was delivered helpless to their greed for spoil. Simultaneously fresh hordes arrived from the far north, Heruli who settled between the Don and Azov by 267, Gepids who took residence in Northern Dacia and so became neighbours of the Western Goths (in 269). Rome was scarcely able to undertake anything of permanence against these waves of peoples, or even against the plundering expeditions which now became the order of the day. Defensive military measures and annual payments to the barbarians momentarily stemmed the tide. But by the close of the third century the Danube again formed the Imperial frontier, as at Augustus' death. It was in this part of the world that settlement and domination by peoples of Germanic stock was at its most widespread.

Their advances were considerably more limited in the west, where they took, besides, a different course. Here too there were plundering raids, as is evident from the operation launched by the Saxons in alliance with the Salians against the coast of Northern France in 286; this is, apart from Ptolemy's early account (see above, p. 307), the first mention of a people probably consisting in the main of Chauci, old hands at this particular game. Somewhat earlier, in the 250s, Franks (now first mentioned) had crossed the Rhine and broken into Gaul, whence, in one great swoop, they got as far as Spain where they sacked Tarraco. Roughly about the same time Alamanni succeeded in reaching the Apennines, where they were brought to a halt, later to be defeated near Milan. All these incursions, simultaneous with the piracies and plundering raids of the Gothic confederacies on the Black Sea and in the Balkans, were only made possible by the continual withdrawal of frontier troops to fight the Sasanid Persians on the eastern frontier of the Empire, as well as rival claimants to the Imperial throne, a process which greatly weakened the Imperial defences.

In no other place and at no other time were quite as many coin hoards so hurriedly hidden as to the rear of the *limes* during the second third of the third century; indeed, no other region suffered such repeated devastation as that comprising the province of Raetia and the former *agri decumates* country. We read of a victory of Caracalla's over the Alamanni in 213, our first introduction to a people consisting in the main of a re-grouping of Suebic confederacies, principally Semnones. In 233 they were already attacking the *limes*, making a deep breach into Raetia itself. After a period of continual advances, this line was finally and permanently abandoned between 254 and 258–60, and the frontier withdrawn to the Rhine, Lake Constance, the Iller system and the Danube, where it was later fortified under Probus and Diocletian. The *agri decumates* country, still inhabited by remnants of the provincial population, was occupied by Suebic groups of settlers. It proved a lasting conquest. In the west too the frontier had been pushed back to its position at the end of Augustus' reign.

List of Emperors

AUGUSTUS	27 BC–AD 14
TIBERIUS	AD 14–37
GAIUS (CALIGULA)	37–41
CLAUDIUS	41–54
NERO	54–68
GALBA	68–69
OTHO	69
VITELLIUS	69
VESPASIAN	69–79
TITUS	79–81
DOMITIAN	81–96
NERVA	96–98
TRAJAN	98–117
HADRIAN	117–138
ANTONINUS PIUS	138–161
MARCUS AURELIUS	161–180
LUCIUS VERUS	161–169
COMMODUS	177–192
PERTINAX	193
DIDIUS JULIANUS	193
SEPTIMIUS SEVERUS	193–211
CLODIUS ALBINUS	193–197
PESCENNIUS NIGER	193–194
CARACALLA	198–217
GETA	209–212
MACRINUS	217–218

Notes

The notes and the bibliographies which follow are intended to be complementary, the bibliographies giving the general works relevant to each chapter, and the notes some specific references to ancient evidence or modern books or articles. Some long titles are given in a shortened form.

Abbreviations

AE   *Année Epigraphique*
ANRW H. Temporini (ed.), *Aufstieg und Niedergang der römischen Welt* 2: *Principat*, Berlin, 1974–
CIL   *Corpus Inscriptionum Latinarum*
FIRA² Riccobono, *Fontes Iuris Romani Anteiustiniani²*
IGR   *Inscriptiones Graecae ad Res Romanas Pertinentes*
ILS   Dessau, *Inscriptiones Latinae Selectae*
JRS   *Journal of Roman Studies*
OGIS Dittenberger, *Orientis Graeci Inscriptiones Selectae*
PIR   *Prosopographia Imperii Romani*
RE   Pauly-Wissowa, *Realencyclopaedie der classischen Altertumswissenschaft*
SEG   *Supplementum Epigraphicum Graecum*

Chapter 1: Introduction

1 G. W. Bowersock, *Augustus and the Greek World*, Oxford, 1965.
2 Strabo, 485; Dio, 68, 24, 1.
3 Fronto, *De feriis Alsiensibus*, 3.
4 H. G. Pflaum, *Carrières procuratoriennes*, no. 247.
5 Aelius Aristides, *Oration* 47: Dindorf, vol. 2, pp. 415–16.
6 Galletier, *Panégyriques Latines* 5, 17.

7 *Huitième congrès international d'archéologie classique (Paris, 1963): Le rayonnement des civilisations grecque et romaine sur les cultures périphériques,* Paris, 1965. See also *Assimilation et résistance à la culture gréco-romaine dans le monde ancien: travaux du VIᵉ Congrès International des Études Classiques (1974),* Bucarest/Paris, 1976.

Chapter 2: Rome, the Roman People and the Senate

1 *CIL* VI 226 = *FIRA²* 3, no. 165.
2 Frontinus, *De aquae ductu urbis Romae,* especially ch. 116–18.
3 I. A. Richmond, *The City Wall of Imperial Rome,* Oxford, 1930.
4 Tacitus, *Annales* 12, 43; Suetonius, *Claudius* 18.
5 Dio, 71, 32, 1.
6 Fronto, *Principia Historiae,* 18.
7 Plutarch, *Moralia* 973E–974A; 968C.
8 M. Sordi, 'L'epigrafe di un pantomimo', *Epigraphica* 15, 1953,104.
9 Dio, 58, 20.
10 Dio, 75, 4.
11 Tacitus, *Annales* 1, 11–13; compare Dio, 57, 2, and Suetonius, *Tiberius* 24.
12 *CIL* VI 930 = *ILS* 244 = *FIRA²* 1, no. 15. See P. A. Brunt, 'Lex de imperio Vespasiani', *JRS* 67, 1977, 95.
13 See P. W. Townsend, 'The Revolution of AD 238', *Yale Classical Studies* 14, 1955, 49.
14 Dio, 70, 1.
15 J. H. Oliver, R. E. A. Palmer, 'Minutes of an Act of the Roman Senate', *Hesperia* 24, 1955, 320.
16 Pliny, *Ep.* 2, 11.
17 Dio, 76, 8.
18 Pliny, *Ep.* 2, 9.
19 Epictetus 4, 10, 20–1. See F. Millar, 'Epictetus and the Imperial Court', *JRS* 55, 1965, 141.
20 Keil, Gschnitzner, *Anz. Öst. Akad. Wiss., Phil.-Hist. Klasse* 93, 1956, 226, no. 8 = *SEG* XVII, 528.

Chapter 3: The Emperors

1 A. H. M. Jones, 'The Imperium of Augustus', *JRS* 41, 1951, 112.
2 *ILS* 264.

3   T. B. Mitford, 'A Cypriot Oath of Allegiance to Tiberius', *JRS*
     50, 1960, 75; S. Weinstock, 'Treueid und Kaiserkult', *Mitt.*
     Deutsch. Arch. Inst., Ath. Abt. 77, 1962, 306; P. Herrmann, *Der*
     römische Kaiserreid, Göttingen, 1968.

4   A. Boethius, *The Golden House of Nero* (Ann Arbor, Michigan,
     1960), ch. 3; W. L. MacDonald, *The Architecture of the Roman*
     Empire I, New Haven, 1965, ch. 2.

5   Fronto, *Ep. ad M. Caes.* 4, 6.

6   M. Durry, *Les cohortes prétoriennes,* Paris, 1938; A. Passerini, *Le*
     cohorte pretorie, Rome, 1939

7   W. G. Sinnigen, 'The Origins of the Frumentarii', *Mem. Am.*
     Acad. Rome 27, 1962, 213; M. Speidel, *Die Equites Singulares*
     Augusti, Bonn, 1965.

8   *ILS* 1514.

9   Philo, *Legatio ad Gaium* 166–77.

10   Pflaum, *Carrières procuratoriennes,* no. 180 *bis.*

11   Dexippus: *Jacoby, Fragmente der griechischen Historiker* 100,
     F6.

12   O. Hirschfeld, 'Der Grundbesitz der römischen Kaiser', *Kleine*
     Schriften, Berlin, 1913, 516; F. Millar, 'The Fiscus in the First
     Two Centuries', *JRS* 53, 1963, 29; P. A. Brunt, 'The "Fiscus"
     and its Development', *JRS* 56, 1966, 75; D. J. Crawford,
     'Imperial Estates', in M. I. Finley (ed.), *Studies in Roman*
     Property, Cambridge, 1976, 35.

13   *ILS* 8870.

14   Dio, 69, 6, 3. See, however, Millar, *Emperor in the Roman World,*
     1977, 1.

15   D. McAlindon, 'Senatorial Opposition to Claudius and Nero',
     American Journal of Philology 77, 1956, 113.

16   Tacitus, *Annales* 3, 55.

17   Marcus Aurelius, *Meditations* 1, 16.

18   *PIR²* H 73; Pflaum, *Carrières procuratoriennes, no. 179.*

19   Dio, 77, 17.

Chapter 4: Government and Administration

1   G. P. Burton, 'The Issuing of *Mandata* to Proconsuls', *Zeitschr.*
     f. Pap. u. Epig. 21, 1976, 63.

1a   A. Stein, *Der römische Ritterstand,* Munich, 1927; cf. M. I.
     Henderson, 'The Establishment of the Equester Ordo', *JRS* 53,
     1963, 61.

2 Tacitus, *Annales* 4, 15.

3 *ILS* 1447; Pflaum, *Carrières procuratoriennes*, no. 37.

4 See G. B. Townsend, 'The Post Ab Epistulis in the Second Century', *Historia* 10, 1961, 375.

5 Pflaum, *Carrières*, no. 162.

6 *PIR²* A 137.

7 W. Kunkel, *Herkunft und soziale Stellung der römischen Juristen*, Weimar, 2nd ed, 1967, 174f; Pflaum, *Carrières*, no. 141.

8 Eusebius, *Ecclesiastical History* 7, 30, 8–9.

9 Fronto, *Ad Antoninum Pium* 7 (Van den Hout, p. 169).

10 Philo, *In Flaccum* 131–4.

11 Dio Chrysostom, *Oration* 35, 15.

12 The inscription is given by D. M. Pippidi, *Dacia* 2, 1958, 227, and re-edited by J. H. Oliver, *Greek, Roman and Byzantine Studies* 6, 1965, 143.

13 *CIL* X 7852 = *ILS* 5947 = Abbott and Johnson, *Municipal Administration*, no. 58.

14 *AE* 1925. 126 = Abbott and Johnson, no. 65a.

15 *IGR* IV 571 = Abbott and Johnson, no. 82.

16 *Digest* 1, 16, 9, *praef.*

17 Statius, *Silvae* 3, 3, 105.

18 Dio, 53, 19.

19 Tacitus, *Annales* 13, 50–1.

20 Statius, *Silvae* 3, 3, 98–102.

21 Statius, *Silvae* 5, 1, 94–8.

22 *AE* 1962. 183. See H. G. Pflaum, *Bonn. Jahrb.* 171, 1971, 349.

23 *Jahreshefte des Österreichischen Archäologischen Instituts* 45, 1960, Beiblatt 80, no. 7, lines 9–14.

24 Philostratus, *Lives of the Sophists* 2, 32.

25 C. Dunant, J. Pouilloux, *Recherches sur l'histoire et les cultes de Thasos* 2, Paris, 1957, p. 66, no. 179.

26 Keil, Gschnitzner, 'Neue Inschriften aus Lydien', *Anz. Öst. Akad. Wiss., Phil.-Hist. Kl.* 93, 1956, 226, no. 8 = *SEG* XVII, 528.

27 Pliny, *Ep.* 10, 107.

28 *ILS* 6870 = *FIRA²* I, no. 103.

29 Text in *Syria* 23, 1942–3, 176f; compare W. Kunkel, *Festschrift H. Lewald*, Basel, 1953, 81.

30 Pliny, *Ep.* 6, 31.

31 See A. M. Honoré, 'The Severan Jurists', *Studia et Documenta Historiae et Iuris* 28, 1962, 162; '"Imperial" Rescripts, AD 193–305: Authorship and Authenticity', *JRS* 69, 1979, 51.

32 *Digest* 1, 18, 8.

Chapter 5: State and Subject: the Cities

1 *Inscriptions Grecques et Latines de la Syrie* 5, 1998.
2 *CIL* III 6866 = *ILS* 6090 = *FIRA²* 1, no. 92 = Abbott and Johnson, *Municipal Administration*, no. 151.
3 J. H. Oliver, 'A New Letter of Antoninus Pius', *American Journal of Philology* 79, 1958, 52.
4 *OGIS* 515 = Abbott and Johnson, no. 133.
5 *OGIS* 527 = Abbott and Johnson, no. 117.
6 A. Piganiol, *Les documents cadastraux de la colonie romaine d'Orange*, Paris, 1962.
7 *Digest* 50, 15, 1 and 8.
8 C. Saumagne, *Le droit latin et les cités romaines sous l'Empire*, Paris, 1965, refuted by J. Desanges, *Rev. Hist. Droit.* 50, 1972, 353 and H. Galsterer, *Epig. Stud.* 9, 1972, 37.
9 Salpensa: *CIL* II 1963 = *ILS* 6088 = *FIRA²* 1, 23. Malaca: *CIL* II 1964 = *ILS* 6089 = *FIRA²* I, 24.
10 *CIL* X 8038 = *FIRA²* 1, no. 72 = Abbott and Johnson, no. 59.
11 *IGR* 4, 1256.
12 Pliny, *Panegyricus* 37–40.
13 C. Sasse, *Die Constitutio Antoniniana*, Wiesbaden, 1958. For a sceptical view see H. Wolff, *Die Constitutio Antoniniana und Papyrus Gissensis 40. 1*, Köln, 1976.
14 See E. Condurachi, 'La Costituzione Antoniniana e la sua applicazione nell' Impero Romano', *Dacia* 2, 1958, 281.
15 *FIRA²* 3, no. 50; *Pap. Oxy.* 1114.
16 S. J. de Laet, *Portorium*, Bruges, 1949.
17 *Digest* 50, 15, 4.
18 Th. Klauser, 'Aurum Coronarium', *Mitt. Deutsch. Arch. Inst., Röm. Abt.* 59, 1944, 129.
19 Babylonian Talmud, *Baba Batra*, 8a.
20 Tacitus, *Agricola* 19.
21 W. H. C. Frend, 'A Third-Century Inscription Relating to Angareia in Phrygia', *JRS* 46, 1956, 46.
22 Epictetus 4. 1. 79.
23 M. Rostovtzeff, 'Synteleia tironon', *JRS* 8, 1918, 26.
24 See W. H. C. Frend, *Martyrdom and Persecution in the Early Church*, Oxford, 1965.

Chapter 6: The Army and the Frontiers

1 J. Baradez, *Fossatum Africae*, Paris, 1949.

2   A. Di Vita, 'Il "limes" romano di Tripolitania', *Libya Antiqua* 1, 1964, 65; P. Trousset, *Recherches sur le Limes Tripolitanus*,Paris, 1974.

3   A. Maricq, 'Les dernières années d'Hatra: l'alliance avec Rome', *Syria* 34, 1957, 289.

4   A. Poidebard, *La trace de Rome dans le désert de Syrie*, Paris, 1934; see L. Dilleman, *Haute Mésopotamie orientale et pays adjacents*, Paris, 1962, pp. 195f.

5   I. A. Richmond, 'Queen Cartimandua', *JRS* 44, 1954, 43.

6   See G. Simpson, *Britons and the Roman Army*, London, 1964.

7   On Hadrian's Wall see I. A. Richmond, 'The Roman Frontier Land', *History* 44, 1959, 13; D. J. Breeze and B. Dobson, *Hadrian's Wall*, London, 1976.

8   A. S. Robertson, *The Antonine Wall*, 2nd ed. Glasgow, 1973.

9   I. A. Richmond, 'Trajan's Army on Trajan's Column', *Papers of the British School at Rome*, 13, 1935 1; L. Rossi, *Trajan's Column and the Dacian Wars*, London, 1971.

10 See C. Caprino, A. M. Colini, G. Gatti, M. Pallottino, P. Romanelli, *La colonna di Marco Aurelio*, Rome, 1955.

11 J. Fitz, 'A Military History of Pannonia from the Marcomann Wars to the Death of Alexander Severus (180–235)', *Acta Archaeologica Acad. Sc. Hung.* 14, 1962, 25.

12 *Michigan Papyri* VIII, 1951, no. 465.

13 F. A. Lepper, *Trajan's Parthian War*, Oxford, 1948.

14 A. Maricq, 'La province d' Assyrie créée par Trajan', *Syria* 36, 1959, 254.

15 F. Kiechle, 'Die "Taktik" des Flavius Arrianus', *45ₑ Bericht der Röm.-Germ. Kommission 1964*, 1965, 87.

16 J. Mann, 'The Raising of New Legions during the Principate', *Hermes* 91, 1963, 483.

16a B. Campbell, 'The Marriage of Soldiers under the Empire', *JRS* 68, 1978, 153.

17 N. Lewis, 'A Veteran in Search of a Home', *Trans. American Philol. Assoc.* 90, 1959, 139.

18 H. Callies, 'Die fremden Truppen im römischen Heer des Prinzipats und die sogenannten nationalen Numeri', *45ₑ Bericht der Röm.-Germ. Kom. 1964*, 1965, 130; M. Speidel, 'The Rise of Ethnic Units in the Roman Imperial Army', *ANRW* 2.3, 1975, 202.

19 K. Kraft, *Zur Rekrutierung der Alen und Kohorten an Rhein und Donau*, Bern, 1951.

20   R. O. Fink, *JRS* 48, 1958, 102; R. Syme, *JRS* 49, 1959, 26; R. O. Fink, *Roman Military Records on Papyrus*, 1971, no. 63.
21   C. B. Welles, R. O. Fink, J. F. Gilliam, *The Excavations at Dura-Europos: Final Report V, 1. The Parchments and Papyri*, New Haven, 1959.
22   H. Schönberger, *The Roman Camp at the Saalburg*[4], Bad Homburg, 1955.

Chapter 7: Italy

1   Pliny, *Panegyricus* 26–7.
2   *Verona e il suo territorio* I: Istituto per gli Studi Storici Veronese, 1960.
3   *CIL* V 5050 = *ILS* 206 = *FIRA*[2] 1, no. 71.
4   O. Testaguzza, 'The Port of Rome', *Archaeology* 17, 1964, 173; *Portus*, Roma, 1970.
5   Tacitus, *Histories* 3, 33–4.
6   On Pompeii: R. C. Carrington, *Pompeii*, Oxford, 1936; A. Maiuri, *Pompeii*[8], Rome, 1956; J. Day, 'Agriculture in the Life of Pompeii', *Yale Classical Studies* 3, 1932, 165; B. Andreae and H. Kyrieleis, *Neue Forschungen in Pompeii*, Recklinghausen, 1975; H. Castrén, *Ordo Populusque Pompeianus*, Rome, 1975.
7   On the alimentary scheme see R. P. Duncan-Jones, 'The Purpose and Organisation of the Alimenta', *Papers of the British School at Rome* 19, 1964, 123, revised in *The Economy of the Roman Empire*, Cambridge, 1974, 288.
8   For all aspects of Pliny and his correspondence see A. N. Sherwin-White, *The Letters of Pliny: A Historical and Social Commentary*, Oxford, 1966. For his finances and property see R. P. Duncan-Jones, 'The Finances of the Younger Pliny', *Papers of the British School at Rome* 20, 1965, 177, revised in *Economy* (see n.7), 17. See also R. Syme, 'People in Pliny', *JRS* 58, 1968, 135 = *Roman Papers*, Oxford, 1979, 694.
9   R. Meiggs, *Roman Ostia*, 2nd ed., Oxford, 1973.
10   M. F. Squarciapino, 'The Synagogue at Ostia', *Archaeology* 16, 1963, 194; *La sinagoga di Ostia*, Rome, 1964.
11   Dio, 76, 10.

Chapter 8: The Western Provinces

1   On the amphitheatre at Lyon see J. Guey, A. Audin in *Gallia* 20, 1962, 117; 21, 1963, 125; 23, 1964, 1; A. Audin, M. Leglay, *Gallia* 28, 1970, 67.

2   E. Will, 'Recherches sur le développement urbain sous l'Empire
    romain dans le Nord de la France', *Gallia* 20, 1962, 79.

2*a* E. Wightman, *Roman Trier and the Treveri*, London, 1970.

3   J. A. Stanfield, G. Simpson, *Central Gaulish Potters*, London,
    1958.

4   P. M. Duval, 'L'originalité de l'architecture gallo-romaine', *VIIIe*
    Congrès international d'archéologic classique 1963, Paris, 1965,
    121.

5   R. MacMullen, 'The Celtic Renaissance', *Historia* 14, 1965, 93.

6   J.-J. Hatt, 'Essai sur l'évolution de la religion gauloise', *Revue des*
    Etudes Anciennes 67, 1965, 80.

6*a* See *Les martyrs de Lyon 177* (Coll. Int. du CNRS, 575), Paris,
    1978.

7   *CIL* XIII 3162; see H. G. Pflaum *Le marbre de Thorigny*, Paris,
    1948.

7*a* See M. Griffin, 'The Elder Seneca and Spain', *JRS* 62, 1972, 1.

8   H. Nesselhauf, *Deutsch. Arch. Inst., Madrider Mitt.* 1, 1960, 148;
    AE. 1962, 288.

9   A. Garcia y Bellido, *Colonia Aelia Augusta Italica*, Madrid, 1960.

10 M. Ponsich, M. Tarradell, *Garum et industries antiques de*
    salaison dans la Méditerranée occidentale, Paris, 1965.

11 For the Northern frontier area see P. Salway, *The Frontier People*
    of Roman Britain, Cambridge, 1965.

12 For the excavations at Fishbourne see B. Cunliffe, *Fishbourne*,
    London, 1971.

12*a* For the new text of the inscription see J. E. Bogaers, 'King
    Cogidubnus in Chichester', *Britannia* 10, 1979, 243.

13 S. S. Frere, 'Verulamium: Three Roman Cities', *Antiquity* 38,
    1964, 103; *Bulletin of the Institute of Archaeology, London,* 4,
    1964, 61; *Verulamium Excavations* 1, Oxford, 1972.

14 P.-M. Duval, *Paris Antique*, Paris, 1961.

15 See A. Balil, 'Hispania en los años 260 a 300 d. J. C.', *Emerita* 27,
    1959, 269.

16 R. M. Butler, 'The Roman Walls of Le Mans', *JRS* 48, 1958, 33.

17 S. Johnson, *The Roman Forts of the Saxon Shore*, London, 1976.

Chapter 9: Africa

1   J.-B. Chabot, *Recueil des inscriptions libyques*, Paris, 1940–1. See
    F. Millar, 'Local Cultures in the Roman Empire: Libyan, Punic
    and Latin in Roman Africa', *JRS* 58, 1968,126.

2   R. Syme, 'Tacfarinas, the Musulamii and Thubursicu', *Studies in Roman Economic and Social History presented to A. C. Johnson,* Princeton, 1951, 113 = *Roman Papers,* Oxford, 1979, 218.

3   G.-C. Picard, 'Civitas Mactaritana', *Karthago* 8, 1957.

4   J. Carcopino, *Le Maroc antique,* Paris, 1943, 200–30.

5   R. P. Duncan-Jones, 'Costs, Outlays and Summae Honorariae from Roman Africa', *Papers of the British School at Rome* 17, 1962, 47; 'Wealth and Munificence in Roman Africa', *ibid.* 18, 1963, 159, both revised in *The Economy of the Roman Empire,* Cambridge, 1974, 63–119.

5*a* See T. D. Barnes, *Tertullian,* Oxford, 1971.

5*b* See C. Saumagne, *Cyprien, évêque de Carthage,* Paris, 1975; M. Sage, *Cyprian,* Cambridge, Mass., 1975.

6   J. Baradez, 'Les nouvelles fouilles de Tipasa et les opérations d'Antonin le Pieux en Maurétanie', *Libyca* 2, 1954, 89.

7   G.-C. Picard, *Castellum Dimmidi,* Algiers, 1947.

8   M. Ponsich, 'Lixus, cité légendaire entre dans l'Histoire', *Archaeologia: Fouilles et Découvertes* 4, May-June 1965, 23.

Chapter 10: Egypt

1   H.-C. Puech, 'Les nouveaux Écrits gnostiques découverts en Haute-Égypte (premier inventaire et essai d'identification)', *Coptic Studies in Honour of W. E. Crum,* Washington, 1950, 91.

2   *Oxyrhynchus Papyri,* no. 1452.

3   M. Hombert, C. Préaux, *Recherches sur le recensement dans l'Egypt romaine,* Leiden, 1952, pp. 27–9.

4   S. L. Wallace, *Taxation in Egypt from Augustus to Diocletian,* Princeton, 1938.

5   H. A. Musurillo, *The Acts of the Pagan Martyrs: Acta Alexandrinorum,* Oxford, 1954.

6   G. Chalon, *L'Édit de Tiberius Julius Alexander,* Olten/Lausanne, 1964.

7   A. Fuks, 'Aspects of the Jewish Revolt in AD 115–17', *JRS* 51, 1961, 98.

8   H. I. Bell, 'Antinoopolis: A Hadrianic Foundation in Egypt', *JRS* 30, 1940, 133.

9   J. R. Knipfing, 'The Libelli of the Decian Persecution', *Harvard Theological Review* 16, 1923, 345.

10 J. Schwartz, 'Les Palmyréniens en Égypte', *Bulletin de la Societé d'Archéologie d'Alexandrie* 40, 1953, 63.

11 T. C. Skeat, E. P. Wegener, 'A Trial before the Prefect of Egypt Appius Sabinus c.AD 250', *Journal of Egyptian Archaeology* 21, 1935, 224.

Chapter 11: The Greek Provinces

1   Preliminary report by Y. Yadin in *Israel Exploration Journal,* 1965. A popular account by Y. Yadin, *Masada,* London, 1966.

2   Y. Yadin, *The Finds from the Bar-Kochba Period in the Cave of Letters,* Jerusalem, 1963; popular account by Y. Yadin, *Bar Kochba,* London, 1971.

3   For a general survey see M. Rostovtzeff, *Dura-Europos and its Art,* Oxford, 1938. See A. Perkins, *The Art of Dura-Europos,* Oxford, 1973; C. Hopkins, *The Discovery of Dura-Europos,* New Haven/London, 1979.

4   I. A. Richmond, 'The Roman Siege-Works of Masada, Israel', *JRS* 52, 1962, 142.

5   See M. Lindner (ed.), *Petra und das Königreich der Nabatäer,* 2nd ed., Munich, 1974, 142–54.

5a C. P. Jones, *Plutarch and Rome,* Oxford, 1971.

6   On Herodes Atticus, P. Graindor, *Un milliardaire antique, Hérode Attique et sa famille,* Cairo, 1930.

7   F. Millar, *A Study of Cassius Dio,* Oxford, 1964.

7a C. P. Jones, *The Roman World of Dio Chrysostom,* Cambridge, Mass., 1978; P. Desideri, *Dione di Prusa,* Florence, 1978.

8   P. Graindor, *Athènes sous Hadrien,* Cairo, 1934.

8a For the Panhellenic League see J. H. Oliver, *Marcus Aurelius: Aspects of Civic and Cultural Policy in the East* (Hesperia, Supp. 13), Princeton, 1970, 92–138.

8b For the evidence on the war see E. Schürer, *History of the Jewish People* 1, ed. Vermes and Millar, Edinburgh, 1973, 534–57.

9   See C. A. Behr, *Aelius Aristides and the Sacred Tales,* Amsterdam, 1968.

10 See J. Schwartz, *Biographie de Lucien de Samosate,* Brussels, 1965; B. Baldwin, *Studies in Lucian,* Toronto, 1973; G. Anderson, *Lucian: Theme and Variation in the Second Sophistic,* Leiden, 1976. No adequate historical study is available.

11 J. Keil, 'Ein ephesischer Anwalt des dritten Jahrhunderts durchreist das Imperium Romanum', *Sitz.-Ber. Bay. Akad. Wiss.* 1956.3 = *SEG* 17, 505.

12 F. Jacoby, *Die Fragmente der griechischen Historiker,* no. 100. See F. Millar, 'P. Herennius Dexippus', *JRS* 59, 1969, 12.

13 H. A. Thompson, 'Athenian Twilight: AD 267–600', *JRS* 49, 1959, 61.

13a For a different chronology see H. R. Baldus, *Uranius Antoninus: Münzprägung und Geschichte*, Bonn, 1971.

14 I.A. Richmond, 'Palmyra under the Aegis of the Romans', *JRS* 53, 1963, 43; M. A. R. Colledge, *The Art of Palmyra*, London, 1976.

15 See F. Millar, 'Paul of Samosata, Zenobia and Aurelian', *JRS* 61, 1971, 1.

Chapter 12: The Balkan and Danubian Provinces

1 See R. Egger, *Die Stadt auf dem Magdalensberg: ein Grosshandelsplatz*, Wien, 1961; A. Obermayr, *Kelten und Römer am Magdalensberg*, Wien, 1971.

2 B. Gerov, 'Römische Bürgerrechtsverleihung und Kolonisation in Thrakien vor Trajan', *Studii Classice* 3, 1961, 107.

3 Text given by D. M. Pippidi in *Dacia* 2, 1958, 227; re-edited by J. H. Oliver in *Greek, Roman and Byzantine Studies* 6, 1965, 143.

4 R. Vulpe, 'Le nombre des colonies et des municipes de la Mésie Inférieure', *Acta Antiqua Philippopolitana: Stud. Hist. et Phil.*, 1963, 147.

4a See H.-C. Noeske, 'Studien zur Verwaltung und Bevölkerung der dakischen Goldbergwerke in römischer Zeit', *Bonner Jahrb.* 177, 1977, 271–416.

5 See J. Garbsch, *Die norisch-pannonische Frauentracht im 1 und 2 Jahrhundert*, Munich, 1965.

6 I. Stoian, 'De nouveau sur la plainte des paysans du territoire d'Histria, *Dacia* 3, 1959, 369.

7 *Inscriptiones Graecae in Bulgaria Repertae* (IG Bulg.) 3.2 1689.

8 E. B. Thomas, *Römische Villen in Pannonien*, Budapest, 1964.

9 E. Swoboda, *Carnuntum*[4], Graz/Köln, 1964.

10 J. Szilágyi, *Aquincum*, Budapest/Berlin, 1956.

11 D.Protase, 'Considérations sur la continuité des Daco-Romains en Dacie post-aurélienne', *Dacia* 8, 1964, 177.

12 D. Tudor, 'La fortificazione delle citta romane della Dacia nel sec. III dell' e.n.', *Historia* 14, 1965, 368.

13 F. Wagner, 'Das Ende der römischen Herrschaft in Raetien', *Bayerische Vorgeschichtsblätter* 18–19, 1951–2, 26.

14 H. Vetters, *Dacia Ripensis*, Vienna, 1950.

Chapter 13: The Empire and the Third-Century Crisis

1 E. A. Thompson, 'Christianity and the Northern Barbarians', in A. Momigliano (ed.), *The Conflict between Paganism and Christianity in the Fourth Century*, Oxford, 1963, 56.

2 J.-P. Callu, 'Les monnaies de compte et le monnayage du bronze entre 253 et 295', *Congresso int. di Numismatica*, 1961, Vol. 2, *Atti*, Rome, 1965, 363; *La politique monétaire des Empereurs romains de 238 à 311*, Paris, 1969.

3 See A. H. M. Jones 'Inflation under the Roman Empire', *The Roman Economy*, Oxford, 1974, 187; T. Pekáry, 'Studien zur römischen Währungs-und Finanzgeschichte von 161 bis 235 n. Chr.', *Historia* 8, 1959, 443; M. Crawford, 'Finance, Coinage and Money from the Severans to Constantine', *ANRW* 2.2, 1975, 560.

4 O. Hirschfeld, 'Die Sicherheitspolizei im römischen Kaiserreich', *Kleine Schriften*, 576. On brigandage see R. MacMullen, *Enemies of the Roman Order*, Cambridge, Mass., 1967, App. B.

5 See A. E. R. Boak, *Manpower Shortage and the Fall of the Roman Empire in the West*, Ann Arbor, Michigan, 1955, and the review by M. I. Finley in *JRS* 48, 1958, 156.

6 See J. Geffcken, *Der Ausgang des griechisch-römischen Heidentums*, Heidelberg, 1920, ch. 2.

7 J. Bidez, *Vie de Porphyre*, Gand-Leipzig, 1913; for this date of writing see T. D. Barnes, 'Porphyry Against the Christians', *Journ. Theol. Stud.* 24, 1973, 424.

8 Eusebius, *Ecclesiastical History* 6, 43, 11.

Chapter 14: Parthia and Sasanid Persia

1 *Catalogue de monnaies grecques et romaines*, no. XII, collection A. de Petrowicz, Geneva, 1926, 133, 137.

2 J. de Morgan, *Manuel de numismatique orientale* 1, Paris, 1923–36, 164, and *Dinkart*, ed, D. M. Madan, 1, Bombay, 1911, 412. The English translation by P. D. B. Sanjana, 9, Bombay, 1900, 577, is wrong.

3 Cf. Frye, *The Heritage of Persia*, London, 1962, 190.

4 Cf. U. Kahrstedt, *Arabanos III. und seine Erben*, Bern, 1950, 80; much is speculative.

5   There are now two schools, one supporting the date of AD 78; e.g.
    S. P. Tolstov and V. A. Livshitz, 'Decipherment of the
    Khwarezmian Inscriptions from Tok Kala', *Acta Antiqua Ac. Sc.
    Hungaricae* 12, 1964, 250; and the other school following AD 225;
    e.g. R. Göbl, 'Zwei neue Termini für ein zentrales Datum der
    Alten Geschichte Mittelasiens, das Jahr I des Kušânkönigs
    Kaniŝka', *Anzeiger der phil.-hist. Klasse der Österreichen
    Akademie der Wiss.*, Wien, 1964, 151. A third, intermediate
    position, either AD 128 or AD 144 (by R. Ghirshman, *Iran*,
    London, 1954, 261) is held by some. On the Khwarezmian
    documents cf. W. B. Henning, 'The Choresmian Documents',
    Asia Major 11, 1966, 166–79.

6   B. Nanjio, *Catalogue of the Chinese Translation of the Buddhist
    Tripitaka*, Oxford, 1883, 381.

7   Frye, *op. cit.*, 182–3.

8   M. E. Masson, G. A. Pugachenkova, *Parfyanskie Ritony Nisa*,
    Moscow, 1956, especially plates 56, 62, and I. M. Dyakonov, V.
    A. Livshitz, *Dokumenty iz Nisy*, Moscow, 1960.

9   D. Schlumberger, 'Descendants non-méditerranéens de l'art
    grec', *Syria* 37, 1960, 136–42.

10 Cf. Frye, *op. cit.*, 156 and R. Ettinghausen, *From Byzantium to
    Sasanian Iran and the Islamic World*, Leiden, 1972, 3–10.

11 J. Neusner, *A History of the Jews in Babylonia. 1. The Parthian
    Period*, Leiden, 1965.

12 Cf. G. Widengren, 'Die Mandäer', *Handbuch der Orientalistik*,
    ed. B. Spuler, Vol. 8, Religion, Leiden, 1961, 83–100.

13 Cf. B. Laufer, *Sino-Iranica*, Chicago, 1919, and E. Schafer, *The
    Golden Peaches of Samarkand*, Berkeley, California, 1963,
    117–55.

14 On the Pazyryk rug, cf. K. Jettmar, *Die frühen Steppenvölker*,
    Kunst der Welt, Baden-Baden, 1964, 114, 123.

15 M. Boyce, 'The Parthian *gōsān* and Iranian Minstrel Tradition',
    RAS, 1957, 10–45.

16 Cf. W. B. Henning, 'Mitteliranisch', *Handbuch der Orientalistik*,
    ed. B. Spuler, Vol. 4, Leiden, 1958, 27–37.

17 B. Simonetta, 'Vologese V, Artabano V e Artavasde',
    Numismatica 19, 1953, 1–4, and F. Cumont in *Comptes-rendus de
    l'Académie des inscriptions et belles lettres*, 1930, 217

18 Cf. Frye, 'The Charisma of Kingship in Ancient Iran', *Iranica
    Antiqua* 6, Leiden, 1964, 46–50.

19   R. Ghirshman, 'Inscription du monument de Châpour Ier', *Revue des arts asiatiques* 10, Paris, 1937, 123–9.

20   Cf. Frye, 'The Middle Persian Inscription of Kartīr at Naqš-i Rajab', *Indo-Iranian Journal* 8, The Hague, 1965, 211–25; M. L. Chaumont, 'L'inscription de Kartir à la Ka'bah de Zoroastre', *Journal Asiatique,* 1960, 339–88, and P. Gignoux, 'Étude des variantes textuelles des inscriptions de Kirdir, genèse et datation', *Le Muséon* 86, 1973, 193–216.

21   Chaumont, *loc. cit.* I amend *mktky,* to *mntky,* although we may have instead an unknown Mesopotamian religion.

22   H. J. Polotsky, *Manichäische Homilien* 1, Stuttgart, 1934, 45, and W. B. Henning, 'Mani's Last Journey', *Bulletin of the School of Oriental Studies* 10, 1939, 948, 952. His name probably was pronounced *Kerdīr.* It should be noted that there were at least two Kartirs or Kerdīrs, both mentioned in Shapur's tri-lingual inscription on the Ka'bah of Zoroaster, Kartir the *herbad* and Kartir Ardavan, both apparently important religious figures.

23   E. Herzfeld, *Paikuli* 1, Berlin, 1923, 208. Perhaps Tōsar (Tansar), mentioned in Islamic sources as the founder of the Sasanian Zoroastrian Church, reflects Kartir.

24   Cf. A. Maricq's translation in *Syria* 35, 1958, 295–360.

24a   This date is provided by the new Greek codex; cf. R. N. Frye, 'The Cologne Greek Codex about Mani', *Ex Orbe Religionum, Festschrift Geo Widengren,* ed. J. Bergman, 1, Leiden, 1972, 424.

25   The date 256 for the capture of Antioch was first proposed in *Bibliotheca Orientalis* 8, 1951, 103–5.

26   R. Ghirshman, *Bichapour* II, Paris, 1956, and A. Christensen, *L'Iran sous les Sassanides,* Copenhagen, 1944, 127.

27   Cf. Frye, 'Development of Persian Literature under the Samanids and Qarakhanids', *Yádnáme-ye Jan Rypka,* ed. J. Bečka, Prague, 1967, 69–74.

28   The distinctive crowns of the various Sasanian kings are of great help to art historians in identifying and dating silver plates and other art objects.

Bibliography

Chapter 1: Introduction

GENERAL

Bleicken, J., *Verfassungs- und Sozialgeschichte des Römischen Kaiserreiches* 1–2, Paderborn, 1978.

Cambridge Ancient History 10, 1934; 11, 1936; 12, 1939.

Mazzarino, S., *Trattato di Storia Romana* 2: *l'Impero Romano*, Rome, 1956.

Petit, P., *La paix romaine*, Paris, 1967 (E. T., *Pax Romana*, London, 1976).

Rostovtzeff, M., *Social and Economic History of the Roman Empire*, 2nd ed., revised by P. M. Fraser, Oxford, 1957.

Syme, R., *Tacitus* 1–2, Oxford, 1958, is essential for the first century of the period.

ECONOMIC DATA

Frank, T., (ed.), *Economic Survey of Ancient Rome* 2, 1936 (Roman Egypt); 3, 1937 (Britain, Spain, Sicily, Gaul); 4, 1938 (Africa, Syria Greece, Asia); 5, 1940 (Rome and Italy of the Empire).

Duncan-Jones, R., *The Economy of the Roman Empire: Quantitative Studies*, Cambridge, 1974.

RELIGION

Beaujeu, J., *La religion romaine à l'apogée de l'Empire*, Paris, 1955.

Chadwick, H., *The Early Church*, Harmondsworth, 1967.

Dodds, E. R., *Pagan and Christian in an Age of Anxiety*, London, 1965.

Latte, K., *Römische Religionsgeschichte*, Munich, 1960.

Liebeschuetz, J. H. W. G., *Continuity and Change in Roman Religion*, Oxford, 1979.

Lietzmann, H., *A History of the Early Church*, London, 1961.

Nilsson, M. P., *Geschichte der griechischen Religion* 2, 2nd ed., Munich, 1961.

SOCIAL LIFE

Balsdon, J. P. V. D., *Romans and Aliens*, London, 1979.

Crook, J. A., *Law and Life of Rome*, London, 1967.

Friedländer, L., *Darstellungen aus der Sittengeschichte Roms*, 9th ed., ed. G. Wissowa, Leipzig, 1919–20.

Gagé, J., *Les classes sociales dans l'Empire romain*, 2nd ed., Paris, 1974.

MacMullen, R., *Roman Social Relations 50 BC to AD 284*, New Haven, 1974.

Chapter 2: Rome, the Roman People and the Senate

ROME AND THE ROMAN PEOPLE

van Berchem, D., *Les distributions de blé et d'argent à la plèbe romaine sous l'Empire*, Geneva, 1939.

Cameron, A., *Circus Factions*, Oxford, 1976, esp. ch. 7.

Coarelli, F., *Guida archeologica di Roma*, Rome, 1974.

Homo, L., *Rome impériale et l'urbanisme dans l'Antiquité*, Paris, 1951.

Paris d'Escurac, H., *La préfecture de l'annone: service administratif impérial d'Auguste à Constantin*, Rome, 1976.

Rickman, G. E., *The Corn Supply of Ancient Rome*, Oxford, 1980.

Veyne, P., *Le pain et le cirque*, Paris, 1976, 593–791.

Yavetz, Z., *Plebs and Princeps*, Oxford, 1969.

THE SENATE

Alföldy, G., *Konsulat und Senatorenstand unter den Antoninen*, Bonn, 1977.

Barbieri, G., *L'Albo senatorio da Settimio Severo a Carino (193–285)*, Rome, 1952.

Bleicken, J., *Senatsgericht und Kaisergericht*, Abh. Akad. Wiss. Göttingen, Phil.-hist. Kl. 3.53, 1962.

Brunt, P. A., 'Charges of Provincial Maladministration under the Early Principate', *Historia* 10 (1961), 189.

Brunt, P. A., 'The Lex Valeria Cornelia', *JRS* 51, 1961, 71.

Campbell, B., 'Who were the "Viri Militares"?', *JRS* 65, 1975, 11.

Cebeillac, M., *Les 'quaestores principis et candidati' aux Ier et IIme siècles de l'Empire*, Milan, 1972.

Corbier, M., *L'aerarium Saturni et l'aerarium militare: administration et prosopographie sénatoriale*, Rome, 1974.

Eck, W., *Senatoren von Vespasian bis Hadrian*, Munich, 1970.

Frei-Stolba, R., *Untersuchungen zu den Wahlen in der römischen Kaiserzeit*, Zurich, 1967.

Halfmann, H., *Die Senatoren aus dem östlichen Teil des Imperium Romanum bis zur Ende des zweiten Jahrhunderts*, Göttingen, 1979.

Hammond, M., 'The Composition of the Senate AD 68–235', *JRS* 47, 1957, 74.

Morris, J., 'Leges Annales under the Principate', *Listy Filogické* 87, 1964, 314.

O'Brien-Moore, A., 'Senatus', *RE* Supp. 6, 1935, 660–812.

Chapter 3: The Emperors

Alföldi, A., *Die monarchische Repräsentation im römischen Kaiserreich*, Darmstadt, 1970.

Baumann, R. A., *Impietas in Principem*, Munich, 1974.

Béranger, J., *Recherches sur l'aspect idéologique du Principat*, Basel, 1953.

Hammond, M., *The Augustan Principate*, 2nd ed., Cambridge, Mass., 1968.

Hammond, M., *The Antonine Monarchy*, Rome, 1959.

Kloft, H., *Liberalitas Principis*, Köln, 1970.

Millar, F., *The Emperor in the Roman World*, London, 1977.

Mommsen, T., *Römisches Staatsrecht* 2.2, 3rd ed., Berlin, 1878.

Parsi, B., *Désignation et investiture de l'empéreur romain*, Paris, 1963.

Taylor, L. R., *The Divinity of the Roman Emperor*, Middletown, Conn., 1931

Wickert, L., 'Princeps', *RE* 22, 1954, 1998–2296.

Chapter 4: Government and Administration

ADMINISTRATION

Burton, G. P., 'Proconsuls, Assizes and the Administration of Justice under the Empire', *JRS* 65, 1975, 92.

Garnsey, P., *Social Status and Legal Privilege in the Roman Empire,* Oxford, 1970.

Hirschfeld, O., *Die kaiserlichen Verwaltungsbeamten,* 2nd ed., Berlin, 1905.

Jones, A. H. M., *Studies in Roman Government and Law,* Oxford, 1960.

Millar, F., 'The Aerarium and its Officials under the Empire', *JRS* 54, 1964, 33.

Millar, F., 'The Emperor, the Senate and the Provinces', *JRS* 56, 1966, 156.

IMPERIAL BUSINESS

Crook, J., *Consilium Principis,* Cambridge, 1955.

Gualandi, G., *Legislazione imperiale e giurisprudenza* 1–2, Milan, 1963.

Kelly, J. M., *Princeps Iudex,* Weimar, 1957.

Millar, F., 'Emperors at Work', *JRS* 57, 1967, 9.

Seston, W., & Euzennat, M., 'Un dossier de la chancellerie romaine: la Tabula Banasitana', *CRAI* 1971, 468.

Williams, W., 'The *Libellus* Procedure and the Severan Papyri', *JRS* 64, 1974, 86.

Williams, W., 'Individuality in the Imperial Constitutions: Hadrian and the Antonines', *JRS* 66, 1976, 67.

EQUESTRIAN OFFICIALS

Brunt, P. A., 'The Administrators of Roman Egypt', *JRS* 65, 1975, 124.

Howe, L. L., *The Pretorian Prefect from Commodus to Diocletian,* Chicago, 1942.

Millar, F., *Historia* 13, 1964, 180; 14, 1965, 362 (on jurisdiction and powers of procurators).

Peterson, H., 'Senatorial and Equestrian Governors in the Third Century AD', *JRS* 45, 1955, 47.

Pflaum, H. G., *Les procurateurs équestres,* Paris, 1950.

Pflaum, H. G., *Les Carrières procuratoriennes équestres* 1–3, Paris, 1960–1.

Pflaum, H. G., 'Zur Reform des Kaisers Gallienus', *Historia* 25, 1976, 109.

Sherwin-White, A. N., 'Procurator Augusti', *Pap. Brit. Sch. Rome* 15, 1939, 11.

IMPERIAL SLAVES AND FREEDMEN

Boulvert, G., *Esclaves et affranchis impériaux sous le haut-empire romain*, Naples, 1970.

Boulvert, G., *Domestique et fonctionnaire sous le haut-empire romain*, Paris, 1974.

Weaver, P. R. C., *Familia Caesaris*, Cambridge, 1972.

COINAGE

Callu, J.-P., *La politique monétaire des Empereurs romains de 238 à 311*, Paris, 1969.

Bolin, S., *State and Currency in the Roman Empire*, Stockholm, 1958.

Mattingly, H., *Roman Coins*, 2nd ed., London, 1960.

Chapter 5: State and Subject: the Cities

Abbott, F. F., & Johnson, A. C., *Municipal Administration in the Roman Empire*, Princeton, 1926.

van Berchem, D., 'L'annone militaire dans l'Empire romain au IIIe siècle', *Mém. Soc. Nat. Ant. France* 8.10, 1937, 117.

den Boer, W., (ed.), *Le Culte des Souverains dans l'Empire romain*, Geneva, 1973.

Deininger, J., *Die Provinziallandtage der römischen Kaiserzeit*, Munich, 1965.

Garnsey, P., 'The *Lex Iulia* and Appeal under the Empire', *JRS* 56, 1966, 167.

Grelle, F., *Stipendium vel Tributum*, Naples, 1963.

Jones, A. H. M., *The Greek City*, Oxford, 1940.

Jones, A. H. M., *The Roman Economy*, ed. P. A. Brunt, Oxford, 1974.

de Laet, S. J., *Portorium*, Bruges, 1949.

MacMullen, R., *Enemies of the Roman Order*, Cambridge, Mass., 1961.

Mitchell, S., 'Requisitioned Transport in the Roman Empire: a New Inscription from Pisidia', *JRS* 66, 1976, 106.

Neesen, L., *Untersuchungen zu den direkten Staatsabgaben der römischen Kaiserzeit (27 v. Chr.–284 n. Chr.)*, Bonn, 1980.

Nörr, D., *Imperium und Polis in der hohen Prinzipatszeit*, Munich, 1966.

Pekáry, T., *Untersuchungen zu den römischen Reichsstrassen*, Bonn, 1968.

Pflaum, H. G., 'Essai sur le cursus publicus sous le Haut-Empire romain', *Mém. prés. à l'Acad. des Ins.* 14, 1940, 189.

Schwahn, W., 'Tributum', *RE* 7A, 1948, 1–78.

Sherwin-White, A. N., *Roman Society and Roman Law in the New Testament*, Oxford, 1963.

Sherwin-White, A. N., *The Roman Citizenship*, 2nd ed., Oxford, 1973.

Sherwin-White, A. N., 'The *Tabula* of Banasa and the *Constitutio Antoniniana*', *JRS* 63, 1973, 86.

Stahl, M., *Imperiale Herrschaft und provinziale Stadt*, Göttingen, 1978.

Chapter 6: The Army and the Frontiers

Barkóczi, L., et al. *Der römische Limes in Ungarn*, Székestehérvár, 1976.

Bogaers, J. E., & Ruger, C. B., (eds.), *Die niedergermanische Limes*, Cologne, 1974.

Bosworth, A. B., 'Vespasian's Reorganisation of the North-East Frontier', *Antichthon* 10, 1976, 63.

Brunt, P. A., 'Pay and Superannuation in the Roman Army', *Pap. Brit. Sch. Rome* 5, 1950, 50.

Cheesman, G. L., *The Auxilia of the Roman Imperial Army*, Oxford, 1914.

Dobson, B., *Die Primipilares*, Bonn, 1978.

Forni, G., *Il reclutamento delle legioni da Augusto a Diocleziano*, Milan/Rome, 1953.

Grosse, R., *Romische Militärgeschichte von Gallienus bis zum Beginn der Byzantinischen Themenverfassung*, Berlin, 1920.

Holder, P. A., *The Auxilia from Augustus to Trajan*, Oxford, 1980.

Kromayer, T., & Veith, G., *Heerwesen und Kriegführung der Griechen und Römer*, Munich, 1928.

Luttwak, E. N., *The Grand Strategy of the Roman Empire from the First Century AD to the Third*, Baltimore, 1976.

MacMullen, R., *Soldier and Civilian in the Later Roman Empire*, Cambridge, Mass., 1963.

Parker, H. M. D., *The Roman Legions*, 2nd ed., Cambridge, 1958.

Richmond, I. A., (ed.), *Roman and Native in North Britain*, Edinburgh, 1958.

Roxan, M. M., *Roman Military Diplomas, 1954–1977*, London, 1978.

Schleiermacher, W., *Der römische Limes in Deutschland*, 3rd ed., Berlin, 1967.

Schönberger, H., 'The Roman Frontier in Germany: an Archaeological Survey', *JRS* 59, 1969, 144.

Watson, G. R., 'The Pay of the Roman Army', *Historia* 5, 1956, 332.

Watson, G. R., 'The Pay of the Roman Army: the Auxiliary Forces', *Historia* 8, 1959, 372.

Webster, G., *The Roman Imperial Army*, 2nd ed., London, 1979.

CONGRESSES ON FRONTIER STUDIES

Birley, E. (ed.), *The Congress of Roman Frontier Studies 1949*, Durham, 1952.

Swoboda, E. (ed.), *Carnuntina*, Graz/Köln, 1956.

Limes-Studien, Basel, 1959.

Limes Romanus Konferenz, Nitra, Bratislava, 1959.

Quintus Congressus Internationalis Limitis Romani Studiosorum 1961, Zagreb, 1961.

Studien zu der Militärgrenzen Rome. Vorträge des 6. Internationalen Limes – Kongress in Suddeutschland. Köln/Graz, 1967.

Roman Frontier Studies 1967, Tel-Aviv, 1971.

Roman Frontier Studies 1969, ed. E. Birley, B. Dobson and M. Jarrett, Cardiff, 1974.

Actes du IXe Congrès International d'Études sur les frontières romaines, 1972, ed. D. M. Pippidi, Bucarest/Köln, 1974.

Studien zu den Militärgrenzen Rome 2: Vorträge des 10. Internationalen Limeskongresses in der Germania Inferior, Köln, 1977.

Limes: Akten des XI internationalen Limeskongresses, 1976, ed. J. Fitz, Budapest, 1977.

Roman Frontier Studies, 1979, 1–3, ed. W. S. Hanson and L. J. F. Keppie, Oxford, 1980.

Chapter 7: Italy

Chilver, G. E. F., *Cisalpine Gaul*, Oxford, 1941.

Eck, W., *Die staatliche Organisation Italiens in der hohen Kaiserzeit*, Munich, 1979.

Kahrstedt, U. *Die wirtschaftliche Lage Grossgriechenlands in der Kaiserzeit*, Wiesbaden, 1960.

Sirago, V. A., *L'Italia agraria sotto Traiano*, Louvain, 1958.

Chapter 8: The Western Provinces

GENERAL

Clavel, M., & Léveque, P., *Villes et structures urbaines dans l'Occident romain*, Paris, 1971.

Harmand, L., *L'Occident romain*, Paris, 1971.

Rupprecht, G., *Untersuchungen zum Decurionenstand in der nordwestlichen Provinzen des römischen Reiches*, Kallinz, 1975.

Ward-Perkins, J. B., 'From Republic to Empire: Notes on the Early Provincial Architecture of the Roman West', *JRS* 60, 1970, 1.

GAUL

Brogan, O., *Roman Gaul*, London, 1953.

Février,P. A., 'The Origin and Growth of the Cities of Southern Gaul to the Third Century AD', *JRS* 63, 1973, 1.

Griffe, E., *La Gaule chrétienne à l'époque romaine*, 2nd ed., Paris, 1964.

Hatt, J. J., *Histoire de la Gaule romaine*, Paris, 1959.

Jullian, C., *Histoire de la Gaule* 4–7, Paris, 1913–26.

Koethe, H., 'Zur Geschichte Galliens im dritten Viertel des 3. Jahrhunderts', *32e Bericht, röm-germ. Kom. 1942*, 1944, 199.

Lafaurie, J., 'L'empire Gaulois. L'apport de la numismatique', *ANRW* 2.2, 1975, 853.

Mackendrick, P., *Roman France*, London, 1971.

SPAIN

Blazquez, J. M., *Economia de la Hispania Romana*, Bilbao, 1978.

Les Empereurs romains d'Espagne, Coll. Int. du CNRS, Paris, 1965.

Étienne, R., *Le culte impérial dans la péninsule ibérique d'Auguste à Dioclétien*, Paris, 1958.

Legio VII Gemina, Leon, 1970.

Menendez Pidal, R. (ed.), *Historia de Espana* 2: *Espana Romana*, 2nd ed., Madrid, 1955.

Sutherland, C. H. V., *The Romans in Spain 217 BC–AD 117*, London, 1939.

Thouvenot, R., *Essai sur la province romaine de Bétique*, Paris, 1940.

Tovar, A., & Blazquez, J. M., *Historia de la Hispania Romana*, Madrid, 1975.

BRITAIN

Frere, S. S., *Britannia: A History of Roman Britain*, 2nd ed., London, 1974.

Liversedge, J., *Britain in the Roman Empire*, London, 1974.

Richmond, I. A., *Roman Britain*, 2nd ed., Harmondsworth, 1963.

Rivet, A. L. F., *Town and Country in Roman Britain*, 2nd ed., London, 1964.

Rivet, A. L. F., & Smith, C., *The Place Names of Roman Britain*, London, 1979.

Thomas, C. (ed.), *Rural Settlement in Roman Britain*, London, 1966.

Toynbee, J. M. C., *Art in Britain under the Romans*, Oxford, 1964.

Wacher, J. S. (ed.), *The Civitas Capitals of Roman Britain*, Leicester, 1966.

Wacher, J. S., *The Towns of Roman Britain*, London, 1975.

Wacher, J. S., *Roman Britain*, London, 1978.

Chapter 9: Africa

Bénabou, M., *La résistance africaine à la Romanisation*, Paris, 1976.

Birley, A. R., *Septimius Severus, the African Emperor*, London, 1971.

Broughton, T. R. S., *The Romanisation of Africa Proconsularis*, Baltimore, 1929.

Dunbabin, K. M. D., *The Mosaics of Roman North Africa*, Oxford, 1978.

Fentress, E. W. B., *Numidia and the Roman Army*, Brit. Arch. Reports., Int. Series 53, Oxford, 1979.

Frend, W. H. C., *The Donatist Church*, Oxford, 1952.

Garnsey, P. D. A., 'Rome's African Empire under the Principate', Garnsey, P., & Whittaker, C. R. (eds.), *Imperialism in the Ancient World*, Cambridge, 1978, 223.

Gascou, J., *La politique municipale de l'empire romain en Afrique proconsulaire de Trajan à Septime-Sévère*, Rome, 1972.

Lassère, J.-M., *Ubique Populus: peuplement et mouvements de population dans l'Afrique romaine*, Paris, 1977.

Pflaum, H. G., *L'Afrique romaine: études épigraphiques*, Paris, 1979.

Picard, G. C., *La Civilisation de l'Afrique romaine*, Paris, 1959.

Romanelli, P., *Storia delle province romane dell' Africa*, Rome, 1959.

Whittaker, C. R., 'Land and Labour in North Africa', *Klio* 60, 1978, 331.

Chapter 10: Egypt

Bell, H. I., *Egypt from Alexander the Great to the Arab Conquest*, Oxford, 1948.

Bell, H. I., *Cults and Creeds in Graeco-Roman Egypt*, Liverpool, 1953.

Bowman, A. K., *The Town Councils of Roman Egypt*, Toronto, 1971.

Bowman, A. K., 'Papyri and Roman Imperial History, 1960–75', *JRS* 66, 1976, 153.

Braunert, H., *Die Binnenwanderung: Studien zur Sozialgeschichte Ägyptens in der Ptolemäer- und Kaiserzeit*, Bonn, 1964.

Jones, A. H. M., *Cities of the Eastern Roman Provinces*, 2nd ed., Oxford, 1971, ch. 11.

Mitteis, L., & Wilcken, U., *Grundzüge und Chrestomathie der Papyruskunde* 1–2, Leipzig/Berlin, 1912.

Montevecchi, O., *La papirologia*, Turin, 1972.

Reinmuth, O. W., *The Prefect of Egypt from Augustus to Diocletian*, *Klio* Beiheft 34, 1935.

Seidl, E., *Rechtsgeschichte Ägyptens als römische Provinz*, Sankt Augustin, 1973.

Turner, E. G., *Greek Papyri*, Oxford, 1968.

Winter, J. G., *Life and Letters in the Papyri*, Ann Arbor, 1935.

Chapter 11: The Greek Provinces

GENERAL

Bengtson, H., *Griechische Geschichte*, 5th ed., Munich, 1977, 519f.

Bernhardt, R., *Imperium und Eleutheria: die römische Politik gegenüber den freien Städten des griechischen Ostens*, Hamburg, 1971.

Bowersock, G. W., *Greek Sophists in the Roman Empire*, Oxford, 1969.

Jones, A. H. M., *The Greek City*, Oxford, 1940.

Jones, A. H. M., *Cities of the Eastern Roman Provinces*, 2nd ed., Oxford, 1971.

Jones, A. H. M., 'The Greeks under the Roman Empire', *Dumb. Oaks. Papers* 17, 1963, 3 = *The Roman Economy*, Oxford, 1974, 90.

Reardon, B. P., *Courants littéraires grecs des 2e et 3e siècles après J.-C.*, Paris, 1971.

Syme, R., 'The Greeks under Roman Rule', *Roman Papers*, Oxford, 1979, 566.

ASIA MINOR

Chapot, V., *La province romaine proconsulaire d'Asie*, Paris, 1904.

Gren, E., *Kleinasien und der Ostbalkan in der wirtschaftlichen Entwicklung der römischen Kaiserzeit*, Uppsala, 1941.

Kraft, K., *Das System der kaiserzeitlichen Münzprägung in Kleinasien*, Berlin, 1972.

Levick, B. M., *Roman Colonies in Southern Asia Minor*, Oxford, 1967.

Magie, D., *Roman Rule in Asia Minor*, 1–2, Princeton, 1950.

SYRIA

Downey, G., *A History of Antioch in Syria from Seleucus to the Arab Conquest*, Princeton, 1961.

Hitti, P. K., *History of Syria*, 2nd ed., London 1957.

Rey-Coquais, J.-P., 'Syrie Romaine de Pompée à Dioclétien', *JRS* 68, 1978, 44.

JUDAEA SYRIA PALAESTINA

Avi-Yonah, M., *The Jews of Palestine: a Political History from the Bar Kokhba War to the Arab Conquest*, Oxford, 1976.

Safrai, S., & Stern, M., (eds.), *The Jewish People in the First Century* 1–2, Assen, 1974–6.

Schürer, E., *History of the Jewish People in the Age of Jesus Christ (175 BC–AD 135)* 1, 1973, ed. G. Vermes & F. Millar; 2, 1979, ed. G. Vermes, F. Millar & M. Black.

Smallwood, E. M., *The Jews under Roman Rule: from Pompey to Diocletian*, Leiden, 1976.

Chapter 12: The Balkan and Danubian Provinces

GENERAL

Mihăescu, H., *La langue latine dans le sud-est de l'Europe*, Bucarest/Paris, 1978.

NORICUM

Alföldy, G., *Noricum*, London, 1974.

PANNONIA

Mócsy, A., *Die Bevölkerung Pannoniens bis zu der Markomannenkriegen*, Budapest, 1959.

Mócsy, A., *Pannonia and Upper Moesia*, London, 1974.
Oliva, P., *Pannonia and the Onset of Crisis in the Roman Empire*, Prague, 1962.

DALMATIA

Alföldy, G., *Bevölkerung und Gesellschaft der römischen Provinz Dalmatien*, Budapest, 1965.
Wilkes, J. J., *Dalmatia*, London, 1969.

MOESIA

Mirković, M., *Rimski gradovi na Dunavu u Gornjoj Meziji*, Belgrade, 1968.
Mirković, M., & Dusanić, S. (eds.), *Inscriptions de la Mésie Supérieure*, Belgrade, 1976.
Mócsy, A., 'Untersuchungen zur Geschichte der römischen Provinz Moesia Superior', *Acta Arch. Acad. Sc. Hung.* 11, 1959, 283.
Mócsy, A., *Gesellschaft und Romanisation in der römischen Provinz Moesia Superior*, Amsterdam, 1970.
Zlatovskaia, T.D., *M'osia v 1–2 v'ekach nashe eri*, Moscow, 1951.

DACIA (see bibliography to chapter 15)

Condurachi, E., & Daicoviciu, C., *Romania*, London, 1971.
Daicoviciu, C., *Siebenburgen im Altertum*, Bucarest, 1943.
Daicoviciu, C., 'Dacia Capta', *Klio* 38, 1960, 174.
Gudea, N. 'The Defensive System of Roman Dacia', *Britannia* 10, 1979, 63.
Mackendrick, P., *The Dacian Stones Speak*, Chapel Hill, N. C., 1975.
Tudor, D., *Oltenia Romană*, 3rd ed., Bucarest, 1968.
Tudor, D., *Orase, tiguri si sate în Dacia romană*, Bucarest, 1968.

THRACE

Hoddinott, R. F., *Bulgaria in Antiquity: an Archaeological Introduction*, London, 1975.
Jones, A. H. M., *Cities of the Eastern Roman Provinces*, 2nd ed., Oxford, 1971, ch. 1.
Velkov, V. J., *Cities in Thrace and Dacia in Late Antiquity*, Amsterdam, 1977.
Wiesner, J., *Die Thraker*, Stuttgart, 1963.

Chapter 13: The Empire and the Third-Century Crisis

Alföldi, A., *Studien zur Geschichte der Weltkrise des 3. Jahrhunderts nach Christus,* Darmstadt, 1967.

Alföldy, G., 'The Crisis of the Third Century as seen by Contemporaries', *Gr., Rom. and Byz. Stud.* 15, 1974, 89.

Jones, A. H. M., *The Later Roman Empire,* Oxford, 1964, ch. 1.

MacMullen, R., *Roman Government's Response to Crisis AD 235–337,* New Haven, 1976.

Rémondon, R., *La crise de l'Empire romain de Marc-Aurèle à Anastase,* Paris, 1964.

Schtajerman, E. M., *Die Krise der Sklavenhalterordnung im Westen des römischen Reiches,* Berlin, 1964.

Walser, G., & Pekáry, T., *Die Krise des römischen Reiches: Bericht uber die Forschung zum 3. Jahrhunderts (193–284 n. Chr.) von 1939 bis 1959,* Berlin, 1962.

Chapter 14: Parthia and Sasanid Persia

For general information and bibliography see R. N. Frye, *The Heritage of Persia,* 2nd ed., London, 1976, 303–10.

Debevoise, N. C., *A Political History of Parthia,* Chicago, 1938, is the standard reference work on the Parthians.

Gagé, J., *La montée des sassanides,* Paris, 1964, has a summary of events with translations from various sources.

Herrmann, G., *The Iranian Revival,* London, 1977, is a good popular account of the cultures of the Parthians and Sasanians.

Luckonin, V. G., *Iran v epokhu pervykh sasanidov,* Leningrad, 1961, gives a good survey of the early Sasanians.

The Cambridge History of Iran, volume three, in preparation, will reflect the latest scholarship in the field.

Walser, G. and Pekáry, T., *Die Krise des römischen Reiches,* Berlin, 1962, give an annotated bibliography of the first half of the third century AD.

Ziegler, K. H., *Die Beziehungen zwischen Rom und dem Partherreich,* Wiesbaden, 1964, is a good summary with extensive bibliography.

Chapter 15: The Dacians in the First Century AD

THE THRACIANS AND THE GETO-DACIANS

Daicoviciu, C., in *Istoria Romanei* (History of Rumania), 1, 1960, 225–338.

Izvoare privind istoria Romanei 1 (*Fontes ad historiam Dacoromaniae pertinentes* 1, *Ab Hesiodo usque ad Itinerarium Antonini*), Bucarest, 1964.

Parvan, V., *Getica. O protoistorie a Daciei*, Bucarest, 1926.

Vulpe, R., *Aşezări getice din Mountenia* (Getic Settlements in Muntenia), Bucarest, 1966.

Wiesner, J., *Die Thraker*, Stuttgart, 1963.

TRANSYLVANIA

Daicoviciu, C., *Transylvania in the Ancient World*, Bucarest, 1945.

THE ROMANS IN THE LOWER DANUBE

Pippidi, D. M. and Berciu, D., *Din istoria Dobrogei* 1 (On the history of Dobrudja), Bucarest, 1965.

HISTORY OF DACIAN CIVILIZATION

Daicoviciu, C., 'The Problem of Dacia and Dacian Culture in the Light of Recent Research', *Recent Historical Studies*, Bucarest, 1955.

Daicoviciu, C. and Daicoviciu, H., *Columna lui Traian*, Bucarest, 1966.

Daicoviciu, H., *Dacii* (The Dacians), Bucarest, 1965.

LATER HISTORY OF THE DACIANS AND DACO-ROMANS

Daicoviciu, C., Petrovici, Em. and Stefan, Gh., *The Formation of the Rumanian People and Their Language*, Bucarest, 1963.

Protase, D., *Problema continuitătii în Dacia în lumina arheologiei şi numismaticii* (The Problem of Continuity in Dacai in the Light of Archaeology and Numismatics), Bucarest, 1966.

Chapter 16: The Scytho-Sarmatian Tribes

Artamonov, M. I., *K. Voprosy o proiskhojhd'eni'e Skifov*, Leningrad, 1950.

Diadema iz Kurgana Khokhlach u Novocher-Kasska Sokrovichsha Ermitazha, Leningrad, 1969.

Ginters, B., *Das Schwert der Skythen und Sarmaten in Sudrüssland,* Berlin, 1928.

Harmatta, J., *Studies on the History of the Scythians,* Budapest, 1950.

Kondakov, N. and Tolstoi, J., *Antiquités de la Russie Méridionale,* Paris, 1891, for details of Novocherkask hoard.

Párducz, M., 'Denkmäler der Sarmatenzeit Ungarns', *Archaeologia Hungarica* 25, 1941; 28, 1944; 30, 1950.

Richmond, I. A., 'The Sarmatae, Bremetennacum Veteranorum and the Regio Bremetennacensis', *JRS* 35, 1945, 15.

Rostovtzeff, M., *Antichnaya Dekorativnaya Zhivopis' na iug'e Rossii.,* St Petersburg, 1914.

—— 'Le culte de la grande déesse dans la Russie méridionale', *Revue des Etudes Grecques* 32, 1919, 462.

Trever, C. V., 'Tête de Senmutv en argent des collections de L'Hermitage', *Iranica Antiqua* 4, fasc. 2, 162–70, Leyden, 1964.

Chapter 17: The Germans

SOURCES

Capelle, W., *Das alte Germanien. Die Nachrichten der griechischen und römischen Schriftsteller,* Jena, 1937. Collection in German translation.

GENERAL ACCOUNTS (HISTORY, CULTURAL HISTORY, ARCHAEOLOGY)

Brøndsted, I., *Nordische Vorzeit,* Vol. 3, *Eisenzeit in Dänemark,* Neumünster, 1963.

Eggers, H. J., 'Zur absoluten Chronologie der römischen Kaiserzeit im Freien Germanien', *Jahrb. d. Röm.-Germ. Zentralmuseums Mainz,* 2, 1955.

Hoops, J., *Reallexikon der germanischen Altertumskunde,* Vols. 1–4, Strassburg, 1911–19.

Müllenhoff, K., *Deutsche Altertumskunde,* Vols. 1–5², Berlin, 1890–1929.

Reinerth, H. (ed.), *Vorgeschichte der deutschen Stämme,* Vols. 1–3, Leipzig, 1940.

Roeren, R., 'Zur Archäologie und Geschichte Südwestdeutschlands im 3. bis 5.. Jahrhundert n. Chr', *Jahrb. d. Röm.-Germ. Zentralmuseums Mainz,* 7, 1960.

Schmidt, L., *Geschichte der deutschen Stämme bis zum Ausgang der Völkerwanderung. Die Ostgermanen*[2], Munich, 1941. *Die Westgermanen*, Part 1[2], Munich, 1938. Part 2, 1[2], Munich, 1940.

Schneider, H. (ed.), *Germanische Altertumskunde*[2], Munich, 1951.

von Uslar, R., 'Bemerkungen zu einer Karte germanischer Funde der älteren Kaiserzeit', *Germania* 29, 1951 (with bibliography of the regional archaeological literature).

—— 'Archäologische Fundgruppen und germanische Stammesgebiete vornehmlich aus der Zeit um Christi Geburt', *Hist. Jahrb.* 71, 1952.

Zwikker, W., *Studien zur Markussäule*, Vol. 1, Amsterdam, 1941.

SOCIAL AND POLITICAL STRUCTURE

Dannenbauer, H., 'Adel, Burg und Herrschaft bei den Germanen', *Hist. Jahrb.* 61, 1941, = *Wege der Forschung*, Vol. 2, Darmstadt, 1956.

Kuhn, H., 'Die Grenzen der germanischen Gefolgschaft', *Zeitschrift der Savigny-Stiftung für Rechtsgeschichte, Germanische Abteilung*, 73, 1956.

Schlesinger, W., 'Herrschaft und Gefolgschaft in der germanischdeutschen Verfassungsgeschichte', *Historische Zeitschrift* 176, 1953, = *Wege der Forschung*, Vol. 2, Darmstadt, 1956.

Wenskus, R., *Stammesbildung und Verfassung. Das Werden der frühmittelalterlichen Gentes*, Cologne-Graz, 1961.

ARISTOCRATIC GRAVES

Eggers, H. J., 'Lübsow. Ein germanischer Fürstensitz der älteren Kaiserzeit', *Prähistorische Zeitschrift* 34/5, second part, 1953.

Schulz, W., 'Leune. Ein germanischer Bestattungsplatz der spätrömischen Kaiserzeit', *Schrft. d. Sektion f. Vor- u. Frühgesch. d. dtsch. Akad. d. Wissensch. Berlin*, Vol. 1, Berlin, 1953.

Werner, J., 'Pfeilspitzen aus Silber und Bronze in germanischen Adelsgräbern der Kaiserzeit', *Hist. Jahrb.* 74, 1955.

ART AND WRITING

Eggers, H. J., *Die Kunst der Germanen in der Eisenzeit*, Kunst der Welt, Baden-Baden, 1964.

Warner, J., 'Die beiden Zierscheiben des Thorsberger Moorfundes', *Röm.-Germ. Forschg.*, Vol. 16, Berlin, 1941.

SACRIFICIAL SITES

Behm-Blancke, A., 'Germanische Mooropferplätze in Thüringen', *Ausgrabungen und Funde* 2, 1957.

—— 'Das germanische Tierknochenopfer und sein Ursprung', *Ausgrabungen und Funde* 10, 1965.

Jankuhn, H., 'Zur Deutung der Moorleichenfunde von Windeby', *Prähistorische Zeitschrift* 36, 1958.

—— 'Moorfunde', *Neue Ausgrabungen in Deutschland*, Berlin, 1958.

MILITARY EQUIPMENT

Jahn, M., *Die Bewaffnung der Germanen in der älteren Eisenzeit*, Mannus-Bibliothek, Vol. 16, Leipzig, 1916.

Raddatz, K., 'Ringknaufschwerter aus germanischen Kriegergräbern', *Offa* 17–18, 1959–61.

—— 'Pfeilspitzen aus dem Moorfund von Nydam', *Offa* 20, 1963.

SETTLEMENT

van Giffen, E., 'Prähistorische Hausformen auf Sandböden in den Niederlanden', *Germania* 35, 1958.

Haarnagel, W., 'Die Ergebnisse der Grabung Feddersen Wierde in Niedersachsen im Jahre 1961', *Germania* 41, 1963.

Hagen, A., *Studier i Jernalderns Gårdssamfunn. Universitetets Oldsaksamlings Skrifter*, Vol. 4, Oslo, 1953.

Hougen, H., *Fra Seter til Gard*, Oslo, 1947.

Jankuhn, H., 'Terra . . . silvis horrida' (on Tacitus, *Germania*, ch. 5), *Archaeologia Geographica* 10–11, 1961–3.

Supplementary Bibliography

Chapter 1
C.M. Wells, *The Roman Empire*[2] (1992)
R. Lane Fox, *Pagans and Christians* (1986)
P. Garnsey and R. Saller, *The Roman Empire: economy, society and culture* (1987)
W.L. MacDonald, *The Architecture of the Roman Empire* II: *An Urban Appraisal* (1986)

Chapter 2
R.J.A. Talbert, *The Senate of Imperial Rome* (1984)

Chapter 3
F. Millar, *The Emperor in the Roman World*, ed. 2, with new Afterword (1992).

Chapter 9: Africa
A.R. Birley, *The African Emperor: Septimius Severus* (1988)

Chapter 10: Egypt
A.K. Bowman, *Egypt after the Pharaohs, 332 BC-AD 642* (1986)
N. Lewis, *Life in Egypt under Roman Rule* (1983)

Chapter 11
S.R.F. Price, *Rituals and Power: the Roman Imperial Cult in Asia Minor* (1984)
M. Wörrle, *Stadt und Fest im kaiserzeitlichen Kleinasien* (1988)

Chapter 14
R.N. Frye, *The History of Ancient Iran* (1983)

Chapter 17
M. Todd, *The Early Germans* (1992)

Chapter 4
P.A. Brunt, *Roman Imperial Themes* (1990)
R. Saller, *Personal Patronage under the Early Empire* (1982)

Chapter 5
J. González, 'The Lex Irnitana: a New Copy of the Flavian Municipal Law', *JRS* 76 (1986), 147
A.R. Burnett, M. Amandry, P.P. Ripollès, *Roman Provincial Coinage* I: *44 BC-AD 69* (1992)

Chapter 6
D. Kennedy, D. Riley, *Rome's Desert Frontier from the Air* (1990)
B. Isaac, *The Limits of Empire: the Roman Army in the East*[2] (1992)

Chapter 7
F. Millar, 'Italy and the Roman Empire, Augustus to Constantine', *Phoenix* 40 (1986), 295
W. Jongman, *The Economy and Society of Pompeii* (1988)

Chapter 8
J.F. Drinkwater, *Roman Gaul: the Three Provinces, 58 BC-AD 260* (1983)
M. Millett, *The Romanisation of Britain: an Essay in Archaeological Interpretation* (1990)
M. Todd and T.F.C. Blagg (eds.), *Research on Roman Britain 1960-1989* (1989)

Index

363